After the Armistice

A century after the Armistice and the associated peace agreements that formally ended the Great War, many issues pertaining to the UK and its empire are yet to be satisfactorily resolved. Accordingly, this volume presents a multi-disciplinary approach to better understanding the post-Armistice empire across a broad spectrum of disciplines, geographies and chronologies. Through the lens of diplomatic, social, cultural, historical and economic analysis, the chapters engage with the histories of Lagos and Tonga, Cyprus and China, as well as more obvious geographies of empire, such as Ireland, India and Australia. Though globally diverse, and encompassing much of the post-Armistice century, the studies are nevertheless united by three common themes: the interrogation of that transitionary 'moment' after the Armistice that lingered well beyond the final Treaty of Lausanne in 1924; the utilisation of new research methods and avenues of enquiry to compliment extant debates concerning the legacies of colonialism and nationalism; and the common *leitmotif* of the British Empire in all its political and cultural complexity. The centenary of the Armistice offers a timely occasion on which to present these studies.

Michael J. K. Walsh is Chair of the School of Art, Design and Media at Nanyang Technological University Singapore and is Professor of Art History. He has published widely on culture at the time of the Great War and has a particular interest in painting and music.

Andrekos Varnava, FRHistS, is Associate Professor in History at Flinders University, South Australia, and an Honorary Professor in History at De Montfort University, Leicester. He is the author of four monographs, eight edited volumes and 50 peer-reviewed journal articles and book chapters.

Routledge Studies in First World War History
Series Editor
John Bourne
The University of Birmingham, UK

The First World War is a subject of perennial interest to historians and is often regarded as a watershed event, marking the end of the nineteenth century and the beginning of the 'modern' industrial world. The sheer scale of the conflict and massive loss of life means that it is constantly being assessed and reassessed to examine its lasting military, political, sociological, industrial, cultural and economic impact. Reflecting the latest international scholarly research, the Routledge Studies in First World War History series provides a unique platform for the publication of monographs on all aspects of the Great War. Whilst the main thrust of the series is on the military aspects of the conflict, other related areas (including cultural, visual, literary, political and social) are also addressed. Books published are aimed primarily at a post-graduate academic audience, furthering exciting recent interpretations of the war, whilst still being accessible enough to appeal to a wider audience of educated lay readers.

Reflections on the Commemoration of the First World War
Perspectives from the Former British Empire
Edited by David Monger and Sarah Murray

The Ottoman Army and the First World War
Mesut Uyar

Renegotiating First World War Memory
The British and American Legions, 1938–1946
Ashley Garber

Spain and Argentina in the First World War
Transnational Neutralities
Maximiliano Fuentes Codera

After the Armistice
Empire, Endgame and Aftermath
Edited by Michael J. K. Walsh and Andrekos Varnava

For more information about this series, please visit: www.routledge.com/history/series/WWI

After the Armistice

Empire, Endgame and Aftermath

Edited by Michael J. K. Walsh and Andrekos Varnava

Routledge
Taylor & Francis Group
LONDON AND NEW YORK

First published 2021
by Routledge
2 Park Square, Milton Park, Abingdon, Oxon OX14 4RN

and by Routledge
605 Third Avenue, New York, NY 10158

Routledge is an imprint of the Taylor & Francis Group, an informa business

British Library Cataloguing-in-Publication Data
A catalogue record for this book is available from the British Library

Library of Congress Cataloging-in-Publication Data
Names: Walsh, Michael J. K., 1968– editor. | Varnava, Andrekos, editor.
Title: After the Armistice : empire, endgame and aftermath / edited by Michael J. K. Walsh and Andrekos Varnava.
Description: New York : Routledge, 2021. | Series: Routledge studies in first world war history | Includes bibliographical references and index.
Identifiers: LCCN 2020053812 | ISBN 9780367487553 (hardback) | ISBN 9781003042761 (ebook)
Subjects: LCSH: World War, 1914–1918—Influence—Great Britain. | World War, 1914–1918—Peace. | Great Britain—Colonies—History—20th century. | Imperialism—History.
Classification: LCC DA577 .A44 2021 | DDC 940.3/12—dc23
LC record available at https://lccn.loc.gov/2020053812

ISBN: 978-0-367-48755-3 (hbk)
ISBN: 978-1-032-00563-8 (pbk)
ISBN: 978-1-003-04276-1 (ebk)

Typeset in Times New Roman
by Apex CoVantage, LLC

For Michael William Clack

Contents

Figures

Contributors

Editors

Michael J. K. Walsh is Professor of Art History and Chair of the School of Art, Design and Media, Nanyang Technological University in Singapore. He is interested in the relationship between culture and conflict, especially in relation to the Great War, and this has led to several books: *This Cult of Violence* (2002), *A Dilemma of English Modernism* (2007), *Hanging a Rebel* (2008), *London, Modernism and 1914* (2010), *Australia and the Great War: Identity, Memory and Mythology* (2016, co-edited with Andrekos Varnava), *The Great War and the British Empire: Culture and Society* (2017, co-edited with Andrekos Varnava) and *Eric Bogle, Music and the Great War: An Old Man's Tears* (2018). mwalsh@ntu.edu.sg

Andrekos Varnava, FRHistS, is an Associate Professor in imperial and military history at Flinders University, South Australia, and an honorary professor at De Montfort University, Leicester, UK. He was born in 1979 and raised in Melbourne to Cypriot-born parents, obtained his BA (Honours) from Monash University (2001) and his PhD (2006) from the University of Melbourne. He is the author of two books: *Serving the Empire in the Great War: The Cypriot Mule Corps, Imperial Loyalty and Silenced Memory* (2017) and *British Imperialism in Cyprus, 1878–1915: The Inconsequential Possession* (2009; paperback 2012). He has edited/co-edited six volumes: *The Great War and the British Empire: Culture and Society* (2017); *Australia and the Great War: Identity, Memory, Mythology* (2016); *Imperial Expectations and Realities: El Dorados, Utopias and Dystopias* (2015); *The Archbishops of Cyprus in the Modern Age: The Changing Role of the Archbishop-Ethnarch, their Identities and Politics* (2013); *The Minorities of Cyprus: Development Patterns and the Identity of the Internal-Exclusion* (2009); and *Reunifying Cyprus: The Annan Plan and Beyond* (2009; paperback 2011). Additionally, he has co-edited a special issue of *Itinerario, 38(3)*, 2014. He has published numerous book chapters and peer-reviewed articles in major journals. andrekos.varnava@flinders.edu.au

Contributors

Bridget Brooklyn is a lecturer in the History and Political Thought discipline in the School of Humanities and Communication Arts, Western Sydney University. Her research interests are late nineteenth- and twentieth-century Australian social and political history, particularly women's political history. She is currently researching the life and work of conservative political activist and eugenicist Dr Mary Booth. Recent publications are 'Claiming Anzac: The Battle for the Hyde Park Memorial, Sydney', *Melbourne Historical Journal* 45, no. 1 and '1954: Did Petrov Matter?' in *Elections Matter: Ten Federal Elections that Shaped Australia*, ed. Benjamin T. Jones, Frank Bongiorno and John Uhr (2018).

Richard Cork is a British art historian, editor, critic, broadcaster and exhibition curator. He has been an art critic for the *Evening Standard, The Listener, The Times* and the *New Statesman*. Cork was also editor for *Studio International*. He is a past Turner Prize judge. He is also the author of *A Bitter Truth: Avant-Garde Art and The Great War* (1994), which won an Art Fund Award.

Dr Andrew C. B. Harrison is a composer, scholar and pianist from Melbourne, Australia. In 2020, he completed a PhD in Music at the Australian National University; his dissertation, 'Sounding Out the Past', won the J. G. Crawford Prize. Harrison's recent research focuses on the composition of a series of works that use narratives from the Great War and Detroit's recent social upheavals as points of creative departure. He has previously composed two works inspired by the First World War: *The drumfire was incessant and continued all night with unabated fury* (2012) for solo piano and *Gassed Shell (Severe)* (2014) for mezzo-soprano and chamber ensemble. His 2016 composition *Hum*, written in collaboration with Detroit-based poet Jamaal May, was commissioned and premiered by contemporary music ensemble New Music Detroit in Michigan, USA.

Matthew Haultain-Gall is a Scientific Collaborator at the Catholic University of Louvain-la-Neuve (UCL), Belgium. His research focuses on the cultural and social impacts of the First World War. He recently completed a PhD at the University of New South Wales (Sydney) in which he traces the memory of the First Australian Imperial Force's battles in Belgium.

Stephanie James: Strong Irish descent and a lifelong interest in history have combined to feed her interest in the lives of Irish Australians. Questions of this minority group's identity and loyalty in an Anglo-dominant society have propelled her research interests. Publications have looked at aspects of early Irish colonists in South Australia as well as issues of Irish-Australian loyalty/disloyalty at times of imperial crisis, such as the Great War, the subject of her PhD at Flinders University in 2014. This focus has led to the examination of parallels with German Australians, who experienced more extreme but unanticipated wartime 'othering'. Her current projects include co-editing diverse multi-author volumes, one dealing with the Irish in South Australia and another examining a broad range of approaches to the history of World War II. Stephanie is an Honorary Research Fellow at Flinders University.

Sarah Midford is a Senior Lecturer in Classics and Ancient History at La Trobe University. Her research interests include war commemoration, the construction of national narratives, and Classical Reception Studies. Currently, Midford is researching the way Anzac commemoration has drawn upon the classical tradition to construct an enduring national narrative.

Colin Milner is a PhD student in the Australian National University's School of History. He is writing a thesis on Robert Randolph Garran, supported by an Australian Government Research Training Program Scholarship. Previously, he worked as an Australian diplomat and civil servant. He holds degrees in Arts and Law from the University of Sydney and is admitted as a Barrister of the Supreme Court of New South Wales. He has published history chapters in earlier publications and appeared as a contributor to Wildbear's documentary series *Rise and Fall: The Turning Points of World War II.*

Dr Rajarshi Mitra is Assistant Professor in the Department of Humanities and Social Sciences, Indian Institute of Information Technology, Guwahati. Before joining IIIT Guwahati, he was Assistant Professor in the Department of English, Central University of Karnataka. He has an MPhil (2010) from the Department of English, University of Hyderabad and a PhD (2014) from the Department of English Literature, The English & Foreign Languages University, Hyderabad. For his PhD, he had worked on natural history narratives from India between 1857 and 1950, and his MPhil was on colonial tiger-hunting narratives. His research interests include food and culture, horror films, Romanticism and literature and colonialism in general.

Kristin O'Donnell focuses on the intersections of history, memory, and art, with a particular focus on embodiment, representation, identity, and the politics of war commemoration in her work. Kristin is currently working towards a PhD through an AHRC TECHNE NPIF–funded studentship entitled 'The Cultural Politics of Commemoration: Participatory Art and Britain's Great War During the Centenary Moment' at the University of Brighton. This research investigates the politics surrounding the memorialisation of the First World War in Britain, particularly during the centenary moment when experiential memory has ceased and commemorative practices that prioritise embodied experiences have emerged as a central mode of commemoration. This research examines how contemporary practices of remembrance are utilised at both an institutional level through the large-scale funding of cultural initiatives to examine the relationship between governments, non-governmental organisations, artists and individuals in the negotiation of war memory and its effect on identity.

Tom Sear is a PhD candidate in the Australian Centre for Cyber Security (ACCS) at UNSW Canberra at the Australian Defence Force Academy (ADFA). Tom's PhD explores cyber temporalities and the warfare information space (notably, interpersonal and social media–based communication) over the last century. It has a particular focus on the convergence and reflexivity between the memory of nodal conflicts from the twentieth century, contemporary Asymmetrical Hybrid Warfare (AHW) ecologies and gaming within planetary scale computation. The purpose of this interdisciplinary research is to advise IT and cyber security specialists, military personnel and educators how to maximise information tools within future conflict by applying historical, social science and digital theory lenses to the analysis. His PhD considers the capacity and methodological impact of new tools for Information War analysis. Sear was selected into the internationally competitive Oxford Internet Institute, Summer Doctoral Programme, University of Oxford, in July 2017. His publications on the commemoration of the First World War as well as his profile can be found at: https://research.unsw.edu.au/people/mr-tom-sear. His academic journalism (including work on China) is available at: https://theconversation.com/profiles/tom-sear-273513. You can follow him on Twitter @tomsear.

Murphy Temple is Dean of Ezra Stiles College, Yale University, New Haven, Connecticut, USA. She holds a PhD in Modern British History from Stanford University, an MPhil in Modern European History from the University of Cambridge, and a BA in history from Yale University.

Ellen Whitton finished her undergraduate degree at Flinders University in 2014 before continuing on to complete a History honours in 2015. Her honours dissertation was a case study on the 1943 British film *The Life and Death of Colonel Blimp*, and it focused on how its creators, Michael Powell and Emeric Pressburger, relied upon multiple resources to create the film's historical settings. Continuing with this thread and filmmaking duo, Whitton began her PhD project in 2016, which focuses on how the style of Powell and Pressburger's history films evolved over their long partnership. In a wider context, Whitton is interested in historically set films and television series' from various decades across the British, Hollywood and Australian industries.

Peter J. Yearwood is Associate Professor and Leader of the History, Gender Studies, and Philosophy Strand at the University of Papua New Guinea and is Joint Editor of the *South Pacific Journal of Philosophy and Culture*. A specialist in the history of the early twentieth century, he is the author of *Guarantee of Peace, The League of Nations in British Policy, 1916–1925* (2009). His latest book, *Nigeria and the Death of Liberal England; Palm Nuts and Prime Minister, 1914–1916*, has just been published.

Acknowledgements

This collection is derived from the conference *Empire, Armistice and Aftermath: The British Empire at the 'End' of the Great War*, which was held at the School of Art, Design and Media, Nanyang Technological University, Singapore, 5–7 December 2018. The editors would like to thank the Centre for Liberal Arts and Social Sciences at NTU for their generous funding and acknowledge the financial contribution also made by Flinders University. The event, and the follow-up projects, have benefitted enormously from the good will and professionalism shown by Margaret 'Meggie' Hutchison (Australian Catholic University) and Romain Fathi (Flinders University). The editors would also like to extend our thanks to Melissa Lovell for the meticulous copy editing. Last, but not least, we would like to extend our thanks to our families – as always!

Introduction

1 *'Britannia Pacificatrix'*

Re-imagining a post-Armistice empire

Michael J. K. Walsh and Andrekos Varnava

'You must get your perspective right. There is no chance of the future resembling the past. England and the empire can never again be the England and the Empire that you knew.'[1]

Introduction

The centenary of the Armistice in 2018, and the eventual realisation of Brexit in 2020, each stimulated a widespread resurgence of interest in the United Kingdom's relationship with the Great War, the European Union, and its own imperial history. A glance at some recent headlines in the popular press offers a diversity of views: 'How the First World War inspired the EU',[2] 'The Imperial Myths Driving Brexit',[3] and 'The EU is the true successor of the British Empire'.[4] If George Orwell had foreseen that Britain without its empire would be a 'cold and unimportant little island',[5] then European Council President Donald Tusk went the distance and declared Brexit to be 'the true end of the British Empire' and anticipated a new status for the UK as 'outsider, a second-class player in an area occupied by China, the USA and the EU'.[6] Danny Dorling has warned accordingly that 'if the British really want to "take back control" they will need to reassess their recent history. Knowledge is power'.[7]

It is clear that a century after the Armistice many issues pertaining to the empire and its emergence from the Great War are not yet resolved, not only within the UK but further afield. Accordingly, Anne Bostanci and John Dubber insist that we *Remember the World as Well as the War*.[8] To focus attention on some of these issues of legacy is the *raison d'etre* of this collection. As a starting point we turn to an artefact of empire, an important 'form of historical evidence',[9] a painting which serves as a lens through which 'Empire, Endgame and Aftermath' can be reconsidered.

Sigismund Goetze's *Britannia Pacificatrix* and historiography

She is a mythical figure, radiating confidence, dignity, and friendship. *Britannia*, a little boyish and theatrically attired in Roman helmet and elaborately woven robe, presides over the Ambassador's Staircase of the Foreign and Commonwealth

Figure 1.1 Sigismund Goetze, *Britannia Pacificatrix*, Mural Decorations at the Foreign Office London, c. 1921.

Source: (Courtesy of the public domain)

Office in London. She was, at the time of her completion, at the very heart of the British Empire. In fact, there are multiple depictions of *Britannia* within the five large murals which were commissioned, conceptualised by the artist, and approved by Earl Beauchamp (H. M. First Commissioner of Works), Sir Edward Grey (Secretary of State for Foreign Affairs), and Prime Minister H. H. Asquith in 1914. The first four panels were completed before the Armistice. It is the fifth, *Britannia Pacificatrix* (Britannia the Peacemaker), finished in 1919 but not actually installed until 1921, which is of particular interest as a microcosm; an embodiment of the emergent disorientation, nostalgia, and anticipation that the post-war era brought to the empire.[10]

William Lygon was clear in his intentions for the five-panel sequence, stating that he wished it to depict 'peace', 'the development of English freedom', and 'the civic virtues of Justice & Mercy', but in a manner that was 'a sober, dignified scheme . . . hinting at rather than realising the greatness of this Island Empire, without bombast, without offence to other people through their Ambassadors'.[11] The artist himself outlined a trajectory for humankind through the progression of panels in yellow ochre, Venetian red, and cobalt flake white, specifically tracing the 'origin, education, development, expansion and triumph of the British Empire, leading up to the Covenant of the League of Nations'.[12] *Britannia*'s role therefore was to inspire, endorse, impress, reiterate, and envisage an imperial vision based, like the empire itself, on a sound 'classicising mentality'.[13] This was an appropriate idiom for a British imperial mission that situated itself in the ethos of Virgil's *Aeneid* (to 'impose culture and peace'), and run by privately educated officers steeped in the classics and unquestioning in their mission as arbiters of international justice.[14] Aesthetically, the composition exuded aspects of pre-war Edwardian taste as promulgated by the Royal Academy of Arts at Burlington House in Piccadilly and, in particular, in the lavish canvases of artists like Frederick Lord Leighton and Edward Poynter. Far from mere decoration, though, David Dimbleby reminds us, 'every image of empire reminded the public that Britain was engaged in a great enterprise which was enriching the nation, raising its international prestige and bringing peace and regeneration to the rest of the world'.[15] Holger Hoock concurred that art 'served the aesthetic performance of politics and helped shape political culture'.[16]

Turning to the image itself, we approach *Britannia Pacificatrix* as a post-war vision of the empire, divinely endorsed by the words inscribed on an Ionic marble colonnade: '*Gloria in excelsis Deo, et in terra pax hominibus bonae voluntatis*' (Glory to God in the highest, and on earth peace to people of good will), which suggests a link between the *Pax Romana* (27 BC–180 AD) and the new *Pax Britannica.* There is a second inscription in English which reads: 'To the motherland they offer aid and counsel. Friends acclaim the righteous peace'. Within the borders of oak leaves, lions' heads, dolphins, seaweed, and shells, the drama plays out. The detritus of conflict is at Britannia's feet, including worthless treaties, a

Figure 1.2 Sigismund Goetze, *Britannia Pacificatrix*, Close-up of title of panel. Mural Decorations at the Foreign Office London, c. 1921.

Source: (Courtesy of Alison Elangasinghe)

pickelhaube helmet, and a discarded crucifix. These are the symbols of a 'righteous peace' borne of war and earned through the sacrifices of the empire. The imperial 'mission civilisatrice' had been paid for, ironically, with the extraordinary brutality and barbarism of the past four years. In her benevolence Britannia, seemingly unscathed by the trauma of 876,064 imperial deaths, is surrounded by her healthy, loyal, confident, partially clad, adult sons. The artist explains, 'having won her position in the world, Britannia's influence is for peace, and [that] her sons, whom she has sent in distant lands, are ready to return to the Motherland, and with counsel and aid be at her side.'[17]

On the right, sun-lit side of the composition (all male, imperial, and mostly Anglo-Saxon) are the Colonies and Dominions: Australia (wearing a bush hat and representing the 332,000 Australian volunteers),[18] New Zealand (draped with a sheepskin representing its 112,000), Canada (crowned with wheat and wearing a loin cloth made out of maple leaves to represent its 458,000 servicemen), South Africa (with the lion skin representing its 136,000), and a youth bearing the Trident, symbolising Newfoundland and perhaps mastery of the seas. India, in light of its colossal war contribution (1.4 million) was depicted as a middle-aged soldier in 'old armour',[19] standing erect and not in the servile kneeling position which an earlier sketch suggests had been its original designation. The newly acquired Middle East is represented by Prince Feisal in the head-dress recently popularised by T. E. Lawrence (together representing the Epic of Arabia), and Africa appears in the form of a tiny fruit-bearing 'Swaheli boy' to remind us, the artist wrote, of 'our obligations and possibilities in the dark Continent'.[20] The composition did not fully capture the imperial commitment of East Africa (34,000) and West Africa (25,000), of the Mediterranean and Middle East, or of the Caribbean and Asia. To the left of the composition (female, fully dressed, and more in the shade), other allies are led by America, dressed in a Phrygian cap of liberty (closely associated with Eugène Delacroix's iconic *Liberty Guiding the People*) and holding the scales of justice close to her breast. Culturally, politically, and economically, the UK and the USA were joining hands across the Atlantic (or was the baton being passed from the old to the new, or, more interesting still, was the prodigal returning to the fold?). A note from the artist makes it clear that 'the handshake of the two sister powers could never have formed the chief incident in the composition had not America eventually thrown in her lot with the Allies'.[21] Although the handshake is firm, Britannia's appearance feels somewhat aloof, staring into the distance and leaning away from the 'sister'. Also to the left are Italy, France (whose intact unsheathed sword points to the 'Scrap of Paper' and garlanded tricolour rises over the ruins of Despotism and Militarism), Greece (holding a statue of Fame aloft), Romania, Portugal, and Russia. Japan is present, too, attired in an imperial robe and bringing the wild cherry blossom that had found such favour in the paintings of James McNeil Whistler (and in W. S. Gilbert and Arthur Sullivan's *Mikado*) in the closing decades of the 19th century in London. At the epicentre of the composition there is Belgium, armed with a broken sword and a crown of thorns, who 'a Psyche-like figure of pure girlhood, personification of the small nation with a great soul, appeals to *Britannia*. She has lost everything, but her honour is safe!'[22] Britannia, by 1918, had certainly paid a high price for that 'honour'. Slightly eclipsed by her, Serbia comforts Montenegro. There is no visual reference to other contributions made by some 16,000 West Indians, 12,000 Cypriots, 8,000 Newfoundlanders, or the proportionately large commitments of smaller territories which had supported the imperial war effort, such as Bechuanaland, Fiji, Hong Kong, Mauritius, Swaziland, the Seychelles, and Malta.[23]

Germany is nowhere to be found either. At least not in this final iteration. One original sketch for the mural had Germany at the centre with France, but that was before the war. Now, as the finishing touches were applied, it was felt that Germany had 'forfeited all right to be included in European and modern civilisation'.[24] The artist, Sigismund Goetze, who had painted the murals without charge as a gift to the nation (the labour of seven years 'to the entire exclusion of all other work'[25]), was treated with scepticism and declared by an over-zealous writer in *Plain English* an enemy 'of this Christian Empire' and a 'foreign Jew', before asking: 'Where were our British artists?'[26] Goetze was neither German nor Jewish, and the writer was jailed for his comments.[27] The artist, nevertheless, was denied permission to paint the cliffs of England as, on account of his name, it might be deemed a security risk.[28] Other traces of anti-German feeling could be felt when Lord Curzon lambasted *Britannia Pacifatrix* for its alleged German beer hall aesthetics, then spent two years trying to ensure that it, and the four other panels, were never installed.[29] No such feeling, either about the art or artist, had been evident at the time of the commission in prewar London.

What had not been clear in 1914 either, but was becoming ever-more evident in the post-Armistice era, was that the painting had imbued within it not only references to a cultured, civilised, imperial past but also by default many of the root causes that had led to the war in the first place and to which now new seeds of future unrest had been added. Familial devotion could no longer be assumed by populations who had made considerable sacrifices of loyalty during the war and now vied for enhanced autonomy or outright independence.[30] Robert Aldrich and Christopher Hilliard noted:

> The reciprocal effects on the colonial world – the establishment of national myths, demands for greater political autonomy and representation, the personal experience of those who had served, the redrawing of colonial boundaries – were dramatic and long-lasting. Colonial concerns did not lie at the heart of the conflict, but the shock of the fighting and its aftermath reverberated throughout the domains conquered by Europeans.[31]

Some of the sons, it appears, were ready to strike out on their own, while others felt an enhanced, strengthened bond through the great bloodletting and were more committed to Britain and her empire at the end of the war than they had been at the outset. Robert Holland described this, saying, 'it united and divided;

it fuelled British solidarities, and defined emergent nationalities; it was driven by continental commitment, yet it reinforced a bias beyond Europe; it encouraged the liberality of reform, but accentuated the temptation of repression.'[32]

In the painting, and among the *dramatis personae* of allies, traces of divergence were not yet evident, but they *were* historically imminent. For example, there was the United States, a non-signatory to Versailles and the League of Nations and author of the problematic Fourteen Points that advocated the 'self-determination' that would deliver 'a world safe for democracy',[33] which sat awkwardly with the fundamental premise of European imperialism. Russia was in mourning after the Bolshevik Revolution, a widespread famine, and its bloody civil war in which almost every key protagonist in the painting was militarily involved (UK, India, Australia, Canada, Italy, USA, Greece, South Africa, Japan, France, and Romania).[34] India disguised the outrage of the 1919 Amritsar Massacre in the Punjab and glossed over the emergence of the Anarchical and Revolutionary Crimes Act and the non-cooperation Movement and Khilafat movement.[35] In the Middle East, Prince Feisal's declarations of sovereignty would cause tremendous strains on relations between the UK and France and undermine the Treaty of Sèvres, leading to long-term instability in Syria and Iraq.[36] Belgium, itself an infamous colonial power in Africa, abandoned neutrality in favour of a military alliance with France while the latter was embroiled in the Franco–Syrian and Franco–Turkish wars, sustaining around 15,000 casualties.[37] Greece reeled from the schism between the pro-Entente liberal Eleftherios Venizelos and King Constantine, then from its Asia Minor 'catastrophe' (with the support of the UK and France), otherwise known as the Turkish War of Independence, from 1919 to 1923, which led to hundreds of thousands of casualties and the misery brought about by the subsequent population exchange between the two countries.[38] Romania had invasion plans in place for Hungary,[39] the Polish–Soviet War was a reality,[40] the Latvian War of Independence (which was followed by the Estonian War of Independence) was underway,[41] the Red Army invaded Georgia and Armenia,[42] the Kronstadt rebellion happened,[43] and Italy was causing grave concerns for Albania and the Kingdom of Serbs, Croats, and Slovenes.[44] Like all the other countries in the mural, Serbia is depicted with extraordinary simplicity and sympathy, largely in keeping with the sentiment of the Serbian Relief Fund, which had Queen Mary as its patron and the Bishop of London as its president.[45] For those more closely acquainted with the ebb and flow of Balkan politics, the innocence and vulnerability were the product of the Great War (and 'art'), whereby:

> The legend of 'gallant little Serbia' . . . which sprang to life as soon as England found herself at war with Germany and Austria-Hungary in August 1914, at once obscured the fact that for the previous decade Serbia had been regarded generally as a thorough-going nuisance, a nest of violent barbarians whose megalomania would sooner or later meet the punishment it deserved. There had been several occasions when the rest of Europe fully expected to see Austria lash out and wipe Serbia off the map.[46]

The allegorical figure of Italy stands unwittingly holding the Roman 'fasces' (Unity) that would, from 1922, become the unwelcome symbol of the fascist nation, and this at about the time the British Empire allowed the 21-year alliance with Japan to lapse, effectively, in retrospect, facilitating the fatal alliance between Italy and Japan.[47] The exquisite figure of 'Japan' in the mural carried with her, alongside the blossoms, a degree of suspicion.

> When the war is at an end, and peace is at last proclaimed, all the leading European nations will be well-nigh bled to death, alike in men and in money. The assumed superiority of Europe will ere long be definitely challenged. The Awakening of Asia is the most important feature in the world-politics of our time.[48]

Even as British troops pulled out of Silesia, the Caucasus, Turkey, and Persia, it was becoming clear that what followed the Armistice was merely the creation of a post-war, not a peace-time, society.[49] Sir Henry Wilson, Chief of the Imperial General Staff, wrote to Lord Esher on 14 November 1919, exasperated, 'it is again pathetic to realise that one year and three days after the Armistice we have between 20 and 30 wars raging in different parts of the world.'[50] For victors and vanquished alike:

> Four uninterrupted years of mass bloodshed in the chief theatres of war did not leave the post-war world a more peaceful place. Revolutions, Civil Wars, wars of independence, ethnic conflicts, and anti-colonial uprisings occurred around the globe. Churchill observed that 'the war of the giants has ended; the quarrels of the pygmies have begun.'[51]

For this reason, Robert Gerwarth and Erez Manela have introduced the idea of the 'Greater War', both spatially and temporally, an imperial war with global consequences, which did not end until at least 1923.[52] Andrekos Varnava has taken this further to suggest that the Treaty of Lausanne officially ended the war.[53] Within these newly defined parameters, we must now view *Britannia Pacifatrix* as an image of war, of the 'Greater War', as opposed to harbouring any notion of it as a peace-time mural.

Having analysed what the mural depicted, we now turn our attention to what it did not. Here the silences are telling. The key allies are lauded, yet the allied coalition depicted is necessarily incomplete. The implied futures, too, omit many of the sacrifices of those who were largely ignored after the war, despite wartime promises, such as the Armenians, for which there is a growing literature.[54] And what of Britannia herself? Her war debts were debilitating, the human cost staggering, and the scale of imperial overstretch now daunting. There was unrest in Egypt under the nationalist Wafd Party, Sharif Hussein's 'Arab Revolt', and the Iraq Revolt of 1920 (which claimed over 2,000 British lives).[55] In Malta, riots led to police shooting demonstrators,[56] there was discontent amongst elites in Burma, Afghanistan, Cyprus, and the Caribbean, while

Ireland was near breaking point.[57] The army of 3.5 million servicemen during the war was reduced to a mere 370,000 in 1921[58] at a time when the empire had acquired vast territories with mandates like Transjordan and Palestine, German Togoland, Cameroon, and East Africa. Even its dominions were sharing in the spoils of victory in a kind of sub-imperialism (Western Samoa went to New Zealand, New Guinea and the Bismarck Archipelago to Australia, and South Africa acquired swathes of the southern portion of that continent). The British government seemed confident, perhaps too much so, with the fact that the empire had grown by 1.8 million square miles and had 13 million new subjects, bringing the total to 32 million square miles and 400 million inhabitants on 6 continents. For sure Britannia's appearance in the mural is in keeping with John MacKenzie's interpretation of the relationship between the Great War and the British Empire, which refutes the notion that the death knell had been rung in 1918 and proposes instead that a new surge of optimism and productivity actually ensued, at least up until the era of the Great Depression.[59] Phillip Buckner and Douglas Francis have found no real hard evidence that the empire was threatened by the Great War either,[60] while Bernard Porter described the immediate post-war by saying 'the flavour was exciting, even intoxicating. If they could build on it after the war, there was no saying what the empire could become.'[61] New Delhi, Lusaka, and Canberra were being built while the Prince of Wales, the future Edward VIII, toured Canada, Australia, New Zealand, India, Burma, Borneo, Sri Lanka, and Egypt in the time between the negotiations for the Treaty of Versailles and the installation of the *Britannia Pacificatrix*. Maybe there was every reason for Britannia's calm optimism in the painting, as it represented a much-needed *rappel à l'ordre*. Or maybe not.

Something as yet undefinable was now emerging in the first years of peace described by Stephen Garton as 'a unique political philosophy of empire nationalism' whereby 'the Great War became not just a war for empire and between empires but also one, in ways many participants may not have understood at the time, against empire.'[62] Aldrich and Hilliard powerfully concluded in a similar vein with 'but the distinctiveness of the sacrifice in each dominion and colony also ensured that in the long run the war experience helped dissolve the bonds of empire on which it had so powerfully drawn.'[63] Within the UK itself, there was plenty of cause for concern, too, as recorded by the Fabian, economist, and social reformer Beatrice Webb, who observed a post-war that offered only uncertainty:

> Burdened with a huge public debt, living under the shadow of swollen government departments, with a working class seething with discontent, and a ruling class with all its traditions and standards topsy-turvy, with civil servants suspecting businessmen and businessmen conspiring to protect their profits, and all alike abusing the politician, no citizen knows what is going to happen to himself or his children, or to his own social circle, or to the state or to the Empire. All that he does know is that the old order is seriously threatened with dissolution without any new order being in sight.[64]

Unemployment climbed to 11.6 per cent, the Communist Party of Great Britain was founded, a national strike brought the nation to a halt, the Representation of the People Act tripled the electorate, colonial troops were excluded from the victory parade, and a steady flow of citizens took their chances by leaving the UK for the empire (with 1,319,206 leaving in the 1920s, and free passage to the dominions being offered to about 86,000 demobilised servicemen and their families between 1919 and 1924). For millions, Britannia's sacrifice during the war had been, as Ezra Pound described, for 'an old bitch gone in the teeth; for a botched civilization'.[65] Maybe it was not so much the war, then, but the peace that was to be feared. Cynthia Asquith caught something of the moment when she confided in her diary a month before the cessation of hostilities: 'I am beginning to rub my eyes at the prospect of peace. I think it will require more courage than anything that has gone before. It isn't until one leaves off spinning round that one realises how giddy one is.'[66] At the time of the Armistice, and far from giddy, Alfred Milner, 1st Viscount Milner, anticipated a collapse, or perhaps even an implosion, writing, 'the war was one thing . . . a perfectly tremendous strain, but one was carried along by the bigness of the thing . . . . Now comes the inevitable slump.'[67] Samuel Hynes noted that 'as war came to an end, as it changed from *now* to *then*, it began to take shape in men's and women's minds as a completed unit of history, a piece of time with a beginning and an end.'[68]

Between 1914 and 1919, the duration of both the war and the execution of the *Britannia Pacificatrix*, the British Empire and perceptions of it had changed and so, accordingly, had its art. Many artists, especially those who had served at the front, had little time for the remnants of such Victorian allegory and nostalgic dreaming. The 'style' of the Royal Academy was now associated with the same society elites that had been responsible for the war itself. The public desired the depiction of an historical reality, a lived truth, which could not and should not be avoided, however grim it may be. A glance at the London shows in the 12 months following the Armistice gives an indication of what the public appetite was for and how imperial history was created: The *Canadian War Memorials Exhibition* took place in Burlington House in January 1919; The *Peace Academy* happened in May 1919 (in which Virginia Woolf famously wrote of the 'brazen din' of 'honour, patriotism, chastity, wealth, success, importance, position, patronage, power');[69] The Nations War Paintings and Other Records 1919–20 (where reviews would enthuse about the 'white tremendous daybreak' of liberty which the Armistice had brought);[70] and a great Hall of Remembrance was planned as a state commission but was destined never to open (see Cork, this collection). Yet at the top of the Ambassadors' Staircase in the Foreign Office is a work that *did* get completed and in which there is very little trace of war or mud or suffering, no hint of the Somme, Gallipoli, or Passchendaele, nor indeed any reference to the crudity and severity of the peace agreements that had followed. There is no hint of the sun setting on an empire now fatally wounded. Were the insistently high-brow aesthetics signs of unwavering resilience or driven by ignorance, romantic nostalgia, or stubborn determination? Was the artist aware that both his method and his message had rapidly become outmoded in four short years and was destined to become irrelevant? Clare Willsdon, in her ground-breaking study of British mural painting, is unambiguous when she says that Goetze's figures are 'at best naïve, at worst an affront, to a nation preoccupied with remembering the dead, caring for the maimed, and rehabilitating – where possible – the traumatised'.[71]

Foreign Secretary Lord Curzon hated the mural of *Britannia Pacifatrix* and wanted it, and the four other murals that accompanied it, to be transferred either to County Hall or to other regional town halls. When that was deemed impossible he compromised, saying that they could be hung in panels (i.e. easily removable at some point in the future), but the artist insisted on *marouflage*, a technique which meant they became part of the wall, embedded in the Foreign Office, an artefact of empire. Even if Lloyd George had declared optimistically that the paintings 'brought light to a tomb',[72] it was soon felt that 'in an era of decolonization, Sigismund Goetz's murals of *Britannia Pacifatrix* on the grand staircase struck an inappropriately triumphalist note.'[73] (One of the sopra-portas was even called *Dulce et Decorum est pro patria mori* – words which are now taught to school children in the context of Wilfred Owen's 'old lie'.) By the 1960s 'the Foreign Office, members of the government and civil servants allegedly averted their gaze, embarrassed by the imperialist sentiments contained in his murals.'[74] Foreign Secretary Douglas Hurd (1989–95) talked of their mixture of 'melodrama, pathos and high camp',[75] while Foreign Secretary Robin Cook (1997–2001) told the *Sunday Telegraph* that he was embarrassed by them.[76] When the restoration of the painting was completed in 1990, Caroline Dakers wrote that the *fin-de-siècle* melodrama embedded in the artist's 'evocation of a past age was revealed in all its absurd glory'.[77] That said, it remains a vital facet of post-colonial enquiry, straddling the years of change in question and providing, as art should, not only some answers about the society that created it but also navigating routes to the questions that remain unasked about empire, armistice, and aftermath.

Methodology and design

This volume represents both a multi- and interdisciplinary approach to help us understand the post-Armistice empire via the broad spectrum of diplomatic, social, ideological, political, cultural, and economic histories. The diverse scholarship presented in these chapters explores aspects of empire and methods of viewing it which might otherwise be overlooked or under-utilised in more conventional studies of empire and Armistice. To begin we have selected scholarship that deals with locations such as Lagos and Tonga (pre- and post-Armistice 'normality' amongst German and British imperial subjects); British Cyprus and the impact of Armenian legionnaires under French command, in a Christian–Muslim island; and China during the transition from the informal influence of Britain to America in the Asia-Pacific region (the resultant cultural appropriation of which may still be witnessed in the era of Xi Jinping). Where the contributions return to more obvious geographies within the empire it has been to prise open new and innovative avenues of enquiry. This includes the debates on pacificism in Bengal in the context of India's militant nationalism, Australia's post-war feminist nationalisms, the influence of the Irish Catholic press, and the long-term impact of state-led commemoration.

To further the originality of this collection the editors have invited scholarship that employs a variety of lenses through which to examine the post-Armistice empire. As such we have offset imperial masculinity with nationalist feminisms; turned our attention to the un-built British Hall of Remembrance in London, and contrasted it with a micro-history of a family-based musical composition written 100 years after the Armistice in Australia; explored the tabloid press and contrasted the sentiments with private memoirs and journals; observed the classicising use of Thucydides by Julia Gillard at Gallipoli and the momentary nostalgia offset by a 1930s fatalism in British film; and concluded with an examination of a notorious act of terrorism in Northern Ireland in the 1980s and an installation work of art in post-Brexit Britain titled *We're here, because we're here*. To attain such diversity, we have drawn upon scholars from Australia, the UK, the USA, Singapore, Papua New Guinea, India, Belgium, and France to undertake the investigation into emergent imperial microcosms and nationalisms, transitionary moments on the imperial periphery, and post-imperial multinational commemorations a century after the Armistice.

Notes

1 Reginald Brett, Viscount Esher, to Cabinet Secretary, Sir Maurice Hankey, February 1919; see Samuel Hynes, *A War Imagined: The First World War and English Culture* (n.p.: Pimlico, 1992), 267.
2 Christopher Booker, "How the First World War Inspired the EU," *The Spectator*, February 8, 2014, www.spectator.com.au/2014/02/how-the-first-world-war-inspired-the-eu/.
3 Alex von Tunzelmann, "The Imperial Myths Driving Brexit," *The Atlantic*, August 12, 2019, www.theatlantic.com/international/archive/2019/08/imperial-myths-behind-brexit/595813/.
4 Ross Clark, "The EU is the True Successor of the British Empire," *The Spectator*, November 14, 2019.
5 Mark Connelly, *George Orwell: A Literary Companion* (Jefferson, NC: McFarland & Company, Inc., 2018), 157.
6 "Britain to Become 'Second Rate' in the World After Brexit, Says EU's Donald Tusk," *Straits Times*, November 14, 2019, www.straitstimes.com/world/europe/britain-to-become-second-rate-in-the-world-after-brexit-says-eus-donald-tusk.
7 Danny Dorling and Sally Tomlinson, *Rule Britannia: Brexit and the End of the British Empire* (n.p.: Biteback Publishing, 2019); see also, Danny Dorling and Sally Tomlinson, "Brexit: How the End of Britain's Empire Led to Rising Inequality That Heled Leave to Victory," *The Conversation*, May 23, 2019, https://theconversation.com/brexit-how-the-end-of-britains-empire-led-to-rising-inequality-that-helped-leave-to-victory-116466; Danny Dorling, "(Mis)Rule Britannia: Brexit is the Last Gasp of Empire," *LSE Brexit 2020 (blog), London School of Economics and Political Science* (February 20, 2019), https://blogs.lse.ac.uk/brexit/2019/02/20/misrule-britannia-brexit-is-the-last-gasp-of-empire/.
8 Anne Bostanci and John Dubber, *Remember the World as Well as the War: Why the Global Reach and Enduring Legacy of the First World War Still Matter Today* (London: British Council, 2014).

9 Annette Becker, "The Visual Arts," in *A Companion to World War I,* ed. John Horne (Chichester, UK and Malden, MA: Wiley & Blackwell, 2010), 338, https://onlinelibrary.wiley.com/doi/book/10.1002/9781444323634.

10 The five panels were: 1) *Britannia Sponsa: The Sea-farers claim Britain as their Bride*; 2) *Britannia Nutrix: She teaches her children the arts of peace*; 3) *Britannia Bellatrix: She teaches her sons the art of war*; 4) *Britannia Colonorum Mater: Mistress of the Seas she sends her sons into distant lands*; and 5) *Britannia Pacificatrix*: ['Britain the Peacemaker'].

11 Caroline Dakers, "Sigismund Goetze and the Decoration of the Foreign Office Staircase: 'Melodrama, Pathos, and High Camp,'" *The Journal of the Decorative Arts Society 1850 – Present* 21 (1997): 55.

12 Sigismund Goetze, *Mural Decorations at the Foreign Office. Descriptive Account by the Artist* (London: Government Publication, 1921, reprinted 1953).

13 Stephen Harrison, "Foreword," in *Classics and Imperialism in the British Empire,* ed. Mark Bradley (n.p.: Oxford University Press, 2010), viii.

14 Ibid.

15 David Dimbleby, *Seven Ages of Britain: The Story of Our Nation Revealed by its Treasures* (n.p.: Hodder & Stoughton, 2009), 187–88. For a fuller discussion see: Timothy Barringer, Geoff Quilley, and Douglas Fordham, eds., *Art and the British Empire* (Manchester and New York: Manchester University Press, 2007), 13. Also: Boris Ford, ed., *The Cambridge Guide to the Arts in Britain: The Edwardian Age and the Inter-War Years*, vol. 8 (London: Cambridge University Press, 1989), 9.

16 Holger Hoock, *Empires of the Imagination: Politics, War, and the Arts in the British World, 1750–1850* (n.p.: Profile Books, 2010), 15.

17 Goetze, "Mural Decorations at the Foreign Office: Descriptive Account by the Artist," Box 2.28.F, 5.

18 Modelled by a randomly selected ANZAC by the name of Bert Hill, complete with slouch hat.

19 Goetze, "Mural Decorations at the Foreign Office," 6.

20 Ibid.

21 "Memorandum on Origin, Scope and Intention of the Foreign Office Staircase Decorations," July 21, 1919, cited in Dakers, "Sigismund Goetze and the Decoration of the Foreign Office Staircase," 60–61, f.n. 31.

22 Goetze, "Mural Decorations at the Foreign Office."

23 Andrekos Varnava and Michael J. K. Walsh, "Colonial Volunteerism and Recruitment in the British Empire During the Great War," *Itinerario* 38, no. 3 (2014): 19–26.

24 Richard Bagot, "Art and War," *Museums Journal* (February 1917): 180, cited in Melissa Hall, "Modernism, Militarism and Masculinity" (PhD diss., State University of New York at Binghamton, New York, 1993), 115.

25 Goetze, "Mural Decorations at the Foreign Office," 2.

26 In fact, Goetze was a London-born devout Christian, teetotaler, and set against turn-of-the-century materialism and had, in his research for the painting, specifically stopped short of the over-the-top presentations on the Neuer Museum staircase by Wilhelm von Kaulbach in preference for Tiepolo's decorations at Warzburg and the work of Puvis de Chavannes in Rouen and at the Musee de Picardie in Amiens. He believed in the morally uplifting power of art and yet did not insert religion into the painting.

27 William D. Rubinstein, *The Palgrave Dictionary of Anglo-Jewish History* (n.p.: Palgrave Macmillan, 2011), 330.

28 Sir Lionel Earle, *Turn Over the Page* (London: Hutchinson & Co., 1935), 196.

29 Alexander Mirkovic, "Imperial History in Pictures: Goetze Murals in the United Kingdom's Foreign Office," *World History Connected* 11, no. 1 (February 2014), https://worldhistoryconnected.press.uillinois.edu/11.1/forum_mirkovic.html.

30 Emma Reisz, "Classics, Race, and Edwardian Anxieties about Empire," in *Classics and Imperialism in the British Empire*, ed. Mark Bradley (Oxford: Oxford University Press, 2010), 210–28.
31 Robert Aldrich and Christopher Hilliard, "The French and British Empires," in *A Companion to World War One*, ed. John Horne (n.p.: Blackwell Publishing Ltd, 2010), 525.
32 Robert Holland, "The British Empire and the Great War, 1914–1918," in *The Oxford History of the British Empire: Vol 4 – The Twentieth Century*, ed. Judith M. Brown and Wm. Roger Louis (Oxford: Oxford University Press, 1999), 114–38.
33 Ross A. Kennedy, *The Will to Believe: Woodrow Wilson, World War I, and America's Strategy for Peace and Security* (Kent, OH: Kent State University Press, 2009).
34 Robert Jackson, *At War with the Bolsheviks: The Allied Intervention into Russia, 1917–1920*, (London: Tom Stacey Ltd., 1972); Ilya Somin, *Stillborn Crusade: The Tragic Failure of Western Intervention in the Russian Civil War, 1918–1920* (London: Routledge, 2018).
35 Sharmishtha Roy Chowdhury, *The First World War, Anticolonialism and Imperial Authority in British India, 1914–1924* (London: Routledge, 2019).
36 Kristian Coates Ulrichsen, *The First World War in the Middle East* (London: Hurst, 2014); Justin Fantauzzo, *The Other Wars: The Experience and Memory of the First World War in the Middle East and Macedonia* (Cambridge: Cambridge University Press, 2020).
37 Pierre Lierneux and Natasja Peeters, eds., *Beyond the Great War: Belgium 1918–1928* (Tielt: Lannoo Publishers, 2018); Robert F. Zeidner, *The Tricolor Over the Taurus* (New York: Peter Lan, 1996); Elizabeth F. Thompson, *How the West Stole Democracy from the Arabs: The Syrian Arab Congress of 1920 and the Destruction of its Liberal-Islamic Alliance* (New York: Atlantic Monthly Press, 2020).
38 Michael Llewellyn-Smith, *Ionian Vision: Greece in Asia Minor, 1919–1922* (n.p.: Allen Lane, 1973 repr., London: C. Hurst & Co Publishers Ltd, 1998).
39 Glenn E. Torrey, *Romania and World War I* (Portland: Centre for Romanian Studies, 1998).
40 Norman Davies, *White Eagle, Red Star: The Polish-Soviet War, 1919–20 and 'the Miracle on the Vistula'* (London: Pimplico, 2003).
41 Anatol Lieven, *The Baltic Revolution: Estonia, Latvia, Lithuania, and the Path to Independence* (New Haven: Yale University Press, 1993).
42 Stephen F. Jones, *The Making of Modern Georgia, 1918–2012: The First Georgian Republic and its Successors* (London: Routledge, 2014); Richard G. Hovannisian, *The Republic of Armenia*, 4 vols (Berkeley: University of California Press, 1971–1996).
43 Israel Getzler, *Kronstadt 1917–1921* (Cambridge: Cambridge University Press, 1993).
44 Vanda Wilcox, ed., *Italy in the Era of the Great War* (Leiden: Brill Academic Publishers, 2018).
45 Andrej Mitrovic, *Serbia's Great War, 1914–1918* (n.p.: Purdue University Press, 2007).
46 Edward Crankshaw, *The Fall of the House of Hapsburg* (London, 1963), 377.
47 James Burgwyn, *Italian Foreign Policy in the Interwar Period, 1918–1940* (Westport: Praeger, 1997); Ian Nish, *Alliance in Decline: A Study of Anglo-Japanese Relations, 1908–23* (London: Bloomsbury, 2013).
48 Henry M. Hyndman, "The Awakening of Asia," *The Fortnightly Review* (October 1916): 690.
49 Richard Bessel, *Germany after the First World War* (Oxford: Oxford University Press, 1993), 283.
50 Keith Jeffery, ed., *The Military Correspondence of Field Marshall Sir Henry Wilson 1918–1922* (London: The Bodley Head for the Army Records Society, 1985), 133.
51 Peter Gatrell, "War after the War: Conflicts, 1919–1923," in *A Companion to World War I,* ed. John Horne (n.p.: Blackwell, 2010), 558.

52 Robert Gerwarth and Erez Manela, *Empires at War: 1911–1923* (Oxford: Oxford University Press, 2014).
53 Andrekos Varnava, *Serving the Empire in the Great War: The Cypriot Mule Corps, Imperial Identity and Silenced Memory* (Manchester: Manchester University Press, 2017); Richard Smith, *Jamaican Volunteers in the First World War: Race, Masculinity and the Development of National Consciousness* (Manchester: Manchester University Press, 2004); Myron J. Echenberg, *Colonial Conscripts the Tirailleurs Sénégalais in French West Africa, 1857–1960* (Portsmouth: Heinemann, 1991).
54 Andrekos Varnava, "Imperialism First, the War Second: The British, an Armenian Legion, and Deliberations on Where to Attack the Ottoman Empire, November 1914 – April 1915," *Historical Research* 87, no. 237 (2014): 533–55; Andrekos Varnava, "French and British Post-War Imperial Agendas and Forging an Armenian Homeland after the Genocide: The Formation of the Légion d'Orient in October 1916," *The Historical Journal* 58, no. 4 (2014): 997–1025.
55 Malak Badrawi, *Political Violence in Egypt, 1910–1924: Secret Societies, Plots and Assassinations* (Richmond: Curzon Press, 2000).
56 Iliya Marovich-Old, "Nationalism as Resistance to Colonialism: A Comparative Look at Malta and Cyprus from 1919–1940," in *Cypriot Nationalisms in Context*, ed. Thekla Kyritsi and Nikos Christofi (n.p.: Palgrave Macmillan, 2018), 261–81.
57 Andrekos Varnava, *British Cyprus and the Long Great War, 1914–1925: Empire, Loyalties and Democratic Deficit* (London: Routledge, 2020); Bill Kissane, *The Politics of the Irish Civil War* (Oxford: Oxford University Press, 2005).
58 Timothy H. Parsons, *The Second British Empire: In the Crucible of the Twentieth Century* (Lanham, MD: Rowman and Littlefield, 2014).
59 John MacKenzie, "The First World War and the Cultural, Political, and Environmental Transformation of the British Empire," in *The Great War and the British Empire: Culture and Society*, ed. Michael J. K. Walsh and Andrekos Varnava (London: Routledge, 2017), 23–38.
60 See Phillip Buckner and R. Douglas Francis, *Rediscovering the British World* (Calgary: Calgary University Press, 2005).
61 Bernard Porter, *The Lion's Share: A History of British Imperialism 1850 to the Present*, 5th ed. (Abingdon: Pearson, 2012), 198. See also Bernard Porter, *The Absent-Minded Imperialists: Empire, Society, and Culture in Britain* (Oxford: Oxford University Press, 2006).
62 Stephen Garton, "The Dominions, Ireland and India," in *Empires at War: 1911–1923*, ed. Robert Gerwarth and Erez Manela (Oxford: Oxford University Press, 2014), 176–77.
63 Aldrich and Hilliard, "The French and British Empires," 532.
64 Beatrice Webb, *The Diary of Beatrice Webb*, ed. N. MacKenzie and J. Mackenzie, vol. 3 (Cambridge: Belknap Press of Harvard University Press, 1984), 315–16.
65 Ezra Pound, "Hugh Selwyn Mauberley," in *New Selected Poems and Translations,* ed. Richard Sieburth (New York: New Directions Publishing Corp., 2010), 109.
66 Cynthia Asquith, *Diaries 1915–1918* (Knopf, 1969), 480.
67 Quoted in Brian Gardner, *Allenby* (London: Cassell, 1965), 252.
68 Hynes, *A War Imagined*, 257.
69 Virginia Woolf, "The Royal Academy," *Atheneum* (August 22, 1919): 774–75.
70 "The Aim of Modern Art," *The New Journalist* (February 18, 1920).
71 Clare Z. P. Willsdon, *Mural Painting in Britain 1840–1940: Image and Meaning* (Oxford: Oxford University Press, 2000), 121.
72 Memo dated November 22, 1921, cited in Earle, *Turn Over the Page*, 198.
73 In her review of: Adam Sharr and Stephen Thornton, *Demolishing Whitehall: Leslie Martin, Harold Wilson and the Architecture of White Heat* (n.p.: Ashgate, 2013); Louise Campbell, *Urban History* 41, no. 3 (2014): 555.

74 Dakers, "Sigismund Goetze and the Decoration of the Foreign Office Staircase," 64.
75 John Ryle, "Britannia Descending the Staircase: A Lost World of Imperial Myth-Making at the British Foreign Office," *The Guardian*, February 9, 1998.
76 *Sunday Telegraph*, January 24, 1999.
77 Dakers, "Sigismund Goetze and the Decoration of the Foreign Office Staircase," 54.

Part I

Imperial endgames

2 Imperial Coercion in Ireland and India 1919–21

Insights for Irish Australians

Stephanie James

'India's case is, in fact, Ireland's case. The 'rebels' in both countries are fighting for freedom and self-determination.'[1]

Introduction

In November 1921, James Vincent (J. V.) O'Loghlin compared India and Ireland in his regular column in Adelaide's Irish Catholic newspaper, the *Southern Cross*. His comment followed rioting in Bombay associated with the visit of the Prince of Wales. O'Loghlin, the founder, first editor and long-term director of the *Southern Cross*, had argued that most Indians feared and hated British rule and that neither 'British officialism' or 'press propaganda' could camouflage popular hostility.

He emphasised the consequences of foreign rule for India, prevented from making its own laws and subject to those made by the British government in India 'in which she has no representation'. O'Loghlin's identification of the parallels between India and Ireland exemplified an important insight about the circumstances confronting the two colonies. In both, Britain was exerting military coercion to reassert control. For Irish Australian readers, similar items in Irish Catholic newspapers magnified the opportunities available for deeper understanding of the empire in the years following the Great War. Before and during the Great War, Australian understanding or engagement with imperial issues beyond the relationship between Ireland and/or Australia and England was limited. The consequences of the war, in particular the Versailles 'peace' conference and treaty-making processes, highlighted the somewhat less-desirable features of the British Empire. This challenged those features as opposed to those which had inspired large forces from both Ireland and India, as well as Australia, to volunteer from 1914 onwards.

Constituting around 25 per cent of Australia's population in 1911, first- and second-generation Irish Australians had limited recognition of some very basic similarities between Ireland and India. For example, that an appointed viceroy was at the apex of British rule in India *and* Ireland and that for both colonies membership of the British Empire involved tight, oppressive power and coercive control. Moreover, probably few people in Australia or Britain realised, that as moves for Irish home rule from the 1880s unfolded, well-educated Indian

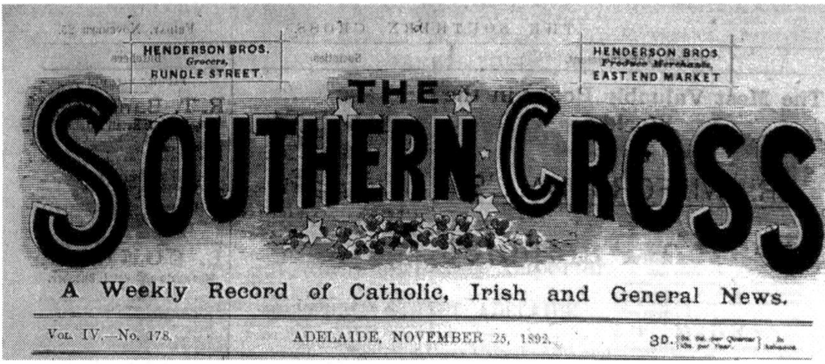

Figure 2.1 Masthead from the Adelaide *Southern Cross*.

Source: (Image courtesy of the Southern Cross, Adelaide)

bureaucrats and professional classes found that this clarified a comparative paradigm of possible pathways for their countries' fight for independence. Somehow, for most Irish Australians, intense focus on the imperial centre resulted in the regular exclusion of drawing meaningful and obvious correlations between the consistently coercive treatment and experience of these two colonies at the periphery of the empire.

Irish Australians, especially the Catholic majority, had limited access to sources presenting Irish news, something of continuing importance for many. The tendency to distrust secular press coverage of Irish affairs was widespread and longstanding. Thus, the Irish Catholic newspapers which existed in all capital cities provided a more reliable conduit for many. One function of these newspapers was to inform readers about Ireland at both religious and political levels. India was often included in items relating to both aspects. The *Southern Cross*, for example, regularly discussed India as a missionary destination, and the consequent growth of Catholicism, in the pre-1914 decades.[2] Sometimes natural disasters like crop failure or famine were featured, seeking reader's generosity;[3] details of potential Catholic appointments to high imperial positions were also frequent.[4] As an imperial possession, India also attracted attention, with British inadequacies often highlighted;[5] the tone usually differed when Irish officials or regiments were involved.[6] Points of comparison between Ireland and India were typically examined under headings such as 'Sisters in Misfortune',[7] but articles describing elements of British policy in India (famine due to level of food exports) and Egypt (barbaric flogging and execution of murderers of British officers) were directly linked to policy in Ireland.[8] That force, or coercion, was frequently used to restore control in both colonies was recognised. The term 'coercion' would have been understood by many Irish Australians as specifically applying to a series of legal measures introduced in Ireland between 1833 (the Suppression of Disturbances

Act) and 1887 (the Criminal Law and Procedure Act). These Acts empowered official restrictions, such as curfews and detention without trial, to prevent or limit disturbances in nominated districts; the 1887 Act remained in force and was used during the early years of the War of Independence.[9] Defining intimidation and conspiracy, it gave magistrates great power in proclaimed districts and facilitated the banning of subversive organisations.[10]

There were both formal and informal connections between Ireland and India. Formally some links of great significance reached back to the nineteenth century. Notably, individuals closely associated with the Indian National Congress (founded in 1885) personified these connections. Dadabhai Naorog, a founder, and later Congress President in 1886, 1893 and 1906, was the first Indian to seek election to Westminster.[11] In 1894, Irishman and Quaker Alfred Webb (a Westminster MP, 1890–95) presided at the tenth National Congress; his role reflected strong and direct peripheral imperial bonds. More informally, the two countries also shared other tactics, for example, India's early twentieth-century adoption of a boycott of British goods. Originally a weapon used against British landowners in the Irish Land Wars of the 1880s, its extension and use in India demonstrates the vulnerability of imperial control when, at the periphery, countries were applying lessons learnt elsewhere in the empire.[12]

Westminster had been the scene of many nineteenth- and early twentieth-century debates about Indian affairs. Prominent Irish MPs familiar to Irish Australians as visitors, writers or officials in Irish Nationalist organisations, such as Michael Davitt[13] and Webb,[14] were vocal parliamentary participants – such items were not always reported in Australia's Irish Catholic press.[15] It took events following the 1916 Dublin Easter Rising and Britain's immediate responses and, longer term, what emerged following the Versailles settlement, as well as episodes of violence in Ireland and India from 1919, to fully enlighten Ireland and its diaspora communities about the shared similarities between the 'Emerald Isle' and India. The war and its legacies inserted a new lens into the framework available to Irish Australians in advancing their understanding of what it was about the imperial structure that placed Ireland and India side by side, despite basic differences, in struggles with London. In this process, Irish Catholic newspapers played a decisive role.

This chapter has three main sections. The first explores the international context, focusing specifically on the backdrop to and impact of World War One in both India and Ireland. The second briefly clarifies the contours of post-war coercion in both countries. The greatest part of this chapter, however, demonstrates how three of Australia's Irish Catholic newspapers, along with their editors and commentators, informed and enlightened readers about the emerging parallels between these imperial associates through an examination of items published between 1919 and 1921. All three papers were weekly publications and existed as official Church organs. The Melbourne *Advocate*, established in 1868; the aforementioned *Southern Cross*, founded in 1889, and Sydney's *Catholic Press*, dating from 1895, all demonstrate the development of a more nuanced understanding of parallels between Ireland and India in the post-war years.

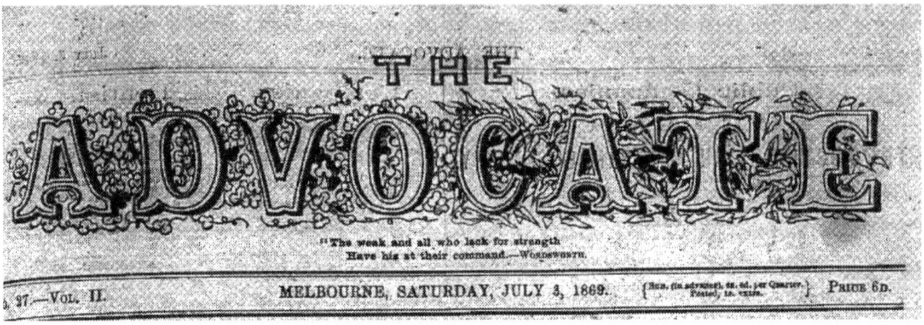

Figure 2.2 Masthead from the Melbourne *Advocate*.

Source: (Image Courtesy of MDHC Archdiocese of Melbourne).

Figure 2.3 Masthead from the Sydney *Catholic Press*.

Source: (Image courtesy of the *Sydney Catholic Weekly*).

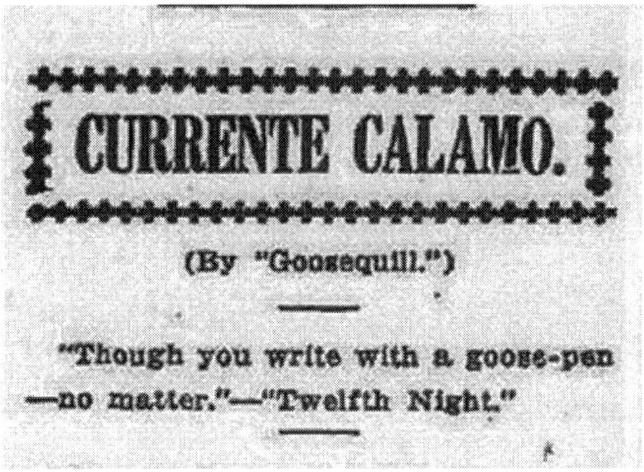

Figure 2.4 Heading from 'Currente Calamo' Column.

Source: (Image courtesy of the *Southern Cross*, Adelaide).

Editors during the years under discussion were all laymen, not clerics, and were experienced newspapermen: Irishman Tighe Ryan in Sydney[16] and Irish Australians Thomas Shorthill and Frederick Martin Koerner in Melbourne[17] and Adelaide respectively.[18] The *Southern Cross* also featured a weekly commentary column – 'Currente Calamo' – penned by founding editor, J. V. O'Loghlin; his material consistently included discussion of imperial issues.[19]

The association between colonial issues and both World War One and the complex Versailles agenda were decisive in transforming Irish Australian awareness of patterns of imperial coercion, unrelated to colour or geography. Irish Catholic newspapers were critical in this process.

Part one

The Great War in Europe was a pivotal experience for the British Empire. The outbreak of the war in August 1914 was accompanied by empire-wide offers of military support. General newspaper coverage was deeply loyal to the empire; this was clearly evident in the Irish Catholic press at the outset. India, Ireland and Australia all responded and encouraged the military participation of their populations; while their armies were termed as volunteer forces, there were significant differences between these imperial associates. Along a continuum of empire membership, with self-governing dominions such as Australia at one end and India as a colonial possession at the other extreme, Ireland was located somewhere towards the centre but in the colonial embrace. Both Ireland and India were ruled by Britain and denied the independent decision-making which existed in the settler colonies.

British policy in India had created major issues which by 1914 were increasingly evident. These can be summarised in three areas: firstly, ethnic issues relating to growing tensions between Hindu and Muslim populations; secondly, limited attempts at reform involving greater local representation which both exacerbated the tensions and failed to satisfy expectations; and thirdly, the hopes for independence which involved the Indian National Congress and, after 1906, the Muslim League. In addition to these complex issues, leaders such as Mohandas Gandhi and Ali Jinna developed followings, alongside the generally inadequate capacity of British officials to negotiate a path forward. On the eve of war, the Balkan military episodes of 191113 ignited concerns among Pan-Islamists who judged British inaction in response to the vulnerability of the Ottoman Sultan as deeply flawed.[20] The Muslim League supported war against Turkey in 1914, but radicals contemplated challenging the Raj. India thus entered the war with potentially dangerous fractures capable of seriously undermining any contribution.

As Keith Jeffery noted, describing India's military contribution as the largest volunteer army ever, was only technically accurate. Without actual conscription, the widespread European colonial method of local subcontracting called into question 'the unforced readiness of individuals to join up'. Edwin Montagu (secretary of state for India, 1917–22) later acknowledged that 'Indian soldiers were . . . persuaded with great vigour . . . to join His Majesty's forces during the war'.[21] The Indian Expeditionary Force was dispatched to France and Belgium in

September 1914; over 1.25 million soldiers left India by 1918. Many prominent Indians believed the goal of independence was best assisted by offering whatever active support for Britain was possible in the empire's military crisis. Expectations of India receiving Dominion status (given the extent of human, financial and supply contribution) comparable to Australia and Canada were widespread. More than 74,000 Indians died in the Great War, and many more were wounded.[22] Shashi Tharour comments that Indian 'assistance exceeded that of any other nation'. He disputes that support was 'offered' by the Indian government, citing in particular 'a lump sum of £100 million as a special contribution' to the war costs. Such generosity, he argues, 'elides the fact . . . that the "Government of India" consisted of Englishmen accountable to His Majesty's Government in Britain'.[23] Commenting on Britain's neglect of these soldiers alongside general ignorance about them in India, he emphasises that the combatants were not fighting for India: 'None of the soldiers was a conscript: soldiering was their profession. They served the very British empire (sic) that was oppressing their own people back home.'[24] The impact of the war years on India was great. Margaret Macmillan argued that war 'had shown Indians that their white masters could be as irrational and savage as anyone else in the world'.[25] Not only did large numbers of Indian soldiers witness action in many theatres of war,[26] but these years were also accompanied by a powerful surge of nationalism, demonstrated by the emergence of nationalist leaders like Mohandas Gandhi. Confirming imperial support at the beginning of the war, as he had previously in South Africa, Gandhi optimistically hoped military contribution would determine India as Britain's 'most favourite partner' with 'racial distinctions . . . becom[ing] a thing of the past'.[27] But in India, war legacies of inflation, the demise of exports and general disillusionment combined to annihilate support from 'even those Indians who had thought that at least British rule provided good government'.[28] The final blow, over 12 million Indian deaths in the post-war influenza epidemic, was appropriated by Gandhi to demonstrate British incapacity to rule.[29]

Meanwhile in simmering Ireland, by mid-1914, home rule seemed imminent. Focused resistance had radiated from Ulster since the 1910 election of a liberal government dependent on labour and Irish minorities, as well as 'commit[ment] to Home Rule as an immediate policy'.[30] Resistance from 218,206 men signing the Ulster Covenant in 1912, with yet more women signing a declaration supporting their men, and the January 1913 formation of the Ulster Volunteer Force, with over 100,000 enlistments by mid-1914, defined the battleground. When the para-military solution was echoed by the nationalists in the south with the establishment of the National Volunteers in November 1913, numbers quickly reached 180,000. In May 1914 the Home Rule Bill passed through Westminster.[31] Addressing cabinet in July, British Prime Minister Asquith articulated the potential imperial ramifications of the Irish situation: 'The issues so far [are] reaching not only civil war, but interests in India, [the] industrial world and throughout [the] empire might be broken up by catastrophe in Ireland'.[32]

At the time it was acknowledged that the Great War saved Britain.[33] In early August, when the European tinderbox ignited, home rule's implementation was delayed until the conclusion of war. Having shepherded home rule, John Redmond, leader of the Irish Parliamentary Party (IPP), now demonstrated the extent of his imperial loyalty by suggesting that the Ulster and Southern Volunteers could combine to defend Ireland. Believing that such an outcome would be good for the empire, he subsequently offered Irish soldiers unconditionally.[34] Trusting that 'common sacrifice for the war effort would create a new basis for Irish unity',[35] he was convinced Ireland's independence would follow. His imperial generosity was rejected by around 10,000 National Volunteers, who moved to form the 'Irish Volunteers'. Their leader Eoin MacNeill, made the statement that these men were not 'bound to serve the Imperial Government in defence of the British Empire', highlighting the gulf in Irish nationalist ranks.[36]

The loyalty and goodwill evident in 1914 quickly dissipated in Ireland, as recognition of differential War Office treatment of volunteer soldiers from Ulster and the South helped animate anti-British sentiment.[37] Although more than 200,000 Irishmen joined Britain's wartime armed forces, the fragility of Irish nationalist commitment was visible in the increasing conditionally expressed loyalties.[38] But by 1916 Irish Volunteer numbers had swelled to 15,000; within that total, the secretive, extremist Irish Republican Brotherhood (IRB) plotted, biding its time. Committed to the need for revolutionary change, their planned but ultimately compromised Dublin Easter Rising of late April 1916 provoked violent British responses.[39] The executions, martial law and deportations destroyed Britain's initial advantage; Irish sympathies gradually shifted towards the rebels.[40] At the imperial centre, as Britain experienced treachery and betrayal from the adjacent Ireland, the 'Irish problem' moved to even greater dominance in the empire. In terms of the Indian periphery, officials there and in London struggled to coordinate varying perceptions of that colony's future.

In the shadow of the Great War, according to Eric Hobsbawm, 'a larger area of the globe . . . [was] under the formal or informal control of Britain . . . but never before had the rulers of Britain felt less confident about maintaining their old colonial supremacy'.[41] Any euphoria after victory in 1918 was short lived. In addition to the myriad issues associated with 'peace-making' at Versailles, Britain soon faced revolt, rebellion and reaction in numerous colonial sites. In Ireland and India the popular expectations of self-determination and independence were heightened.

Part two

Hobsbawm also argues that the Great War 'was the first set of events which seriously shook the world of colonialism'.[42] In January 1919, when the victors met in Paris to grapple with peace, redraw borders and penalise Germany, both Ireland and India attached disproportionately high hopes to the gathering. Much of the optimism related to President Wilson's Fourteen Points on which the negotiations were supposedly centred. Macmillan judged that 'Indian nationalists noted... [his] talk of self-determination with approval'.[43] But of the Fourteen Points, she also designated this point 'as one of the most controversial and opaque'.[44]

In Ireland, events flowing immediately from Britain's December 1918 general election (the first in five years) highlighted voter rejection of the IPP. Against the paltry 6-seat return for the IPP, Sinn Féin garnered 73; those elected (55 of whom were in British jails) refused to grace Westminster.[45] Within Sinn Féin there were former home rule supporters, those committed to physical force, and others totally opposed to such actions. From the first Dáil Éireann, convened in Dublin on 21 January, came the Declaration of Independence, a statement overtly connecting Ireland to 'President Wilson's espousal of self-determination'.[46] It stated that

> Ireland today asserts her historic nationhood the more confidently before the new world emerging from the War, . . . because . . . permanent peace . . . can never be secured by perpetuating military dominion for the profit of empire but only by establishing the control of government in every land upon the basis of the free will of the people.[47]

Recognising the importance of the Paris Peace Conference, the Sinn Féin leadership dispatched a delegation to place Ireland's case on the agenda. But Ireland was allowed no voice; British resolve to ensure Ireland remained a domestic rather than an international item was powerful, and Wilson's disinterest in that small Irish nation eventually became clear. The imprecision of self-determination led to Sinn Féin's appeal for Wilson's support, but by March, the president accepted that Ireland was 'a domestic affair of the British Empire' in which external intervention had no place.[48] The presence of Sinn Féin delegates in Paris, however, laid effective groundwork for subsequent promotion of their cause.[49] By the turn of 1919–20, moderate Sinn Féin members recognised that Versailles could not deliver peaceful achievement of Irish independence; in conjunction with the September banning of the Dáil and the December passage of a new home rule act effectively partitioning Ireland, the space for the extremist domination of Sinn Féin was now clear.[50]

Thus, January 1920 marked a new phase in Irish Volunteer (now termed the Irish Republican Army (IRA)) violence against British authority when two policemen were ambushed and shot. By mid-1920, a sequence of arms seizures, attacks on police, guerrilla-type raids and ambushes resulted in 55 police deaths, the destruction of 16 barracks and many others abandoned. Despite rising violence, increased British expenditure and troop deployment, London resisted referring to the conflict as war. But when the British began advertising for temporary constables in January 1920 to assist the Royal Irish Constabulary (RIC), the situation changed. The Black and Tans first arrived at the end of March; in July the Auxiliaries followed, signalling new directions on the ground.[51] Thus bolstered, the RIC was able to pursue the IRA more aggressively, and 'the government, at first tacitly and then openly, condoned reprisals by the police'.[52] According to Maurice Walsh in *The News from Ireland*, early correspondent coverage of the violence largely accepted Britain's interpretation, was more sceptical by 1919, and following the involvement of the two paramilitary forces, 'the reporting of the British campaign became even more hostile'.[53] By mid-1921, escalating violence had left

405 police, 150 military and possibly 750 IRA and civilians dead. In July a truce enabled a path towards negotiation of the Anglo-Irish Treaty. This was signed on 6 December and established the Irish Free State as a self-governing Dominion within the British Commonwealth.

Unlike Ireland, India was allowed its own delegation in Paris. However, delegation membership –Montagu and two Indians 'chosen for their loyalty' – was hardly reflective of 1919 India.[54] Hobsbawm's reference to India from 1918 to 1922 as 'revolutionary years'[55] encompasses both increasing Indian demands for home rule instead of limited self-government and imperial inability to generate relevant reforms. In 1919 legislative responses veered from the power-sharing ideals of the Government of India Act[56] to the overtly coercive Rowlatt Act designed to bolster imperial authority and suppress any opposition.[57] One unintended consequence of the tighter security came from Gandhi's civil disobedience campaign and a non-violent general strike called for in April 1919. Again, Bengal emerged as the focus of protest. The extreme measures employed in Amritsar by Reginald Dyer (the temporary commander of a British Infantry Brigade), of unprovoked violence that led to and shadowed the Jallianwala Bagh Massacre – an event described by Tharour as 'a conscious deliberate imposition of colonial will'. Continuing, Tharour expounds

> it represented the worst that colonialism could become, and by letting it occur, the British crossed that point of no return that exists only in the minds of men – that point which, in any unequal relationship, both master and subject must instinctively respect if their relationship is to survive.[58]

Thus, the Amritsar Massacre was a post-war turning point – for ordinary Indians in terms of their imperial identity; among the prominent were Rabindranath Tagore, the Hindu figure of international literary significance, who returned his imperial knighthood; and Gandhi, who became convinced of the 'moral righteousness . . . of independence'. It 'turned loyalists into nationalists and constitutionalists into agitators'.[59] Ireland was implicit in this crisis; the Punjab Lieutenant Governor Michael O'Dwyer was Anglo-Irish, and Dyer, himself educated in County Cork, received loud support from Sir Edward Carson. Derek Sayer argues that the Ulster leader's 'advocacy of Dyer [at Westminster] was not unrelated to considerations of methods of government for Ireland'. Going further, he contends that 'the whole Dyer controversy was a thinly coded discussion of Ireland, then in open revolt'.[60]

By 1920 Gandhi's control of Congress enabled the launch of the non-cooperation campaign, followed by the civil disobedience drive of 1921, which involved a boycott of British goods. Widespread peasant attacks against landlords, sectarian violence and increasing conflict between the largely Hindu Congress and the Muslim League added further combustible elements to the Indian periphery of empire.

In Britain the press was acknowledged as the basic source of information about the empire. At the imperial centre, then, negative newspaper reports about Ireland or elsewhere across the empire became increasingly sensitive issues. In assessing the ways the British government attempted to control news from India – for example, by suppressing details about Amritsar for six months – Chandrika Kaul demonstrated the interdependence of the press and parliamentary views.[61] Walsh suggests the same framework also applied to Ireland.[62] He comments that amidst the imperial revolts occurring in association with the signing of the treaties, it was Ireland 'that received . . . inordinate . . . attention' and suggests that 'conflict [became] a highly visible test of some of the most cherished imperial illusions'.[63] An alternative perspective, however, comes from Tharour. Referencing A. J. P. Taylor's judgement that the Amritsar Massacre represented the fulcrum of Indian detachment from empire, he differentiates between 16 post–Easter Rising executions in Dublin and the hundreds at Jallianwala, emphasising 'how little the British valued Indian lives'.[64]

Part three

At the antipodean periphery of the empire, for many Irish Australians the Great War changed their perspectives on Britain and its empire. The treatment of Ireland and the experiences of the Irish population after the Easter Rising continued to challenge Irish Australians. But the war and Britain's subsequent actions in Ireland operated as an ongoing process of revelation for them. Despite decades of criticism of Britain's policy legislation and behaviour in Ireland, it was now becoming clear to many Irish Australians that this coercive framework applied across the empire and that the Irish struggle for independence replicated conflicts underway in other imperial locations. In this environment, the educative, connecting role of the Irish Catholic press was of unparalleled importance.

One consistent theme was evident in Irish Catholic newspapers – complaints about the veracity of daily papers in relation to Ireland. Numerous examples describing these papers as 'cable-liars', misrepresenting the truth or altering news items, dotted the colonial and early twentieth-century papers.[65] Cumulatively, the secular press was distrusted. Overseas cables always emanated from London; thus Irish Australian readers recognised filtering at the centre of the empire as well as potential alteration from Australian editors. But, in 1919 Australia wartime censorship still applied to all incoming news cables. This further curtailed readers' or the public's understanding of emerging links between Ireland and India and represents an underlying feature of this chapter.

Without a history of the religious press in Australia, and with sparse archival records apart from the newspapers themselves, aspects such as circulation figures and detailed knowledge of editorial processes have proved disappointingly elusive.[66] However, important elements for the *Advocate*, *Southern Cross* and *Catholic Press* can be enunciated: their Catholic focus was strong, their coverage of Irish religious and socio-political and also international Church news (especially from Rome) was prominent, and detailed local news of Church events with more limited insights into national Catholic happenings were all presented to readers. The balance between religious and secular items was weighted towards the former. Importantly, there was a time delay in receiving news items from overseas, the significance of which emerges in the following discussion.

All the editors used the practice of exchanging copies of their publication with like-thinking colleagues around the world.[67] Occasional references to material drawn 'from our exchange table' conjures visions of well-loaded and important office furniture; items were usually attributed to their original source. The mechanism of exchange was informal, one specifically arranged between individuals, which certainly facilitated the interchange of news and commentary across the diaspora.[68] To some extent it offset the previously mentioned London-centred bias in cables and the secular press.

The items from these newspapers referencing both India and Ireland have been generally examined in terms of five different perspectives. These are: 1) allusion to or mention of imperialism/British Empire, 2) direct links between Ireland and India, 3) specific acts of violence, 4) issues of skin colour and/or race and 5) symbolism. Some items incorporate more than one perspective. From April 1919, all three editors display more nuanced understandings of imperial issues. Sydney editor Tighe Ryan directly linked Ireland and India by suggesting that that Indian nationalists were 'to a certain extent' inspired by the Irish nationalist leader C. S. Parnell's policies of 40 years prior, showing how both were involved in struggles for autonomy.[69] One week later, Ryan specifically challenged a conservative Sydney paper's characterisation of popular unrest in India; his perception of Britain's differential imperial responses emphasised the precision of his recognition of racial and skin colour issues.

> England recognises that liberty wears a different complexion, according to the strength or weakness, the race or colour of those who claim its blessings. . . . The overthrow of British rule in Ireland . . . or India, on the same sacred plan [of Great War type overthrow] would . . . be rank blasphemy.[70]

In what seems an early reference to the mid-April Amritsar Massacre, a one-line reference in the *Southern Cross* of late May 1919 to 'four thousand casualties in Indian Rising' was unusual, given censorship, and demonstrated the paper's close focus on Indian items.[71] Significantly, no further discussion of the violence nor its victims followed. One reason for official silence about the events in the Punjab emerged in August. O'Loghlin's column explained that 'cable censorship' had allowed Britain's coalition government to limit both Irish news and 'unpleasant proceedings' elsewhere in the empire. But he explained the recent arrival of overseas newspapers clarified many 'things [relating to the empire] of which the cables gave us not even dim intimation'. By then, the 'peace-making' had concluded, and the reality of proceedings in Paris was clearer. O'Loghlin described experiences of the unofficial Irish and Egyptian delegations, and the nature of some imperial inconsistencies: 'they have found out that pious platitudes and professions about 'the liberties of peoples' and 'government by consent of the governed' are kept by British statesmen for foreign consumption, and are not for use within the British Empire'.[72]

Such a powerful condemnation from a former self-described imperial patriot, whose longstanding militia experience had propelled an offer to volunteer during World War One (despite being in his early sixties) and then involved him accompanying troop ships overseas, reflected an informed imperial critique. And this, too, from a proud Irish Nationalist.

In August, Shorthill's *Advocate* editorial contrasted the gap between the 'peace' treaty and imperial 'hotspots.' He claimed that

> what has happened and is happening in Ireland, India, [and] Egypt . . . forces on us the realisation that the Peace Treaty has not been of a nature to bring a real and lasting peace to the war-stricken world.[73]

In September Koerner reported approvingly of 'the great Hindu poet and mystic', Rabindranath Tagore, 'begg[ing] to be relieved of . . . [his 1915 British] knighthood'. As already suggested, Tagore's international standing ensured his public rejection of the imperial honour earlier bestowed on him, had immediate impact. It was a powerful symbolic act. His desire to stand beside 'those of . . . [his] countrymen, who for their so-called insignificance, are liable to suffer a degradation not fit for human beings', explicitly rebuked Britain.[74] It can be seen, then, that in 1919 the editors of these three newspapers managed to draw insights from the confused imperial template. This was amidst the post-war coming to terms with peace-making realities and international uncertainty, despite censorship issues and consistently delayed overseas news.

The state of war between Britain and Ireland, something reflected in the intensifying violence, was clarified in these Irish Australian newspapers during 1919. In April, as the exclusionary contours of Versailles were understood, both the *Catholic Press* and O'Loghlin's column in the *Southern Cross* used material from Britain's *Daily News* speculating about Britain's potential for going to 'war in Ireland for the suppression of the cause of freedom and the denial of the doctrine of self-determination'.[75] Later, when the *Advocate* and *Southern Cross* both used this language as a reality – September for the former[76] and November for the latter,[77] their readers were familiar with notions of war in Ireland. In September, military action in Fermoy appeared under the headline 'The War in Ireland' and described as the 'Reign of Terror in Ireland'[78] and later in Melbourne as 'The Sack of Fermoy';[79] after the military reprisals which followed a Sinn Féin attack, readers quickly recalled descriptions of World War One. Terminology associated with Great War violence increasingly permeated reports in the Irish Catholic papers with, for example, references to 'A Hunnish Government' or Prussianism.[80]

The year 1920 was marked by increasing IRA raids and ambushes in Ireland. This resulted from the shift towards more extremist domination of Sinn Féin, which followed the multiple frustrations of more moderate hopes for Ireland being settled internationally and peacefully.[81] Glaring examples of violence between the IRA and incoming forces further assisted editorial understanding of similarities between Ireland and India.[82] Late in January 1920 Koerner penned an important, lengthy editorial titled 'The Indian Peril'. In this he examined the 'striking' parallel between Ireland and India, arguing that both 'had trusted the promises of British rulers' in relation to the fruits of wartime generosity – that is the granting of self-determination. Koerner viewed this as imperial deception and opined that the justified Indian 'protest was registered in rebellion'. He again referred to Tagore's response, endorsing his return of the empire's knighthood – a hallowed symbol. His editorial comments not only embodied the shocking violence in and symmetry between the two colonies but also attributed blame to cables and newspapers for limiting reader understanding of the depth of discontent. Koerner wrote:

> The British answer to these aspirations [towards independence] in India as in Ireland, has been ruthless repression and military rule [and] . . . it is evident that the causes of disaffection in India, as in Ireland, are more deep-seated than the cables and the daily papers would have us believe.

Amid the unusual reminder to readers of India's importance to Australia in terms of proximity, as well as imperial trade and commerce – factors he stressed as being impossible to ignore – he incorporated some early understanding of the nascent League of Nations. Expressing optimism about its ability 'to deal with cases like those of Ireland and India,' he continued, 'If not its usefulness will be greatly curtailed'.[83] Although consequences of the increasing application of British force to protect the empire and fears of its 'dismemberment' should the Irish resolve for freedom succeed were both apparent, revelations about the events at Amritsar propelled intense anxieties at the periphery of the empire. And these editorials accelerated Irish Australian recognition of Ireland and India occupying the same plane of imperialist thinking and action, thus experiencing similar violent repression.

In early February 1920, in a newspaper 'exchange' dated 13 December 1919, Irish Australians finally read details of the April 1919 massacre at Amritsar in Bengal.[84] As suggested earlier, here the delay reflected in the publication lag between 13 December in Liverpool and 6 February in Adelaide was significant.[85] Koerner cited the Liverpool *Catholic Times* in his editorial, titled 'British Military Crime in India. Inhuman Massacre in the Punjab'. Clearly disturbed by the gap from April to December 1919 in terms of any public knowledge of the violence, he decried the fact that 'the public at home were kept . . . without any knowledge of the affair'. At the end of the item which connected violence, imperialism and both countries, he observed:

> We need hardly point out how the above bears out the parallel between militarism in Ireland and India drawn in our leading article on 'The Indian Peril' last week. The silence of the cable agencies and our great dailies about this awful British crime, while Irish crime is daily starred, is significant.[86]

Koerner's selection of 'exchange' material from 'Irish and English files' concerning Ireland in early February, was headed: 'Prussianism in Excelsis: The Reign of Terror in Ireland.' Stating these were 'carefully camouflaged and minimised by the cable agencies . . . [presumably] under directions from the anti-Irish propaganda department of the British Government'.[87] His focus on levels of imperial violence was closely informed by the Great War.

The emergence of further details of violence over following weeks provoked Koerner's scorn about both news suppression and imperial patriotism. By mid-February in an editorial, 'The Irish Reign of Terror,' Koerner questioned why '[t]he particulars [of the horrible British massacre in the Punjab] were made known in England early in December, but either nothing was cabled to Australia or it was carefully suppressed by "patriotic" (?) editors'. His sarcastic tone about the 'preserved silence [of the local press] for nine months', reflects personal horror as well as 'the parallel between events in Ireland and India'. However, he recognised that:

> Though English soldiers cannot be charged with such an awful crime as that of Amritsar during the present reign of terror in Ireland, they have gone as far as to loot towns like Fermoy and Thurles, and inflict heavy loss and suffering on innocent civilians for deeds attributed to Sinn Féiners. . . . It is not for want of incitement by British journals and jingoes that an Amritsar has not been recorded in Ireland.[88]

Koerner's acknowledgement that the Irish were 'the only white race . . . which another nation holds in subjection and oppression by . . . brute force' represented a critical turning point. He saw the situations of Ireland and India as offering 'striking correlations'.[89] Local Commonwealth Investigation Bureau (CIB) files show surveillance personnel were dismissive of Koerner's comments, judging him as 'trying to make political capital'.[90]

Unusually in relation to other Irish Australian newspapers, the *Advocate* sometimes utilised cartoons; in early March 1920, it published the faded, but now famous, David Low cartoon – 'The situation in Ireland and India'.[91] Low was noted as a political cartoonist, his depictions were explicit in their critiques.[92]

The cartoon depicted a scene evoking General Dyer's infamous demand that Indians crawl on hands and knees down a street where an English woman had been assaulted prior to the Amritsar massacre. Low showed Ireland and India as crawling under Britain's boot. The *Advocate*'s April summary painted Lloyd George's government as a 'terrorist', arguing 'It is playing this role not only in Ireland, but in other parts of the world – in India and in Egypt'. In his critique of the imperial centre, Shorthill insisted England needed a new government, one of 'justice and not of oppression, one which will give, Ireland, India and Egypt their rights and thus relieve England of her reputation for tyranny and oppression'.[93]

In July Koerner categorised police firing into an Irish crowd at the town of Milltown Malbay in County Clare as 'Ireland's Amritsar'.[94] Another connection to Ireland and violence existed in the stationing of the Irish regiment, the Connaught Rangers, in the Punjab. In protest against accounts of British paramilitary repression in Ireland, 300 members of this old Irish regiment refused to obey orders and handed in their arms and ammunition in early July 1920.[95] While the militia-experienced O'Loghlin acknowledged this as a 'deplorable event', he also judged it as unsurprising 'in view of the dragooning of their countrymen in Ireland'. He thought it must have been 'galling' for such brave soldiers 'after fighting for liberty and self-determination abroad to find the Prussian methods against which they had struggled heroically . . . ruthlessly applied in their own beloved land'.[96] The following week, responding to the gushing comments over the visiting Prince of Wales and the proclaimed benefits of the empire even to 'the refractory minorities', O'Loghlin stressed that 'the empire is held together by naked force and that alone'.[97]

In a September account of an 'Irish Self-Determination Fund' meeting in Wollongong, *Advocate* readers were presented with some of the glaring discrepancies in terms of the 'small nation' justification for the Great War and the contemporary situation. A Sydney Irish cleric, Fr. M. J. O'Reilly, integrated comments about violence in Ireland with issues of the wider empire. He stated that:

> The Irish question today is a world question. The whole world is crying shame on the British military clique that is calling out for more machine guns, more tanks, against a small nation – Ireland. . . . In India – who could hear of the bloody happenings at Amritsar without a shudder? – Egypt, Mesopotamia or Ireland. It does not matter where the oppressed stood up for freedom, his sympathies would be with them. The Irish people were out for self-determination.[98]

By late 1920, editors of both the *Advocate* and the *Southern Cross*, in a linguistic adaptation from Amritsar needing no explanation for most readers, utilised the term 'Dyerism'.[99] Sayer also discusses this term's wider associations in Britain: meaning 'indiscriminate shooting', something increasingly seen as synonymous with RIC policy.[100] By December 1920, comparing imperial coercion in India and Ireland was, for O'Loghlin, unequivocal:

> There is much similarity between the situations in India and Ireland, and in the policy adopted in each country to meet the trouble. Both countries are held down by a foreign despotism, the same in each case.[101]

In 1921 O'Loghlin frequently used his 'Currente Calamo' column to comment about Ireland and India in terms of their imperial similarities. In discussing 'bonds of loyalty and service' in January, he differentiated between the empire's function as 'a Commonwealth of free nations' and

> a domination of subject nations, held down by force – where its sceptre is not freedom but the sword – then it secures neither, love nor loyalty. Who can say truthfully that this is not the case in India [and] in Ireland . . . today?[102]

In response to daily paper discussion of and astonishment about Gandhi's opposition to India's post-Amritsar reform by instalment process, O'Loghlin's disillusion about empire was apparent: 'After all the glorification of British justice and beneficence to subject nations we have the cynical admission that India is held by force. Might is *Right*. This, then is "The Ethics of Empire"'.[103] In early 1921, Shorthill and O'Loghlin both quoted an explicit statement from prominent Irish literary figure, George Bernard Shaw, about what he would say if able to attend a London Indian gathering. As well as linking Ireland and India, he presented a succinct perspective about imperial policies.

> If I could attend . . . I should move a resolution simply calling the attention of the Government to the fact that India is a somewhat larger and more populous place than Ireland, and that a policy which involves finally the extermination of its inhabitants presents great difficulties under twentieth century conditions.[104]

The *Catholic Press* report of an Indian National Congress resolution 'which paid homage to the late Lord Mayor of Cork (Mr MacSwiney) and . . . [sent] sympathy to the Irish people in their struggle for independence', clearly established that, on the ground, close understanding existed between these countries.[105] In May at a meeting for Irish Self-Determination in Ballarat, a large regional town in Victoria, Federal MHR Frank Brennan disputed accusations that Sinn Féin leaders intended to dismember the empire.[106] This staunch Irish Australian argued that the 'Irish question was tearing up the whole fabric of the empire, and if it was not settled the empire was in danger'. His co-speaker, William Watt MHR, referred to India as giving 'ominous signs of the dismemberment'.[107]

To explain the significance of Gandhi to his readers in September, O'Loghlin used well-known Irish figures and history. He characterised Gandhi:

> to all intents and purposes an Indian Sinn Féiner – another Padraig Pearse or De [sic] Valera aiming, like the Young Irelanders, to 'create and foster public opinion, and make it racy of the soil' . . . . He is the most formidable antagonist that British rule in India has yet encountered.[108]

Later that month, at a well-attended public Self-Determination for Ireland meeting in Adelaide, O'Loghlin addressed a resolution responding to Australia's wartime participation in support of that principle. He challenged Britain's offering to Ireland. In his powerful finale, a ringing 1921 condemnation of imperialism, although India was not mentioned, his words clearly applied: a disaffected and discontented Ireland was no good to the empire, and an empire not founded on freedom and justice was no good to the world.[109]

In Victoria, a letter from a local 'Loyalist' presented challenging details from an August 'International Convention of 15,000 Negroes [sic]' in New York. Integrating realities of imperial domination with challenges to racial assumptions, the writer explained the assembly:

> Telegraphed . . . King George asking him to use his influence to free Ireland, India and Egypt, and to prevent future race wars. How truly Christian and

kindly! Yet what a satire upon the much vaunted civilization and 'superiority of the white races'.[110]

In an era when letters to these newspapers were few, this item indicates the broader reading of some Irish Australians and their recognition of international racial nuances into which Irish and Indian self-determination demands slotted.

During the November visit of the Prince of Wales to India, Shorthill commented on 'the serious outbreak of rioting', discussing the possibility of Britain having drafted a number of Black and Tans to the colony. Clearly alarmed by this threat and connecting issues of race, violence and direct imperial actions, he argued that 'Their murderous activities among whites in Ireland indicate very clearly the manner in which they are likely to act towards the downtrodden and despoiled natives of India'.[111] By late 1921 the sharpness of the parallels between Ireland and India had led to their editorial treatment as largely interchangeable, something exemplified by O'Loghlin's summation at the introduction of this chapter.

Conclusion

Between 1919 and 1921, in the confusing aftermath of the Great War, the Sydney *Catholic Press*, the Melbourne *Advocate* and the Adelaide *Southern Cross* all negotiated the demands of censorship and the many post-war uncertainties. These newspapers played an important role in both informing and challenging their readers about the ways the post-war experiences of Ireland and India at British hands were similar, if not identical. Looking at the framework through which the newspapers were examined, it is unsurprising that the empire and its policies dominated newspaper items, given the visibility of Ireland under British assault framing their relationship in response to Irish demands for self-determination. Insights resulting from this violence facilitated greater recognition of previously unrecognised connections between the colonies. Among these understandings the issue of race and skin colour, previously a marker of difference, could now be viewed differently. Symbolic contributions such as that reflected in the return of a knighthood or in a prominent writer's public statement helped reinforce inter-colonial similarities.

Using a counter-factual framework as a mechanism to conclude this discussion, removing the Great War accentuates its role in unsettling the empire.[112] Without the war, troops would not have been mobilised in either country, Ireland would have achieved home rule, the Rising and its related consequences culminating in the War of Independence would not have occurred then and Ireland would possibly have evolved towards a more settled imperial position. Alongside lesser Muslim/Hindu tensions and more targeted reforms, the possibility of Gandhi not returning and the reduction of independence pressures may have facilitated India's development within the empire. The war happened; however, it was a turning point, and the histories of both Ireland and India were shaped along violent pathways which were ultimately destructive for the empire. Within this construct, readers of Australia's Irish Catholic newspapers were exposed to insights which located Ireland and India as targets of comparable imperial policies of coercion.

Notes

The author would like to thank the Flinders University Postgraduate Reading Group for helpful responses to an early version of this material and more recently to colleagues Dr Janet Scarfe and Susan Arthure for their generous assistance.

1 James Vincent O'Loghlin, "Currente Calamo," *Southern Cross*, November 25, 1921, 12 (hereafter cited as *SC*).
2 "The Church in India: Growth in the Middle of Famine," *SC*, August 10, 1900, 4.
3 *SC*, February 5, 1897, 7. This 'topic' or sub-editorial suggested that local sympathy for India should be 'special' because Adelaide's Sir Charles Todd, a much-revered astronomer, superintendent of telegraphs and responsible for the overland telegraph connecting Australia to the world via the undersea cable at Darwin, stated that 'the drought cycles are much the same in each country' so 'suffering comes synchronously to both'.
4 *SC*, May 22, 1891, 3.
5 "English Rule in India," *SC*, September 24, 1897, 3. This item opened with the statement that 'England has brought nothing but ruin to India'.
6 "The Priest and Soldier," *SC*, October 18, 1895, 3.
7 *SC*, July 16, 1897, 3.
8 *SC*, July 13, 1906, 10.
9 The Irish War of Independence is conventionally dated from 21 January 1919 and continued until the truce of 11 July 1921 allowed the negotiation of the Anglo-Irish treaty, signed on 6 December 1921; it was ratified in Dublin on 7 January 1922.
10 S. J. Connolly, ed., *Oxford Companion to Irish History* (Oxford: Oxford University Press, 2007), 104.
11 Jennifer Regan-Lefebvre, "Imperial Politics and the London Irish," in *Ireland in an Imperial World: Citizenship, Opportunism and Subversion*, ed. Timothy G. McMahon, Michael de Nie and Paul Townsend (London: Palgrave Macmillan, 2017), 121–25.
12 J. M. Roberts, *The Penguin History of the Twentieth Century* (London: Penguin Books, 1999), 229. See Connolly, *Oxford Companion to Irish History*, 57; for the derivation of this practice from the Land Wars of the 1880s. An English-born former soldier, Captain Charles Boycott, an agent for a Co Mayo estate, became the first prominent victim of the Land League policy of 'consigning those who broke from the League's code of conduct into moral Coventry'.
13 Michael Davitt (1846–1906), well known as a Fenian after his 1870 arrest, and later as founder of the Land League and his role in Ireland's agrarian struggle. His 1895 visit to Australia followed a series of proposed visits; none of the earlier plans came to fruition, causing intense local disappointment. His election to Westminster occurred while in Australia; his opposition to the South African War received much local focus, reinforcing his recognition among Irish Australians.
14 Alfred Webb (1834–1908), an Irish-born Quaker, was in Australia from 1853 to 1855 and again in 1895, following his resignation as an elected IPP member at Westminster. On the IPP Executive with Michael Davitt, and as treasurer of the Tenant's Defence Association in 1891, he regularly received donations from Australia.
15 See for example, *SC*, May 17, 1907, 12 which comments on IPP leader John Redmond's protest about 'coercive methods . . . [being] as useless in promoting good government in India as they had been in Ireland'.
16 Ryan (1870–1922) was born in Tipperary; his family emigrated around 1881. He was educated by the Christian Brothers and by 1893 was involved in Sydney's newspaper world. In 1897 he was invited to edit the *Catholic Press*.
17 Shorthill (1859–1934) was born in Adelaide to Irish parents who moved to rural Victoria. After an early career in the police force, in 1887 he became a travelling correspondent for the *Advocate*, then a regular contributor. Some years of editing regional

newspapers led to a role as deputy *Advocate* editor in 1915 and editor from 1917 until his retirement in 1920.

18 Koerner (1857–1943) was born in Victoria; his father was German-born and his mother was Irish. Involved in newspapers all his career, from 1889 he worked on Broken Hill's *Barrier Miner*, then Sydney's *Evening News*, before becoming the third editor of the *Southern Cross* in May 1903. He retired in 1933.

19 O'Loghlin (1852–1925) was born in South Australia to parents who had emigrated from Co Clare in 1840. His early career involved farming, a wheat sales position, owning / editing a country newspaper and local council membership before his 1888 election to the Legislative Council. In 1889 he founded, then edited, the *Southern Cross* for seven years until his appointment to Cabinet; later he was elected as a Federal Senator representing South Australia. His *Southern Cross* column, 'Currente Calamo', appeared until his death in December 1925.

20 Pan-Islamists adhered to a political ideology advocating the unity of all Muslims under one Islamic country or state, something the British were suspicious of in relation to India's Muslim community.

21 Keith Jeffery, *1916: A Global History* (London and New York: Bloomsbury, 2015), 196. Montagu was speaking to his British Cabinet colleagues in 1920.

22 Tharour, *Inglorious Empire*: *What the British did to India* (Victoria: Scribe Publications, 2018), 74.

23 Ibid., 74–75. He cites food, cash and ammunition generated from British taxation of India and from princely states, a sum of £3.5 million for the 'war gratuities' of British officers and men 'of the normal garrisons of India'. Indian revenues also contributed another £13.1 million for the war effort, stating that contemporary estimates of India's contribution were £146.2 million, perhaps £50 billion today; some dispute this as too low.

24 Tharour, *Inglorious Empire*, 75.

25 Margaret Macmillan, *Women of the Raj: The Mothers, Wives and Daughters of the British Empire in India* (London: Thames & Hudson, 2018), 274.

26 As well as Europe and the Mediterranean, Indian troops served in Mesopotamia and North and East Africa.

27 Tharour, *Inglorious Empire*, 76.

28 Margaret Macmillan, *Paris 1919: Six Months that Changed the World* (New York: Random House, 2002), 402.

29 Macmillan, *Paris 1919*, 404.

30 Robin Wilson, "Imperialism in Crisis: The 'Irish Dimension'", in *Crises in the British State 1880–1930*, ed. Mary Langan and Bill Schwarz (London: Hutchinson in association with the Centre for Contemporary Cultural Studies University of Birmingham, 1985), 151.

31 Sometimes described as the third Home Rule Crisis, the first attempt came in 1886 when Gladstone was PM. He also led the next attempt in 1893; this was defeated in the House of Lords. In 1912, when the third bill was introduced (the liberals being dependent on IPP votes), it had to pass three times in the Commons in the same term to avoid going to the House of Lords. This was achieved in May 1914.

32 Wilson, "Imperialism in Crisis," 163–64.

33 Ibid., 164.

34 Jeffery, *1916*, 107–8. Speaking at Woodenbridge in Co Wicklow, Redmond fully pledged Nationalist Ireland to the war effort.

35 Connolly, *Oxford Companion*, 501.

36 F. X. Martin, ed., *The Irish Volunteers 1913–1915*: *Recollections and Documents* (Dublin: Duffy, 1963), 168.

37 Jeffery, *1916*, 109. Kitchener's disinterest in providing equal treatment in terms of separate divisions for both sets of volunteers was clear; this happened for Ulster but not for Redmond's followers.

38 Jeffery, *1916*, 110.
39 Sinn Féin (founded in 1905) was publicly associated with anti-British policies, especially in relation to opposing recruitment. It was thus typically held responsible for the Rising, despite Sinn Féin itself taking no part in the events of April 1916.
40 Diarmid Ferriter, *A Nation and Not a Rabble: The Irish Revolution 1913 1923* (London: Profile Books, 2015), 168–69.
41 Eric Hobsbawm, *Age of Extremes: The Short Twentieth Century 1914–1991* (Great Britain: Abacus, 1995), 211.
42 Ibid., 210.
43 Macmillan, *Paris 1919*, 402.
44 Ibid., 11.
45 Although Sinn Féin was successful in wartime by-elections, its threat was not fully understood by IPP leadership, so when it won only six seats in 1918, many nationalists seemed incapable of adjusting.
46 Maurice Walsh, *The News from Ireland: Foreign Correspondents and the Irish Revolution* (London: IB Taurus & Co Ltd, 2011), 60.
47 Ronan Fanning, Michael Kennedy, Dermot Keogh, and Eunan O'Halpin, eds., *Documents on Irish Foreign Policy, 1919–1922*, vol. 1 (Dublin: Royal Irish Academy, 1998), 2.
48 Walsh, *The News from Ireland*, 151.
49 Ibid., 106–9.
50 Michael Hopkinson, *The Irish War of Independence* (Dublin: Gill & Macmillan, 2004), 25–29, 38–46.
51 Training for both – drawn from British ex-soldiers and sailors and demoblised British officers – was paltry. By the end of 1921, attracting 9,500 and 1,900 respectively, their inadequate supervision and the resultant brutality contributed to rising international horror about the Anglo-Irish War.
52 Connolly, *Oxford Companion*, 50.
53 Walsh, *The News from Ireland*, 181.
54 Macmillan, *Paris 1919*, 49.
55 Hobsbawm, *Age of Extremes*, 210.
56 Montagu expended great effort into this legislation, negotiating with Gandhi and Jinna, the Muslim leader, but the outcome was criticised for both its inadequacy and its excessive generosity.
57 The full title was the Anarchical and Revolutionary Crimes Act.
58 Tharour, *Inglorious Empire*, 170.
59 Ibid.
60 Derek Sayer, "British Reaction, to the Amritsar Massacre 1919- – 1920," *Past and Present* 131 (May 1991): 153.
61 Chandrika Kaul, *Reporting the Raj: The British Press and India, c.1880–1922* (Manchester: Manchester University Press, 2003), 100.
62 Walsh, *The News from Ireland*, 94–95.
63 Ibid., 182.
64 Tharour, *Inglorious Empire*, 170–71.
65 Stephanie James, " 'From Beyond the Seas': The Irish Catholic Press in the Southern Hemisphere," in *Ireland in the World: Comparative, Transnational and Personal Perspectives,* ed. Angela McCarthy (New York: Routledge, 2015), 88–90.
66 For explanation about limited circulation figures for both *Advocate* and *Southern Cross*, see Stephanie James, " 'Deep Green Loathing?' Shifting Irish-Australian Loyalties in the Victorian and South Australian Irish-Catholic Press 1868–1923" (PhD diss., Adelaide: Flinders University, 2013), 94–8.
67 James, "From Beyond the Seas," 86–90.

68 Heather McNamara, "The *New Zealand Tablet* and the Irish Catholic Press Worldwide, 1898–1923," *New Zealand Journal of History* 37, no. 2 (2003): 160; for details of exchanges from notebooks of *Tablet* editors.
69 *Catholic Press*, April 24, 1919, 22 (hereafter cited as *CP*).
70 *CP*, May 1, 1919, 22. The *Sunday Times* operated in Sydney from 1885 to 1930.
71 *SC*, May 30, 1919, 14. The figure was in a regular feature termed 'Twinklings', a list of between 20 and 30 news items presented as succinct single-line summaries.
72 *SC*, August 1, 1919, 17.
73 *Advocate*, August 2, 1919, 21.
74 *SC*, September 19, 1919, 12. Tagore (1861–1941), a Bengali polymath, had a distinguished publishing career; in 1913 he was awarded the Nobel Prize in Literature.
75 *CP*, April 3, 1919, 10; and *SC*, April 18, 1919, 12. A longer section was published in Sydney, a smaller one in Adelaide.
76 *Advocate*, September 20, 1919, 8.
77 *SC*, November 21, 1919, 6.
78 *CP*, September 11, 1919, 19. The article refers to daily papers of 9 September, Ryan arguing the story 'shows that Ireland is swarming with soldiers' and mentioning that the Sinn Féin activities were described as 'outrages' in the cablegrams.
79 *Advocate*, September 20, 1919, 8.
80 *CP*, May 7, 1919, 5; *SC*, February 6, 1920, 2.
81 Hopkinson, *The Irish War*, 38, 41–42, 71–74.
82 Ibid., 27–28.
83 *SC*, January 30, 1920, 10.
84 *SC*, February 6, 1920, 7.
85 James, "From Beyond the Seas."
86 *SC*, February 6, 1920, 7.
87 *SC*, February 6, 1920, 2. Koerner emphasised that the descriptions were taken from London's *The Tablet*, a conservative English Catholic paper, 'because we can be sure it is not too highly coloured'.
88 *SC*, February 13, 1920, 10.
89 *SC*, February 6, 1920, 7.
90 National Archives of Australia Adelaide (NAA): D1915 SA29 Pt.1., March 15, 1920.
91 *Advocate*, March 6, 1920, 7. The cartoon came from the London *Daily News*; Low, a New Zealander, was wrongly described here as an Australian.
92 Low (1891–1967) was born in Dunedin and first worked there as a political cartoonist; he moved to Australia in 1911 to work for the *Bulletin*. In 1919 he was invited to work for the *London Star*; he died in London.
93 *Advocate*, April 8, 1920, 16.
94 *SC*, December 17, 1920, 15.
95 One private was shot, others received lengthy sentences but were released in early 1923. See "A Letter from a Mutineer in the Connaught Rangers," *CP*, September 29, 1921, 5; for later focus on the incident.
96 *SC*, January 21, 1921, 11.
97 *SC*, February 25, 1921, 4.
98 *Advocate*, September 2, 1920, 14. The event raised £170. Born in Co Cork, Fr O'Reilly had arrived in Australia in 1892 and was located as a teacher in Sydney; later he was Rector of a Sydney University College. A close associate of Archbishop Mannix, O'Reilly was prominent and outspoken on Irish issues.
99 *Advocate*, September 16, 1920, 7; *Advocate*, November 25, 1920, 19; *SC*, November 26, 1920, 2; and *SC*, December 3, 1920, 2.
100 See Sayer, "British Reaction," 145, 153, 163.
101 *SC*, December 17, 1920, 15.

102 *SC*, January 21, 1921, 11.
103 *SC*, February 25, 1921, 4.
104 See *Advocate* of February 10, 1921, 17; and *SC*, March 4, 1921, 6.
105 *CP*, March 24, 1921, 40. Previously somewhat hostile to each other, Brennan (1873–1950) and Watt (1971–1946) spoke here as unlikely associates.
106 The Self-Determination for Ireland League was first established in 1920. Australian branches attracted large numbers in 1921 and 1922; an internationally based organisation, it had the backing of Eamon de Valera.
107 *Advocate*, May 5, 1921, 14.
108 *SC*, September 9, 1921, 17.
109 *SC*, September 23, 1921, 18.
110 *Advocate*, October 13, 1921, 12.
111 *Advocate*, November 24, 1921, 22.
112 Niall Ferguson, ed., *Virtual History* (London: Penguin Books, 2011), 1–90.

3 Native Kings and German Traders on the British Imperial Peripheries

Lagos and Tonga

Peter J. Yearwood

Empires place different peoples in different relations to a shared overlord. They are necessarily collections of anomalies. This was particularly so for the largest empire, that of Great Britain. This chapter looks at two of its most anomalous territories and how the war changed them.[1] Both were insular. Lagos was a small island with a population of about 70,000 persons at the entrance to a great West African lagoon. Tonga comprised three groups of Pacific islands, with a total population of roughly 20,000: Tongatapu in the south, with the capital Nuku'alofa; Ha'apai, in the centre; and Vava'u in the north.[2] During the war their traditional rulers and indigenous elites had vigorously asserted their support of the British war effort and their devotion to British values. They hoped to use this wartime loyalty to advance their position within the empire and enhance their autonomy.

Lagos had long been a British colony, while the rest of Nigeria, of which it was the capital, was only a protectorate. Tonga's status was less well defined. At a pinch it might be considered part of the British Empire, but it certainly was not a colony. Lagos and Tonga each had indigenous rulers. The descendant of King Dosunmo, who had ceded his rule to the British in 1861, still lived in his palace, called himself Eleko (Lord of Lagos), and retained the loyalty of Lagosians. While he received a meagre stipend, he had no role in the administration, which in the language of imperialism was 'direct'. Tonga's anomalies were quite different. There was no British governor and no colonial administration. The British presence was formally diplomatic, the agent and consul. Tonga's relations with Great Britain were regulated by the Treaty of Friendship of 1900 and a Supplementary Agreement of 1905. The scope and status of these were both disputable and disputed. Tonga's king had a full government, with Europeans in several senior positions. As the British Consul had on his staff only a clerk, an interpreter, a carpenter, and a labourer, who were paid in total £216,[3] there could be no question of his running the country. Whatever needed to be done in Tonga had to be done by the Tongan government. The consul might advise the King, but whether that advice had to be sought and accepted was one of the matters of dispute.

As it controlled access to Western Nigeria, Lagos was a major commercial centre with a vigorous African commercial elite. Few of these were indigenous Awori. Most were from other Yoruba groups or from the Yoruba diaspora. The city exported the bulk of Nigeria's palm kernels, though that trade had passed into the hands of the large German and British firms: G. L. Gaiser, Witt und Büsch, and John Holt. Tonga was less important in the global economy, as evidenced by the fact that it had neither radio nor telegraph connection with the rest of the world. Copra was its only significant export. The trade had been pioneered by German companies of which the Deutsche Handels und Plantagen Gesellschaft der Südsee Inseln zu Hamburg (DHPG) remained a major commercial presence, along with the Australian Burns Philp and the British Lever Brothers. Both kernels and copra went to Germany, which was the world centre for the crushing of hard oleaginous materials. Therefore, at the outbreak of the war, both Lagos and Tonga had significant German communities.

These communities were very different. The Germans of Lagos were employees of the big firms and of the shipping company Woermann Linie. While leaders of the African community had regarded them as friends,[4] they were not integrated into that community and did not marry Africans. By contrast, many German families in Tonga had been settled for three generations and had intermarried locally with British, Tongan, and other Polynesian families. There was a significant 'half-caste' population, especially in Vava'u. The distinction between 'European' and 'native' was important, as they were subject to different laws and different courts, which caused problems for unacknowledged children. Few bothered about the difference between Germans and British. Some Germans believed that 'little brown Germans' should be sent to school in 'the home country . . . in order to learn something proper'.[5] Others sent their children to Australia. In May 1914 the expatriate community established the (still existing) Nuku'alofa Club with British Consul H. E. W. Grant as president and German Vice Consul Waldemar von Treskow, a man of 72 who had been *en poste* since the 1880s and was married to a Samoan, as the vice president.

The German communities of Lagos and Tonga had quite different fates in the war. In Lagos, after some vacillation and reversal of policy, German trade was stopped in November 1914. Almost all the Germans were reservists in the army and would be deported in conditions of some discomfort even for the 'better class people'.[6] They would spend the war as prisoners of war in England. The colonial authorities feared that the elimination of the German commercial presence would give a small number of British, mainly Liverpool, firms control over the Nigerian export trade. There were also complaints from African merchants trying to break back into produce exporting that the British shipping company Elder Dempster, which now had a monopoly, was conniving with the big firms (now aptly named the Lagos Ring) to exclude them. The Lagos authorities rejected the Ring's attempt to take over the stocks of the German companies, employing an African auctioneer to ensure that they were sold openly. When in 1916 London authorised the sale of the sites, Lagos, backed by the Colonial Office and the Colonial Secretary, Bonar Law, held the auction in London with high publicity to attract neutral (American and Dutch) capital into Nigeria. The large British firms responded with an agitation on ostensibly patriotic grounds. This was taken over by the leading oppositional politician Sir Edward Carson and culminated in the famous 'Nigeria Debate' of 8 November 1916. The parallel agitation of the Lagos merchants, who had sent a representative to England, and the smaller British firms created the impression of a colony about to be taken over by a greedy cartel that had to be broken. This helped Law win the debate and re-establish himself as the effective leader of the Conservative Party, though, paradoxically, it also began the process which brought down H. H. Asquith and established Lloyd George as the new prime minister in coalition with Law.

Despite their parliamentary defeat, the Ring firms secured almost all the sites up for auction, excluding foreign competitors. Nevertheless, smaller companies, British and Lagosian, did acquire a share of shipping. Far from being crushed, they thrived after 1916, with many new ones joining them. The main threat they faced as the war ended came from the elaboration of schemes for the control of raw materials and for an 'economic' offensive in which their interests would have been sacrificed to 'the claims of efficiency and expediency in the organisation of a scheme of purchase by the Imperial Government'. Such plans were quickly abandoned after the Armistice. A year later they would be regarded with bemusement by most in the Colonial Office.[7] The crash of 1920 shook the big firms and destroyed most of the small ones. Eventually Germany became again a major, though no longer the only, market for Nigerian palm kernels. G. L. Gaiser would return to Lagos, but Germans no longer formed a significant community in Lagos and are now hardly remembered.

The pattern of the German diaspora in Tonga was much different. While King Tupou II was quick to declare his support for Great Britain and its war aims, the German–Tonga Treaty of Friendship of 1876 was not denounced. Trade with firms based in enemy territory was prohibited for everybody. Germans had to swear not to do anything which might lead to unrest among the 'native' population, but they were not made to register as enemy aliens, and no special restrictions were placed on their commercial activities. Tonga was therefore considered legally neutral. This changed in 1916. The Tongan government was told to denounce the 1876 treaty, to introduce registration of alien enemies, and to restrict their movements. London wanted to root out the Deutsche Handels und Plantagen Gesellschaft,[8] though, unlike in Nigeria, it could not liquidate its fixed assets during the war, as its headquarters were in German Samoa, which was occupied territory, and measures taken there might have created precedents for German action in occupied Belgium and France. While the DHPG was made to stop trading in May, the Colonial Office opposed interference with smaller local traders, especially 'half-castes whose connection with Germany is very remote'.[9] Nevertheless, the Tongan government did encourage them to sell up to British traders, which they did, often on the understanding that they would buy back the businesses after the end of the war.[10] The three managers of the DHPG – Hellfritz in Nuku'alofa, Ohle in Ha'apai, and Schultz in Vava'u – were deported. London told Tonga to treat them courteously before deportation, but conditions would be different in internment in New Zealand, where they protested against their expulsion from a neutral country.[11] Their families remained in Tonga. If they did not have plantations, arrangements were made for their maintenance. No other Germans were deported from Tonga. Unlike in

Nigeria, persons of German descent remain a significant element in the population today.

While the grievances of the Lagos merchants resonated powerfully in England, they created little stir in Lagos itself. One who did take up their cause was James Bright Davies, at 68 the old lion of the city's journalism and editor of the *Times of Nigeria*. Affirming British values at the start of the war, he charged that the governor, Sir Frederick Lugard, was inspired by a German 'rancorous negrophobism'. In August 1916 he asserted that there was an 'undercurrent of sympathy for the German cause' among the native population, who hoped for German rule 'if only to be saved from the tyranny and exploitation of the British merchants'.[12] This was his second offence and earned him a six-month sentence for sedition, but the authorities rightly felt that as an Igbo he had 'no local influence in Lagos'.[13]

Other forces would drive the politics of the city. Yoruba political systems are complex and convoluted. This had particularly been the case in Lagos, where the ruling dynasty had come from Benin, but land was controlled by the indigenous Awori 'white cap' chiefs, whose rights had been set aside by the colonial administration. As an instinctive authoritarian sympathetic to the Muslim rulers of the North, Lugard had little time for the urbanised Yorubas of Lagos. This was evident in the Courts Ordinance and the Provisional Criminal Code that he tried to push through. Of even more immediate significance in 1916 was the rate to be levied for a tapped water supply coming from works, which the only official from the Colonial Office who went out to Nigeria in this period compared to those of ancient Rome.[14] The long-delayed imposition of this tax in September led to a boycott of the taps and then to a few hours of rioting in Lagos. Told by the acting governor, A. G. Boyle, to send out his bellman to condemn the boycott, Eleko replied evasively. After the riots the administration stopped his stipend and those of all but three of the white cap chiefs.[15] Minor as the disturbances may have been in comparison to what had happened five months before in Dublin and five months later in Petrograd, they had a similar effect in discrediting those who had previously claimed the leadership of popular politics but had stepped back at the decisive moment. Instead, they brought to the fore a very different sort of man. Lagosians now followed the flamboyant, aggressively moustachioed Herbert Macaulay, even though he had not been prominent in the water rate agitation. Regarded by the Colonial Office as a 'dangerous man' capable of leading an 'anti-European movement on American negro [Garveyite] lines',[16] he had an instinctive grasp of what would move the indigenous population but little concern for the grievances of the largely outsider educated elite. He played no part in the National Conference of British West Africa, which had originated in Sierra Leone and the Gold Coast but would be weak and bitterly factionalised in Lagos as '[c]hairman came after chairman, officers in galore as lieutenants in the Hytian [*sic*] army'.[17] He took up instead the causes of the House of Dosunmo and of the land rights of the white cap chiefs. In January 1918 Lugard restored Eleko's stipend, feeling that he had broken with 'all the bad advisers who surrounded him last year and made the "Palace" the centre of intrigue against the Government'.[18] This attempted reconciliation did not last. Instead, in 1919 Eleko turned to the Jamat faction which commanded the loyalty of most of the city's majority Muslim population. He displaced most of the chiefs, replacing them with Jamat supporters. This led again to the cancelling of his stipend. However, this was soon restored by the new governor, Sir Hugh Clifford, who was eager to undo most of whatever Lugard had done. Meanwhile, the white cap chiefs' land case finally reached the Judicial Committee of the Privy Council in London in 1921. The delegation was led by Amadu Tijani, Chief Oluwa, with Macaulay as his secretary. He had with him the staff of office, which Eleko claimed had been given to his ancestor Dosunmo by Queen Victoria in 1852. Surprisingly the chiefs won their case, gaining a decision which throughout the empire would be 'the *locus classicus* on the whole subject of Crown ownership of colonial times'.[19] More immediately sensational, Oluwa and Macaulay, with the staff prominently displayed, had been photographed by the recently established periodical *West Africa* having a 'chat' with King George V at a garden party at Buckingham Palace shortly after Macaulay had given an interview to the *Daily Mail* describing Eleko as 'acclaimed by the 17 million Nigerians, as the titular King of Lagos', and therefore entitled by treaty to a pension equal to Nigeria's revenue of £4 million. The Colonial Office was aghast. If the palace gave any explanation, it does not appear in the files.[20] Eleko was illiterate, but he could understand the photograph. With the support of the king and the British people, he felt he could now safely defy the Lagos authorities. As in 1916, he was told to send his bellman round to disavow actions taken in his name. As in 1916, he refused to do this. Again, his stipend was stopped.[21] This time it would not be restored, but when electoral politics were introduced into Lagos, Macaulay would master them for a generation and is now regarded as the grandfather of Nigerian independence.

While Eleko was despised as incompetent and treated with contempt by the colonial administrators in Lagos, Tupou II in Tonga had to be taken seriously. Senior officials in Whitehall regarded Tongan administration as a 'curious anomaly' which should eventually be 'interred in a decent and appropriate fashion', but during the war they should 'keep up the idea of playing at a Royal independence'.[22] Tupou II was notoriously profligate and certainly lazy. Nevertheless, he was both intelligent and well advised. 'Not a bad letter, for a king' minuted Lewis Harcourt, a colonial secretary who came from a family which could regard even European monarchs as vulgar upstarts.[23] The Supplementary Agreement of 1905 required him to seek and follow the consul's advice on important matters. This had been imposed on him under threat of deportation. Considering it contrary to the 1875 Constitution, he was determined to ignore it as much as possible. An ill-advised attempt, in 1910, by an overzealous Consul William Telfer Campbell, to force the government to suppress an emergent co-operative, the Tonga Ma'a Tonga Kautaha, led to an expensive court case, which had to be abandoned but cost about a sixth of government revenues.[24] As the Colonial Office considered Campbell 'perfectly well meaning but stupid', a post was eventually found for him in the Gambia where he would have less room to act at his own discretion.[25] The high commissioner of the Western Pacific, Sir Francis May, had to intervene to resolve the matter, but, as the Colonial Office long remembered, the King 'gave him a bad fall'.[26] From 1911 it was accepted that while Tupou had to listen to the consul's advice he was not required to follow it.

The relationship between Tonga and the British Empire would now follow Tongan rather than British lines. The foundations were laid by the new Acting Consul, Islay McOwan, an Australian whose career had been with the Fiji Police. With few weapons other than 'tact and respect' he quickly re-established working relations with the King, which had completely broken down.[27] He approved the appointment as premier of the recently ennobled Tu'ivakano, who had previously been an enemy of the king. McOwan had hoped, with British backing, to become the first president of a Tongan republic but now worked closely with Tupou II to enhance Tongan autonomy against Great Britain. While the previous premier had been treated as something of a figurehead, McOwan considered Tu'ivakano capable of running the country without constant British interference. Rather than trying to control the government by placing his own man as European Secretary in the Premier's Office, the consul agreed to the appointment of the long-settled Tasmanian lawyer George Scott, also someone who had been a bitter enemy of the king but was now his ally. McOwan achieved so much so quickly that the European merchants petitioned for him to be kept on.[28] Instead, the high commissioner, Sir Bickham Sweet Escott, secured the appointment of his protégé, H. E. W. Grant,[29] a man nearing the end of his career who wanted to keep things quiet. Grant's approach was well exemplified at the outbreak of the war. He would have received the circular despatch instructing him to deport enemy consuls but instead allowed von Treskow to close his vice-consulate and retire to his plantation, where he died at the end of 1915. Meanwhile Grant prided himself that 'by the exercise of much good sense among those of the best standing in the European community, no difficult situations have arisen'.[30]

Tonga's legal neutrality co-existed with strong political support for British war aims, declared by the King as soon as news of the outbreak reached Tonga at the beginning of September. Those aims were defined as protecting the independence of small nations, Tonga as much as Belgium.[31] Essentially rhetorical in 1914, this would have practical consequences from 1916. The liquidation of the DHPG and the registration of Germans and restriction of their movements required Tongan legislation and the active involvement of the king and government. It would also cost money, which might more easily come from Nuku'alofa than from the British Treasury. As was noted in the Colonial Office, 'this will please the king who is not at all likely to demur'.[32] Tupou II and Tu'ivakano would emphasise that they were acting at the behest of their protector, and this would strengthen their case for protection, not so much against Germany as against annexationist pressures in London and Wellington. Support for the war was not just a matter of high-level diplomatic calculation. Tongans backed it. Financial contributions to the war effort had initially been disappointing from islands repeatedly devastated by hurricanes and had come mainly from Europeans. From 1916 the royal family, the nobles, and the commoners contributed £4,202/8/8 to the Lord Kitchener Memorial Fund, significantly more than the £3,525/4/1 (pounds/shillings/pence) which Europeans contributed to all the funds together.[33] This was done quite independently of the government, which, with good harvests and new markets for copra in America, was 'flush' as the war ended and able then to invest £4,000 in British war bonds and a similar sum in Australian.[34]

Nevertheless, in the short run, the strategy failed. It was overshadowed by Tupou II and Tu'ivakano's persistence over appointing George Scott to the vacant chief justiceship against the judgement of Escott, who considered him not socially qualified. The Colonial Office agreed that the appointee should be a decent person. It concluded that the consul's diplomatic approach had failed.[35] Grant's retirement through illness then came at a difficult time for staffing. Fortunately, one man on leave in London, Geoffrey Bingham Whistler Smith-Rewse, whose career had stalled in the Gilbert and Ellice Islands, was anxious for promotion and eager to go out as acting consul.[36] Noted for zeal rather than discretion, he was determined to 'see an efficient government and the rights of the Tongan commoner safeguarded and the spirit of British justice inculcated into the minds of all'. He intended to break Scott and Tu'ivakano.[37] He quickly forced a crisis and charged the King with violation of the 1905 agreement when he refused to dismiss them, even though the high commissioner had warned him of the limits of his powers.[38] The Colonial Office wrote disapproving minutes, noting correctly that he had quarrelled with 'most . . . people white or brown in Tonga'.[39] As in 1911, the King and the consul were not on speaking terms.

Fortunately, Acting Consul Smith-Rewse then moved on to his next posting as Administrator of Nauru. A well-known aphorism had it that the empire would be lost because it was Buggins's turn. The Patronage Committee of the Colonial Office duly offered the consulship to Buggins, but he declined to go out. Islay McOwan was the second choice.[40] Aware that careers might be broken by rejecting an offer, he accepted, despite the unattractive salary.[41] As in 1911, he managed to restore a broken relationship. He endorsed a rather fudged resolution of the crisis that Smith-Rewse had created[42] and worked closely with Tu'ivakano, whose original appointment he had approved and whom he praised as a persistent reformer whose 'broader outlook, clear vision, the courage of his convictions, and his noble rank made him the dominant figure in Tongan politics'.[43] Smith-Rewse had taken the opprobrium of imposing a British Chief Justice. McOwan could move on to work with the king and the premier in furthering the war effort. Nevertheless, Tu'ivakano had had a severe shock. His report for 1916 passionately defended Tongan independence against Europeans ignorant 'of the language, custom, traditions, and the method of the ways of working, and manner of deliberation of the Tongans'. Going beyond British wishes, he called for the deportation of all the Germans 'because they form part of a nation whose records of rapine, murder and brutality has never been exceeded'. He would maintain this policy well past the Armistice.[44] In Fiji, from where many Germans had been deported, returned servicemen forcibly stopped them from coming back.[45] Ex-servicemen in Tonga, including at least two Tongans, considered this a precedent to follow.[46] So did the British settlers in Vava'u, where there was a large, young German half-caste population. Disturbances there in September 1919 were serious enough for McOwan to make the first consular visit since 1912. His report sympathised with the call for deportations. The Colonial Office took it as showing the 'feeling against Germans in the Pacific, but, while the Peace Treaty did now permit the complete liquidation of the DHPG, it ruled out the expulsion of resident Germans and allowed them to resume trading, policies which McOwan and the Tongan government reluctantly had to accept.[47]

Meanwhile Tupou II had arranged the marriage of his young daughter Salote to Uiliame Tungi, who came from a family long favoured by the British and, as rank in Tonga was determined by female ancestry, he was arguably of higher status than she. With a good claim to the throne, he had been regarded as the heir[48] at a time when Salote was noted mainly for her ability in basketball as a schoolgirl in Auckland.[49] As her father was in his mid-forties with a younger wife who had given birth to his second daughter in 1912, she had not been considered a person of much significance. The marriage was repeatedly delayed because of the recurrent illnesses of the king, which Smith-Rewse had considered malingering.[50] It eventually took place on 17 September 1917, just after McOwan's arrival. He felt that the union of the two families 'eliminated the possibility of any controversy arising on the death of the present king as to the succession'.[51]

The German question and the war effort remained one on which consul and premier might work together. Nuku'alofa took over paying the maintenance of a German family made destitute by Smith-Rewse's closure of his wife's bakery on the grounds that it was being used to spread disaffection, even though he had not told the government at the time.[52] The Colonial Office re-imbursed Wellington for the deportation and internment of the three DHPG managers 'as it is not desirable that the Dominion should have any claim to control Tongan affairs'.[53] In his report for 1917 the premier noted that: 'Practically the whole of the English speaking races are now engaged in fighting for the principles so ably expressed by President Wilson and Mr Lloyd George. . .; and these principles affect Tonga deeply'. Recognition of its right to exist as a small nation was 'practically world policy'. He had 'no fear whatever that Great Britain will ever want to interfere with the national right, provided we carry out our obligations to her'.[54]

Tu'ivakano was emulating the famous Fourteen Points address of 8 January and the British Prime Minister's war aims statement of 5 January 1918. Their principles are usually characterised as 'national self-determination'.[55] This phrase had been used by the new Russian Soviet Government in calling for a peace conference in 1917. Although it would come to be so much associated with him, President Wilson did not use the phrase until February, as he feared what might happen if non-Europeans adopted it. Instead, in the Fourteen Points, he called for an impartial adjustment of colonial claims balancing the interests (not the wishes) of colonised peoples against the 'equitable claims of the governments whose title is to be determined'.[56] Although Lloyd George had spoken of self-determination, specifically with relation to the inhabitants of the occupied German colonies, his intention was to block their return to Germany. Whitehall promptly set about ascertaining that these peoples were indeed opposed to the restoration of German rule.[57] It had no intention of promoting colonial independence or of allowing the colonised to choose their masters. Tonga would benefit from this, as it was already a protected state. London would continue to protect it against its most serious threat, New Zealand. The policy which Nuku'alofa had followed during the war allowed it to take advantage of what historians have called the 'Wilsonian moment' after the war. For most non-European peoples (as well as the Irish), that moment would be brief, ending in bitter disillusionment and a turn to more violent strategies. Tonga's post-war history would be much different. Great Britain would no longer play with keeping up a show of Tongan autonomy. It would instead work with a strengthened, stable, and increasingly powerful monarchy. As part of this strengthened relationship, Tu'ivakano agreed to restore a procedure that had lapsed after 1911, whereby the consul would vet the estimates before their consideration by the Privy Council, and praised this placing of 'our finances on such a footing that absolute reliability may be placed upon our expenditure'.[58]

In his report for 1919 the premier was almost complacently optimistic. The protector's victory had won for Tongans 'the right to have a voice in their own affairs, and the fact that small nations such as Tonga have a right to exist'. McOwan's statements had given him confidence that Great Britain would not change its form of government. Indeed, Tongans 'have a peaceful and contented people; and very few people in the various states of the world have these things with which we are contented at the present'.[59] Nevertheless, McOwan's position had been weakened by the death of Tupou II on 5 April 1918. The consul had counted on the king's 'powerful influence' to control the noisy and disaffected nobles in the Legislature, who had never accepted the Supplementary Agreement of 1905.[60] While in November 1918, after the coronation, McOwan had reported that 'the new reign opens under the most optimistic circumstances', he felt that Salote (now Tupou III) was 'inexperienced and incapable'.[61] He stuck with Tu'ivakano, helping him to recover pension rights, which had been lost because of his broken service with the Tongan government.[62] Eventually the queen overcame her initial diffidence, acquired experience, and with Tungi, who succeeded Tu'ivakano as premier in 1923, began to assert herself against a still powerful opposition. Until then it was uncertain whether the system which McOwan had created could be made to work, especially as he had to counter attempts to sideline him by Europeans in the government who no longer saw the need for his supervision.[63]

Historians learn as much from the experiences of ordinary persons as from the activities of those in power. Therefore, the rest of this chapter shall deal not so much with general policy as with particular cases, mainly with two Germans who conspicuously did not fit into the patterns just outlined. Charles Guilleaume Lucien Ungebauer was the only German not deported from Lagos. Heinrich Schultz was one of only three deported from Tonga but the only one of these to return after the war. Ungebauer had gone out to Lagos in 1877. He was the longest-established European merchant in the colony but had not been very successful. In 1914 he was the representative of Sachse and Company, which had its head office in Bohemia and specialised mainly in beads. He was recognised as a 'famous character' in the city.[64] He had evidently married locally, as his daughter lived in Porto Novo, in French Dahomey, and his son-in-law required a Yoruba interpreter when he returned to give evidence in Lagos. This degree of integration would have been unremarkable in Tonga but seems to have been unique in Nigeria. He was also a strong Freemason, which linked him with leading Lagosians, both African and European. As Ungebauer was in his mid-fifties and not an army reservist, he was not deported with the other Germans in 1914. Instead, he took advantage of Lagos's status as British soil to gain naturalisation, for which he would have been ineligible in a protectorate. With a change of name, he managed to keep his business going. Although it was suggested that he was at heart a 'very loyal German',[65] his deepest loyalties were to his firm, his family, and to Freemasonry. Unfortunately, his naturalisation could be called into question, as it should have been granted only if he had been continuously resident in Lagos for a full year prior to his application. Ungebauer also had business interests in Porto Novo, where he was the German consular agent. He had been there in August 1914 and had been deported to Lagos when war broke out between France and Germany. He was not the man to master legal technicalities. He had not tried to deceive the Lagos authorities. He had provided information on the other German firms to the British and had 'written the views I hold of the German methods of warefare [*sic*]'.[66] He feared deportation to Germany and repeatedly said that he would kill himself rather than leave Lagos. The authorities there recognised that he was 'not quite sane'[67] and made sensible and humane decisions whenever his case came up. Unfortunately for Ungebauer, this did not last. His business began to flourish as economic conditions improved in Lagos after 1916. Rivals moved against him. Carson's agitation in 1916 had exploited fears of German influence over the British government. Lloyd George's promise of a more vigorous conduct of the war fed on and enflamed this Hun-hating. Its noisiest leader was Gershom Stewart, a Conservative MP who was prominent in the small Trading with the Enemy Committee. He had Ungebauer very much in his sights. The leadership of the Colonial Office readily caved to his pressure. Lugard was forcefully told to push through legislation revoking Ungebauer's naturalisation in June 1918. Ungebauer committed suicide on the night before he was due to be deported to Great Britain. In a letter to the Lagos merchant Samuel Pearse, he gave an 'assurance as a man and Mason that never either in word or deed have I do [*sic*] anything wrong to the British Government'.[68]

The much greater integration of the Germans in Tonga produced many more anomalous situations. At the highest level, the leading 'German' family, the Riechelmanns were intermarried with the leading 'British' family, the Cockers, with whom they shared business interests. Lilla Riechelmann was married to William Bagnall, who was assistant treasurer in the Tongan government. She would become Queen Salote's personal secretary.[69] Peacetime choices for children's education had unexpected consequences once war broke out. Here are two cases to consider. Although Hermann Wolfgramm's mother was Tongan, he was sent to school in Germany in 1909, when he was eight or nine. He spent the war in the internment camp for British civilians at Ruhleben near Berlin. Destitute when he was finally released, he was able to return to Tonga only after the British consul in Berlin compassionately gave him a British passport and repatriated him to Great Britain.[70] By contrast, the Hettigs were equally long established in Tonga, but W. Hettig's son was educated in Australia. He returned in July 1914 to become a clerk in Grant's office, where he served until March 1915, when he began to work in his father's business. His national status was uncertain. Von Treskow had refused to register him as German because he had not performed military service.[71]

However, the most striking Tongan anomaly was that of Heinrich Schultz, a man as different from the unfortunate Charles Ungebauer as can be imagined. He was the DHPG agent in Vava'u and therefore one of the three Germans deported in 1916. He was the only one considered potentially dangerous, as it was felt that he 'was capable of murdering the [DHPG] liquidator by means of a hired assassin'.[72] McOwan described him as a 'drunken blustering Prussian',[73] even though, like Ungebauer, he came from Hamburg. Whereas Emil Hellfritz, the agent at Nuku'alofa, accepted deportation to Germany, despite having family in Tonga, and Emil Ohle, the agent at Ha'apai, went to Samoa after the war, Schultz insisted on returning to Vava'u. As he had an educated mixed-race wife, Wellington refused to deport him to Germany on 'ground of humanity', and London agreed.[74] Neither McOwan nor the Tongan government wanted him back in Tonga. London wavered. At first it was inclined to back Wellington but then considered that as a 'half-caste Tongan [Schultz's wife] differs little from a European', and as two of Schultz's children were already being educated in Germany, there would be no hardship in shipping them back there.[75] However, by then Wellington had gone ahead with his deportation to Vava'u. Despite the objections of the Tongan government, the British consul, and the high commissioner for the Western Pacific, he had to be allowed to stay and to resume trading along with the other Germans. The Colonial Office considered this 'most unfortunate'.[76]

For the German communities in these two anomalous parts of the British Empire, the war ended very differently. The Germans of Lagos and of the rest of Nigeria had been deported. The only man sufficiently well-integrated to stay was eventually driven to suicide by a xenophobic campaign in London which overwhelmed the Nigerian government. By contrast, the Germans of Tonga survived. Only three had been deported, and the most obnoxious of these made his way back. His influence over 'unruly half-castes' was feared, as 'Strong racial prejudices have been aroused by the war'.[77] Despite the tension before Schultz's return, his wife's protest against the display of British and American flags at the celebration of the birthday of Queen Salote's son, the future Tupou IV, in June 1919 attracted very little support from indigenous Tongans in Vava'u.[78] Hopes for the continued integration of the Tonga Germans into the wider community were largely fulfilled. Some families retained a connection with Germany and continued to send children there for education. During the Second World War, some men were interned in New Zealand and the Solomon Islands as being potentially subversive. Berlin accepted them as German nationals, as Polynesians were not considered non-Aryan. They declared loyalty to the Third Reich and received German 'pocket money' through the Protecting Power. In 1944, fearing post-war deportation to Germany, they declared themselves to be Tongan through their mothers. Although descent in Tonga is patriarchal, this choice was not questioned.[79] The restoration of the 1876 Treaty of Friendship in 1976, shortly after Tonga became fully independent, is a source of pride in both countries.

Notes

1 A much fuller account of the situation in Nigeria is in my recently published Peter J. Yearwood, *Nigeria and the Death of Liberal England, Palm Nuts and Prime Ministers, 1914–1916* (n.p.: Palgrave Macmillan, 2018). I intend shortly to publish an article on Tonga in the First World War. Currently the best published account is Elizabeth Wood-Ellem, *Queen Sālote of Tonga, The Story of an Era 1900–1965* (Auckland: Auckland University Press, 1999); but Penelope A. Lavaka, "The Limits of Advice: Britain and the Kingdom of Tonga, 1900–1970" (unpublished PhD thesis, Australian National University (ANU), 1981), remains valuable, especially for the pre-war period.

2 In researching Tonga, I have benefitted from correspondence with Professors Clive Moore, Ian Campbell, and Christine Winter, and from Declan O'Reilly's diligence in checking out details from the British Archives.

3 The National Archives (TNA): Colonial Office (CO) 225/155/59793 High Commission of the Western Pacific Estimates, 1917–18.

4 *Nigerian Pioneer,* August 28, 1914, quoted in Akinjide Osuntokun, *Nigeria in the First World War* (London: Longman, 1979), 72.

5 This remark was by a long-term German settler in Samoa, recorded in Arthur Berger, *Talofa, Sturm- und Sonnentage auf Samoa* (Dresden, 1919), quoted in Christine Winter, "Changing Frames, Identity and Citizenship of New Guineans of German Heritage during the Interwar Years," *The Journal of Pacific History* 47, no. 3 (September 2012): 357, https://doi.org/10.1080/00223344.2012.714092.

6 TNA: CO 583/47/38607 Acting Director, to Director, Nigeria Marine, April 7, 1916, in Sir Frederick Lugard (Governor General, Nigeria) despatch 607, July 24, 1916.

7 TNA: CO 554/40/41765,47653 George Grindle (Assistant Under Secretary, Crown Colonies Division) minute., September 9, 1918 (quotation); Charles Dixon (Dominions Division) min., September 6, 1919. In the Colonial Office, the Western Pacific came under the Dominions Division.

8 TNA: CO 83/134/3808 Sir George Fiddes (Permanent Under Secretary, C. O.) min., February 28, 1916.

9 TNA: CO 225/146/24347 Charles Tennyson (Assistant Legal Adviser, C.O.) min., May 29, 1916 (quotation); C. O. to Sir Eyre Hutson (Acting High Commissioner, Western Pacific) telegram, June 5, 1916.

10 TNA: CO 225/256/63950 Report for 1916; TNA: CO 225/161/37831 Islay McOwan (Agent and Consul, Tonga) to Sir Bickham Sweet Escott (High Commissioner, Western Pacific) secret, April 22, 1918.

11 TNA: CO 225/147/34006 Hellfritz to Escott, June 5, 1916; TNA: CO 225/148/43345 Grant to Hutson, s. d., Hanssen protests, June 30, 1916; TNA: CO 225/149/58522, September 14, 1916.

12 *Times of Nigeria*, September 15, 1914, 15–19; and February 1916, quoted in Osuntokun, *Nigeria in the First World War*, 68–69, 82–83.

13 TNA: CO 520/130/19439 A. G. Boyle (Acting Governor) to Lugard, May 12, 1913.

14 TNA: CO 583/34/35972 Charles Strachey (Head, Niger Department, C.O.) min., August 10, 1915.

15 TNA: CO 583/48/49544 Boyle confidential 23 September, with copy conf. report by T. F. R. Parry, Acting Inspector General of Police, September 22, 1916.

16 TNA: CO 583/94/63713 A. J. Harding (number 2 in the Niger Dep't) min., January 11, 1921.

17 *Lagos Weekly Record* (J. D. Adebayo) November 27, 1920, quoted in C. O. Olusanya, "The Lagos Branch of the National Congress of British West Africa," *Journal of the Historical Society of Nigeria* 4, no. 2 (June 1968): 331.

18 TNA: CO 583/65/11411 Lugard conf. January 31 (covering Moorhouse (Administrator of Lagos) to Lugard January 2, 1918) (quotations).

19 T. O. Elias, *Nigerian Land Law*, 4th ed. (London: Sweet & Maxwell, 1951, 4th ed. 1971), 10.
20 *Daily Mail*, July 8, 1920; *West Africa*, July 31, 1920 (clipping); TNA: CO 583/96/40999 Harding min. 2 August and correspondence between the C. O. and the Palace, August 13–18, 1920.
21 TNA: CO 583/94/. 63713 Clifford conf., December 12, 1920.
22 TNA: CO 225/152/17069 C. A. Harris (Chief Clerk, C.O.) min., March 16, 1917.
23 TNA: CO 225/103/1626,8437 Harcourt min., March 22, 1912.
24 Space allows only a bare mention of this turning point in Tongan history. Fuller treatments are, Lavaka, "Limits of Advice," ch. 6; Noel Rutherford, "Tonga Ma'a Tonga Kautaha: A Proto-Cooperative in Tonga," *Journal of Pacific History* 16 (1981): 20–41; and Ian. C. Campbell, *Island Kingdom, Tonga Ancient and Modern* (Canterbury: Canterbury University Press, 2015 (1997)), 147–49. The case cost £8,169 out of government revenues of £51,050. TNA: CO 225/117/37459 Grant Report, 1911–12.
25 TNA: CO 225/112/24990 G. W. Johnson (Principal Clerk, Dominions Division) min., August 23, 1912 (quotation), endorsed by his superiors. See also the minutes in TNA: CO 225/103/1626.
26 TNA: CO 225/145/9816 Johnson min., March 14, 1916.
27 See the documents in file TNA: CO 225/114/9950, which is unfortunately incomplete; Wood-Ellem, *Queen Sālote of Tonga*, 29.
28 TNA: CO 225/106/40843,1423 Cowley (President, Public Committee of Tonga) letter/petition, November 30, 1911. Of the 44 signatories, 10 had conspicuously German names.
29 TNA: CO 225/149/58551 Escott desp. 443, November 3, 1916.
30 TNA: CO 225/142/1163 Grant conf., October 21, 1915.
31 TNA: CO 225/129/28190 Loyal Message, September 17, 1914.
32 TNA: CO 225/146/13454 Tennyson and Johnson (quotation) mins., March 22, 1916.
33 Sir Cecil Rodwell (High Commissioner, Western Pacific) desp. 252 and enclosures, November 21, 1919; TNA: CO225/166/594.
34 TNA: CO225/161/14378 McOwan to Rodwell, October 1, 1918, OG.R. Williams (Clerk, Dominions Dep't) min., April 4, 1919 (quotation).
35 TNA: CO 225/148/39661 Escott desp. 286, 13 July, H. C. M. Lambert (Assistant Under Secretary, Dominions Division) min., September 2, 1916.
36 Details on Smith-Rewse's appointment and earlier career are in TNA: CO 225/148/33157 and TNA: CO 225/146/20567.
37 TNA: CO 225/152/10769 Smith-Rewse to Escott January 8, 1917.
38 The main documents are in TNA: CO 225/154/41298. See also TNA: CO 225/152/10769 Escott to Smith-Rewse conf., December 12, 1916 (copy).
39 TNA: CO 225/154/30726 J. N. Green (Principal Clerk, Dominions Division) min., July 30, 1917. The reference to 'white' reflects Smith-Rewse's relations with the Liquidator of the DHPG appointed by Wellington.
40 The material on this is in CO225/149/58551.
41 TNA: CO 225/161/56720 McOwan desp. 129, September 28, 1918.
42 TNA: CO225/156/4850 McOwan to Escott October 20, 1917; Escott to McOwan November 15, 1917.
43 TNA: CO 225/161/56706 McOwan desp. 105, August 8, 1918.
44 TNA: CO 225/256/63950 Premier's Report for 1916, forwarded October 22, 1917, (quotation); TNA: CO 225/170/1919 Report for 1919, March 25, 1920.
45 TNA: CO 83/149/59922 Press clipping December 19, 1919 in Rodwell tel., December 15, 1919 (quotation). TNA: CO 83/147/71305. These may refer to separate incidents.
46 TNA: CO 225/171/64055, Petition of Tonga Returned Sailors and Soldiers Association 11 July (copy), McOwan to Rodwell, July 23, 1920 (carbon).

47 TNA: CO 225/166/63054. C. O. to Rodwell tel. November 4, 1919, McOwan desp. 113, September 15, 1919; TNA: CO 225/169/18705 Rodwell to McOwan desp. 220, November 27, 1919; H. F. Batterbee (Private Secretary, C.O.) min., April 23, 1920 (quotation).
48 TNA: CO 225/105/31019 McOwan to Escott conf., June 22, 1912 (copy).
49 Wood-Ellem, *Queen Sālote*, 16.
50 TNA: CO 225/153/33083 Smith-Rewse conf. report to Escott, April 10, 1917.
51 TNA: CO 225/156/17 McOwan desp. 123, September 25, 1917.
52 The main documents on this are in TNA: CO 225/159/26976.
53 TNA: CO 225/161/45817 Green draft 10 October of C. O. to Treasury, October 18, 1918.
54 TNA: CO 225/161/48749 Premier's Report for 1917, March 28, 1918.
55 The literature on this is enormous. Erez Manela, *The Wilsonian Moment, Self-Determination and the International Origins of Anticolonial Nationalism* (Oxford: Oxford University Press, 2007), has become foundational. For the military diplomatic context, see David Stevenson, *The First World War and International Politics* (Oxford: Oxford University Press, 1988), 183–98; for the wider context, Eric D. Weitz, "Self-Determination: How a German Enlightenment Idea Became the Slogan of National Liberation and a Human Right," *American Historical Review* 120, no. 2 (April 2015): 462–96. Lloyd George's speech is in George, *War Memoirs of David Lloyd George*, vol. 2 (London: Odhams Press Ltd, 1933), 1510–17.
56 Arno J. Mayer, *Wilson vs. Lenin, Political Origins of the New Diplomacy 1917–1918* (Cleveland and New York: Meridian Books, 1964 (1959)), 362.
57 W. R. Louis, *Great Britain and Germany's Lost Colonies* (Oxford: Oxford University Press, 1967), 97.
58 TNA: CO 225/161/48749 Premier's Report for 1917.
59 TNA: CO 225/170/42362 Premier's Report for 1919.
60 TNA: CO 225/176/14982 McOwan desp. 103, December 6, 1920 (copy).
61 TNA: CO 225/151/14381 McOwan to Rodwell November 5, 1918 (1st quotation). TNA: CO 225/160/29379 McOwan no. 41, April 12, 1918 (2nd quotation).
62 The material on this is in TNA: CO 225/160/37756.
63 Wood-Ellem, *Queen Sālote*, 79. This view had support within the C. O., Green min., TNA: CO 225/169/24095, May 25, 1920.
64 TNA: CO 583/27/44446 Strachey min., November 14, 1914.
65 TNA: CO 583/38/55087 Thomas F. Burrowes (Liquidator of Enemy Property, Lagos) memo, October 23, 1915.
66 TNA: CO583/66/34961Ungebauer to Central Secretary, Lagos 2 June in Lugard desp., June 19, 1918.
67 TNA: CO 583/38/55087 Burrowes memo, October 23, 1915.
68 TNA: CO 583/73/13285 Ungebauer to Pearse June 15, 1918, in copy of Inquest in Moorhouse (Acting Governor, Nigeria) desp. 143, February 8, 1919.
69 Wood-Ellem, *Queen Sālote*, 62.
70 The material on Hermann Wolfgramm is in TNA: CO 225/173/37754.
71 TNA: CO 225/140/33306 Grant desp., May 6, 1915.
72 TNA: CO 209/287/18424 Earl of Liverpool (Governor-General, New Zealand) tel., April 17, 1916. Escott discounted this, as Schultz had had a violent quarrel with a man who had returned to New Zealand threatening to arrange his deportation. Tel. TNA: CO 225/147/29939, April 20, 1916.
73 TNA: CO 225/171/64055 McOwan desp., July 23, 1920.
74 TNA: CO 225/169/6170 C. O. to Rodwell, February 12, 1920.
75 TNA: CO 225/169/9249 Green min., February 2, 1920.
76 TNA: CO 225/176/18354 Green memo, April 21, 1921.

77 TNA: CO 225/171/64055 McOwan desp., July 23, 1920; (1st quotation); TNA: CO 225/169/18705 McOwan to Rodwell September 15, 1919; (2nd quotation).

78 TNA: CO225/169/18705, McOwan desp. 113, September 15, 1919.

79 I owe this information to Christine Winter. It builds on what she has written in Winter, "Changing Frames," 347–67.

4 Imperial masculinity and racial pacification

'Martial Bengalis' in the Great War

Rajarshi Mitra

> The 49th Bengali Regiment may perhaps be regarded as one of the many tangible evidences of the wave of patriotic favour which swept over India at the declaration of the Great War. The movement for the formation of a Bengali unit was inaugurated at a great demonstration in Town Hall over which Lord Carmichael presided.[1]

In College Square in central Kolkata[2], a monument commemorates the death and sacrifice of Bengali men of the 49th Bengali Regiment who died during the Great War. Addressed to 'the glory of God, King and Country', the marble monument was erected in 1924 at a cost of 4,500 rupees. Inscribed on it are names of the 56 soldiers who fell in the war. In separate columns, it lists registration number, rank, name, date of their demise and the district they hailed from. In a society where caste equations mattered, a look at the names reveal an overwhelming presence of upper-caste Hindus from Bengal. The erection of the monument was a cause for celebration, though, as much as the formation of the regiment became a matter of racial pride. Bengalis had not been in the British Indian Army since they were not considered worthy of martial service. The martial race theory adopted by the army establishment in the late nineteenth century designated certain races in India as fighting material. Bengalis were considered a non-martial race. The First World War provided Bengalis a unique opportunity to prove their allegiance to the British Empire. Despite a steep rise in anti-colonial revolutionary activity in Bengal, newspaper reports from both before and after the First World War reveal a feverish patriotic zeal among a section of Bengalis to serve the king and country. For the colonial government, this was a felicitous occasion to improve its public perception as a benevolent ruler in India. For Bengalis, this was a perfect opportunity to shake off the stigma of non-martial race.

This chapter sketches the involvement of Bengalis as a race in the Great War. It unearths secret intelligence files, newspaper reports and personal memoirs to understand the dynamics of a community's racial identity during the war. Inspired by war propaganda, Bengali civil society mobilised support to raise an ambulance corps in 1915 and a battalion in 1916 to serve at the Mesopotamian front. The colonial culture around the formation and disbandment of both the ambulance corps and the Bengali Battalion serve as good examples of how racial theory shaped the aspirations of the colonised. The Bengali Battalion was the result of a civilian project to gain political prominence. It is unique because the colonial government invested little in its formation. British attitude to Bengal's racial pride during the war was akin to colonial appeasement policies followed elsewhere. Within the limits of martial race theory, colonial authorities began by encouraging a community to serve the king. Unlike the criminal tribes[3] in British India, martial race theory was never a statutory set of rules, yet the army and police departments followed it as a conventional recruitment policy. Its extensive use has been traced to the days following the mutiny in 1857, when the rebellious factions within the Bengal army were disbanded. The army establishment now sought new recruits among the North Indian peasant communities, the Sikhs in Punjab, the Muslims in the North West Frontier and the Nepalese.[4] Thomas Metcalfe writes that 'the logic of martial races' had become so compelling that by the 1880s the entire army had been 'organized into units based on caste and ethnicity'.[5] Absorbing Victorian notions of masculinity, martial race theory considered certain communities to have inherited a superior physical and psychological culture suited for combat. The army would reason that these communities would have the necessary fighting spirit and therefore the natural propensity to follow orders to remain loyal to the empire. A typical debate in favour of or against the martial race theory considered a community's major profession and its past involvement in combat. Lobbies in favour of it proposed to recruit individuals from traditional labour and agricultural communities. Lobbies against felt that certain communities, for want of better combat experience, had become more peace-loving and therefore unfit for being in the army. Pro–martial races lobbyists were always in favour of keeping the army as a homogeneous racial unit, whereas those against the martial races argued that to counter racial monopolization, the Indian army had to be multi-racial and multi-ethnic. In 1914, the social composition of the British Army was overwhelmingly 'martial' – filled with individuals from the martial races. The Army Committee, set up in 1912, made explicit links between the ethnic qualities of a community with a specific sort of warfare in its 1913 report.[6] However, the government had to tweak their recruitment policy when the protracted war required new soldiers and military labourers. Several 'non-martial' races were opted into the army, especially in 1916, and later when mobilisation in India became no more an option but a necessity.[7] As the war drew to a close, facing discontent and political pressure, the British government gradually distanced itself from the military aspirations of the Bengali community all the while maintaining a charade of patronage.

An 'effeminate race'

Perception of Bengalis as an intellectual and 'effeminate' race was quite well established by the early twentieth century. In John Alexander Hammerton's encyclopaedic text, *People of All Nations*, Valentine Chirol described the 'intellectual quality' of Bengalis as superior to other Indian races: 'For readiness to learn, for retentiveness of memory, for intellectual flexibility and for the facile eloquence they have few rivals and no superiors in India'.[8] Chirol writes that in Bengal's largest city of Calcutta, Western learning is greatly valued and the city's universities have provided an opportunity for a blend of Western and Eastern traditions:

> However, the conditions in which such education is disseminated are morally and physically deleterious. Consequently, most students remain misguided. Despite western education producing a sizeable set of intellectuals, it has also swelled the population of unemployable and 'dangerous' intellectual proletariat. Their comical flights of English rhetoric and their swarthy figures are the worst qualities of their character, whereas 'when they care' they can play football bareheaded and barefooted against British teams and defeat them.[9]

Chirol was referring to a moment of considerable racial pride for Bengalis when a Calcutta-based football club defeated the East Yorkshire Regiment and won the Indian Football Association Shield in 1911. This win momentarily disproved an imperial myth about Bengalis as lacking strength and physical character. Bengalis responded euphorically and celebrated their masculine strength with flowing rhetoric. The win was finally a weapon to fight the stigma of effeminacy. In fact, anxiety over one's masculine powers had developed into a fairly well-structured 'Bengali Hindu political project of recovering' the race's martial character through physical culture.[10] There were myriad cultural manifestations of this masculine project of disciplining a Bengali body and mind. Martial monks, for example, became a staple in popular imagination. Monks symbolised sacrifice, restraint, discipline and spiritual awakening. In a charged atmosphere of masculine ideals, Swami Vivekananda, the famous Hindu monk from Bengal, in his speeches encouraged Hindus to shake off their weakness and embrace *Kshatra-Virya* (warrior strength).[11] Popular tastes veered to the *Bir* (gallant and heroic) cult that sought to root out weakness and effeminacy and embrace bravado and adventure.

The late nineteenth century had a proper beginning of Bengali heroic romances in the hands of novelist Bankim Chandra Chatterjee. Several writers, including Chatterjee's descendants, carried forward his legacy of writing heroic historical fictions located India's golden age of masculine chivalry and warrior code of conduct in a precolonial past. Bankim's rhetoric of heroism was adopted by secret revolutionary societies in Bengal during the rise of militant nationalism in the province. Pramathanath Mitra, an established barrister, adopted Bankim Chandra and Vivekanada's rhetoric to run *Anushilan Samiti* – an organisation that would have a considerable role to play in anti-colonial activities and armed insurrection in Bengal. Bankim, in his *Dharmatattwa*, had developed a scheme of Hindu self-culture where *anushilan* (practice) meant a cultivation of physical and spiritual powers. When the war broke out, the Bengali cult of heroism remained divided between one's loyalty to the king and one's allegiance to the Bengali revolutionary ideal of an independent nation. Sentiments that went into the formation of the 49th Bengali Regiment hung between British racial gaze and Bengali resistance to that gaze. Bengalis participating in the Great War became part of this cultural project of bringing back lost heroism. Early editions of historian Upendranath Bhattacharya's popular text *Banger Bir Santan*[12] included life histories of members from the Bengal Ambulance Corps (BAC) and the 49th Regiment. During the Great War, popular magazines and journals celebrated this opportunity that was presented to Bengali men to shake off their effeminacy. In the autumn of 1916, after the departure of the 49th Bengali Regiment for Basra, *Kushdaha*, a monthly Bengali magazine, celebrated that Bengal had risen to the occasion. Bengali mothers were smilingly sending their sons to war. The stigma of weakness was no more.[13]

Texts about Bengali involvement in the Great War travelled between two universes: Bengali adulation of their war adventure and a taciturn government watching the events carefully. Imperial texts can be notoriously consistent in their intertextual patterns of repeating collective knowledge. Government secret files about the regiment abound in references to racial anthropology popular during the early twentieth century. Mrinalini Sinha has demonstrated that since the late nineteenth century, the colonial cliché 'effeminate Bengali' was a complex set of racial and cultural investment in colonial masculinity that permeated through colonial policies and colonial culture in general.[14] For the Western-educated Bengali elite, the *bhadralog*, self-perception of effeminacy, led to periodic cultural movements to prove one's masculinity. During a widespread Russian war scare in the late nineteenth century, prodded by the viceroy's call for volunteers to raise the number of standing armies in India, native volunteer movement had occasioned vitriolic debates in the press about relative martial merits of Bengali babu and manly Englishman.[15] The Great War too witnessed a re-enactment of congealed cultural attitudes towards masculinity. What must be borne in mind is the connection empire drew between effeminacy, physical weakness and political unrest.

Valentine Chirol's powerful *Indian Unrest* made it clear that behind the 'storm' in Bengal in the early twentieth century lay a sustained native effort to revive Hinduism and wrong methods of dissemination of European education.[16] British attempt at intellectual emancipation of Indians has led to frustrations and disappointments with British political authority. A disastrous scheme of partitioning Bengal province in 1905 for better governance backfired when the Bengali elite started organising opinions against it. According to Chirol, the ill-trained Bengali students joined in the protest. He mentions correctly, however, that a large number of deeds of violence against the British followed in the aftermath of the anti-partition agitation.[17] Among various political visions about India that emerged during the anti-partition movement was the concept of sovereign independence as a national goal. Writings of extremist leaders within Congress, such as Aurobindo Ghose and Bepin Chnadra Pal, became extremely popular. Both of them encouraged Bengalis to rise up against English rule. If the revolutionaries felt that the war was a great opportunity to challenge British supremacy, Bengali moderates in the Indian National Congress felt the need use the war to establish better ties with Britain. Working as a pressure group of civilians supporting the war effort, moderates wanted to show their influence among the masses, especially the respectable bhadralog class.

'Storm' in Bengal and the Great War

While the then colonial government was responsible for the construction of the war monument in College Square, it is known that various civil society organisations based in Calcutta lobbied for and raised money to support its erection. Subedar Monbahadur Sinha's memoir, *Sainik Bangali*, furnishes excerpts from contemporary newspapers regarding large gatherings during the meetings of the Bengali Ex-Soldier Association.[18] In February 1920, the Association met for the first time in Indian Association Hall and formed a committee to look after its activities. It was instrumental in raising public support for the construction of the monument in 1924.[19] This was the same year the British government was busy framing an ordinance to contain revolutionary movement in Bengal. The Bengal Criminal Law Amendment Ordinance became a notorious bill in 1925 which enabled the British government to deal with widespread revolutionary activities of secret societies like *Anusilan Samiti* and *Yugantar*. During the war years, Bengal required special attention for the rise in revolutionary activities and general disorder in the province. Colonial bureaucracy prepared copious reports about the political situation in Bengal, which were preludes to the Defence of India Act in 1915. By this act the police were given special power to unleash repressive measures, like detention without trial. With the First World War, Bengali revolutionary activities entered a new phase. The revolutionaries now looked beyond India to locate their anti-British activities. There was a fairly well-coordinated German plan to support simultaneous uprisings in Bengal and Ireland and fuel Islamic misgivings against the British occupation of territories in the Middle East.[20]

Three years before the war had begun in 1914, Bengal had lost its political prominence in the empire when the British Raj relocated its capital from Calcutta, a major city in Bengal, to New Delhi. Amidst uproar on what prompted the transfer, what was evident was that the Bengal province, without a doubt, was becoming too unstable a province from which to rule India. Throughout the early twentieth century, Bengal witnessed the rise and growth of violent revolutionary terrorism.[21] It was triggered by protests against the then viceroy Lord Curzon's infamous decision in 1905 to divide Bengal presidency. Later in 1911, intense protests forced Lord Hardinge, who had assumed office as the viceroy of India in 1910, to reunify Bengal. The same year saw the relocation of the Indian capital from Calcutta to New Delhi. Lord Hardinge, as ambitious as Lord Curzon, tried to emulate him by arranging another imperial durbar to mark the relocation of the capital in New Delhi. Forces unleashed during the division and reunification of Bengal continued to shape the political culture of the province, often plunging it in internecine fight and chaos. Attacks against what were deemed colonial symbols were too common throughout the province. The most audacious of all – an assassination attempt on the viceroy himself – was masterminded by Bengali revolutionary Rashbehari Bose. In 1912, while travelling on the streets of Delhi on an elephant, a homemade bomb killed the mahout and wounded Lord Hardinge severely. Known in Indian history as the Delhi–Lahore Conspiracy Case, the incident was followed by an empire-wide effort to bring the perpetrators to justice.

Colonial intelligence went after the revolutionary groups and secret societies from Bengal and Punjab.

In Bengal, underground organisations like *Anusilan Samiti* and *Yugantar* had been pro-active in recruiting young men and women into their revolutionary doctrine. During the war, both the societies were reportedly involved in Hindu–German conspiracy to destabilise the British Empire. They helped Germany to make elaborate but imprecise plans to ship arms to different parts of British India. As a consequence, conspiracy theories festered in Calcutta. Members of Ghadr, a revolutionary group from Punjab raised in the United States, chose to secretly land in Calcutta in 1914 only to be arrested by the British police. A member of the *Yugantar party*, Jatin Mukherjee, popularly known as Bagha Jatin in Bengal, was arrested while offloading German military aid in a remote seashore in Orissa, south of Calcutta. War allowed an international edge to the entire revolutionary movement – an edge to be explored by a sedition committee in 1917. The committee was famous in Indian history as the Rowlatt Committee, for its president, Sidney Rowlatt, evaluated political terrorism in Bengal and Punjab provinces.

What emerged in the intelligence reports in the years leading to the war was a certain perception of Bengali bhadralog as a gentlemanly terrorist. These were elite Western-educated Bengali men who embraced revolutionary violence as a method to challenge the Raj. The detective departments started listing bhadralog dacoity as a special form of seditious activity. These dacoities were undertaken by well-dressed, well-educated and high-caste Bengali men who were disenchanted by colonial limits on their social, economic and political evolution.[22] The incidents of bhadralog dacoity became a constant unease among the moderates in the Indian National Congress, who argued that introduction of liberal reforms would greatly change the attitude of a section of bhadralogs. When moderate leaders in Bengal began to mobilise support for the war effort, they had a dual task: to salvage bhadralog identity and to prove Bengali masculinity as capable of heroic deeds.

Bengal Ambulance Corps

Manbahadur Sinha's memoir would have us believe that support for the king and country remained strong in Bengal during and after the war. In fact, the 49th Bengali Regiment was formed as a voluntary corps without any financial help from the government to prove that Bengalis supported the British cause. Vilified as a non-martial race, Bengalis, probably unlike any other community, needed to prove their fighting spirit. This need had arisen almost a year into the war – Bengal's first phase of war effort – when Bengal had decided to raise an ambulance corps for field service. Its commendable service in the field in Mesopotamia egged Bengalis to pitch for the raising of the 49th Regiment in 1916. The first phase had followed a nation-wide call for mobilisation when King George V, in a stirring message to his Indian subjects, announced that: 'I find in this hour of trial a full harvest and a noble fulfilment of the assurance given by you [Indian subjects] that the destinies of Great Britain and India are indissolubly linked'.[23] Indian princely states and British provinces had lent their support to the British Empire as soon as the war was declared in 1914. Most highly placed Bengalis, who ran the moderate faction of the Indian National Congress, were in favour of patriotism through their show of loyalty to the empire.[24] They disparaged the revolutionaries, who had adopted violent means to overthrow the government. Prominent moderate Sir Surendranath Bannerjea – the founder of *The Bengalee*, an established English newspaper from Bengal – in one of his speeches even said that 'Indians were loyal because they were patriotic'.[25]

For the 1.5 million Indians who would serve in Europe and Mesopotamia during the war, the imperial call for mobilisation and support was primarily a recruitment opportunity in a country plagued by chronic poverty. In 1915, Dr Suresh Prasad Sarvadhikari would regret that Bengalis living as they are in relative peace, are hardly bothered about the war in Europe. Hailing from a distinguished Bengali family, Dr Sarvadhikari was an eminent surgeon and one of the Indian representatives at the International Medical Conference in London. If *The Hindoo Patriot*, another popular Bengali civil society newspaper in English, was correct, he was begging door to door to raise money for the Bengal Ambulance Corps. The British government did not ask Dr Sarvadhikari to raise the corps, though; he was raising it because Bengali civil society wanted to help Europe in whatever way possible. The cost of the corps was borne by the Bengal province. Dr Sarvadhikari chaired several meetings to seal a deal with the empire. He brought the wealthy Bengalis together, raised money, chose the volunteers himself and asked the British governor of Bengal to lend his moral support to the cause. *The Hindoo Patriot* projected a beleaguered Dr Sarvadhikari appealing to its readers in an article on 28 June 1915 titled 'An Appeal to Bengali Patriotism'. The article reminded Bengalis of their patriotic duty to serve the British Empire during its hour of need. Bengalis needed to be aroused with a bombardment like the one that happened in Madras Harbour in 1914. 'But this won't do', the newspaper wrote,

> the good name of the Bengalees [sic] is now at stake. Dr Sarvadhicari only wants thirty-five thousand rupees to make up his deficit. . . . After all the Ambulance Corps is the special contribution of the Bengalees. It is their own creation. Its claims are therefore paramount.[26]

Several meetings and fundraising drives had supported the raising of the corps. The volunteers were trained in first aid and emergency medical care by Colonel A. H. Nott of the Indian Medical Service in Alipur Civil Lines. Colonel Nott also saw the corps through the colonial bureaucracy and arranged for the final send off in June 1915. Almost a month before their departure in May 1915, the BAC's steamer, observably titled *The Bengalee*, capsized off the coast of Madras, thankfully without a crew member on it. The appeal in the previous paragraph appeared when Dr Sarvadhikari needed to commission another boat for the BAC, which could work as a field hospital at the front. *The Hindoo Patriot* carried detailed reports concerning the formation and status of the BAC. Those who joined the corps were mostly young, educated Bengali men, including Shishir

Prasad Sarvadhikari, the brother of Dr Sarvadhikari. Years later, Shishir Prasad Sarvadhikari would write one of the few extant Bengali memoirs from the First World War. His *Abhi Le Baghdad*[27] records his experience as a volunteer at the Mesopotamian front. Prafulla Chandra Sen, another volunteer who served in the corps, would write a well-documented memoir in 1935 titled *Bengal Ambulance Corpser Katha* (roughly translated, the History of Bengal Ambulance Corps). The memoirs constantly reflect on the sense of honour the volunteers drew from serving the king and country. They parallel the enthusiasm and disappointment evident in the pages of *The Hindoo Patriot*. Bengali enthusiasm was particularly evident while sending off the corps in June 1915. The members were showered with gifts and food, and passers-by wished them luck. They reached Iraq in July 1915 and served in Tesiphon, Baghdad and Kutt Al Amarra, eventually earning praise from the British authorities.[28]

In September 1916, a section of the corps was attached to the second Field Ambulance and sent to take part in the battle in Kut. They were imprisoned by the Turks when General Townsend surrendered following a gruelling, four-month-long siege in Kut between December 1915 and April 1916. This was one of the worst defeats of the allies, ending in terrible suffering for the Indian troops garrisoned there. Those who lived through the horrifying marches and appalling conditions as prisoners of war were able to return home after the Armistice in 1918.[29] The section not sent to Kut, returned home on 27 July 1916. *The Bengalee*, another civil society English newspaper, reported how the volunteers were received with warmth by the founding members of the corps. They went to a temple to offer prayers and cheered for the king and country.[30] By the time the BAC returned home, efforts to recruit Bengalis for a double company were in progress.

Raising the 49th Bengali Regiment – a 'bhadralog' regiment

Long before Mahatma Gandhi's call for supporting the empire's war efforts, Bengali civil society leaders, several of them affiliated with the Congress, had formed a pressure group in early 1916 to mobilise Bengali youth. The recruitment process in Bengal was rather unique in its character. The Indian National Congress and its leaders, like Mahatma Gandhi, supported the empire's war effort to gain better representation of India in the British government following the war, whereas, in Bengal, the encouragement to join the war was meant to glorify Bengali masculinity and the loyalty of the bhadralog. In Bengal the recruitment process required the governor of the province, Lord Carmichael, to address the crowd and thank them for their enthusiasm. The rhetoric for mobilisation was pitched high enough by enthusiastic activists like Sarala Devi to arouse a dizzying patriotic fervour for service in the Great War.[31] It required the formation of an executive committee for raising a company for voluntary service, and the committee agreed in its first meeting on 22 August 1916 that all war expenses would be borne by it. The members of the pressure group were primarily upwardly mobile, educated Hindu middle-class men who had gathered under the presidency of Maharajadhiraj Bahadur of Burdwan. This committee held public meetings and issued instructions to the interested recruits. In its first meeting, the committee worried about the homogeneous identity of the battalion and announced that enlistment must not be confined to the bhadralog class but must be open to anyone who came forward. It was felt that there were other Bengali castes, like Gowalas, who were fighting material. Bengali recruits must not bargain for better emoluments since bargaining would collapse the noble intentions of the committee. Instead, participation in war should be looked upon with pride and as a 'voluntary undertaking'.[32]

A very aware English-language press in Calcutta covered the recruitment process for a double company. *The Bengalee* was constantly engaging with the sentiments expressed in British-backed newspapers. On 10 August 1916 it quoted both *The Statesman* and *The Englishman*, which praised Bengalis for contributing to the war effort but warned of an inevitable failure unless Bengalis suppress their non-martial racial character. If the experiment of the Bengali regiment was successful, then Bengal, which had long been ignored as a recruitment ground for the British Indian Army, would be opened up. What the province demanded was to be granted equal opportunity like other provinces to serve the empire. *The Statesman* referred to the common perception of Bengalis as a non-martial race with Lord Macaulay's seal on it. Indeed, Lord Macaulay in his 1841 essay on Warren Hastings had disparaged Bengali character as passive enough to allow his country to be overrun by dacoits without offering any resistance. With his characteristic imperial snobbery, Macaulay wrote that Bengalis didn't offer themselves as soldiers to the East India Company but as deceitful money lenders, usurers and as sharp legal practitioners. They were a weak and effeminate race.[33] *The Englishman* warned that terms of enlistment must be clearly read out to the recruits so that there was no misunderstanding. It was time to put the claims of the Bengali people to a 'real and thorough test'.[34]

On the 17 August, *The Bengalee* wrote back to the empire that, as ordered by the British government, the double company had been recruited primarily from the 'bhadralog', or the literate class, and that highly placed Englishmen from the military establishment were part of committees that recruited Bengalis.[35] Salvaging the bhadralog identity was uppermost in the minds of the recruiters. This identity had been a sort of cultural project of the English-educated Bengali middle class in the nineteenth century. The term 'bhadralog' – gentlefolk – presupposed both a law-abiding subject and a 'new, egalitarian, speaking legal subject' who had received liberal European education.[36] During the war, empire expected loyalty from the bhadralogs, yet, as secret intelligence files in the Home Department would have it, the bhadralogs were responsible for several revolutionary activities in the aftermath of Bengal partition in 1905. When the double company was formed, more than Bengalis' martial nature, what was at stake was the bhadralog identity. The memoirs of Bengali soldiers also reflect on this dual project of salvaging the Bengali race's martial as well as bhadralog identity. But the secret reports about the regiment would have an entirely discouraging story to tell to the empire.

Once the recruits were formed into a double company, the requirements of war meant their movements were rapid. In September 1916 they were sent to

Nowshera to train with other Indian troops. In December the same year they were sent to Karachi for garrison duty. It would be in Karachi where the rest of the troop would remain while a section was sent to Mesopotamia later in 1917. Meanwhile, members of the Working Committee for Bengalee Double Company published letters exchanged with the commanding officers supervising the training of the recruits. One such letter from a commanding officer mentioned the rapid advancement in progress and that the recruits were 'willing, well-behaved and anxious to do credit to their class'.[37] The order for transforming the company into a battalion immediately occasioned further civilian mobilisation in Bengal for financial support. A wave of donations followed. Several women's organisations began collecting funds for the battalion. In fact, the Mahila Samity (women's organisation) would book-keep their account until the end of the war and purchase provisions for the battalion throughout.[38]

Arriving in Basra in July and August 1917, the regiment served on the Lines of Communication for three years before their return and disbandment in India on 30 August 1920. The regiment did not see action, but a section was deployed in Kurdistan to contain Sheykh Mahmud's uprising against the British in May 1919. In Kurdistan the unit primarily performed long marches and were employed on escort duty. Memoirs of Bengali soldiers repeatedly refer to racial pride and honourable bearing of the regiment's men. Particularly significant are the writings of popular Bengali poet Kazi Nazrul Islam, who enlisted in mid-1917 and was stationed in Karachi until the disbandment of the regiment in August 1920. He found the patriotic fervour of 1916 and 1917 in Bengal especially appealing and enlisted to show his fighting spirit.[39] There is reason to believe that the British government was generally favourable to Bengali enthusiasm for enlisting in the army. On 19 July 1917 a letter from the Chief of the General Staff wrote to the commanding officer of the Mesopotamian Expeditionary Force that great importance was being attached to the Bengali bhadralog regiment. If the experiment of bhadralog soldiers was successful, it could open new grounds of recruitment for the British Army. The Chief of General Staff asked the commanding officer to take personal interest in looking after the training of the soldiers.[40]

Subedar Sinha's memoir is remarkably detailed in explaining how Bengalis bore themselves with courage and honour through difficult garrison routines, war manoeuvres and marches. Being a subedar, which meant a native commissioned official in the Indian Army equivalent to that of a captain, Sinha had a clear knowledge of the war and the 49th Regiment's position in it. To support his experiences in Iraq, Sinha included letters and newspaper reports about the regiment beginning with the days of mobilisation to its disbandment and aftermath. Sinha wrote highly of the camaraderie among Bengali soldiers. He regretted that the intensity of war was waning when the Bengali regiment had been sent to Iraq. If the war was in its prime, Bengalis could have proved themselves in the battlefield. Sinha pays due attention to training exercises and encouragements received during parades and marches from commanding officers. His aim was to show how Bengali men were strong, willing and ready to face any physical challenge.

'Elemdar paltan'

Amiya Halder's memoir *Paltan Chauni* is a more humane portrait of the Bengali Battalion in Iraq.[41] Amiya Halder was a soldier, not an officer. Therefore, his knowledge of the war was limited to garrison duties and general sentiment about war. From him we get an altogether different picture of Bengali soldiers, who, though enthusiastic and willing, were under considerable psychological strain. We get to know that severe demands of army training would make the recruits homesick. Some found ways to get dismissed and go home. Men fell sick and sought ways of emotional release in the trying climate of Iraq. The soldiers seem anxious about their pay and food or, rather, the lack of it. They participate in military sports, earn medals and plan mischievous escapades. Rumours of supernatural presence fuel 'latrine fear'. Men see ghosts, and daredevils face dares. In Baghdad, Bengali soldiers celebrate the autumn festival Durga puja with utensils borrowed from Jewish families and drums borrowed from the Maratha Regiment. Halder records how mental illness ruins the health of certain Bengali soldiers and how they are secretively sent home. And yet, Halder was proud to be part of the Bengali Battalion. He presents Bengali soldiers as fun-loving but well-disciplined men very alert to their duties. If Sinha was bent on presenting to his readers what important officials thought about Bengali soldiers, Halder shows how infantrymen from other regiments looked upon the battalion. The Bengali Battalion came to be called Bengali paltan – paltan meaning soldier in several Indian languages. Indian soldiers from other regiments respectfully call them 'elemdar paltan', meaning very capable soldiers who have joined the war not out of necessity but of personal interest. Halder portrayed an egalitarian image of military camps where young privates from British regiments eagerly exchanged food with Indians.

Halder's observation on the battalion's physical condition is more consistent with the two war diaries for the 49th Bengal Infantry kept between July 1917 and April 1920. The diaries show several cases of illness, death from diseases and general withdrawal from soldiering. During their stay in Iraq, several men were invalidated due to physical reasons and were sent home. The year 1918 saw invalidations in greater frequency. Further, the diaries report cases of accidental gun shots. These observations in the war diaries, though not very unique for a battalion during the Great War, did not go down well in the confidential reports sent to the headquarters. Just before being transferred to Aziziyeh in January 1918 a medical board inspected the regiment and found most soldiers unfit. Jemadar A. N. Chatterji and 57 Indian Other Ranks remained in camp in Baghdad in segregation owing to infectious diseases.[42]

Confidential reports

The British Library holds two top-secret files on the 49th Bengali Regiment and a file on a shooting affray. Both the secret files are summarily dismissive of the military ability of the Bengali troop. The file about a shooting affray in the regiment reports an unfortunate incident in 1918 – an incident neither Sinha nor

Halder mentions in his memoir. Sinha briefly points out that soldiers ran amok one day but does not furnish the details. On 9 June 1918, a few months after the 49th was sent to Basra, personal jealousy drove two soldiers to attack and wound three Bengali officers while they were sleeping. One of them, Subedar Mitra died of a wound he received from a revolver shot. The unpopular Subedar D. K. Sen was implicated in the incident and arrested immediately but was released later in September. The entire incident was labelled as mutiny, insubordination and misconduct worthy of court-martial. A court of enquiry found Naik S. Choudhury and Sepoy S. Sidhanto guilty of firing shots. They were both subjected to death by hanging on 17 October 1918. The incident coincides with a host of activities undertaken by Mahila Samity in Bengal to raise funds for the 49th Regiment. The Samity had organised a fair in May 1918 to raise money, and by July 1918 they had a considerable bank balance to carry on supporting the battalion.[43] As the moderate politicians in Bengal continued to support the war effort, quite understandably, the shooting affray was downplayed and unreported.

The mood and tone of the secret files remained totally opposite to the public enthusiasm shown by the civil society in Bengal. The second file carries a devastating set of reports on the unworthiness of Bengalis as troopers.[44] Their commanders find them unsuitable for responsible military action at the front because of their higher intellectual ability. They write that Bengalis, being more suited to administrative jobs and other intellectual pursuits, do not possess any military instinct. Some of them are very keen, but in general they cannot be relied upon for any army duty. As to the question of preferential treatment, British officers debated on how to look after the troops. Being from bhadralog class, they found Bengali soldiers constitutionally weak. One of the reports mentioned the prevalence of venereal diseases among bhadralog soldiers – a clear indication of lack of moral standards and self-control.

In December 1917 Commanding Officer Lt Col A. L. Barrett had been so bemused with the battalion's general health standards that he had divided the 49th Bengali Regiment into 'the Measles Squad', 'The Whooping Cough Squad' and so on. General Sir William Marshall, the Commander-in-Chief of British Forces in Mesopotamia, mentioned this with some element of surprise in his memoir.[45] The fortunes of the Bengali regiment began changing in November 1917, after the death of popular Commander-in-Chief General Stanley Maude. General Maude, to believe Sinha, loved Bengali troopers so much that even on his deathbed he had sought them. General Marshall, who assumed command after General Maude passed away, would soon push for demobilisation. With the end of war in sight, any regiment without proper credentials would have to be disbanded. The 49th Regiment became part of the demobilisation scheme. In December 1918 General Marshall sent unsatisfactory reports about the 49th to the Indian government, stating clearly that the experiment of Bengalis had failed and there was no need to keep them in Mesopotamia.

Earlier, on 5 September 1918, Lt Col Barrett sent to the headquarters in Simla a report that must have decided the future of the battalion. He reiterated the racial slur common in British documents about Bengalis. Lt Col Barrett wrote that the 49th were terrible in physique and lacked any ability to obey, execute and give orders. Many soldiers suffered from venereal diseases like syphilis and gonorrhoea – suggesting the propensity of a bhadralog Bengali to visit whorehouses. He reported that they looted shops in bazaars and stole rations for the sick. He recommended that flogging be allowed to discipline the Bengalis. In his opinion, 'the Bengali can never make a soldier'.[46] On 26 February 1920, a few weeks before the disbandment of the regiment, Commanding Officer in Mesopotamia Major General G. F. MacMunn wrote another unfavourable report about the 49th Bengali Battalion. Before the war, MacMunn, who was posted in India, had considered the martial race theory to be of supreme importance in his *Armies of India*.[47] Bengalis belonged to non-martial type and, like Kashmiris, were 'hopeless poltroons'.[48] His pre-war opinion was reconfirmed in Mesopotamia. He repeated most of the observations made by Lt Col Barrett, reiterating that Bengalis were incapable of any military duty, though there were individuals who were keen and enthusiastic. Many Bengali soldiers had petitioned to be released from duty. Since no one wanted to command the Bengalis in Mesopotamia, MacMunn had sent a unit to Kurdistan 'in the hope of giving them a chance to distinction'. Twenty five per cent of the regiment volunteered and carried themselves well. If they had gone as a regiment they would have failed, he wrote.[49]

Disbandment

British military establishment looked upon the 49th as a sort of liability but hesitated to announce its disbandment because incorporation of the regiment in the army was a political arrangement between moderates and the government of India. But by 1918, moderates, who championed the 49th, had become less popular in Indian politics. The revolutionaries, both within and outside the Indian National Congress and the Home Rule movement between 1916 and 1918 had brought new leaders to the fore. The moderates, who were increasingly aligning themselves with British liberals, were being looked down upon by the Indian public. Major moderate leaders and supporters of the 49th, like Surendranath Bannerjea, were being labelled as pro-British. The British government sought political support from Bannerjea and his sphere of influence, especially after the proposal to introduce dyarchy through the Government of India Act in December 1919. The political situation had worsened in India in that year. Severe repression of Indian opinion before the passing of the act had led to the infamous Jalianwala Bagh massacre in April. In the same year, when units in the 49th Regiment were still stationed in Iraq and Kurdistan, Bannerjea left the Indian National Congress and formed the Indian National Liberal Federation. He would be part of the reformed Bengal Legislative Council in 1921 and knighted the same year. Confidential letters reveal how highly placed British officials were reminding each other to be very diplomatic with the 49th. Unfavourable reports about the regiment should not be leaked to the public, even if Bengalis projected the regiment as successful.[50] Preparation for disbandment of the regiment was in full swing, though. War diaries reveal that most sepoys and officers were being sent to Karachi for demobilisation by early 1920. However, the military establishment wanted the disbandment to wait until the visit of Duke of Connaught in India. When the royal visit was postponed, the disbandment of the regiment was immediately announced in August 1920.

Matters did not rest with disbandment in Bengal. Prominent citizens, supporters of the Liberal Federation, sent letters to the government to express their disappointment. From these letters, it becomes evident that the public in Bengal knew that the disbandment was due to financial constraints.[51] The reports about unsatisfactory performance were never made public in Bengal. Yet, as confidential reports work in administrations, secrets hardly remain proper secrets. Parts of the report must have been leaked to *The Morning Post* on 8 April 1919, five days before the Jallianwala Bagh massacre. The paper lampooned Bengali babus who were clamouring for better political representation in India without proving themselves in the battlefield. At least one prominent Bengali in imperial administration, Lord Satyendra Prasanno Sinha, knew about these reports. Lord Sinha was a member of the Imperial War Cabinet and Conference and was close to the moderate faction in the Indian National Congress. In early August 1920, on enquiry from Lord Ampthill, Lord Sinha had replied that the 49th was not well reported 'whilst in duty in Mesopotamia'.[52]

Barring few who wrote memoirs, it is difficult to ascertain the whereabouts of nearly 4,000 men who had enlisted in the 49th Regiment. Most men must have been absorbed in the political life of Bengal after their return from Mesopotamia. A political report in March 1924 from Chittagong, a district in Bengal, observes that Jasoda Pal, an ex-soldier of the regiment, was involved in revolutionary activities.[53] The gradual disappearance of the 49th from Bengali public memory further points to the failure of a political arrangement between the moderates and the British Raj. The 49th, however, was a very distinct regiment since it engaged with the ideologies of the empire and tried to prove them wrong. The 49th was doomed to failure from the start. It was never taken seriously, and the non-martial tag meant that most British officers were not eager to command them.

It would be wrong to consider Bengali involvement in the Great War as merely a response to war propaganda. Their war effort was part of various political mobilisations within the province. This chapter has shown that colonial culture around formation and disbandment of both the ambulance corps and the Bengali Battalion serve as good examples of how racial theory shaped and frustrated the aspirations of the colonised. College Square's Bengali War Memorial still serves as a reminder to a political culture that sought greater self-representation within empire.

Notes

1 *The Statesman*, August 5, 1924, quoted in Manbahadur Sinha, *Sainik Bangali* (Kolkata: M. B. Sinha, 1939), 224.

2 Calcutta was renamed as Kolkata in 2001. In this chapter, Calcutta will be the preferred reference for the historical events before 2001. However, the city has always been referred to as Kolkata in Bengali language.

3 The British government passed the first Criminal Tribes Act in 1871 and subsequently revised it in 1911 and 1924. According to the act, certain tribes in India were considered habitual criminals. For more, see Brown Mark, “Ethnology and Colonial Administration in Nineteenth-Century British India: The Question of Native Crime and Criminality,” *The British Journal for the History of Science* 36, no. 2 (2003): 201–19.
4 Liebau, Heike, “Martial Races, Theory of (Version 1.1),” in *1914–1918-online. International Encyclopedia of the First World War*, ed. Ute Daniel, Peter Gatrell, Oliver Janz, Heather Jones, Jennifer Keene, Alan Kramer, and Bill Nasson (Berlin: Freie Universität Berlin, February 15, 2017).
5 Metcalf, Thomas, *Ideologies of the Raj* (New Delhi: Cambridge University Press, 1998), 126.
6 Kaushik Roy, *Indian Army and the First World War 1914–18* (New Delhi: Oxford University Press, 2018), 42–45.
7 Ibid., 52–55.
8 John Alexander Hammerton, *People of All Nations* (London: The Fleetway House, 1922); Valentine Chirol, “India I,” in *Peoples of All Nations*, ed. J. A. Hammerton, vol. 4 (London: The Fleetway House, 1922), 2840.
9 Hammerton, *People of All Nations*, 2840–54.
10 Sikata Banerjee, *Mascular Nationalism: Gender, Violence and Empire in India and Ireland, 1914–2004* (New York: New York University Press, 2012), 57.
11 Ibid., 59.
12 Upendranath Bhattacharya, *Banger Bir Santan [Great Sons of Bengal] 1929, 1940* (Kolkata: Brindaban Das and Sons Ltd., 16th ed., 1945).
13 *Kushdaha* (1916), 211.
14 Mrinalini Sinha, *Colonial Masculinity: The ‘Manly Englishman’ and the ‘Effeminate Bengali’ in the Late Nineteenth Century* (New Delhi: Kali for Women, 1997), 4–25.
15 Sinha, *Colonial Masculinity*, 80–81.
16 Valentine Chirol, *Indian Unrest* (London: Macmilan and Co., 1910).
17 Ibid., 96.
18 Sinha, *Sainik Bangali*.
19 Ibid., 226–30.
20 Thomas G. Fraser, “Germany and Indian Revolution, 1914–18,” *Journal of Contemporary History* 12, no. 2 (1977): 255–72; Matthew Plowman, “Irish Republicans and the Indo-German Conspiracy of World War I,” *New Hibernia Review* 7, no. 3 (2003): 81–105.
21 Partha Chatterjee, “Bombs and Nationalism in Bengal,” conference paper in *Subaltern Citizens and their Histories: South Asia and the U. S.* (Atlanta: Emory University, 2006), 1–33, http://sarr.emory.edu/subalterndocs/Chatterjee.pdf; Sumit Sarkar, *The Swadeshi Movement in Bengal, 1903–1908* (New Delhi: People’s Publishing House, 1973); Peter Heehs, *The Bomb in Bengal: The Rise of Revolutionary Terrorism in India* (New Delhi: Oxford University Press, 2004).
22 Durba Ghosh, *Gentelmanly Terrorists: Political Violence and the Colonial State in India, 1919–1947* (Cambridge: Cambridge University Press, 2017), 6–8.
23 National Archives of India (NAI), Home Political: NA1924NAF-74 Internal-A: Proceedings, February 1915, nos. 66–95.
24 Shrabani Basu, *For King and Another Country: Indian Soldiers on the Western Front 1914–18* (New Delhi: Bloomsbury, 2015), 12–13.
25 Lord Sydenham of Combe, *Indian and the War* (London: Hodder and Stoughton, 1915), 73.
26 Dr Sarvadhikari, “An Appeal to Bengali Patriotism,” June 28, 1915.
27 Shishir Prasad Sarvadhikari, *Abhi Le Baghdad* (Kolkata: privately printed, 1958).
28 Manbahadur Sen, *Sainik Bangali* (Kolkata: M. B. Sinha, 1939), 24–30.
29 Roy, *Indian Army and the First World War 1914–18*, 212–60.

30 "Bengal Ambulance Corps," *The Bengalee*, July 28, 1916, 3.
31 Abhishek Sarkar, "The Great War, Communal Identity and Personal Emotions in the Fiction of Kazi Nazrul Islam," *South Asian History and Culture* (2019): 4–5.
32 Sinha, *Sainik Bangali*, 57–60.
33 T. B. Macaulay, *Essay on Warren Hastings* (Boston: Houghton Mifflin Company, 1910), 111.
34 "Bengali Troops: Press Comments," 1916, 5.
35 "The Bengali Regiment," *The Bengalee*, August 17, 1916, 2.
36 Anindita Mukhopadhyay, *Behind the Mask: The Cultural Definition of the Legal Subject in Colonial Bengal (1775–1911)* (New Delhi: Oxford University Press, 2006), 4–5.
37 Sinha, *Sainik Bangali*, 92.
38 Ibid., 113–15.
39 Sarkar, "The Great War, Communal Identity," 1–14.
40 British Library (BL): IORLMIL717030.
41 Amiya Halder, *Paltan Chauni* (Kolkata: Dasgupta and Co., 1960).
42 The National Archives (TNA): WO-95–5020–5: 24.
43 Sinha, *Sainik Bangali*, 114–15.
44 BL: IORLMIL717768.
45 Ashok Nath, "The 49th: A Bengali Infantry Regiment in the Great War," in *The British Indian Army: Virtue and Necessity*, ed. Rob Johnson (Newcastle: Cambridge Scholars Publishing, 2014), 73.
46 BL: IORLMIL717768.
47 Major General G. F. MacMunn, *Armies of India* (London: Adam and Charles Black, 1911).
48 Ibid., 130.
49 BL: IORLMIL717768.
50 BL: IORLMIL717030.
51 Ibid.
52 Ibid.
53 NAI: NA1924NAF-74 Home Political.

5 Society and identity in the former Ottoman world

Encounters between Cypriots and Armenians of the *Légion d'Orient* in Cyprus in 1917–18

Andrekos Varnava

Introduction

On 25 April 1918, 2 French non-commissioned officers and 15 Armenians camped outside Lefkonico, a Cypriot village in the Famagusta district, a considerable distance from the base of the *Légion d'Orient* at Monarga village. In the evening, four Armenians on leave visited the house of an old Muslim woman asking for her daughter-in-law, reputed to be of 'immoral character'. She was away, and when the Armenians refused to leave, three Muslims came to the old woman's aid, but the Armenians attacked them with their bayonets. Then an Orthodox Cypriot trooper arrived, but the Armenians persisted, and while he went for reinforcements, much of the primarily Orthodox Christian village[1] descended on the house and roughed up the Armenians, who left before the police arrived. The villagers threatened to attack the Armenians at their camp, but the police subdued them. Then the police had to pacify the Armenians, who were fixing their bayonets to attack the villagers. Later, the police were notified about the serious stab wounds on the stomach of the 70-year-old Mulla, Osman Suleiman, who had initially aided the old woman and now required life-saving surgery.[2] How was this possible, given that elsewhere in the Ottoman Empire Christians and Muslim society had disintegrated?

This chapter unpacks this story and situates it within broader, as well as local, contexts to better understand it. This necessitates understanding the history of the island, especially as regards identity formation and rural life under British rule since 1878 and the understanding of the Christian–Muslim 'divide' in the island, particularly in the rural lower classes, which is little explored alongside the nationalism of the educated urban upper and middle classes. Also, this requires an understanding of the broader imperial and regional picture, namely, of the Balkan Wars, the Great War in the region and the role of Cyprus within British and French military strategy and post-war imperial agendas, as well as of the Armenian Genocide and French (and British support for) co-option of the Armenians into the coalition against the Central Powers.

The chapter draws upon various archives from London, Paris and Nicosia, and the relevant historiographies, to answer the three questions posed in the abstract.

To explain the violence and criminality of some members of the *Legion d'Orient*, it is important to understand the nature of these acts and their context, namely, the Armenian Genocide and how survivors and those Armenians in the diaspora reacted to the Ottoman policy of extermination. Additionally, one must also appreciate the nature of such volunteer forces and the various factors that can often lead to such behaviour, for which there is an existing historiography.[3] Answering the second question, on the role of the British and French imperial powers, necessitates an understanding of their relationship to and views on the people of the former Ottoman Empire and their actions in prosecuting the war effort and achieving their post-war imperial ambitions.[4] Thirdly, and perhaps most importantly, is unpacking the Lefkonico incident to show that the banding together of Cypriot Christians and Muslims goes beyond merely a response to this one example of violence and criminality. This can only be concluded by understanding the historical syncretism between Christians and Muslims in Ottoman Cyprus and how this continued under British rule, despite British modernization, especially in rural Cyprus, while it began to collapse in other parts of the Ottoman Empire and former Ottoman Empire from the Balkan Wars, as shown by Nicholas Doumanis.[5] Cypriot society, especially rural society, had not split along the religious or ethnic divide, and the differences between classes remained greater than differences between the two main ethno-religious communities.

Published sources on the *Legion d'Orient* fall under two distinct historiographies, connected here for the first time because the *Légion* was stationed in Cyprus: the history of Cyprus, in which the *Légion* is mentioned by a select few, and the history of the *Légion* within the broader context of the Armenian Genocide. In the published Cypriot primary sources, the *Légion* was first mentioned in 1930 in *A Chronology of Cyprus* by the governor from 1926 to 1932, Sir Ronald Storrs. He stated that in 1916 a camp was established at Monarga in the Famagusta District for training the *Légion d'Orient*, mostly composed of Armenians.[6] This factual information can be juxtaposed with the memoirs of Sir Harry Luke (Lukach at the time), who in 1918 was the District Commissioner of Famagusta.[7] Published decades later, he mentioned that he often lunched with Commandant Louis Romieu at the camp and that the chaplain of the *Légion*, an elderly Armenian archbishop, was a refugee from Asia Minor.

> Hook-nosed and emaciated, bowed and long-bearded, the poor old man looked, I thought, utterly incongruous in a French *soutane* with the two thin gold stripes of a Lieutenant on a most inappropriate forage-cap. He was styled, in equally incongruous conjunction, 'Sa Béatitude Monseigneur l'Archevêque-Lieutenant-Aumonier' Hagopian'.[8]

Luke's racist overtones were clear, yet the behaviour of the Armenian Légionnaires was omitted.

Interestingly, there are not many primary sources from the Armenian perspective that refer to the *Légion*; in fact, there are only three autobiographies. The first, by Sarkis Torossian, a fascinating and controversial figure, was published in English in the United States in 1947, in which Torossian claimed that he had served in the Ottoman armed forces for much of the Great War and was decorated for his bravery while in charge of the first fort at the Dardanelles entrance and later served in the *Légion d'Orient* after discovering that his family had died during the Genocide. His memoirs, however, say little about his time in the *Légion.*[9] On the other hand, the autobiography (in Armenian) of Dikran Boyadjian gives much detail on life in Cyprus for the Légionnaires and their relations with their French officers and the Cypriots. He also details their impatience to fight yet gives little military information.[10] The third autobiography, by Mikael Garougian, also a Légionnaire, who died in 1958, was not published until 2005 after his daughter translated his memoirs. They complement Boyadjian's, since Garougian's account provides invaluable insights into the motivations of the Légionnaires and their time as part of the French Army of Occupation in Cilicia, with the Armenian Genocide looming large in the mind of Garougian and others as the overarching motivation to enlist to find family and friends who survived and to help France in creating a safe homeland for the survivors.[11]

The secondary literature has only in recent years developed, while there have also been divisions within the historiography of the Armenian Genocide about the *Légion.* In the Cypriot historiography, Georghallides incorrectly gave the village in which the camp was based as Monagri, which is in the Limassol district.[12] A book on Agios Elias, a village near Monarga, provides some raw information, some of which is incorrect because of the limited archival research from local researchers.[13] The historiography of the *Légion* in the broader historiography of the Armenian Genocide is more complex. In the historiography that does not accept the term 'Armenian Genocide', the *Légion* is portrayed as an example of 'the provocation thesis' first put forward by Stanford Shaw,[14] which claims that the Armenians provoked the Ottoman government into suppressing them, or the 'Civil War thesis' put forward by Justin McCarthy.[15] These theories fall into the denialist camp in the Armenian Genocide debate and two denialists, Ulvi Keser and Halil Aytekin, discuss the *Légion* at length, yet both were flawed because they used the existence of the *Légion*, not formed until October 1916, to justify the Ottoman 'deportation' policy of 1915, confusing the chronology of events and the context of French and British decisions.[16] Keser's book is more interesting for including aerial photographs of the camp taken by the Ottomans, confirming the post-war discovery that Muslim Cypriots had betrayed military secrets to the Ottomans.[17] Additionally, in 2010, the Utah Series in Turkish and Islamic Studies, which specializes in publishing denialists, published a book by a Turkish diplomat that attempted to explore the relationship between the Armenians and the Allies as regards Cilicia between 1914 and 1923, which claimed that the formation of the *Légion* belonged to a long-term British and French plan to destroy the Ottoman Empire.[18]

Only in recent years has a historiography on the *Légion* emerged independent of both the Cypriot and Armenian Genocide historiographies and which situates the *Légion* in the broader contexts of British and French imperialism and the Great War. The focus here has been on exploring the proposals to form the *Légion*, the British and French positions and their various rejections, until it was finally formed in the aftermath of the Sykes–Picot Agreement.[19] Additionally, there has been comparative analysis between the British rejection of a Cypriot legion and acceptance of the Jewish Legion and between those two cases and British support for the French forming the *Légion*.[20] In 2018, anthropologist Susan Paul Pattie published the first book on the *Légion* to attempt to comprehensively cover the subject; however, it was largely based on the memoirs of Boyadjian, it lacked the comprehensive archival base (limited archives from the UK, France or Cyprus were consulted, with a mere 152 footnotes in the entire book) and reads like an hagiography of those who sacrificed their lives to volunteer only to be betrayed by the allies.[21] Her coverage of the incidents in Cyprus was taken from my earlier publications, sighted in this article, which merely touch upon the subject.[22] This chapter thus breaks new ground by fully exploring the incidents from a social, imperial and military perspective.

Background: the formation of and reactions to the *Légion* in Cyprus

By the time of the Lefkonico incident, the *Légion d'Orient* had been in Cyprus for 18 months. Established at the end of 1916, it was the first time since the British occupied the island in 1878 that so many troops were stationed and trained in the island for a military expedition.[23] Ironically, it was the French and not the British who organized this force, and indeed there were more Armenian Légionnaires in the island than British.[24] Armenian political elites in the diaspora had pushed for an Armenian legion under British auspices since November 1914. The British rejected it when they were considering a landing at Alexandretta (January to March 1915), when in April 1915 they landed troops at Gallipoli and the Armenian Genocide became internationally known. The French also rejected the scheme in late 1915, while the Armenians did so when the British and French came around in early 1916. The British and French (and by 1916 prominent Armenians elites) worried that the proposal would result in the killing of non-combatant Armenians before and during the Genocide.[25] Also, the British were cool about the formation of such legions as the Armenians proposed, having previously rejected Cypriot and Jewish legion proposals.[26] The situation changed when the French military authorities decided, in the aftermath of the Sykes–Picot Agreement of May 1916, to form an Armenian Légion under French auspices. For the French, such a force would be useful because they could not inject French troops into the Middle East after having committed to establishing an empire in Syria, Cilicia and the surrounding areas, where Armenians lived (with Kurds, Turks and Greeks). The French promised Armenian elites autonomy under French control but were told that they had to fight for it. The British accepted the French line, allowed the training to be undertaken in Cyprus under the command of Louis Romieu and helped transport Armenians from Egypt, Mesopotamia and India to the camp.[27]

The camp was on the land side of the main Famagusta-Karpass road in the Cypriot Muslim hamlet of Monarga until its closure in February 1919. Over 4,000

Armenians were trained in this camp, and about a third came from the United States, with many reaching Marseilles deemed medically unfit and rejected.[28] The French and British used the small anchorage at Boghaz to embark and disembark the Armenian volunteers and various provisions. The *Légion d'Orient* first served in the Palestine Campaign, specifically in the Battle of Arara, for which General Edmund Allenby commended their service.[29] Renamed 'Armenian Légion' in 1919, it controversially served in the French Army of Occupation of Cilicia and other former Ottoman provinces, ostensibly protecting the returned survivors of the Armenian Genocide.[30] There it met a hasty end when the French pulled out in 1921 after Kemalist nationalist forces defeated the combined French–Armenian forces, ending the centuries-old Armenian presence in Cilicia and neighbouring areas of the former Ottoman Empire.[31]

The British authorities in Cairo, London and Cyprus largely supported the formation of the *Légion* under French auspices, but not all supported locating the training camp in Cyprus. The British authorities in Cairo believed the Cypriot government would oppose the move.[32]

Yet, Sir John Clauson, the high commissioner of Cyprus, had agreed, or as one Foreign Office minute put it, implied a 'grudging acceptance'.[33] Indeed, he warned about the 'political difficulties attending the reception of Armenian refugees in Cyprus' but hoped that this would be 'minimised in the case of a military corps under strict discipline and without families'.[34] This concern was reflected in the letter by Paul Cambon, the French ambassador to London, to the French Foreign Minister and Prime Minister, Aristide Briand, that the British did not oppose the creation of the *Légion* but wanted it camped in northern or eastern Cyprus where there were fewer Muslims.[35] Selecting Monarga, with 35 Cypriot Muslims in 1911 (and no Christians), contradicted this. Yet, the presence of Muslims near the camp did not make the Armenians any more or less prone to misbehave since their outrages were not linked to ethnic or religious prejudice.

Meanwhile, the assumed ethnic concerns, along with the obvious military issues, necessitated the British authorities insisting that the presence of the *Légion* in Cyprus be kept secret. Public knowledge that the French army was using a British island to train Armenian volunteers to increase French imperial power in the eastern Mediterranean could have been seen as detrimental to British strategic interests, even though France was a wartime ally. Most importantly, there was the threat that information on allied military activities in Cyprus could be leaked to the enemy, as indeed happened.[36] Accordingly, London ordered Clauson to keep a 'strict watch' on the correspondence from Cyprus with a 'view to suppressing reference to the Armenian Corps at Monarga', which was to be 'styled a Detachment of the *Légion d'Orient*' in case mention of its Armenian element (there were some Arabs) caused an Ottoman reaction.[37]

A comprehensive survey of various Cypriot newspapers shows that the British authorities did well to prevent the local newspapers, which were censored, from mentioning the *Légion d'Orient*. The first reference was in *Ελευθερία* (Freedom), which mentioned a report in *The Spectator* of 23 September 1916 that volunteers from the refugees in Syria and Anatolia would be trained in Cyprus and that it was estimated to attract 50,000 men.[38] Since at the time the Armenian Légionnaires had not yet arrived in the island, this must have been leaked by the authorities or by Armenian sources. The second report was in February 1917, and it stated that 400 refugees were being housed at Bogaz and that the French were preparing accommodation for 5,000 men. The article also reported that the Commander of the *Légion* (Romieu) had visited the high commissioner.[39]

Since the *Légion* was a joint British and French concern (under French auspices, on British territory, as part of their agreed post-war imperial aims), it was no surprise that the British played a vital role in recruitment. Firstly, the British authorities in Egypt had pressed the French to take the Armenian refugees from Musa Dagh (or 'Moses Mountain', today in Hatay, Turkey) ever since they had been taken to Egypt by the French,[40] and so they were only too ready to facilitate the transfer of the men to Cyprus. This nucleus was amplified by the British transfer of Armenian POWs they held in Mesopotamia and India. British shipping also facilitated the transfer of Armenians from the United States, who formed a significant cohort in the *Légion* and were considered, at least by the French, as especially undisciplined.[41]

Romieu, an infantry officer, had particular ideas about discipline. As early as 28 October 1916 he told the War Ministry that the camp had to be well set up so the Armenians had no need to leave it, so as to avoid contact with locals, which Clauson had insisted on, because of fear of possible clashes, but also for secrecy.[42] Romieu agreed with Armenian leaders in Cairo to keep the *Légion* a secret, with no written propaganda, because the Armenians did not want to incite further Ottoman killings of Armenians.[43] Consequently, local French agents in the Americas were to use discretion in recruiting.[44] Although the discipline of the early recruits, mainly from Musa Dagh, was good, Romieu warned about the lack of discipline of the potential recruits from America. Volunteers needed identity papers and a character reference from the local French consul.[45] He also wanted to cut the ties between them and the Armenian committees recruiting them as soon as they arrived in Cyprus.[46] The French authorities worried about French officers who could not adapt to 'commanding Orientals', and those Romieu deemed unsuitable were returned to France.[47] By May 1917 Romieu reported that discipline and morale were good but wanted to form a discipline committee because the 'prison and the cells in the camp were not enough', and he wanted to refer some cases to court-martial. To this someone in the War Ministry pencilled, 'if we need troops to guard them, we would rather expel them'.[48] A month later, Romieu reported that he had released for general 'insufficiency' 35 volunteers and 10 from Musa Dagh, 3 others were in gaols in Egypt and Marseilles, and others would be court-martialled. He wanted officers and NCOs with the ability to adapt to commanding and training 'Orientals' without using too much discipline.[49] Romieu took strict measures against the French auxiliaries, and any resistance would result in them being returned to France.[50] Although the main incidents involved Armenians, the behaviour of French auxiliaries may have encouraged the misbehaviour of Armenians. Romieu tried to limit the disciplinary problem while wanting officers and NCOs who would use less discipline.

The Armenians were also generally enthused by the formation of the *Légion*. Boghos Nubar, the founder and first president of the Armenian General Benevolent Union (1906–28), and the head of the Armenian National Delegation in Paris from December 1912, first pushed for the formation of a Légion in 1914 but then thought otherwise after the Genocide, accepting the British and French position that it might lead to more Armenian deaths. He was only won around during the summer of 1916 by the promises of an Armenian homeland under French protection. The Musa Dagh refugees were also pleased since they had been promised by the French naval commander who had evacuated them that they could go back to fight the Ottoman enemy, and when this promise had not materialized, they had become restless in Egypt. Armenian POWs willingly enlisted since they would have been spared the harshness of POW life in Mesopotamia and India and would have welcomed the opportunity to fight against the government that had attempted to exterminate their people.[51] This last motivation was important for the Armenians in the diaspora, mainly the United States (like Garougian), who were anxious to find family and friends and help to create a safe homeland for the survivors after the war.

In Cyprus, the Légionnaires became frustrated. At the Monarga camp, they undertook intense military and physical training from 7 a.m. to 5 p.m. each day for anywhere between 8 and 16 months. Little evidence remains of what life was like for them in and outside the camp. According to Boyadjian, there was much frustration because the men were anxious to fight and because they had an uneasy relationship with their French commanders, who opposed having senior-rank Armenian officers, despite the eligibility of several. Also, Garougian's memoirs highlight that many men were anxious to find out whether their families and friends had survived the Genocide. In their free time, the Armenians tried to take their mind off their anxieties and frustrations, organizing various events and activities: there were amateur musical, song, poetry, theatrical and sporting events; national celebrations; and excursions to the various ancient sites and, of course, to the beach. But mostly the volunteers spent their time in the restaurant The Boghaz, a ten-minute walk from the camp, which had French and Armenian newspapers. They kept their morale up by corresponding with their womenfolk (wives, fiancées, mothers, sisters, etc.) in Egypt, who would provide words of encouragement and occasionally send clothing they had made. Boyadjian reported one incident with the local population when the Légionnaires got into a drunken brawl with Greek Cypriots over the carriage they wanted to take back to the camp from Famagusta. Several of the locals were injured, and the Légionnaires returned to the camp the next morning surprised that their French superiors had not punished them.[52]

Initially, however, the locals were positive about the establishment of the *Légion* because it would serve as part of the broader coalition against the Central Powers and for the economic benefits of having such a large force. When the Cypriot government announced the establishment of the camp in late 1916 at Monarga, the local rural lower classes, consisting of the peasants and labouring classes, both Christians and Muslims, welcomed the initiative for economic purposes and because the Armenians would be trained for the civilizing purposes espoused by the war (i.e. in opposition to 'German militarism').[53] The Cypriot peasant and labouring classes thus accepted the opportunities presented by British rule and the Great War and broadly agreed with the principles underpinning the allied war effort.[54] But immediately the Armenian Légionnaires posed problems for the Cypriots, as numerous clashes, disturbances, thefts and assaults were reported to police. Cypriot 'Greek' Christians and 'Turkish' Muslims jointly appealed to the Cypriot government to deal with the Armenian outrages and took matters into their own hands by roughing up troublesome Armenians. These incidents and others were the last straw for local leaders. On 30 March 1918, the Azas and Muktars of seven villages near the Monarga camp (Trikomo, Agios Elias, Patriki, Agios Theodoros, Gastria, Avgolida and Ovgoros) appealed to Clauson to move the camp, claiming that the 'orgies of the Armenian soldiers . . . and the terror they have inspired into all the people of the neighbouring villages, and . . . [to] those who travel the Karpas Road', could only be stopped by their removal. They did not care anymore about the economic advantages but for the safety of villagers and travellers. They accused Armenian soldiers of entering villages and people's homes at night; stealing sheep and produce from their fields, which they were forced to abandon; damaging property and beating and robbing travellers on the Karpass Road. As British subjects, the village representatives appealed to Clauson for protection for the inhabitants of the area and for those travelling through the region.[55]

These actions show a limited colonial agency in the face of an alien group introduced, albeit it temporarily, by the British colonial power; and, more importantly for the purposes of this chapter, that village-community and class identity, which crossed religious differences, still trumped ethno-religious identity in a colonial Cyprus still transitioning from a pre-modern Ottoman system to a mildly modernist British system. Any affinities or sympathies Cypriot Christians may have had for Armenians went out the door when it came to choosing whether to support their Turkish Cypriot neighbours.

The incidents and reactions

A file in the State Archives in Nicosia on the *Légion* reveals a story of continued clashing between the Armenians and the Cypriot inhabitants of the nearby villages starting from February 1917. This caused serious tensions between the Légionnaires and Cypriots and anxiety for the British and French authorities trying to keep the *Légion* a secret. Most of the incidents occurred in villages near the camp, yet there were incidents as far as Varosha, when Armenians went on leave, or in villages in other parts of Famagusta District where the Armenians went for training purposes. The incidents involved thefts, assaults (including sexual assault) and damage to property. The French commanders defended their Armenian prodigies or blamed the incidents on drunkenness, the antipathy of the locals to Armenians and even on the 'orientalism' of the Armenians, especially those from the United States. The British did not want to take any responsibility, were annoyed about stretching police resources, wanted these incidents hushed and were indifferent to local concerns.

Numerous incidents occurred between the Armenians and the villagers of Agios Elias, the closest Orthodox village to the camp, almost as soon as the Armenians arrived. On 9 February 1917, Francis Baxendale, the district commissioner of Famagusta, informed acting Chief Secretary John Fenn of a 'fracas, not of a serious nature' on 3 February between the villagers of Agios Elias and numerous Armenians, caused by drunken Armenians using obscene language and making indecent proposals to married women. Police inquiries found that the Armenians broke the peace, while the French Commandant blamed both sides but advised the closure of licensed places and a ban on liquor trading to Armenian soldiers.[56] The local Commandant of Police at Famagusta, Major H. J. Thorne, reported to Nicosia and enclosed the reports by T. Wilson, Inspector of Police, and the acting French Commandant, Captain P. Nanse. Wilson concluded that the Armenians were lying because one who was allegedly stabbed in the face had only a surface wound, while another who claimed he was bitten later denied it. Nanse was adamant that the villagers were equally to blame, especially the shopkeeper, Zenos Orphanides, for insulting the French colours by saying 'this is shit' ('*αυτό σκατά είναι*'). When Wilson investigated, however, the Armenian claiming that this was said did not speak Greek, and the other who relayed this denied that he had. Initially Nanse blamed the Cypriots, listing another seven villagers from Agios Elias, particularly the priest, Papa (Father) Pavlos (although Wilson believed that he had had a calming influence), for aggravating the situation by gesticulating with a stick. Later Nanse agreed with Thorne that the Armenians were solely to blame, and he sent eight to Port Said for court-martial and placed Agios Elias out of bounds.[57]

The mischief of the Armenian soldiers, aided by their increasing numbers and idleness, spread to other villages and towns in the region. On 16 April, the Muktar of Trikomo, Demetrios M. Zavou, and his three Azas, Panayis Hajji-Demetris, Demetrios Hajji-Zannetos, and Spyros Hajji-Antoni, implored Clauson to end the scandalous behaviour of the Légionnaires. They accused them of visiting their town, with or without the permission of their French officers, for the sole purpose of plundering and assaulting the inhabitants.[58]

Then in July a more serious clash occurred at Agios Elias. Thorne reported to the Chief Commandant of Police in Nicosia that on 21 July the Muktar of Agios Elias, together with a deputation, protested about the conduct of the Armenians. Romieu counter-claimed that one of his soldiers, Garabet Bektashian, was beaten, stoned and robbed of over 100 francs at Agios Elias on 15 July. When another incident occurred between Armenian soldiers and villagers from Trikomo, Thorne opined that a 'very difficult situation is developing between the Armenian soldiers and the surrounding villagers'. He strengthened the patrols near the Armenian camp and placed Sergeant-Major Stylli from Yialousa at Trikomo.[59] Six weeks later, Wilson, who was in charge of the Bektashian case, reported to Nicosia that eight men from Agios Elias were taken before the Magisterial Court of Famagusta for the assault, but the charges against one were dropped, owing to insufficient evidence. The rest were committed to trial on 10 October 1917.[60] The newspapers did not report on the case, but on 3 October there were allusions to it in *Kypriakos Phylax*. It detailed the night-time destruction of parks and gardens at Trikomo during September by people with 'wild and animal instincts' ('*άγρια και κτηνώδη ένστικτα*').[61] Given the ensuing narrative, it is almost certain that the article was referring to Légionnaires.

Then over two weeks in December 1917 and January 1918, the Armenians went on a rampage.[62] In all, Armenian soldiers committed 13 offences: (1) on 22 December three Armenians stole an ewe from Papa Pavlo Christofi of Agios Elias, and (2) Armenians fired three revolver shots at the *Zaptieh* trying to effect arrest; (3) on 23 December there was an attempted theft of an ewe from the house of Achillea Nicola at Agios Elias, (4) the theft of four rafters from the Government Timber Store at Boghaz (and another two, two days later) and (5) stones were stolen from the property of Antoni Elengous near Trikomo; (6) on 24 December the house and store of W. H. Colson was forcibly occupied at Perivolia tou Trikomo, causing damage to his tobacco, and (7) Yanco Antoni was stabbed at a Varosha café; (8) 20 cartloads of stones were stolen from Varnavas Yiorghi of Agios Elias on 28 December; (9) the police were obstructed from executing their duty at Boghaz on 31 December; (10) on New Year's Eve, a 12-year-old boy, Chrisanthos Evangeli of Agios Elias, was indecently assaulted near Monarga (probably the 'scandal' Romieu refers to in his letter of the 1st of January);[63] (11) Private Nisiforos, a *Zaptieh*, was insulted whilst on duty on New Year's Day; (12) 50 oranges and an oke of bread were stolen from Sabri Ali of Galatia on 2 January and 13) on 6 January, an Armenian attempted to assault Mrs Alexandrides (wife of an advocate) at Varosha.[64] Petty theft at Famagusta was prevalent while intoxicated Armenians were causing havoc at these places and at the villages of Patriki, Gastria, Komi Kebir, Ardana, Syngrasi and Agios Theodoros after the weekend closure of the licensed places at Trikomo, Agios Elias and Boghaz. More authority was required to avert a major clash, as the Armenians had 'made themselves most unpopular by their unseemly conduct'.[65]

Romieu replied to the Chief Secretary, Malcolm Stevenson, that there was 'for all civil populations certain inconveniences in the vicinity of a military camp [but] these . . . are partly compensated by pecuniary advantages which the inhabitants derive from such military clientelage'. He claimed that he could not 'guarantee the morality' of 3,000 'Oriental volunteers', particularly 'those coming from America have, as all other inhabitants of new worlds, a rather lively temper'. He had established pickets at Famagusta and, at Agios Elias and Trikomo, a provostship to facilitate the orderly visiting of troops to distant villages and a commission to inquire into property damage. Romieu, however, also defended his men. He blamed the 'ill-will' of a 'population racially and instinctively antipathetic to them' – the Greeks.[66] Although Greeks and Armenians lived side by side across Asia Minor,[67] Romieu accused the Greeks of being spiteful and habitual complainers. The only serious incident, he believed, was the attempted murder of one of his men near Agios Elias (Bekstashian case).[68]

Harry Lukach, the new district commissioner of Famagusta from January 1918, was indifferent to what he called 'exaggerated' complaints and 'fabrications'.[69] This was no surprise since he frequently lunched with Romieu.[70] Lukach had a reputation on the island for being pro-Turkish, as reported in 1913 to the Colonial Secretary, Lewis Harcourt, by J. C. C. Davidson, later 1st Viscount Davidson and Conservative politician.[71]

> It is unfortunate . . . that Sir Hamilton (Sir Hamilton Goold-Adams, the high commissioner), owing to the undue influence exercised by his own private secretary – Mr Lukach – manifested on his arrival such strong anti-Greek sympathies, especially as he appears just before I arrived in the island to have made in this respect a complete *volte-face*. He is hated – there is no other word which I can really use – by the Greeks, and I think there is only one man in the island of whom this can be said in a greater degree and that is Mr Lukach.[72]

This explains that, in his reply to Stevenson, Lukach claimed that because the Légionnaires volunteered in order to avenge the Turks, they were not well disposed to the 'Turkish' Cypriot villages and therefore were to blame. He did not mention that the Muslim hamlet of Monarga had never complained or that of the seven villages that protested to Clauson, only two were Muslim – Avgolida and Ovgoros. This showed the solidarity of the Cypriots on this issue but also that most of the incidents, contrary to Lukach's statement, were perpetrated against Orthodox Christians. This was primarily because the two largest villages in the proximity of the camp were Christian: Agios Elias and Trikomo. Nevertheless, Lukach agreed with Romieu that the offences were trivial compared to the actions of other such corps Lukach had seen. Lukach showed little interest in the welfare of the local inhabitants and more for the harassment of the police and the convoy of wood fuel for the Forest Department coming from Kantara and the Karpass forests near Rizokarpasso.[73]

Within ten days of Lukach's reply to Stevenson, the situation worsened. On 21 April three Armenians violently beat Yorghios Zanis, a mounted coastguard who patrolled the coast from Cape Greco to Boghaz, while taking his dinner in the custom guardroom at Boghaz.[74] This could have had severe repercussions for military intelligence, given the victim's job.

The Lefkonico incident

By the time of the next incident at Lefkonico, the inhabitants of the region were at the boiling point. As previously discussed, at Lefkonico the peace was threatened and the Mulla, Osman Suleiman, was critically wounded. The report of Inspector Tilliro, of the Famagusta Police, and Judge Mustafa Effendi, to the Local Commandant of Police, A. M. Fleury, was damning. Four out of the eight Armenians given leave by their French superiors on 25 April wanted to have 'their way' with the 'immoral' daughter-in-law of an old Muslim woman living at Lefkonico and refused to leave when told that she was away, proceeding to assault the three Muslim men, including the Mulla, who came to the old woman's aid. Still refusing to leave when an Orthodox Cypriot policeman arrived, they did so only after much of the predominantly Orthodox Christian village then descended on the old woman's house and attacked the Armenians. Then the villagers threatened to attack the Armenians at their camp, while the Armenians were found fixing their bayonets to come after the villagers, but the police stopped any further violence. Later, the police were notified that Suleiman required life-saving surgery.[75]

Lukach took little interest in the case, rejecting Osman's claim that the government or the French pay his doctor's fees.[76] Six weeks after Osman's claim, Lukach advocated to the government that it pay Osman's doctor's bills (the surgeon charged 54 pounds, and the Royal Medical Officer and local doctor charged 6 pounds and 5 pounds respectively) out of the funds allocated for war expenditure.[77] If this were not possible, Osman should allow the two private practitioners to sue him and allow the courts to decide a fair sum.[78] Not only did Lukach not recommend that the *Légion* pay, as was the case with property damage, but he claimed that owing to the soldiers being on active service, no court action could be taken.

This meant that the resources of the local police were even more stretched since in peacetime such behaviour would have been punished and hopefully deterred by court action. The police chief

> was compelled to have the temporary stations established at Pervolia tou Trikomou and Agios Elias opened up to the end of February 1919 owing to the existing troubles given by the Armenian soldiers encamped at Monarga to the neighbouring villages for the purpose of affording protection to the villages and travellers by. Serious assaults and insults and thefts have been the most prevalent connected with the Armenians stationed at Monarga.[79]

The Lefkonico incident was not the first or the last involving the Armenian Légionnaires, as the British and French responses were inadequate to stop the conflicts and misbehaviour. The British and French reactions and responses have been explained, but how can the actions and reactions of the Armenians and Cypriots be understood?

Explaining the Lefkonico incident

The behaviour of the Armenian Légionnaires was not unusual, nor is it difficult to understand, given their psychological state. It was not the result of racial characteristics or racist attitudes against Cypriots, Christians or Muslims. First, all forces, volunteer or not, put into a military situation of isolation will inevitably become bored and restless and become mischievous in looking for ways to pass their time; in this case the extensive training with the delays in seeing combat made matters more mundane and acute. There are numerous examples from the Great War to show this, even from the Cypriot Mule Corps.[80]

Distinguishing the *Légion*, however, is the complex psychological state of the men caused by the Genocide. This is evident in the memoirs of Garougian, who spends most of his time while in the *Legion* thinking about whether any members of his family and his friends had survived. There was no real difference between Armenian Legionnaires from Musa Dagh or those from the diaspora in the United States when it came to this feeling of potential loss (i.e. this is not merely felt by those who physically survived from the Musa Dagh defence or otherwise but applies to those who were in America, too). When mixed with feelings of revenge against those responsible, it created a complex psychological state, especially given the monotony in Cyprus and the delays in their seeing combat. All this combined caused some of the men to misbehave; indeed, the Lefkonico incident occurred three years and a day after the Armenian Genocide had been unleashed in 1915. This also could explain, too, why their victims were indistinguishable by ethnicity or religion. Although revenge has been discussed before, this has been either from a perspective of denying the Genocide or from an Armenian nationalist perspective of fighting against the Turks to create a homeland.[81] The unusual psychological state, that is, revenge, restlessness and longing to know what happened to friends and family, has never been fully discussed, let alone have the consequences of this state on the behaviour of the men.

Equally complex is explaining the reaction of the locals. The presence of the Armenians in the *Légion d'Orient*, aside from making life difficult for the local Cypriot population in the Famagusta district, especially nearby villagers, reveals an identity based on religious affiliation and the village and opposition to 'outsiders'. The case study indicates differences between the expected results of introducing Armenians into a Christian and Muslim community living together for centuries and the actual results, with the British expecting trouble between the Armenians and the Cypriot Muslims, while the French (and Lukach) blamed the 'Greek' Cypriots for the troubles. Thus the British concerns produced one type of racial profiling, while the French explanations produced another. These reflected Western attitudes of the perceived Christian and Muslim religious divide on the one hand and, on the other, the perceived 'Greekness' of the Cypriots and the broader racial profiling of Greeks as troublemakers.[82] This ignored the 'Eastern' realities in an Ottoman Cyprus that still lingered during the British period and which meant that the island was largely untouched by the fall-out of the Balkan Wars and the Armenian Genocide. Understanding these realities will help to comprehend why a Christian and Muslim community united against a Christian foreigner.

The answer lies within how the Ottoman Empire administered its subjects, the synergies this produced in the Ottoman Empire where mixed Christian–Muslim populations existed and how this continued in Cyprus during the Great War, while it had fallen apart in other parts of the Ottoman and former Ottoman worlds. The way the Ottoman Empire had traditionally administered its non-Muslim subjects was driven by Ottoman religious law. To understand this, one must understand the Ottoman *dhimmi* and later *millet* systems. The Koran distinguishes between Muslims, followers of other Abrahamic religions and people belonging to other polytheistic religions (sometimes referred to as pagans). The nature of true Islamic thought and practise in relation to other 'people of the book' that they ruled. Christians and Jews were considered 'People of the Book' and afforded a protected status known as *dhimmi*, derived from a theoretical contract, *dhimma*, or 'residence in return for taxes' and loyalty. In essence, Christians and Jews were allowed religious freedom (including religious laws) and a measure of communal autonomy (including personal laws) under their religious leaders in exchange for paying their tax and ensuring their loyalty to the Sultan and his government.[83] Thus, as one Ottomanist has put it: 'The millet system in the Muslim world provided the pre-modern paradigm of a religiously pluralistic society by granting each religious community an official status and a substantial measure of self-government'.[84] For Orthodox Christians, until the 19th century, such religious leaders – usually archbishops or bishops and referred to as *ethnarchs* – wielded considerable power.

This did not mean that the lower classes in each *millet* identified with their more privileged *millet* leaders. In fact, the lower class identified with those in their identical socio-economic situation, whether they were Christian or Muslim, which led to socio-cultural integration between them. This occurred in both urban and rural areas, but in the latter it was deeper and longer lasting. This did not, however, lead to a common 'national' identity, and with the formation of nation states, such as Greece, this socio-cultural integration, in time, was threatened and eventually fragmented, first in urban areas and then in rural. In the 1830s, when it was still together, the Ottoman authorities decided to create an Ottoman identity, when on 3 November 1839 the Edict of Gülhane (*Hatt-i Sharif of Gülhane*) proclaimed the principle of equality among all subjects regardless of religion. Yet this changed little on the ground, merely giving legitimacy to the political and social structures which had given rise to the haves and have nots in the Ottoman Empire. Until the Great War, the ideologies emanating from the various newly formed Balkan nation-states and other parts of Europe had not penetrated to the peasant and labouring classes in the Ottoman Empire: this would happen only after the Great War, with the rise of Communism and Fascism. Yet, as Doumanis has aptly shown, the synergy between Christian and Muslim lower classes (and indeed across other classes) began to change immediately before the Great War, when the Ottoman Empire and its former subjects and now members of independent Christian nation-states, in some cases for many generations (i.e. Greece and Serbia), fought the Balkan Wars. The first Balkan War led to many Balkan Muslims finding refuge in Ottoman cities (such as Constantinople/Istanbul and Smyrna/Izmir), only to tell their harrowing stories of expulsion at the hands of their Christian neighbours and incoming Christian armies.[85]

The experience of Cyprus was similar to other parts of the Ottoman Empire, with the exception of other variables resulting in differences. The difference was that there were very few Muslims and Christians who settled in the island as a result of various wars between Greece and Turkey, such as the Balkan Wars (at least until a good number of Orthodox Christians settled in the island after the Greco–Turkish War of 1921). In Cyprus the Ottoman socio-political structures gave rise to an even more insular society, partly because of the independence of the Cypriot Orthodox Church and partly because of the protection from outside forces afforded by the fact that it is an island. The Ottoman *millet* system allowed the Cypriot archbishop and the higher clergy to become secular as well as spiritual leaders, with the archbishop becoming the *ethnarch* (and not subordinate to the Ecumenical Patriarch). So the Eastern Orthodox Church elite were willingly co-opted into the ruling class and their power derived from the Ottoman imperial system. Within the context of this 'contract', they received power in exchange for guaranteeing the loyalty of their people, the lower-class Christians (i.e. peasants and rural agricultural labourers). They guaranteed this loyalty by either suppressing revolts led by the lower class or representing them to the imperial government during droughts, locust plagues and famine. Thus Christian and Muslim elites relied on each other for power and control over the Cypriot masses.[86]

The Christian and Muslim lower classes also relied on each other and were also integrated into what can only be described as a religiously syncretized society. The increase in mixed villages exemplifies integration: the 1832 Ottoman census recorded 172 mixed villages;[87] in 1858 the British consul estimated 239;[88] in 1891, in the second British census, there were 346 out of 702 villages.[89] They shared economic and social hardships brought on by droughts, bad harvests, locust plagues and a lack of technological advancement and government and private investment in industries and infrastructure. Together they opposed high taxes in memorials and revolts. They also shared a folklore, a commonly spoken language (i.e. Cypriot Greek), cultural events (even religious), and even intermarried[90] and went off to serve together in the Great War as part of the Cypriot Mule Corps.[91] Lukach (now Luke), in another book on Cyprus, related the story of an Orthodox Christian woman living near Adana and Konya who lost her son, 13 years old. Seventeen years later St Andreas (Andrew) appeared to her and told her to make a pilgrimage to the St Apostolos Andreas Monastery on the tip of the Karpass Peninsula in Cyprus. On the vessel she chatted with a dervish, her son. They made the pilgrimage together and the story spread far and wide, and the monastery became a source of worship and veneration for Cypriot Christians and Muslims[92] ever since, and they celebrated (and more recently since the checkpoints have opened) his feast day together.

British Cypriot society continued to resemble Ottoman Cypriot society. This explains why the Lefkonico incident happened. Ottoman Cypriot society was divided along class/social lines: (1) the Ottoman Muslim elites; (2) the Eastern Orthodox Christian elites, mostly the higher clergy and government employees; (3) the Muslim peasant and labouring classes and (4) the Christian labouring and peasant classes. To be sure the Christian elites sometimes exercised more power than the Muslim elites, who were not a consistent staple and often relied on the local knowledge of the Christians. But when the Christian elites were considered to have broken 'the contract' and fermented revolt, as they were falsely accused of doing in 1821 in support of the 'Greek' revolt, the imperial government agreed to the execution of leading Cypriot Orthodox Christian elites.[93] This isolated event did not harm the synchretism between Christians and Muslims in the rural parts of the island. And neither did the change in administration in 1878, with the partial modernization implemented by the British. The differences between classes continued to be far greater than any differences across the two main religions.

Conclusion

The Lefkonico incident in Cyprus in April 1918 is an example of how a small incident can shed light on broader world themes, in this case on imperialism and colonialism and on Christian–Muslim relations and encounters in the Ottoman and former Ottoman world. Based on this incident, made possible by the Great War, there are three broader lessons. Firstly, the case shows how Armenian survivors of the Genocide dealt with being survivors, how they coped and did not cope, how revenge stirred them to volunteer for the *Légion d'Orient* to fight the Ottomans and how they were desperate to find their family and friends. This created a psychological condition, coupled with boredom in their training camp and delays in their combat, creating a toxic mix for some that led to criminal, including violent, behaviour in the island. Secondly, the case highlights how the colonial mentalities of the British and French racialized the Armenians, Cypriot Orthodox 'Greeks' and Cypriot Muslim 'Turks', and placed their strategic interests before the colonial peoples and proxies they were meant to protect. And finally, the case shows how rural Cypriot Christians and Muslims united against the outrages of the Armenians because they had not experienced the fragmentation of the Christian–Muslim society in other parts of the Ottoman or former Ottoman Empire. Even as late as 1917, they acted as one community – not as one would expect Greeks and Turks to behave and as they did in the Balkans and Anatolia at the time – but as Cypriots to oppose both morally and physically a troublesome foreign element disturbing the peace. This was not a racist response since Armenians were largely welcomed only a few years later as refugees. But as the Lefkonico incident shows, when only one group, in this case Cypriot Muslims/Turks, were threatened, the entire community, including the Christians/Greeks, were moved to act.

Notes

1 The 1911 Census found 1,901 Orthodox Christians and 135 Muslims. *Cyprus: Report and General Abstracts* of *the Census of 1911 Taken on the 2nd April 1911* (London: Waterlow & Sons Limited, 1912).

2 TNA: SA 1/1068/1916 A. M. Fleury, "Local Commandant of Police, to Commandant," *Légion d'Orient*, April 30, 1918. For other reports see TNA: SA 1/1068/1916.

3 Peter Stanley, *Bad Characters: Sex, Crime, Mutiny, Murder and the Australian Imperial Force* (Sydney: Pier 9, 2010).

4 Andrekos Varnava, "French and British Post-War Imperial Agendas and Forging an Armenian Homeland after the Genocide: The Formation of the *Légion d'Orient* in October 1916," *The Historical Journal* 57, no. 4 (2014): 997–1025.

5 Nicholas Doumanis, *Before the Nation: Muslim-Christian Coexistence and its Destruction in Late-Ottoman Anatolia* (Oxford: Oxford University Press, 2012).

6 Sir Ronald Storrs, *A Chronology of Cyprus* (Nicosia: Government Printing Office, 1930), 35.

7 Lukach changed his name to Luke on 13 April 1919. TNA: CO 67/195/29254/1919.
8 Sir Harry Luke, *Cities and Men: An Autobiography,* vol. 2 (London, 1951), 44.
9 Sarkis Torossian, *From Dardanelles to Palestine: A True Story of Five Battle Fronts of Turkey and her Allies and a Harem Romance* (Boston: Meador Publisher Co., 1947). There is some controversy about Torossian, but this does not relate to his service in the Legion. Taner Akçam, "A Short History of the Torossian Debate," *Journal of Genocide Research* 17, no. 3 (2015): 345–62; Edhem Eldem, "A Shameful Debate? A Critical Reassessment of the Torossian Debate," *Journal of Genocide Research* 19, no. 2 (2017): 258–73; Ayhan Aktar, "A Rejoinder: The Debate on Captain Torossian Revisited," *Journal of Genocide Research* 19, no. 2 (2017): 279–91; Edhem Eldem, "A Reply to the Responses by Taner Akçam and Ayhan Aktar," *Journal of Genocide Research* 19, no. 2 (2017): 292–97.
10 Dikran Boyadjian, *Haygagan Lekeone: Badmagan Hushakrutiun* (*The Armenian Légion: A Historical Memoir*) (Watertown: Bayker Press, 1965).
11 Varteres Mikael Garougian, *Destiny of the Dzidzernag: Autobiography of Varteres Mikael Garougian,* trans. and ed. Mariam (Garougian) Sahakian, Gomidas Institute (Princeton and London, 2005).
12 George Georghallides, *A Political and Administrative History of Cyprus, 1918–1926* (Nicosia: Cyprus Research Centre, 1979), 89.
13 Andreas Georgiades and Christakis Zographou, *Άγιος Ελίας του Karpassι και Μπογάζι: παραδόσεις, ιστορία και άνθρωποι* (*Agios Elías of the Karpass, and Bogazi: Traditions, History and People*) (Nicosia, 2001).
14 Stanford Shaw, *History of the Ottoman Empire and Modern Turkey*, vol. II (Cambridge: Cambridge University Press, 1977); Stanford Shaw, "The Armenian Légion and its Destruction of the Armenian Community of Cilicia," in *The Armenians in the Late Ottoman Period*, ed. Turkkaya Ataov (Ankara: Türk Tarih Kurumu, 2001), 155–206.
15 Justin McCarthy, *Death and Exile: The Ethnic Cleansing of Ottoman Muslims* (Princeton: Darwin, 1995); Justin McCarthy, Esat Arslan, Cemalettin Taskiran, and Omer Turan, *The Armenian Rebellion at Van* (Salt Lake City: University of Utah Press, 2006).
16 Halil Aytekin, *Kıbrıs'ta Monarga (Boğaztepe) Ermeni Lejyonu Kampı (Monarga Camp of Armenian Légion in Cyprus)* (Ankara: Turkish Historical Association, 2000); Ulvi Keser, *Kıbrıs 1914–1923: Fransız Ermeni kampları İngiliz esir kampları ve Atatürkçü Kıbrıs Türkü (Cyprus 1914–1923: French Armenian Camps, British Prisoner Camps and Kemalist Cypriot Turks)* (Istanbul: Akdeniz Haber Ajansı Yayınları, 2001); Ulvi Keser, *Kıbrıs-Anadolu ekseninde Ermeni doğu Lejyonu (Armenian Eastern Légion in the Cyprus-Anatolia Axis)* (Ankara: Cyprus Turkish Cultural Association, 2007).
17 See various photos in Keser, *Kıbrıs 1914–1923*, 229–49; For the breech see TNA: SA 1/806/1917.
18 Yücel Güçlü, *Armenians and the Allies in Cilicia, 1914–1923* (Salt Lake City: University of Utah Press, 2012); Andrekos Varnava, review of *Armenians and the Allies in Cilicia, 1914–1923*, (review no. 1419), accessed October 19, 2017, www.history.ac.uk/reviews/review/1419.
19 Andrekos Varnava, "Imperialism First, the War Second: The British, an Armenian Légion, and Deliberations on where to Attack the Ottoman Empire, November 1914 – April 1915," *Historical Research*, 87, no. 237 (2014): 533–55; Varnava, "French and British Post-War Imperial Agendas and Forging an Armenian Homeland after the Genocide."
20 Andrekos Varnava, "The Politics and Imperialism of Colonial and Foreign Volunteer Legions during the Great War: Comparing Proposals for Cypriot, Armenian and Jewish Legions," *War in History* (2015): 344–63.

21 Susan Paul Pattie, *The Armenian Legionnaires: Sacrifice and Betrayal in World War I* (London: I. B. Tauris, 2018).
22 Varnava, "The Politics and Imperialism," 53–55.
23 Andrekos Varnava, *British Imperialism in Cyprus, 1878–1915: The Inconsequential Possession* (Manchester and New York: Manchester University Press, 2009).
24 TNA: SA 1/60/1916, Return of Officers and other Ranks at Cyprus, November 30, 1916; TNA: SA 1/60/1917, Return of Officers and other Ranks at Cyprus.
25 Varnava, "Imperialism First, the War Second"; Varnava, "French and British Post-War Imperial Agendas."
26 Varnava, "The Politics and Imperialism of Colonial and Foreign Volunteer Légions during the Great War."
27 Varnava, "French and British Post-War Imperial Agendas."
28 By 15 June 1917 there were 5,000 Armenians from Boston and New York City ready to leave for France to the Legion. See *Service historique de la Défense* (SHD) GR/7/N/2148, Vincennes, France, Armenian delegate to War Ministry, June 15, 1917; and GR/7/N/2148, Foch, to Briand, Foreign Affairs Secretary, August 11, 1917; The list of the members of the *Légion* are held at the Nubarian Library (Armenian General Benevolent Union Papers, 1912–1924), Paris, and show that many men embarked at Bordeaux and other Atlantic ports, indicating that they had travelled from the US. See also *Forgotten Heroes: The Armenian Légion in World War I*, Armenian Library and Museum of America, 2007. Traveling exhibition.
29 WO 32/5128, no. 31087, Advance copy of *Supplement to The London Gazette*, General Allenby, December 30, 1918.
30 Letters from the governor of Adana in May 1920 to the Interior Ministry showed that the Armenians who had returned to the province were unsafe because of the nationalist forces, while the Légionnaires were causing problems for local Muslims. See HR/SYS/2557/3, May 2, 1920, 8, Governor of Adana, to Interior Ministry, May 5, 1920; HR/SYS/2557/3, May 2, 1920, 10–11, Governor of Adana, to Interior Ministry, May 13, 1920; HR/SYS/2557/3, May 2, 1920, 14, Governor of Adana, to Interior Ministry, May 17, 1920; HR/SYS/2557/3, May 2, 1920, 17–18, Governor of Adana to Interior Ministry, May 17, 1920. In his letter of 2 May, the governor stated that the members of the Armenian *Légion* belong to the 'families of those Armenians who were deported and died or were killed in the desert or who could flee to the Syrian coast and from there to Cyprus and Egypt'. They received military training in Cyprus to 'hate Muslims and especially Turks because of these events'.
31 Stanley E. Kerr, *The Lions of Marash: Personal Experiences with American Near East Relief, 1919–1922* (Albany: State University of New York Press, 1973), 61–196; Robert F. Zeidner, *The Tricolor over the Taurus 1918–1922* (Ankara: Turkish Historical Society, 2005).
32 TNA: CO 67/183/49486, 2, R. Graham, Ministry of the Interior to McMahon, September 19, 1916.
33 FO 371/2769/1800004, minute, September 12, 1916.
34 SA 1/1068/1916, Clauson, November 7, 1916.
35 Ibid., Cambon to FM, September 13, 1916, 114.
36 Andrekos Varnava, "British Military Intelligence in Cyprus during the Great War," *War in History* 19, no. 3 (2012): 353–78; For the Turkish Cypriots who stole the vessel and made it to Antalya, where they revealed military activities in Cyprus, see SA1/806/1917.
37 SA1/1068/1916, confidential, Fenn to the Officer Commanding Troops, Cyprus, December 18, 1916.
38 *Ελευθερία* (freedom), October 21, 1916, 3.
39 *Ελευθερία* (freedom), February 3, 1917, 3.

40 Andrekos Varnava and Trevor Harris, "It Is Quite Impossible to Receive Them: Saving the Musa Dagh Refugees and the Imperialism of European Humanitarianism," *Journal of Modern History* 90, no.4 (2018): 834–62.

41 See SA1/1068/1916.

42 GR/7/N/2148, secret, Romieu to War Ministry, October 28, 1916.

43 GR/7/N/2148, secret, Romieu to War Ministry, November 10, 1916.

44 GR/7/N/2148, secret, Roques, War Secretary to Briand, Foreign Affairs Secretary, November 25, 1916.

45 GR/7/N/2148, Instructions to Armenian delegates sent to the Americas to recruit, undated.

46 GR/7/N/2148, secret, Romieu to War Ministry, January 1, 1917; GR/7/N/2148, secret, Romieu to War Ministry, January 19, 1917; GR/7/N/2148, secret, Romieu to War Ministry, March 31, 1917.

47 GR/7/N/2148, Hamelin, Army Staff, African and Oriental Section to War Secretary, March 19, 1917.

48 GR/7/N/2148, secret, Romieu to War Ministry, May 1, 1917.

49 GR/7/N/2148, secret, Romieu to War Ministry, June 1, 1917.

50 GR/7/N/2148, Excerpt of report n°24 by Romieu, January 1, 1918.

51 Varnava, "Imperialism First, the War Second"; Varnava, "French and British Post-War Imperial Agendas and Forging an Armenian Homeland after the Genocide"; Varnava and Harris, "It Is Quite Impossible to Receive Them."

52 See Boyadjian, *Haygagan Lekeone*; Garougian, *Destiny of the Dzidzernag*.

53 See SA1/978/1916/3, Ioannis Haji Georji, Livadia, Larnaca, to High Commissioner Stevenson, November 15, 1921. Georji served in the Cypriot Mule Corps. See also Varnava, *Serving the Empire in the Great War*.

54 Andrekos Varnava, "European Subaltern War Asses: 'Service' or 'Employment' in the Cypriot Mule Corps During the Great War?" *Britain and the World* 10, no. 1 (2017): 6–31.

55 SA1/1068/1916, 179–82, Muktars and Azaes of Trikomo, Agios Elias, Patriki, Gastria, Agios Theodoros, Avgolida and Ovgoros, to Clauson, March 30, 1918.

56 SA 1/1068/1916, Baxendale to Fenn, February 9, 1917.

57 SA 1/1068/1916, Thorne to Chief Commandant of Police, Nicosia, February 10, 1917, including a report by Captain P. Nanse, Acting Commandant of the Monarga Camp, February 6, 1917, and T. Wilson, Inspector of Police, Famagusta, February 7, 1917. Others accused included Elias Chrysostomos, a blacksmith; Elias Periklis, the cafe owner; Yannakis Hadji-Christofi, Photis Christofi (Papa Pavlos' brother), and Vassili Michael, all labourers; and Michael Georghaki.

58 SA 1/1068/1916, leaves 54–55, Muktar and Azaes of Trikomo to Clauson, April 16, 1917.

59 SA 1/1068/1916, Thorne to Chief Commandant of Police, Nicosia, July 27, 1917.

60 Ibid.

61 *Κυπριακός Φύλαξ* (Cypriot watchman), October 3, 1917, 3.

62 SA 1/1068/1916, Wilson to Commandant, *Légion d'Orient*, January 8, 1918, with statements and reports.

63 SA 1/1068/1916, statement, Chrisanthos Evangeli, Agios Elias, and statement of Panagi Yiannakou, Agios Elias. This is the most striking of the 12 offences. The boy often worked in his father's fields near Monarga and slept there at night. While working on 31 December 1917, an Armenian soldier approached him and asked for wine or zuki. Chrisanthos replied that he had none, and the soldier sat down. In the afternoon, when the other villagers working in the fields had gone home, the Armenian grabbed Chrisanthos and made an indecent proposal to him. The boy escaped, but the Armenian exposed himself, and in fear, Chrisanthos ran away but was chased by the Armenian until he saw a fellow villager. The Armenian promptly

ran off. The third son of Evangelis I. Zographou, who had been charged with the assault of Garabet Bektashian, Chrisanthos Evangeli Zographou was one of the few villagers of Agios Elias to emigrate (two other fellow villagers had left for Chile in 1912). Chrisanthos went to Argentina in the 1920s before settling in the United States. His older brother Yiannis named his fifth son after him, but of more interest is that Chrisanthos's younger brother, Alexandros, named his first child after him and not after his father, as is the custom. Possibly Chrisanthos left Cyprus because of this incident. See Georgiades and Zographou, *Άγιος Ελίας του Karpassι και Μπογάζι*, 188, 306–7.

64 SA 1/1068/1916, Local Commandant of Police, Famagusta to Commandant, *Légion d'Orient*, January 8, 1918, with statements and reports on each case.

65 SA 1/1068/1916, Wilson, Local Commandant of Police, Famagusta to Commandant, *Légion d'Orient*, January 8, 1918.

66 SA 1/1068/1916, Romieu to Chief Secretary, undated (between 16 and 20 January).

67 Doumanis, *Before the Nation*.

68 SA 1/1068/1916, Romieu to Chief Secretary, undated (between 16 January and 20 January).

69 SA 1/1068/1916, confidential, Lukach to Chief Secretary, Malcolm Stevenson, April 16, 1918.

70 Luke, *Cities and Men*, 44.

71 J. C. C. Davidson, *Memoirs of a Conservative: J. C. C. Davidson's Memoirs and Papers, 1910–1937*, ed. Robert Rhodes James (London, 1969), 13.

72 Ibid., 14.

73 SA 1/1068/1916, confidential, Lukach to Stevenson, April 16, 1918.

74 SA 1/1068/1916, Statement by Yorghios Zanis of Derynia, to Tilliro, April 23, 1918.

75 SA 1/1068/1916, Fleury to Commandant, *Légion d'Orient*, April 30, 1918. For other reports see SA 1/1068/1916.

76 SA 1/1068/1916, Statement of Mulla Osman Suleiman of Lefkonico, October 25, 1918; SA 1/1068/1916, Lukach to Stevenson, December 11, 1918.

77 SA 1/1068/1916, Suleiman's statement, October 25, 1918.

78 SA 1/1068/1916, Lukach to Stevenson, December 11, 1918.

79 CO 67/192, Cyprus 1919, II, 34189, Report on Police Force, 1918 and 1919, for year ended March 31, 1919, by Major G. C. Bayly, Acting Chief Commandant of Military Police.

80 For Australia see Stanley, *Bad Characters*; For Maori see P. S. O'Connor, "The Recruitment of Maori Soldiers, 1914–18," *Political Science* 19, no. 2 (1967): 48–83; For Canada see: Fay Wilson, "Booze, Temperance, and Soldiers on the Home Front," *Canadian Military History* 25, no. 1 (2016): 1–36; For the Ottoman army: Erik Jan Zürcher, "Between Death and Desertion: The Experience of the Ottoman Soldier in World War I," *Turcica: Revue d'Etudes Turques* 28 (1996): 235–58; For the Cypriot Mule Corps, see Andrekos Varnava, *Serving the Empire in the Great War: The Cypriot Mule Corps, Imperial Identity and Memory* (Manchester: Manchester University Press, 2017), 161–79.

81 Shaw, "The Armenian Legion and its Destruction of the Armenian Community of Cilicia," 155–206; *Forgotten Heroes*.

82 See Andrekos Varnava, "Martial Races in the Isle of Aphrodite," *Journal of Military History* 74, no. 4 (2010): 1047–67.

83 Kemal Karpat, *An Inquiry into the Social Foundation of Nationalism in the Ottoman State: From Social Estates to Classes, From Millets to Nations* (Princeton: Center of International Studies, Princeton University, 1973).

84 Abdulaziz Abdulhussein Sachedina, *The Islamic Roots of Democratic Pluralism* (Oxford: Oxford University Press, 2001), 96–97.

85 Doumanis, *Before the Nation*.

86 See generally Andrekos Varnava and Maurice Walsh eds., *The Archbishop's of Cyprus in the Modern Age*.
87 N. Kizilyurek, "The Turkish Cypriot Upper Class and Question of Identity," *Turkish Cypriot Identity in Literature* (London, 1990), 21.
88 FO 198/13, consular report, 1858.
89 Richard A. Patrick, *Political Geography and the Cyprus Conflict: 1963–1971* (Ontario: University of Waterloo Press, 1976), 12; Census, 1891.
90 Achilles Aimilianides, "Η Εξέλιξει του Δίκαιου των Μικτών Γάμων εν Κύπρω," *Kypriakai Spoudai* 2 (1938): 197–236, 209; Paschalis Kitromilides, "From Coexistence to Confrontation: The Dynamics of Ethnic Conflict in Cyprus," in *Cyprus Reviewed*, ed. Michalis Attalides (Nicosia, 1977), 35–70; Paul Sant Cassia, "Religion, Politics and Ethnicity in Cyprus During the Turkocratia (1571–1878)," *European Studies of Sociology* (1986): 3–28; Kemal Cicek, "Living Together: Muslim-Christian Relations in Eighteenth-Century Cyprus as Reflected by the Sharia Court Records," *Islam and Christian-Muslim Relations* 4, no. 1 (1993): 36–64; Theodore Papadopoullos, *Δημώδη Κυπριακά Άσματα εξ Ανεκδότων Συλλογών του ΙΘ' Αιώνος* (Nicosia, 1975), 63, 151–57, 213–6, 220–5, 239–41, 243–50; K. Giagoullis, "Ο Χριστοφής τζε η Εμινέ," *Laographiki Kypros* XXIII (1972): 15–21.
91 Varnava, *Serving the Empire in the Great War*; Varnava, "European Subaltern War Asses."
92 Harry Luke, *City of Dancing Dervishes and Other Sketches and Studies from the Near East* (London, 1914).
93 Michalis N. Michael, *Η Εκκλησία της Κύπρου κατά την οθωμανική περίοδο (1571–1878): Η σταδιακή συγκρότηση της σε θεσμό πολιτικής εξουσίας (The Church of Cyprus During the Ottoman Period (1571–1878): The Gradual Establishment of an Institution of Political Power)* (Nicosia: Cyprus Research Centre, 2005), 215–40; Varnava, *British Imperialism in Cyprus*, 153–55.

6 Mary Booth's imperial nationalism in the aftermath of the Great War

Bridget Brooklyn

During the two aftermath decades following the end of the Great War, Australia came to terms with its wartime loss and evaluated its contribution to the war through grief and memorialisation but also through a sense of national identity that honoured its contribution to this imperial war. The decades that follow show how much Australia had changed in its nationalist aspirations since the nineteenth-century emergence of radical, or 'bush', nationalism that sought separation from the British Empire. While radical nationalism represented a minority of Australians, the zeitgeist in the Federation era had been more accommodating of ideas of independence.[1] In 1887, Alfred Deakin coined the term 'independent Australian Briton', establishing a distinction between both radical nationalism and craven imperial loyalty, but in the aftermath decades, this independent, middle way became less so – many who shared these dual loyalties nevertheless placed greater emphasis on the 'Briton'.[2] Parliamentary leadership was more often than not conservative, and returned servicemen, if they identified themselves as part of a group, the two most prominent of these, the officer-class Legacy and the rank-and-file Returned Sailors' and Soldiers' Imperial League of Australia, were politically conservative. The decade of the 1920s also saw the rise of rural conservatism in the formation of the Country Party so that the previous century's association of radicalism with the bush, for all its urban associations, was overtaken by 'countrymindedness'.[3] Meanwhile, among the radical rural working class, the twentieth century saw an internationalist trend, reflected in the continuation of the radicalism of the 'nomad tribe' of radical rural workers in international movements such as the Industrial Workers of the World (IWW).[4]

The term 'imperial nationalism' to describe the values of my subject, Mary Booth, requires explanation; at some level, it is an oxymoron. Krishan Kumar observes how nationalism – or, more accurately, national identity – which is essentially monoethnic, can exist within a larger imperial entity, constituting an imperial nationalism.[5] Building on Kumar and others, Kevin Colclough discusses examples of nationalist movements in Scotland and British Canada, putting them into the category of movements 'seeking greater voice for the nation within an empire and claiming this will benefit both the nation and the empire'.[6] While Booth's nationalism did not form part of a similarly large-scale political movement, her beliefs about Australia as a nation, drawing on the deeds of the First AIF as a superior imperial fighting force, constituted a 'nationalism with a small N'[7] that saw in the First AIF, expressed symbolically in the word 'Anzac', a national claim for a greater voice within the empire. Booth's small-N nationalist vision was shared by others in her circle, notably, the official historian of the Great War, C. E. W. Bean, albeit with some differences, which are discussed briefly in this chapter. I have chosen 'imperial nationalism', then, as an accurate reflection of Booth's sense of national mission within an imperial framework. Booth's imperial nationalism was also idiosyncratic, partly because her feminism led her to make a place for women in this national vision at a time when the most prominent feminists of her generation were moving in an internationalist direction. Bessie Rischbieth, Vida Goldstein and Marguerite Dale were some of the prominent Australian feminists who took their feminism into the global arena.

In this global environment, although the Great War in so many ways spelled the end of empires, the British one was not quite done yet, with its territorial occupancy being at its height in the post-war years.[8] In Australia, the mainstream of conservative thought could still assert pre-war imperial certainties and Australia's importance in vindicating those certainties, while at the same time dealing with the war's catastrophic impact. In the aftermath of the Great War, imperial loyalty offered solace to those who put their faith in empire: the sense of an emerging national pride could be balanced against the enormity of that wartime loss and provide reassurance that it was not in vain.[9] Booth shared with other imperial nationalists a fusion of Australian and imperial mission but added to it her own strain of combined Australian and British identity, which incorporated 'Anzac' – in its figurative sense, symbolising Australia's contribution to the war – into British ethnic and cultural tradition. Booth's nationalism reflects the general aims of post-suffrage Australian feminists to establish their place in the polity. This active citizenship could take several forms, ranging in political stripe from the radical to the conservative.[10] Booth partly directed her citizenship aims towards the emerging nationalist symbol of Anzac by constructing an idea of nationalism that included a place for women, even in that most masculine of national symbols. I have discussed this goal in greater detail elsewhere.[11] Booth's nationalist goals in the post-war period combined a continuation of her activities in support of soldiers and their dependents during the war and her post-war organisation, the Anzac Fellowship of Women. This chapter aims to discuss Booth's activities in this post-war nationalist environment and how she developed a form of nationalist thinking that fit within the broader framework of feminist citizenship goals.

Dr Mary Booth was a political conservative from the professional middle class, whose lifetime activities were centred in Sydney, New South Wales.[12] She has been variously described as feminist, physician, eugenicist and welfare worker – she was all of these. She has also been described as both a patriot and a nationalist, a distinction explored further here. The scholarship on Booth remains fairly sporadic, although several historians have discussed her activities in some depth.[13] The work of Jill Roe, beginning with her entry on Booth in the *Australian Dictionary of Biography*, has been foundational, and so has a particularly interesting and wide-ranging essay of hers on feminism and nationalism: 'What has Nationalism Offered Australian Women?'[14] According to Roe, if post-suffrage feminists were to develop an essentially feminist nationalism, Booth was the one to do it. But she failed. Part of the explanation for this failure (but not all of it) was the fact that feminism, in the aftermath of the Great War, was more internationalist than nationalist: Roe observes that from the time white Australian women gained access to the vote, they 'oscillated between nationalist and internationalist strategies in an ongoing struggle for enhanced status'.[15] Finally, it was internationalism that captured the imaginations of the country's leading feminists in the post-suffrage years.[16]

Since the publication of Roe's essay, the scholarship on feminist internationalism has borne out this observation.[17] But there is more to be said on Booth's nationalism. Her melding of feminism, nationalism and imperial loyalty that looked backward to British traditions that pre-dated the British settlement of Australia stood apart from the more progressive organisations being formed in the interwar years, even those whose focus was also domestic – such as the Australian Federation of Women Voters and the United Associations of Women. Booth nevertheless asserted women's entitlement to equal citizenship, an issue that was uppermost for feminists, generally in the post-suffrage decades. One aim of this chapter is to suggest that Roe's answer to her own question: 'What has Nationalism Offered Australian Women?' – essentially, not a lot – needs revising. While Booth's particular brand of imperial nationalism, refined in the decades after the Great War, did not give rise to an identifiably 'feminist nationalism', its blending of the Anzac tradition with British cultural symbols added a distinctive voice to interwar feminists' calls for equal citizenship.

We cannot think of the evolution of Australian nationalism without reference to Britain, and much of the scholarship centres on the extent to which we see our nationalism as an embrace or a repudiation of Britishness.[18] The work of Neville Meaney has been influential. Maintaining the position that the very notion of an Australian identity in this period is laughable,[19] Meaney's focus is on foreign policy as entwined with cultural nationalism conceived of Australian national identity as existing in symbiosis with Britain. The cultural aspect of our nationalism was so overwhelmingly British that it led to Australia identifying its political interests with British ones, even when crucial events in the twentieth century demonstrated they so patently were not.[20] Our view of ourselves as British, not Australian, led to a romantic conception of Britishness that was quite removed from what was to be found in Britain itself. Meaney points out that it was only in the dominions that an amorphous 'Britishness' existed. In the so-called mother country, English, Scottish, Irish and Welsh rubbed along together in uneasy union – and not a small degree of resentment of English dominance.[21]

It is important, however, to acknowledge this Britishness as an intrinsic part of Australian nationalism. This has been the subject of much scholarship on Australian nationalism. To mention just a couple of examples, Bob Birrell has decried the 'revisionist' Federation histories as interpreting 'Britishness' as precluding Australian sentiment.[22] Russell McGregor has argued that it was a component of even radical nationalism and must not be seen as cancelling out 'Australianness'.

Rather, Australian nationalism is best described as ethnographically 'thick'. His use of this term draws on the work of anthropologist Clifford Geertz in identifying the layers of meaning conveyed through ethnic symbols. Applying Geertz to Australian nationalism means British ethnic symbols gave Australian national symbolism its ethnic thickness.[23] While some relationship between Britishness and Australianness is a given in any analysis of Australian nationalism, the question of the degree of imperial allegiance in the mix has been central. The decision about whether to consider nationhood in its more political sense, as Meaney does, or its more ethnic sense, as McGregor does, hinges on the accepted division of nationalism into two broad categories: the 'civic' and the 'cultural'. Turning to Mary Booth's imperial nationalism, it was very much a cultural nationalism, based on ethnic symbols drawn from an amorphous conception of Britishness but with the addition of an important Australian symbol, that of Anzac – it, too, was more than a little British.

Scholarship on the ethnic basis of nationalism offers a way of conceiving Booth's views as nationalist, rather than simply a collection of patriotic views assembled within an imperial framework. Among the key scholars in the area of ethnosymbolist nationalism, Anthony Smith emphasises the variations in nationalism, which is 'an eminently malleable nexus of beliefs, sentiments and symbols'.[24] Anthropologist Bruce Kapferer has used the Anzac tradition to illustrate this ethnic nationalism. To summarise necessarily briefly and therefore somewhat crudely, Kapferer sees it as a component of national ideology, particularly egalitarianism, which exists – not always harmoniously – at the level of both the individual and the state.[25] Many others have discussed the ethnic basis of nationalism. John Hutchinson, another ethnosymbolist, has defined cultural nationalism as, among other things, the dramatisation of 'rediscovered myths and legends' and the evocation of 'heroic ages as a critique of present degeneration'.[26] Smith's and Hutchinson's views are pertinent to Booth's nationalism, but before exploring it further, let us return briefly to the internationalism that galvanised many interwar feminists.

The union of feminism and internationalism incorporated causes that ranged from the specifically feminist suffrage campaigns to women's international citizenship, to peace movements that also addressed global issues of race. Fiona Paisley and Angela Woollacott, among others, have undertaken detailed studies of the relationship between feminism, race and internationalism among Australian feminists.[27] Leila Rupp's work on women's international organisations has demonstrated how internationalism at this time, exemplified in the formation of the League of Nations, was at a 'crescendo', facilitating a collective feminist 'we' that could tackle at an international level such issues as the vote, labour legislation, married women's citizenship and morality.[28] Although subjects such as peace, race and class were important in their own right to many feminist internationalists, they existed within the aim of securing a more feminist-influenced future globally. That these matters could throw up contradictions and paradoxes for women of the British and other empires has also been the subject of scholarship on the complicated ways in which women of the British Empire navigated their status as politically disadvantaged within their own race while using their imperial advantage to pursue the 'uplift' of colonised women, thus traversing the intersection between gender and race that reflected the power advantage of the feminist colonisers.[29]

Leila Rupp has noted the maternalist nature of international feminism.[30] A form of feminism that was very successful across the Western world in the interwar years, maternalist feminism was based on the view that women's innate maternal qualities made them better equipped than men to further the rights and wellbeing of women and children. In Australia, it had a sufficiently broad set of premises to bring together feminists whose other political beliefs ranged widely, from the New South Wales nationalist politician Millicent Preston Stanley to Western Australian Aboriginal rights activist Mary Montgomerie Bennett. It was broad enough to offer feminists of varying political persuasions the chance to exercise power within the Australian polity, including entering into parliamentary politics.[31]

While the complexities and contradictions of international feminism have been discussed at length in the scholarship, the relationship between ideas categorised as 'progressive' (both contemporarily and by historians) and those categorised as 'conservative', warrants further exploration in this interwar context of nationalism and internationalism. As Kate Laing's insightful analysis of Australian internationalist feminism indicates, not all women who became active in the movement for international peace held views that we would necessarily describe as 'progressive'. Building on the scholarship mentioned briefly earlier, Laing outlines how the goal of racial purity, shored up by immigration restriction, was accepted by a range of internationalist Australian feminists, alongside the internationalist goal of greater equality – both with men and among all women everywhere. At the same time, they sought to redress racial discrimination at a domestic level. Such distinctions could be manifested, for example, in the support given to non-white mothers already resident in Australia, while its advocates remained opposed to the dilution of Australia's white population through an open immigration policy.[32] Even in identifying conundrums and paradoxes, however, the danger of whiggery or presentism lurks. Laing's findings indicate just how exacting a task it is to map the history of feminist ideas in that turbulent period; what we interpret as paradoxes would not have seemed so to the women holding those views and who regarded themselves as progressive.

Laing's observation that many progressive internationalist feminists, such as Vida Goldstein, held 'nuanced' views of race, highlights the overlap of values that characterised interwar feminism. While Mary Booth's activities were carried out in different arenas, the pervasively cultural nature of Australia's racial policies created points of similarity between the imperially nationalist Booth and feminists who were opposed to nationalism and 'war sentiment'.[33] Laing's analysis reminds us that, for all Australians' ventures onto the world stage, from the Great War to Versailles to feminist internationalism, Australia remained in many ways insular and fearful. While this was a time in world history when white societies generally put whiteness at the apex of humanity, Australia's unique racial policies were a reflection of an inward-looking culture. Feminists' agreement on White

Australia reflects this inwardness, which was not just about race, but where race was a pervasive threat. David Walker's comprehensive sweep of Australian cultural history from the mid-nineteenth century to the outbreak of the Second World War continues to provide a solid reference point in its exploration of a culture where national anxiety was characteristically expressed in racial terms.[34] Even more interesting from the point of view of how ideas gain traction is Laing's discussion of Eleanor Moore, a relatively conservative peace activist. Drawing on her biography by Malcolm Saunders and Moore's own memoir, Laing reports how Moore's exposure to women beyond White Australia through the Pan-Pacific Women's Conferences led to a change in her views about race.[35] Internationalism, then, brought the world in.

Booth's world was narrower. Another difference between her and the majority of internationalist feminists is that her feminist beliefs were not the principal motive of her activities and her activism. There is no explicit declaration of feminist goals or principles that guided them. Indeed, the exact nature of Booth's feminist beliefs over the course of her lifetime is not always clear. Instead, nationalist goals are at the centre of her activities, albeit with the underlying message that women deserved an equal say in anything to do with citizenship. The strongest contrast with the internationalist feminists was that the link between women's citizenship and women's nationalism began with activities that supported war, rather than peace. These included charitable work in support of soldiers and their dependents, many commemorative activities and a wide range of other activities and campaigns aimed at keeping the sacrifice of Australian servicemen to the fore in the nation's thinking. These were not actively bellicose but stemmed from the view of the war as a just one because imperial and Australian interests were the same. The feminist component is evinced through activities that demonstrate that in nationalist terms, men's and women's contributions were also the same, or equivalent. From 1918, under the auspices of her Centre for Soldiers' Wives and Mothers, she inaugurated what was to become a tradition in the 1920s and 1930s: a women's march, which left from the principal Anzac Day gathering in Sydney's Domain and proceeded down the hill to No. 1 Wharf, Woolloomooloo, the departure point of the troopships. In 1921, under the regulations of the War Precautions Repeal Act 1920 (Cth), she successfully applied for permission to use the word 'Anzac' in the name of the organisation that became the very successful Anzac Fellowship of Women. Through these activities, she made a place for women within the celebration of Anzac as a national symbol, while admitting Anzac into her own pantheon of Britishness, discussed here further.

It is important to bear in mind that, even as feminism continued to look beyond national and imperial borders, Booth was not alone in her choice to keep her activities within the purview of empire and dominion. Many feminists' gaze was local, rather than internationalist, with maternalist reforms spearheading the evolution of the welfare state within a number of countries.[36] This they did within parliamentary politics and without, in party-political and in non-party-political ways.[37] For a conservative feminist such as Mary Booth, the interwar consolidation of this maternalist feminist agenda, combined with women's greater prominence as a result of their home-front support during the war as well as their personal sacrifice of loved ones,[38] offered greater opportunities to shape Australian nationalism. Booth's rhetoric evinces maternalist feminist values to a limited degree – what is important here is the way in which the widespread acceptance of maternalist values fostered a receptive environment for women who could be identified with these values. This was the same environment that had affirmed Australia's imperial ties in the recent war. In the aftermath, when imperial loyalty and patriotism had all but silenced feminists who were against Australia's involvement in the war, the field was left open to its supporters, such as Booth.[39] This environment may well have galvanised her in the years following its end. In her 1920 campaign for political office, she stood as an 'independent feminist candidate'; a campaign pamphlet contains both politically conservative rhetoric and policies that could fit within a maternalist feminist program. These policies included education, health, town planning and the care of war widows and stated:

> What women may do we have a promise of, through the work accomplished through the opportunities the war made for them. Women ask now for further opportunities to serve the State – to make their voices directly heard in public affairs. On consideration, these affairs of the State are those of the family writ large.

Elsewhere, the pamphlet, much of it set out in the form of an open letter to voters, exhorts them to 'apply the lessons of the war' to shore up Australia's borders and 'to keep fit and sound within'.[40] The rhetoric shows the influence of her political sympathies and her eugenicist background – only a well-defended and fit populace will be able to withstand threats from beyond Australia's borders. But despite the legacy of women's war work, Booth was unsuccessful and did not campaign again, so this possible avenue for the broadcast of nationalist ideas was then closed.[41]

As Jill Roe observes, the conservative temper of the interwar times should have provided the ideal climate for Booth's nationalism, but it did not. Instead, Booth's many projects aimed at advancing her nationalist sympathies gradually ground to a halt in the 1920s.[42] As already suggested, feminist scholarship since Roe's essay appeared in 1994 has vindicated her argument that the tendency of feminism has been towards internationalism rather than nationalism. But this is partly because there is still work to be done on the relationship between Australian women and nationalism; it has not commanded as much attention.[43] This is one reason why Roe's wide-ranging and erudite exploration of the subject is nevertheless somewhat pessimistic in its conclusions about Mary Booth's activities, as is some subsequent Booth scholarship. Tanja Luckins argues in a similar vein to Roe that Booth's post-war organisation, the Anzac Fellowship of Women, 'never made the transition from wartime patriotism to post-war nationalism', with 'little continuity with the War years, having been founded several years after the Armistice'.[44] To be precise, it was founded in the third year after the Armistice, at a time when Booth was still prominent through the continuation of two of her very successful organisations, the Soldiers' Club and the Centre for Soldiers' Wives and Mothers. Given this continued prominence, and the impact of the idea of both sacrifice and of 'Anzac' as a symbol of Australian heroism throughout the 1920s, the time lapse is not unduly long.

In her analysis of what she, like Roe, sees as Booth's failure to seize the nationalist moment, Luckins makes a distinction between 'wartime patriotism' and 'postwar nationalism' but does not expand on the significance of the distinction between patriotism and nationalism. Understandings of the difference vary, and the two terms are often used interchangeably. One definition of patriotism is that it denotes allegiance to a territorial entity, including a strong wish to defend it and its institutions. The urge to patriotism is often felt when in a state of war. Nationalism, to some degree, grows out of those patriotic feelings, but, since its advent around the late eighteenth century, 'has annexed these universally held sentiments to the service of a specific anthropology and metaphysic', in which national differences are defined not in terms of territory or institutions but of cultural and ethnic factors.[45]

Despite the fact that Luckins does not pursue in detail her reasons for regarding Booth's nationalist goals as unrealised, there is merit in her assertion that Booth 'never found a defining symbol or motif'.[46] While Booth's many public activities suggest that she was strongly political by nature, her 1920 campaign does not demonstrate a concerted attempt to disseminate her nationalist ideas to reach even the New South Wales polity generally – possibly because she had not formulated these ideas yet. Her efforts in the aftermath decades to develop an Australian nationalism were nevertheless quite strenuous. Luckins homes in on the use of language in connection with Booth's memorial activities to draw on the pioneer legend, which in the new century was enjoying an ascendancy over the more radically nationalist bush legend.[47] While Booth's (frequent) invocation of the pioneer legend might have struck a chord, this alone is unlikely to have been sufficient ground on which to build a nationalist platform. Although Roe argues that the nationalist moment was hers for the asking, perhaps it was not – Roe sees a lack of political support as significant.[48] Or perhaps, despite her strenuous activities and a political atmosphere that was receptive, Booth's message was too narrow, too representative of an older generation of feminists or too idiosyncratic to attain the kind of mass reach necessary for a successful nationalist movement, particularly when the global feminist trend was in the other direction. But while Booth's time in the sun was brief, there is considerable evidence of her impact on ideas of remembrance, nation and women's citizenship in these aftermath decades.

Of what, then, did Mary Booth's nationalism consist? A key aspect of nationalism is some wish for independence. Accordingly, radical nationalism had set itself against the British Empire; yet, Booth's nationalism was all in favour and does not even echo the 'independent' in 'independent Australian Briton'. Even war historian Charles Bean, who shared many of Booth's imperial views, attributed a broad 'Britishness' – as opposed to Englishness – to the formation of an Australian type. Both nevertheless placed Australian identity within an imperial one, thus subscribing to the notion of the Australian as the 'better Briton', which gained part of its impetus from the perception of the threat of Asian incursion – a fear frequently voiced by another of her associates, W. M. Hughes.[49] While not as strident as Hughes in her support of White Australia, Booth's promotion of Britishness forms part of the racial underlay in her conception of an ethnic form of nationalism around the idea of 'Anzac' – an Australian version of British, particularly English, national character. While this entailed no programme of nation-building as such, her ideas resemble many at the basis of what Anthony Smith and others have identified as ethnonationalist thought, particularly in its identification of an ethnic community, which Smith refers to by the French word *ethnie* as the closest in meaning to the Greek *ethnos*.

Smith identifies four principles of the 'sacred properties' of the nation:

1 a belief in ethnic election, the idea of the nation as a chosen people, entrusted with a special mission or having an exclusive covenant with the deity;
2 an attachment to sacred territory, an ancestral homeland sanctified by saints, heroes and sages, as well as by the tombs and monuments of the ancestors;
3 shared memories of 'golden ages', as the high points of the nation's ethnohistory, ages of material and/or spiritual and artistic splendour; and
4 the cult of the 'glorious dead', and of their heroic self-sacrifice on behalf of the nation and its deity.[50]

Not all of these characteristics are reflected equally in Booth's nationalism, but what Smith describes as 'ethno-histories' are relevant: the memories of a community that seeks a rediscovery of an 'authentic' communal past. This 'authenticity', much like 'tradition', usually contains at least some component of invention. British ethno-symbolism was, of course, not limited to the dominions. It is also evident in English war commemoration, notably, Adrian Jones's Cavalry Memorial in London's Hyde Park depicting, instead of a twentieth-century cavalryman, 'an armoured figure of St George', with the slain dragon at the feet of his horse.[51]

The ethnic origins and properties of nations are themes that form the core of Smith's work on nationalism and which he has returned to and refined many times. In *National Identity*, he gives a variation of the previous list, being:

1 a collective proper name;
2 a myth of common ancestry;
3 shared historical memories;
4 one or more differentiating elements of common culture;
5 an association with a specific 'homeland'; and
6 a sense of solidarity for significant sectors of the population.[52]

This second list highlights aspects of nationalism that home in more closely on aspects of Booth's nationalism, particularly points 2–5. Although there was a strong sense of common British ancestry, the dominant English – rather than broadly British – culture is at the forefront. Of the other components of Booth's

Britishness, Scottishness is far more prevalent than Welshness, while Irishness, perhaps following her imperial sympathies, does not appear to figure at all.

In the pursuit of an Australian–British cohesion, Booth drew on the myths of the ancient British past, rather than, say, the record of Britain's eighteenth- and nineteenth-century imperial prowess, to develop a sense of ethnic solidarity and foster a sense of tradition. As a subject of historical enquiry, the analysis of the 'invention' of tradition is related to the work of political scientists on the ethnic basis of nationalism. Eric Hobsbawm comments that the invention of tradition occurs more frequently in times of rapid social change and has clustered in the period of profound change over the past couple of hundred years.[53] David Cannadine, in his study of that most British (or perhaps mostly English) of traditions, the veneration of the monarchy, observes that much of this tradition originated in the last quarter of the nineteenth century. Rather than ritual rehearsed over millennia, much royal pageantry was a relatively recent response to Britain's waning international power in the face of the rise of European empires, particularly that of Germany.[54]

The growth in interwar Australia of a nationalist sentiment that eclipsed radical nationalism relied considerably on British institutions, such as the monarchy, but also on identifying the growing Anzac tradition with a conservative, rather than a radical, statement of 'Australianness'. Booth's nationalist sentiments fit well into this context but challenged the dominant masculinism of Anzac by offering something for women. The beginnings of an Australian nationalist fusion of Britishness and the Anzac tradition took place in tandem with the wide range of activities that she undertook through her Anzac Fellowship of Women. The organisation was formed on Anzac Day 1921, just one sign of the ways in which this organisation, comprised entirely of women, saw itself as imbued with the Anzac spirit. The organisation's constitution set out the following objectives:

1 To provide the comradeship of women who were engaged in war work during the Great War
2 To foster the spirit and traditions of Anzac Day
3 To have regard for the welfare of soldiers and their bereaved
4 To be helpful and friendly to new comers from the Old Country
5 To enlist the sympathy of others who are sympathetic with the above objects.[55]

The link between 'Anzac' as an ideal and the activities of Booth's organisation is not immediately obvious. The Anzac Fellowship's second objective, to foster the spirit and traditions of Anzac Day, is the only one that actually mentions Anzac, and it is unspecific. Booth nevertheless had certain things in mind that embraced a range of activities – political, social and cultural – that fell within the purview of this second object and which incorporated aims both for the Australian nation and for women's active participation as its citizens. I have described the more political of those activities elsewhere;[56] the focus of the present discussion is cultural.

In the 1930s, Booth established her Anzac Festival, a cultural event held on Anzac Eve which celebrated both Britishness and Anzac – again, the sense of the latter is figurative. The festival was organised by the Anzac Fellowship of Women with a view to 'link up the younger generation with the story of the past, + [sic] to cherish in unbroken continuity, the glorious traditions of our race'.[57] Thus the new Anzac tradition links up with older ones attached to 'race' or, more precisely, the British *ethnie*. The term 'race', so widely and variously used in the nineteenth and twentieth centuries, better fits Smith's description of an *ethnie* as an ideal type of ethnic community; the confusion of *ethnies* with 'races', the latter being groups sharing inherited biological traits, is a product of the racial thinking in the years from 1850 to 1945, which incorporated shared cultural and historical attributes into a 'racial' hierarchy.[58] Booth used the term 'race' in that ethnonational sense common to her times; the Anzac Festival articulated and celebrated qualities that Booth associated with Britishness. More than this, it represents both a commemoration and a redemptive form of salvation and self-renewal, which Smith identifies as part of nationalist myths of ethnic election – a sense of 'chosenness linked indissolubly with collective salvation'.[59]

The Anzac Festival was founded at a meeting in the Sydney Town Hall in October 1931. Once a committee was formed, it was decided to commission an Anzac Day song, with words by poet Dora Wilcox and music by composer Alfred Hill. While the words of the song itself, typical of much doggerel glorifying Anzac, does not make any specifically British references, it represents one part of Booth's pairing of Anzac with a British cultural tradition, which she developed further in 1933, as discussed next.

Once the song was completed in 1932, a competition was held early in April of that year, in which school choirs from both state and independent schools sang the Anzac song. The winning choir, North Sydney Girls' High School Choir, then sang it that Anzac Day at Booth's annual get-together for returned servicemen, held in the basement of the Sydney Town Hall. In addition, a pageant, 'The Spirit of Anzac', was held in the City Mission Halls in what were described as 'the congested areas of Chippendale and Newtown', with no admission being charged.[60] These suburbs being predominantly working class by 1932, it is possible that Booth was attempting to broaden her nationalist message by sending it out to the labor class.

The next Anzac Festival, held in the following year of 1933, had the format that it was to retain, more or less, for the next two decades. This was the year in which the festival began to be held at the Sydney Conservatorium of Music. A more ambitious affair, the 1933 festival looks to have been aimed at middle-brow audiences of Booth's class, with vocal performances of a song about the Menin Gate and of Handel's 'Rejoice Greatly' from *Messiah*. Importantly, the new venue suggests that the target audience had narrowed, with no apparent attempt to go forth into the 'congested areas'. If there was an initial mission to take the message to the working class, possibly this had not been successful and/or Booth had changed direction to make the festival more of a celebration of certain values within her own class. If the latter, then Booth's nationalism must also be seen as having a class dimension that intersected the implied collective cultural identity of ethnonationalism. Class distinctions and values in Australian history are difficult to unravel in both historical and sociological analysis,[61] so the question of exactly how class and nation intersect in Booth's worldview must await future analysis.

A significant aspect of the 1933 festival was its enhanced educative character. Booth's excursions in the previous year into the Mission Halls of Chippendale and Newtown can be interpreted as educative; with this following year's Anzac Eve competition, there was an increased number of categories in which school-children could compete. The centrepiece was a one-act play competition, its brief as follows:

> a one-act play lasting not more than twenty minutes, non-militant but embodying the idea of Valour, Truth, Beauty, and Endeavour as exemplified in the lives of St. George, Shakespeare, Captain Cook, and the Anzacs. It will stir the imagination of the competitors to know that these four characters, so great in British history, have made the last week of April a concentrated focus of human interest.[62]

Here is where Anzac becomes imbued with a sense of British ethnohistory – part of the amorphous Britishness that could only exist in the far-flung dominions. It is accurate to call it Britishness, but we can see here how English it was. Leaving aside the Anzacs for a moment, the triumvirate of St George, Shakespeare and Cook appears frequently in Booth's papers – these men are the carriers of British tradition that she held most dearly. The Anzacs, too, performed a symbolic function within this tradition. In drawing together a sense of a 'golden' ethnohistorical age, Booth's ethnosymbolism was assisted by fortuitous timing.

Shakespeare's birthday and St George's Day both occur on 23 April, and Cook's landing at Botany Bay on the 29th of that month.[63] The sense of a special mission – another of Smith's sacred properties of the nation – that she was keen to impart, if not to the working class then to the rising generation of her own class, is suggested in Booth's concluding line about the final week of April as 'a concentrated focus of human interest'. It was serendipitous for Booth that the Gallipoli landing was also in the last week of April.

In keeping with this British ethnosymbolism, the winners of the choral section of the Anzac Festival were awarded a grail-like trophy, the Silver Cup of Remembrance – ethnically thick indeed![64] Thus ancient ethnic symbols were cross-fertilised with new ones: the Anzac ideal had both British and Australian origins. 'Anzac' stood for the heroism that represented the best in the British character. As the brief for the Anzac Festival play competition sets out, the values of 'Valour, Truth, Beauty, and Endeavour' were continued through the Anzac spirit. Again, in comparison to Bean, who shared many of Booth's views that Australian soldiers were born of good British stock, Booth's Australian Briton did not represent a new Briton, shaped by Australian egalitarianism. More, the Australian was a revitalised Briton not vastly different from the old one.

Booth's Anzac Festival continued to grow through the 1930s, continuing also to merge a British (usually English) tradition with an Australian one. It managed to survive the Second World War but did eventually peter out in the 1950s, probably due to a lack of interest from the schools. And so we return to Roe's claim that Booth, while perfectly poised to develop a conservative feminist nationalism on a large scale, failed to do so. This is perhaps not entirely because her feminism swam against the tide of internationalism in the post–women's suffrage decades. It is noteworthy that, whereas during the aftermath of the Great War, when she had been in many ways in the thick of the action, much of Booth's activity either did not survive the Second World War or emerged from that conflict in a weakened state. The Second World War represents something of a hiatus or at least a change of direction for many aspects of an incipient Australian identity, including nationalism. With the final demise of the British Empire, this was a nationalism both sure and unsure about where it stood.[65] Although Curtin's wartime turn to the United States is often misconstrued as a turn away from Britain, the nation's position in the wake of the Pacific War, combined with the post-war loss of key British colonial territories to independence, was not one in which such imperial certainties could flourish.

The Great War, occurring a short time after white Australian women gained the vote, both intervened in and enhanced post-suffrage citizenship. For many women on the home front during the war, Booth included, the voluntary activities undertaken in those years provided unprecedented opportunities in public life, if not in formal political life. Mary Booth, whose imperial nationalist sentiments emerged during and after the war, took a different route from the peace activism of so many internationalist feminists, who had come together for the Congress of Women in 1915, even as war raged.[66] Instead, the war was a call to the dominions, and in its aftermath, Anzac was a tradition in the making that Booth used to create a place for women in Australia's post-war nationalism. She achieved this, for example, through her women's commemorative activity and her use of the word 'Anzac' in her post-war organisation, the Anzac Fellowship of Women.

Given that Booth's activism did not produce a strong, feminist imperial nationalism, what can we say that nationalism offered Australian women? Or, more pertinently, what did this woman offer Australian nationalism? As mentioned, a number of factors have to be considered as contributing to Booth's failure to ignite the polity – or even the feminist part of it – in an enduring way. Booth, like many others who shared her political values, saw the Great War as a testing time for the new Australian nation within the British *ethnie*. Whereas other feminists looked beyond the British *ethnie*, even while accommodating contradictory (to us, at least) views about race, Booth maintained a gaze that was consistent in its reliance on the certainties of empire, nation and race that characterised conservative thinking.

For women, access to the vote in both Commonwealth and state legislatures from 1902 and access to state political office after the passage of the Women's Legal Status Act in 1918 (NSW) offered new political opportunities. Like other feminists, Booth could seek a platform for her views that had not been possible in colonial New South Wales. That her form of nationalism was not able to make use of these greater political opportunities could be attributed to several causes, including women's difficulty in achieving political success in the parliamentary arena, whether aligned with a party or not. Initial success in parliamentary politics was gained in state legislatures, and the 1920s saw several women achieve varying degrees of political success in this decade: Edith Cowan with the Western Australian Nationalist Party, Millicent Preston Stanley with the New South Wales Nationalists and Irene Longman with the Progressive National Party in Queensland. These were all non-Labor women, although in many ways not deeply conservative. They nevertheless reinforce Jill Roe's surprise that conservative women did not seize the post-war political agenda to a greater extent than they did. The fact that women did enjoy some success in parliamentary politics, however, does attest to the appeal of maternalist politics. All three of the examples mentioned earlier had affiliations and programmes that reveal the influence of maternalist feminism, all of them supporting a range of initiatives that demonstrate the diversity of maternalist feminist programs. To mention just a few, there was infant welfare, motherhood endowment and a housewives' union for Cowan; child endowment and a long campaign to equalise child custody legislation – both during and after her parliamentary career – for Preston Stanley; and the welfare of women, children and the disabled for Longman.[67] Although some maternalist feminist policies could be radical – for example, advocacy of motherhood endowment, which constituted a payment to mothers, rather than families – a large number of maternalist feminist policies fell sufficiently comfortably within the parameters of consensus politics to bolster political success. The strength of maternalist feminism offers a possible cause for the lack of enduring feminist interest in nationalism. Apart from a milieu in which internationalist ideas were in the vanguard of feminist thought and action, there were perhaps other things that feminists in the domestic arena saw as more pressing to make the post-war world order more responsive to women's needs.

While Booth also espoused values that can be described as maternalist feminist, she concentrated her attention elsewhere. She was aided by the fact that her conservatism fit the interwar times. In her beliefs and activities, apart from conceiving of a distinct Australianness, albeit derived from Britishness, she also asserted that women were central to nationalism, for all the masculine character of its principal symbol of Anzac. In doing so, she crafted a nationalism that drew together post-suffrage feminism and interwar imperial nationalism. In the longer term, a nationalism based on Britishness did not fit the times. Following the Second World War, with what Curran and Ward describe as 'three interlocking processes' – briefly, decolonisation, Britain's reduced economic and strategic position in the post-war world and its eventual turn towards Europe – the way was paved for an Australian identity that was far less British than it had ever been.[68] If Booth's moment had by then passed, she had nevertheless contributed to the Australian nationalism that developed in the aftermath of the Great War.

Notes

1 J. B. Hirst, "'Destiny,' ch. 1 and 'Identity,' ch. 2," in *The Sentimental Nation: The Making of the Australian Commonwealth* (Melbourne: Oxford University Press, 2000).

2 Neville Meaney, "Britishness and Australian Identity: The Problem of Nationalism in Australian History and Historiography," *Australian Historical Studies* 32, no. 116 (2001), doi:10.1080/1031461010859614879-80.

3 Don Aitkin, "'Countrymindedness' – The Spread of an Idea," *Australian Cultural History* 4 (1985): 34–41. For the debate on whether 'bush' nationalism was essentially urban, see Graeme Davison, "Sydney and the Bush: An Urban Context for the Australian Legend," *Australian Historical Studies* 18, no. 71 (1978), doi:10.1080/10314617808595587191-209; Bill Garner, "Bushmen of the Bulletin: Re-examining Lawson's 'Bush Credibility' in Graeme Davison's 'Sydney and the Bush,'" *Australian Historical Studies* 43, no. 3 (2012): 452–65, doi:10.1080/1031461X.2012.706626; and Graeme Davison, "Just Camping Out? A Reply to Bill Garner," *Australian Historical Studies* 43, no. 3 (2012): 466–71, doi:10.1080/1031461X.2012.706623.

4 See, for example, Rowan Day, *Murder in Tottenham: Australia's First Political Assassination* (Spit Junction, NSW: Anchor Books Australia, 2015), 1, 31–39, 157.

5 Krishan Kumar, "Nation and Empire: English and British National Identity in Comparative Perspective," *Theory and Society* 29 (2000): 577–79, www.jstor.org/stable/3108547. I have also discussed elsewhere my reasons for this terminology. See B. Brooklyn, "Mary Booth and British Boy Immigration: From Progressivism to Imperial Nationalism," in *Australia, Migration and Empire. Britain and the World*, ed. P. Payton and A. Varnava (Cham, Switzerland: Palgrave Macmillan, 2019), 230, https://doi.org/10.1007/978-3-030-22389-2_10.

6 Kevin Colclough, "Imperial Nationalism: Nationalism and the Empire in Late Nineteenth Century Scotland and British Canada" (PhD thesis, University of Edinburgh, Edinburgh, 2006), 70.

7 Ibid., 71.

8 Kumar, "Nation and Empire," 588.

9 Carolyn Holbrook, "Nationalism and War Memory in Australia," in *The Great War and the British Empire: Culture and Society*, ed. Michael J. K. Walsh and Andrekos Varnava (London: Routledge, 2017), 224, https://doi.org/10.4324/9781315557502.

10 See, for example, Marilyn Lake, "Childbearers as Rights-Bearers: Feminist Discourse on the Rights of Aboriginal and Non-Aboriginal Mothers in Australia, 1920–50," *Women's History Review* 8, no. 2 (1999): 347–63; Ozich Clare, "'The Great Bond of Motherhood': Maternal Citizenship and Perth Feminists in the 1920s," *Studies in Western Australian History* 19 (1999): 127–38.

11 Bridget Brooklyn, "Claiming Anzac: The Battle for the Hyde Park Memorial, Sydney," *Melbourne Historical Journal* 45, no. 1 (2017): 112–30.

12 By 'conservative feminist', I mean that Booth was politically conservative and also a feminist. The sense in which I use it here is not to condescend, as Hilary Carey, in a discussion of 'female collectivism' indicates can be the case in feminist scholarship, although the scholarship has moved on since Carey's intervention. Hilary M. Carey, "'Doing their Bit': Female Collectivism and Traditional Women in Post-Suffrage New South Wales," *Journal of Interdisciplinary Gender Studies* 1, no. 2 (1996): 102.

13 Apart from the work of Jill Roe, noted in the following paragraph, other principal works that discuss Booth are Joy Damousi, *The Labour of Loss: Mourning, Memory and Wartime Bereavement in Australia* (Cambridge: Cambridge University Press, 1999); Bruce Scates, "The Unknown Sock Knitter: Voluntary Work, Emotional Labour, Bereavement and the Great War," *Labour History*, no. 81 (November 2001): 29–49, www.jstor.org/stable/27516802; Tanja Luckins, *The Gates of Memory: Australian People's Experiences and Memories of Loss and the Great War* (North Fremantle: Curtin University Books, 2004); and Tanja Luckins, "The Ugliness of Anzac: Mary Booth," in *World War One: A History in 100 Stories*, ed. Bruce Scates, Rebecca Wheatley, and Laura James (Melbourne: Viking and Penguin, 2015).

14 Jill Roe, "What Has Nationalism Offered Australian Women?" in *Australian Women: Contemporary Feminist Thought*, ed. Norma Grieve and Ailsa Burns (Melbourne: Oxford University Press, 1994).

15 Roe, "What Has Nationalism Offered Australian Women?" 30.

16 Ibid., 32.

17 Fiona Paisley, *Glamour in the Pacific: Cultural Internationalism and Race Politics in the Women's Pan-Pacific* (Honolulu: University of Hawaii Press, 2009), 1; Angela Woollacott, "Inventing Commonwealth and Pan-Pacific Feminisms: Australian Women's Internationalist Activism in the 1920s – 30s," *Gender and History* 10, no. 3 (November 1998): 425; Angela Woollacott, *To Try her Fortune in London: Australian Women, Colonialism, and Modernity* (Oxford: Oxford University Press, 2001); Catherine Fisher, "World Citizens: Australian Women's Internationalist Broadcasts, 1930–1939," *Women's History Review* 28, no. 4 (2019): 626–44, doi:10.1080/09612025.2018.1506554.

18 James Curran, *Curtin's Empire* (Cambridge: Cambridge University Press, 2011), 12–18; J. J. Eddy and Deryck Schreuder, "The Edwardian Empire," in *The Rise of Colonial Nationalism: Australia, New Zealand, Canada and South Africa First Assert their Nationalities, 1880–1914*, ed. John Eddy and Deryck Schreuder (Sydney: Allen and Unwin, 1988); Meaney, "Britishness and Australian Identity"; Russell McGregor, "The Necessity of Britishness: Ethno-cultural Roots of Australian Nationalism," *Nations and Nationalism*, 12, no. 3 (2006): 493–511, https://doi.org/10.1111/j.1469-8129.2006.00250.x; Neville Meaney, "'In History's Page': Identity and Myth," in *Australia's Empire*, ed. Deryck M. Schreuder and Stuart Ward (Oxford: Oxford University Press, 2008), ch. 15; James Curran and Stuart Ward, *The Unknown Nation: Australia after Empire* (Carlton, Victoria: Melbourne University Press, 2010).

19 Neville Meaney, "The Search for Security in the Pacific, 1901–14," in *A History of Australian Defence and Foreign Policy, 1901–23*, vol. 1 (Sydney: Sydney University Press, 1976), vii.

20 Meaney, "Britishness and Australian Identity," 86–89.

21 Ibid., 82.

22 Bob Birrell, *Federation: The Secret Story* (Sydney: Duffy and Snellgrove, 2001), 186–88 and *passim*.

23 McGregor, "The Necessity of Britishness," 494–95, 497–99.

24 Anthony D. Smith, *National Identity* (London: Penguin, 1991), 79.

25 Bruce Kapferer, "When the World Crumbles and the Heavens Fall in War, Death, and the Creation of Nation," in *Legends of People, Myths of State: Violence, Intolerance, and Political Culture in Sri Lanka and Australia*, new and rev. ed. (Washington: Smithsonian Institution and Berghahn, 2012), ch. 5, 121–48; Anthony D. Smith, *Nationalism: Theory, Ideology, History*, 2nd ed. (Cambridge: Polity Press, 2010), 156.

26 John Hutchinson, *Modern Nationalism* (London: Fontana, 1994), 45, 50. See also Walker Connor, *Ethnonationalism: The Quest for Understanding* (Princeton, NJ: Princeton University Press, 1994).

27 Fiona Paisley, "Citizens of their World: Australian Feminism and Indigenous Rights in the International Context, 1920s and 1930s," *Feminist Review* 58 (1998): 66–84, https://search.proquest.com/docview/1300489612?accountid=36155; Woollacott, "Inventing Commonwealth and Pan-Pacific Feminisms"; Woollacott, *To Try her Fortune in London.*

28 Leila J. Rupp, *Worlds of Women: The Making of an International Women's Movement* (Princeton: Princeton University Press, 1997), esp. 6–7, 175, 194–95 and ch. 6.

29 See, for example, Antoinette Burton, *Race, Empire and the Making of Western Feminism* (London: Routledge, 2016); Clare Midgeley, "Bringing the Empire Home: Women Activists in Imperial Britain, 1790s – 1930s," in *At Home with the Empire: Metropolitan Culture and the Imperial World,* ed. Catherine Hall and Sonya O. Rose (New York: Cambridge University Press, 2006), ch. 11, 230–50.

30 Rupp, *Worlds of Women,* 85–86.

31 See, for example, Marilyn Lake, "A Revolution in the Family: The Challenge and Contradiction of Maternal Citizenship," in *Mothers of a New World Maternalist Politics*

and the Origins of Welfare States, ed. Seth Koven and Sonya Michel (New York: Routledge ebook, 2016), 378–95; and Lake, "Personality, Individuality, Nationality, Feminist Conceptions of Citizenship 1902–1940," *Australian Feminist Studies* 19 (Autumn 1994): 26–28.

32 Kate Laing, "'The White Australia Nettle': Women's Internationalism, Peace, and the White Australia Policy in the Interwar Years," *History Australia* 14, no. 2 (2017): 223–25, doi:10.1080/14490854.2017.1319736.

33 Ibid., 230.

34 David Walker, *Anxious Nation: Australia and the Rise of Asia, 1850–1939* (Queensland: University of Queensland Press, 1999).

35 Laing, "The White Australia Nettle," 233.

36 See, for example, Theda Skocpol, *Protecting Soldiers and Mothers: The Political Origins of Social Policy in the United States* (Cambridge, MA: Belknap Press of Harvard University Press, 1992); Seth Koven and Sonya Michel, eds., *Mothers of a New World Maternalist Politics and the Origins of Welfare States* (New York: Routledge ebook, 2016, 1st ed., 1993), doi:10.4324/9781315021164; Marilyn Lake, "The Independence of Women and the Brotherhood of Man: Debates in the Labour Movement over Equal Pay and Motherhood Endowment in the 1920s," *Labour History* 63 (1992): 1–24.

37 Marilyn Lake has discussed the many obstacles to women's participation at a party-political level. The legitimacy of that position notwithstanding, it is important to acknowledge women's achievements in these decades, seeking entry into the polity through a variety of means, both party and non-party political. Marilyn Lake, *Getting Equal: The History of Australian Feminism* (St Leonards, NSW: Allen & Unwin, 1999), ch. 6, cf; J. Baker, "Woman to Woman: Australian Feminists Embrace of Radio Broadcasting, 1930s – 1950s," *Australian Feminist Studies* 32, no. 93 (2017): 292–308, doi:10.1080/08164649.2017.1407643; B. Brooklyn, "The 1920s: A Good Decade for Women in Politics," in *Seizing the Initiative: Australian Women Leaders in Politics, Workplaces and Communities* (Parkville: eScholarship Research Centre, University of Melbourne, 2012), 156–70.

38 Damousi, *The Labour of Loss*.

39 Judith Smart, "Feminists, Food and the Fair Price: The Cost of Living Demonstrations in Melbourne, August – September 1917," *Labour History* 50 (May 1986): 131, doi:10.2307/27508786.

40 National Library of Australia (NLA): MS2864, Box 12, Folder 7, Mary Booth Papers, 'Letter from Dr. Mary Booth, O. B. E.' Election booklet [ca.1920].

41 Roe's entry in the *Australian Dictionary of Biography* (*ADB*) mentions a second attempt, but I have been unable to find evidence of this, including through examination of Roe's *ADB* file notes held at the Australian National University.

42 Roe, "What has Nationalism Offered Australian Women?" 30–35.

43 With some exceptions; see, for example, Marilyn Lake, "Women and Nation in Australia: The Politics of Representation," *Australian Journal of Politics and History* 43, no. 1 (1997): 41–52.

44 Luckins, *The Gates of Memory*, 198.

45 Elie Kedourie, *Nationalism*, 4th, expanded ed. (Oxford and Cambridge, MA: Blackwell, 1993), 68.

46 Luckins, *Gates of Memory,* 198.

47 Ibid., 165–66; Richard Waterhouse, "Australian Legends: Representations of the Bush, 1813–1913," *Australian Historical Studies* 31, no. 115 (2000): 220–21, doi:10.1080/10314610008596127; and Richard Waterhouse, "The Pioneer Legend and its Legacy: In Memory of John Hirst," *Journal of the Royal Australian Historical Society* 103 (pt. 1) (2017): 1–17.

48 Roe, "What has Nationalism Offered Australian Women?" 35.

49 Curran & Ward, *The Unknown Nation,* 12.

50 Smith, *Nationalism: Theory, Ideology, History*, 155.
51 Richard Cork, "Foreword," in *The Great War and the British Empire*, ed. Michael J. K. Walsh and Andrekos Varnava (London: Routledge, 2017), xix.
52 Smith, *National Identity*, 21.
53 Eric Hobsbawm, "Introduction: Inventing Traditions," in *The Invention of Tradition*, ed. Eric Hobsbawm and Terence Ranger (Cambridge: Cambridge University Press, 1983), 4–5.
54 David Cannadine, "The Context, Performance and Meaning of Ritual: The British Monarchy and the 'Invention of Tradition', c.1820–1977," in *The Invention of Tradition*, ed. Eric Hobsbawm and Terence Ranger (Cambridge: Cambridge University Press, 1983), 133.
55 NLA MS2864: Box 13, Folder 10, Mary Booth Papers, Anzac Fellowship of Women.
56 See, for instance, Brooklyn, "Claiming Anzac," 112–30; and Brooklyn, "Mary Booth and British Boy Immigration."
57 Mitchell Library, State Library of NSW (ML), MSS 2109, Box 4, Item 2, notes, 'The Anzac Festival', n. d. [ca. 1933], Mary Booth papers, 1905–1957.
58 Smith, *National Identity*, 21–22; Birrell, *Federation*, 286–88.
59 Smith, *National Identity*, 37.
60 Notes, "The Anzac Festival."
61 Chris Chamberlain, *Class Consciousness in Australia* (Sydney: George Allen & Unwin, 1983), 39.
62 ML: MSS 2109, Box 4, Item 2. Information pamphlet, "Anzac Festival Competitions 1933", Mary Booth Papers.
63 Luckins, "The Ugliness of Anzac: Mary Booth," 271.
64 ML: MSS 2109, Box 4, Item 2, notes, "The Anzac Festival," Mary Booth papers.
65 Curran & Ward, *The Unknown Nation*, 16–21.
66 Rupp, *Worlds of Women*, 3.
67 Margaret Brown, "Cowan, Edith Dircksey (1861–1932)," *Australian Dictionary of Biography*, vol. 8 (National Centre of Biography, Australian National University, 1981), accessed February 1, 2020, http://adb.anu.edu.au/biography/cowan-edith-dircksey-5791/text9823; Heather Radi, "Preston Stanley, Millicent Fanny (1883–1955)," *Australian Dictionary of Biography*, vol. 11 (National Centre of Biography, Australian National University, 1988), accessed February 1, 2020, http://adb.anu.edu.au/biography/preston-stanley-millicent-fanny-8107/text14153; Wendy Michaels, "The Final Factor: What Political Action Failed to Do," *Lilith* 19 (January 2013): 18–31, http://search.ebscohost.com/login.aspx?direct=true&db=30h&AN=113818593&site=ehost-live&scope=site; Mary O'Keeffe, "Longman, Irene Maud (1877–1964)," *Australian Dictionary of Biography*, vol. 10 (National Centre of Biography, Australian National University, Published First in Hardcopy, 1986), accessed February 1, 2020, http://adb.anu.edu.au/biography/longman-irene-maud-7228/text12515.
68 Curran and Ward, *The Unknown Nation*, 15.

7 Shanzhai 山寨 nationalism 中国民族主义

Reflexive empires and digital commemoration in China from Ah Q to AI

Tom Sear

> 'These past two weeks have certainly been strenuous days for me. The President was suddenly taken violently sick with the influenza at a time when the whole of civilization seemed to be in the balance.'[1]

So wrote Rear Admiral Cary T. Grayson, personal physician to US President Woodrow Wilson, in a letter to a friend. The seriousness of the president's illness was not disclosed to the media; instead, the public were advised he had a cold.[2]

In April 1919, during the Versailles negotiations, the President of the United States was struck down with the Spanish Flu. Wilson's post-viral weakness may have contributed to the outcome of negotiations with Clemenceau over reparations and for control of East Asia, both accelerating the likelihood of the 1937–45 war.[3] Between January 1918 and December 1920 the pandemic killed tens of millions around the world. The official state-coordinated and popular commemorative traditions that arose from the First World War in France and Britain's Dominions for the military losses of the Great War overshadowed the centenary of the flu epidemic. Historians and epidemiologists noted the anniversary, but it did not deeply penetrate popular consciousness or trans-national state activity.[4]

By early 2020 an uncanny centenary correlation to the Spanish Flu pandemic was beginning to emerge. The outbreak in late 2019 of the novel coronavirus SARS-CoV-2 in Wuhan, People's Republic of China (PRC) and the subsequent rapid, contagious, global spread of the related disease COVID-19 brought the period of the earlier pandemic back into stark popular focus.

Here I explore, through the PRC-ruling Chinese Communist Party's (CCP) incorporation of Western commemorative practices into its own remembrance forms, the rise and character of shanzhai (山寨) nationalism (中国民族主义) in China – an intrinsically originless, deconstructionist nationalism that enables the incorporation of Western technologies at the same time as it rejects Western influence.

Investigating the fusion of technological and cultural change in China in the Armistice and aftermath of the First World War reveals a history of empire which incorporates the importance of ontologically aware cosmotechnics within the post-colonial spatial model to explore how power contestation of the twenty-first century not only has arisen but is reflexively integrated into earlier historical disruptions. In 1919 China's response to the aftermath of the Great War integrated the shock of modernism through the principles of Qi and Dao (道器合一) and the process of shanzhai to express an emergent political consciousness. The materiality and temporality of telegraphic media and communication technology, along with the crystallisation of a character, or 'spirit', in the New Culture Movement, provided new meaning to traditional conceptions of 'absence', 'presence' and 'originless origin'. The promethean moment of 4 May 1919 defined a century of constant change in China. On its centenary, in the contemporary era of the revisionist, vectoralist leadership of Chairman Xi Jinping, a similar process of change is being undertaken through the adoption of the 'new' within a Chinese computational cryptoinfosphere but with the recursive, ironic twist that a cultural imaginary of memory (and forgetting) is being reconfigured not through the events of 4 May 1919 in Beijing, but rather the First World War commemorative social technologies China was resisting – those of the British Empire. This chapter analyses this reflexive nationalism – and distinctly twenty-first-century technological structures – to assert a new concept of empire nationalism not just in the present but how such hegemonic power transferrals have their origin in the past. In so doing this chapter argues for an increased importance for time as well as space, technology as well as culture in the aftermath of the First World War.

The uncanny centenary of 1919, COVID-19 and an imagined planetary community

The practices which the CCP executed in 2020 arose and were adapted from post–First World War British Empire formulations. The era 1919–20 saw the emergence and codification of commemorative forms like the 'unknown soldier' and the 'minute's silence' accepted across the British Empire. A century later, in the wake of COVID-19, there was a resurgence of global public memorialisation and mourning of death, even collective protest and civil disorder.[5]

In the PRC, the CCP endorsed a new practice during the period of Qingming in 2020.[6] Qingming Jie (清明节) or 'Tomb Sweeping Day' falls on fourth or fifth of April each year. In 2020 Qingming was declared a day of mourning, and a period of three minutes of silence was conducted nationally.[7] This rare event was in remembrance of the loss of life arising from the COVID-19 outbreak. In Beijing, Chairman Xi Jinping stood, head bowed, with the politburo. In Wuhan, the site of the outbreak, Vice Premier Sun Chunlan led mourners. The officially mandated silence was declared 'in mourning for martyrs and compatriots who lost their lives in the COVID-19 pandemic'.[8] National moments of silence had been officially reserved in China before, for political mourning, such as at the funeral of Chairman Mao or for earthquake victims in 2008.[9] However, in the Xi Jinping era, silences have become associated with the new Second World War–related annual tradition of Martyrs' Day at Tiananmen Square in Beijing.[10]

Chinese collective moments of silence, in particular the intensification of state-centric memory, cultured under the leadership of Chairman Xi Jinping were adopted from a twentieth century, chiefly British diaspora, Western cultural form, which was first developed in 1919.[11]

On 8 May 1919, King George V declared 'for the brief space of two minutes, a complete suspension of all our normal activities'. So that 'in perfect stillness, the thoughts of every one may be concentrated on reverent remembrance of the Glorious Dead'.[12] New industrial technologies, from tanks to poison gas, radically changed the scale, speed and global impact of warfare between 1914 and 1918. Afterwards, what psychologist Steven D. Brown calls 'social technologies' emerged to cope with the trauma. The seemingly timeless commemorative practices of silence, poppies and poetic odes were invented and globally accepted between 1919 and 1922.[13] Material memorials provided an architecture for the spatial imaginary of an emergent diasporic, post-colonial nationalism within empire. Located in the metropole centre, the cenotaph and 'Unknown Warrior' were made permanent by November 1920. Tombs of opposing absence, in the form of the symbolically empty cenotaph, and the anonymous presence of an Unknown Warrior, provided the foci for an imaginary community of sacrifice. The subsequent annual application of the new social technology of silence during Armistice Day at 11 a.m. on the 11th month of the year became a ritual for the temporal integration of the imaginary: becoming the space/time continuity of a social technology.

The centre-periphery structure of empire was vital to the development of this social technology of silence. Two men usually share the credit for proposing the two-minute silence: South African author and politician Sir Percy FitzPatrick and Australian soldier and journalist Edward Honey. Honey and FitzPatrick grasped the power that technologies of telesthesia had for a wounded empire emergent from the First World War.[14] Coming from Britain's colonial periphery, both men understood the capacity of mediatory suspensions of time and space to create a unified globalised political imaginary – qualities that made the commemorative collective silence trope accessible and adaptable across the twentieth century and beyond.

The simultaneous nationalist, and global diaspora–unifying, qualities of the social technologies of commemoration, emergent in the aftermath of the First World War were evident to the leadership of the CCP in recent times. The 2020 CCP COVID-19 three minutes of silence had multiple purposes. A primary function reflected the metropole-periphery structure of empire. The collective, highly visual act firstly supported internal political CCP messaging within the PRC itself. The silence was an event integrated into communication media projected out into the world and then deliberately refracted through global media reactions and reflected back into the PRC. The stillness also demonstrated that China – the origin of the virus – was back in motion while the rest of the world was still in a phase of frozen stasis.

The silence also co-opted other features of the 1919 social technology which processed political aspects of the COVID-19 global pandemic. The rituals of silence developed in Anglophone countries arising from the First World War carry with them an 'economics of sacrifice'.[15] These rituals took account of the costs of sacrifice: who had paid the highest price, who was in debt to whom and from whom reparations might be owed.[16] In a 2020 global, highly visually mediated social and economic crisis, the deployment of such commemorative strategies had multiple political implications.

In Anglophone nations moments of silence are observed annually and adopted for collective tragedies other than war. Equally, a diversity of nations globally have also adopted the form on occasions of national trauma, most recently in relation to terrorist events. The key lineage in the PRC for commemoration was the collective silence of Mao's funeral in 1976, an event largely beyond living memory in 2020 China. The COVID-19 silence lacked the remembrance infrastructure of the funeral of a revolutionary leader. Without it this instant community vanishes. Many photographed in 2020 appeared awkward and confused. Other complexities may have been cultural. As Brown indicates, a 'commemorative silence disposes of the dead'.[17] If the dead are processed and returned to the past through silence, then this may be at odds with the ongoing presence of the 'spirits' within traditional Chinese rituals of annual commemoration and presence.

The traditional Chinese conception of 'spirit' is, however, itself undergoing transition in the Xi Jinping era. The 2020 official moment of silence in the PRC was an aural expression of a wider aesthetic and a paradoxical apparatus of an invisible presence in plain sight. The silence called attention to the public secrecy of the cryptocractic CCP state.[18] While the silence mourned and acknowledged the sacrifice of those who were missing, it also processed their dangerous exiled spirit back into a sacred state-sanctioned memory. Wuhan whistle-blower Dr Li Wenliang (李文亮), who was persecuted locally for raising early concern about SARS-CoV-2 on social media, was converted into an official martyr and acknowledged during the silence.[19] The silence was a piece of British Empire Armistice social technology deployed a century later in China, towards a specific objective. Li Wenliang's role as SARS-CoV-2 'whistle-blower' was initially disruptive, but when the pandemic spread, his victimisation by local authorities became an issue for the CCP. His subsequent recognition in the silence served to repress this contradiction. Whereas the artifice of the Armistice silence ostensibly seeks to heal and seal a rupture, the CCP used the same technology but instead to affirm a continuity.[20] The 2020 PRC silence and martyrdom of Li Wenliang surfaced Qingming within a surveillance apparatus of continuity that is epistemological: 'knowing what not to know'. In addition, the deployment of technologies of exile integrated the 'so-called hidden rules (*qian guize* 潜规则)' of public secrecy with the spirit of Qingming.[21]

Digital amnesia, analogue ancestors and social media politics in an era of cyber sovereignty

The aftermath of the Great War introduced new annual traditions and commemorative 'days' to the British diaspora calendar. Chinese culture – in the form of

Qingming – already possessed a central day of commemoration. Qingming is a time of jì zǔ (祭祖), the sacrificial rituals of ancestor worship. Rituals even more than any religious identity have played a pivotal role in the organization of China.[22] Ancestor praxes infer the presence of an eternal soul. The burning of paper money is suggestive of ensuring such souls are provided for.[23] Qingming influences temporal focus and spacetime mapping. The day itself leads Chinese people to conceptualise the 'past as in front of them'.[24] Qingming is a heterotopic spacetime. The ritual opens a potential for deviation and social memory activation and mobilisation which paradoxically – for a day centred around tradition – may threaten the CCP.

Qingming, particularly when associated with recent mourning, has been historically a trigger for political unrest in modern China. The events of 4 June 1989 arose from the death of Hu Yaobang just after Qingming. A prior smaller-scale Tiananmen protest occurred on Qingming after the death of Premier Zhou Enlai in 1976. This repeated pattern of behaviour may have triggered the CCP to first declare Qingming a national holiday in 2007 and then closely associate it with the new phenomenon of officially recognising military martyrdom.[25] The official holiday, called Martyrs' Day, commenced in 2014. The politicisation of the term 'martyr' coincided with the two other newly formally ratified commemorations later in the year associated with the war against Japan.[26] As historian Ian Johnson has observed, China is not immune to the presence of memory in the present. The Chinese government, Johnson argues, does 'not just suppress history, it recreates it to serve the present'.[27] Xi Jinping, more than any other leader since the First World War, has emphasised tradition. The images featured in the 'China Dream' advertising campaign hark back to the kitsch clay figurines of centuries-old arts and crafts.

The internet has played a critical role in accelerating engagement with this new memorialisation. China is increasingly digital. Seventy one per cent of people use the internet regularly and own a smartphone. Eighty four per cent of people use online social networking sites. Ninety four per cent of people aged 18 to 34 own a smartphone.[28]

Chinese social media is dominated by two key platforms. Weibo (微博), also known as Chinese Twitter, has 100 million daily users. WeChat (微信) known as the 'Super App', had an estimated 1 billion active users in 2018 – in China and within the Chinese diaspora.[29]

Use of WeChat for social interaction is now so prevalent that traditional practices like 'Tomb Sweeping' – the burning of money and symbolic material goods and pouring rice wine on graves – are often experienced remotely via video conferencing on the app. Marketplaces for simulated paper objects to burn for relatives to use in heaven now even feature iPads, phone chargers and Wi-Fi routers. Some cemeteries offer live-streamed remote worship with live crying set at 300 yuan for ten minutes.[30]

Social media platforms offer a huge arena for influence and propaganda. Digital media accelerated the potential threat of politicised memory leading to civil unrest in China. The CCP have developed coordinated censorship mechanisms in response. Despite the perception, censorship of social media in China is not uniform, and the regulations continue to evolve. However, it has widely been thought the Chinese government has been actively involved in 'astroturfing', that is, the practice of crowdsourcing what appear to be unsolicited comments to create influence. Such posts in China have become known as 50c comments because of the rumour that posters were paid 5 jiao (角) or .08 US cents for each post.

China's internet and social media are notoriously difficult to research. In a landmark study published in 2017, a US team proved the existence of these posts, timing and content and estimated their total volume.[31] Their study shows that digital technologies are central to all these activities. Qingming and Martyrs Day are the largest target for what many argue are government-influenced social media posts.[32] It is estimated there are around 750 million social media users in China, and the study suggests that the Chinese government encouraged at least 2 million people to post propaganda on social media as though it was real opinion.

This study presented quantitative evidence that estimates the Chinese government fabricates around 448 million so-called 50c social media comments every year.

By far the biggest spike of these posts occurs to commemorate those who sacrificed their lives for China on Qingming Day and Martyrs Day. Such posts

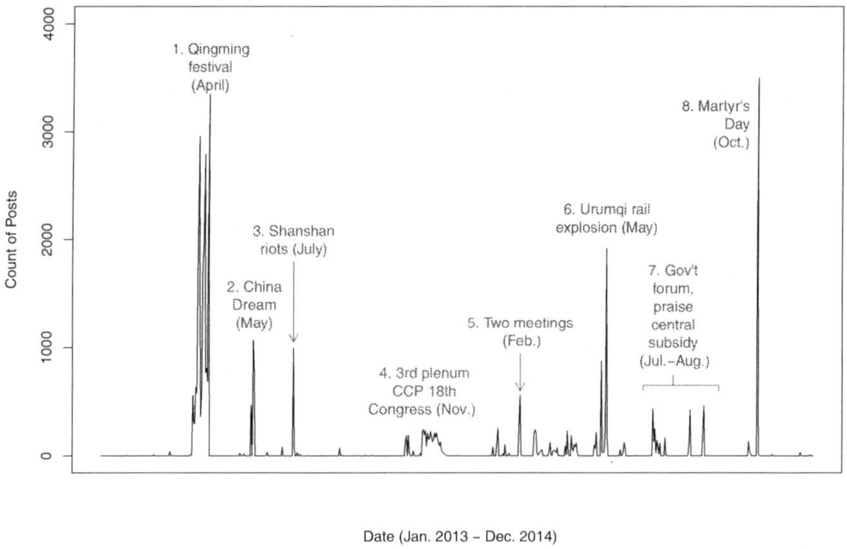

Figure 7.1 Gary King, Jennifer Pan and Margaret E. Roberts. Time series sample of 43,797 known 50c social media posts, with qualitative summaries of the content of volume bursts.

Source: (Courtesy of author)

declared: 'Many revolutionary martyrs fought bravely to create the blessed life we have today!' or simply, 'Respect these heroes.'[33]

Qingming has historically been a time of protest. The researchers suggest the massive volume of war commemoration posts are 'consistent with a strategy of distraction'. Leaked e-mails from propaganda departments request 50c party members to 'promote unity and stability through positive publicity'. King et al., argue the strategy of the Chinese government is distraction because the key necessity is to stop discussions with collective action potential.[34]

More recent CCP events of collective unification draw on much older forms. China has recently begun to establish new commemorative events around past conflicts of contemporary relevance, using practices apparently learned from Western war commemoration, merged with existing cultural practices of ancestral worship and accelerated by digital information activities.

WWI, the WWW and revisionist hegemonic geopolitics

This book explores a centenary moment of Armistice and aftermath for the British Empire in a period of significant change. A hundred years ago power was being negotiated and transferred from Britain to the United States as emergent Asian powers tested their influence.[35] Similarly, in the present, Indo-Pacific nations are immersed in a 'long-term, strategic competition' which has re-emerged as China rises to challenge the hegemony of the United States.[36]

A revisionist contest of power between empires is commensurate with a commemorative moment. From 2014 to 2018, while an Anglophone West reflected on the end of the Great War through commemorative rituals established a century ago, the Chinese government looked forward to the commemoration of an impact of the Armistice itself: the May Fourth Movement of 1919 and the inception of the CCP in 1921.[37]

The era of Chairman Xi Jinping (commencing in November 2012) coincides roughly with the centenary of the First World War globally. The Xi Jinping era has seen an emphasis upon memory as a form of state-sponsored national cohesion, and pivotal memorial 'days' in the calendar are commemorated on social media.[38]

While the historical response in China to the end of the First World War between 1919 and 1923 took forms and symbolism radically different than those of the British Empire, and China struggled against the cultural influence of the West in the 1920s, today the politicised memory technologies of the CCP draw on the memory traditions and cultures the British Empire invented in 1919–20.

Anglophone empire memory practices are being integrated into a new form of colonial domain emergent in the present day: digital empire. The internet and social media have transformed political participation within nation states and empire politics between states. China and the United States are involved in a geostrategic technology competition.[39] Artificial Intelligence (AI), quantum computing and biotech will be central to future national power. Just as there is Baidu, Alibaba and Tencent (BAT) versus Google, Apple, Facebook and Amazon (GAFA), 'Stack on Stack' conflict will take place over access to hemispherical data archives for machine learning.[40] Whether these digital empires will replace nation states in the future is an open question. However, for the moment at least, the Westphalian system of nation states prevails.[41]

Over the last 30 years a period of adaptation has evolved geopolitical competition to a suspension just below the threshold of outright conflict. Major revisionist powers have learnt from the asymmetrical adaptations of conflicts and changes since the end of the Cold War.[42] Such changes have witnessed a new understanding of the role of deconstruction, disintegration and non-binary constellations in historical understanding of empires.

The apex of this period of geopolitical evolution of nation states and insurgent state-building enterprises was the period 2013–15.[43] Coalitions of expeditionary security and nation-building military in the Middle East from 2001 have provided a context for the re-examination of empire. As Heather Streets-Salter has pointed out, the last decade saw a methodological shift in the study of war and empire. The historiography of empire had previously focussed primarily upon the locations of and interactions between centre and the periphery, viewing these polarities of relationship as of primary importance. Such a binary focus not only excluded more lateral interactions but emphasised discrete national experiences within confined periods. Streets-Salter argues for a 'conceptualization of modern empires which is messier, more multilateral than the colony/metropole model allows'.[44]

I concur with Streets-Salter that the colonies and metropoles, particularly via diplomacy and the alliance system of the First World War and the armistice process, were more connected than we might have imagined and that peoples were active participants in larger global movements and revolutionary nationalism. To this reformulation I would like to add three other processes. One is not just the error of studying empires as discrete units but to stress the importance of exploring empires in friction and entanglement as change occurs. The second is to explore how memory in the present and technological change and commemorative practices have weaponised the historical period 1918–23 as forms of contemporary nation state–based reflexive political mobilisation and censorship. Finally, as great powers begin to be defined by digital borders and their power is articulated through porous firewalls and entangled domains, we may need to look to consider the media archaeology of empires within our methodologies. The telegraph was just as important to creating connections in the British Empire as the internet is today to the integration of Chinese metropole with diaspora.

Postcolonial theory has emphasised how hegemony has functioned through imposition of universals. The Armistice and its aftermath are useful periods to examine how resistance is also an assertion of a local culture and politics, adapting specific universalising modernist ideas from the culture of the coloniser.[45] The May Fourth Movement in 1919 illustrated this complexity, and the New Culture Movement revealed this tension. The New Culture Movement of 4 May was interested in the twin Western Modernist forces of 'Mr Science' and 'Mr Democracy'.[46] The work of Streets-Salter is useful in locating these connections on a global scale which de-emphasises the importance of the metropole and locates important events occurring at a distant periphery. However, in the case of Beijing, the emphasis upon space within the post-colonial period may lead us to miss other forces at work in our present which can be explored through historical examples. These examples are less about space and more about the technologies which connect space.

Information communication technologies were integral to maintaining a British empire as they were vital to the events of 4 May in China. Lord Curzon described British interests of empire as 'commercial, political, strategical and telegraphic'.[47] The network and telegraphic connection was vital to the British hegemony of empire through space. Curzon made this statement in 1899. In 1919 he was in charge of the British Foreign Office when actions at Versailles reverberated globally.[48]

Armistice, media archaeology and the topology of empire telesthesia

The British Empire's diplomatic and political efforts at Versailles sought to simultaneously maintain influence in China, placate the rising naval power of Japan and reward that nation for its assistance in the First World War while blunting the power of the United States in the Asia Pacific as power was transferred. This had unforeseen circumstances in China.[49]

A definitive transfer of global power and influence from Britain to America had commenced during the Great War. But in 1919 how such a transfer might manifest itself in the Asia Pacific was far from certain. The lasting representation of this change is the image *Britannia Pacificatrix* – a mural by Sigismund Goetze finished in 1919.[50] The centrepiece of *Britannia Pacificatrix* is a handshake between the United States and Great Britain and her empire. The handshake symbolises the central exchange of Versailles and the years from 1919 to 1923 – the peaceful transition of global hegemonic power from Britain to the United States. The United States strives forward confidently. Britannia's body language is diffident and defensive, almost untrusting.

British historians typically see the transfer of power as one of succession, conducted in a handshake between civilisations. As Adam Tooze has pointed out, this is somewhat flattering as it was less a succession than a paradigm shift. In an era of coronavirus and climate change we are familiar with governance by the curve, and an intersection on one curve is one key indicator of how the paradigm shifted.[51] Sometime in mid-1916 the combined GDP of the British Empire was overtaken by that of the United States.[52] Two years earlier, in September 1914, Japan occupied the German concession in the city of Qingdao on the Shandong Peninsula, China. Japan had been allied with Britain since 1902, declaring war on Austria-Hungary in 1914, subsequently taking control of Qingdao (Tsingtao) in China's Shandong peninsula and helping Britain suppress an uprising in Singapore in 1915.[53] Japan leveraged the alliance. In January 1915 Tokyo submitted to Beijing a list of 21 imperialist demands, provoking outrage amongst students and the wider Chinese community.

Throughout the war China cultivated relations with the United States, hoping it might prove a bulwark against the Anglo-Japanese Alliance when peace came.

Because China had supplied 140,000 labourers to the Western Front this earned the nation a role in the peace negotiation.[54] China was to be disappointed at Versailles. London, with so many resources tied up in China, and, equally frightened of a Japan–US conflict in Pacific waters, was supportive of Japan. Using its leverage with Britain and President Wilson's fears of a walkout and of Japanese naval power, Wilson, Clemenceau and Lloyd George buckled and gave Japan control of Shandong until 1922. On 3 May, Lù Zhēngxiáng (陸徵祥) the head of the Chinese delegation in Paris, telegrammed Beijing that the 'conference was unprecedentedly authoritarian' and the delegation 'definitely could [not] sign' the peace treaty.[55] That night and for the day after, enraged students held a protest on 4 May 1919 at Tiananmen Gate. It was this moment that was central to a chain of events that created the Communist Party.[56]

The historiographical narrative of 4 May has typically positioned events located in major cities like Beijing and Shanghai as the simultaneous expression in colonial cultures of the 'Wilsonian Moment'.[57] Recent work has explored the circulation of ideas within China and across other locations globally, slightly de-emphasising a unidirectional pulse from centre to periphery.[58] Post-colonial approaches have tended to empathise spatial dimensions, and, indeed, 4 May involved the construction of Tiananmen Gate as political space.[59] Few, however, have examined the role the technology of the telegraph played in creating political time.[60]

The telegraph from the nineteenth to early twentieth century was critically important to the hegemonic re-organisation of space.[61] Global communications infrastructure, such as the telegraph, influenced the shape and agenda of public life and diplomacy.[62] In the period up to 1911 the widespread use of telegrams for political nationalist mobilisation in China and Qing administration attempts to suppress their circulation is well documented.[63] While the telegrams of 3 May were a vital trigger for the 4 May incident, the telegraph was an essential and constant form of communication to and from Versailles, both before and after the incident itself.[64]

The fourth of May is frequently represented as a nation-building anti-foreign movement. Genuine pro-foreign cosmopolitanism[65] was evident, in addition to the more frequently emphasised nationalism which sought to 'externally preserve Chinese sovereignty and internally eliminate national traitors'.[66] Multiple internal interests were also in effect. Representatives of China's warlords (*junfa*) of the Guangzhou Military Government were present at Versailles itself and actively pursued their interests both in France and within China, where they responded to Paris events via a coordinated armed network. From late April it was a dedicated telegram communications campaign to and from military governors to organise events and protests that both escalated and provided a structure of security for activity around and following 4 May.[67]

Technical, reproducible media were integral to the mobilisation of bodies and ideas in protest during the incident of 4 May. At a higher level of abstraction via the telegraph medium – the incident of 4 May was a mediation of encoded cultural presences and absences.[68] 4 May was a dual transcultural technical telegraphic experience of 'presence' and the 'Nietzsche-Heidegger axis of deconstruction' of moral and metaphysical traditions.[69] The telegraph enabled telesthesia: perception at a distance. To theorist and writer McKenzie Wark, 'modern telesthesia . . . starts with the telegraph. It is the first vector that moves information faster than people or things. It becomes the means via which to organise those movements.'[70] However, the milieu of 4 May also saw a transition of representational, literate forms of semantic meaning through the New Culture Movement. In this way, 4 May contains two key processes for China's 'modernisation' as both a technical and a symbolic transition within a framework of culture.

The New Culture Movement epitomised this latter form of change. New Culture was a movement which embraced Western ideas of Marxism, democracy and the use of vernacular Chinese language in culture.[71] New Culture was fundamentally a literary movement: its enduring literary figure was Lu Xun 鲁迅 (1881–1936). Lu Xun's intention was 'wén yǐ zài dào' (文以载道), 'literature as a vehicle for moral message'.[72] In 1921 he penned: 'The True Story of Ah Q', an allegory of the 1911 revolution and a metaphorical parody of traditional culture. The central character of Ah Q has been influential for a century. So much so, that 'the spirit of Ah Q' remains a cliché.[73] Famous for his self-deception and perverse superiority, Ah Q was a figure embraced as a critical symbol of the Chinese national character. The 'Q', which is not able to be translated into Chinese, is symbolic of the ambiguous feelings for Western culture present at the time.[74]

Techne, spirit and the ontology of hauntological nationalist lost futures

The figure of Ah Q is known for his 'problematic modernity'.[75] Ah Q is a national allegory, a 'meta-fiction of a crumbling imperial China drawn into the vortex of modernity', where 'China as a phenomenology of crumbling and dispersal takes shape through the frenzied but aimless activities of Ah Q as ghost – through its roaming around; its self-negating search for an identity'. It is via Ah Q as the '"real story" of the nameless ghost of China, seeking in vain its return and reinvention, that the origin of Chinese modernism surges into being . . . as a radical, nihilistic phenomenology of decay, void, dispersal, and, dialectically, as renewal, rebirth, and hope'.[76]

Ah Q is hauntological. Jacques Derrida's theory of hauntology is a form of and play upon ontology and temporality. Derrida argued that while cultural ideas may seem to have disappeared into history, their spectre remains in the form of spirits and ghosts.[77] Like the technical aspect of the telegraph, inherent to what today we might name 'the digital', 'teetering at the borderline of absence and presence, these revenants give rise to a sense of temporal disjuncture as well as ontological uncertainty'.[78] Hauntology's greatest proponent is Mark Fisher.[79] He writes: 'What haunts the digital cul-de-sacs of the twenty-first century is not so much the past as all the lost futures that the twentieth century taught us to anticipate.'[80] Hauntology is oscillatory, as Fisher explains, that which is absent is no longer present from the past 'but which remains effective as a virtuality'. While, 'the second sense of hauntology refers to that which . . . has not yet happened, but which is already effective in the virtual.'[81]

Ghosts figured prominently in imagery following the Great War. For Anzac Day 1925 Australian artist Will Dyson drew a cartoon for *Punch* of a soldier returning home to women with the caption suggesting on Anzac Day the spirits of the nation's dead return home for leave. For Anzac Day 1927 he produced an popular image of two ghostly diggers declaring a 'voice from Anzac': "Funny thing Bill – I keep thinking I hear men marching!" '[82] In July 1927 Australian official war artist Will Longstaff was present at the unveiling ceremony of the Menin Gate Memorial, Ypres, Belgium.[83] Unable to sleep that night Longstaff returned to the gate and claimed to have had 'a vision of spirits of the dead rising out of the soil around him'.[84] Upon returning to his London studio Longstaff painted *Menin Gate at Midnight* (also known as *Ghosts of Menin Gate*) in a single session.[85]

If Australia invented a figurative 'spirit' of Anzac after the First World War as an iconic twentieth-century civic persona,[86] Chinese political culture in a parallel time of political violence enabled the 'Spirit of Ah Q'.[87] The 'Anzac spirit' of Gallipoli to convert a military defeat into a moral victory is mirrored in Ah Q. 'Ah Q is famous for his "spiritual" victory method' (精神勝利法) – his ability to transform apparent defeat and humiliation into a symbolic victory by re-narrativising events in a way that is more favourable to him. A form of Nietzschean ressentiment, Ah Q's strategy transformed objective weakness into a form of symbolic strength.[88] However, Lu Xun enclosed national deconstruction as his 'real' protagonist. The ' "real" story of Ah Q can only be a ghostly invention evoking the void, not the reality, of its socio-ontological being', in which the True Story is one of a ' "bedeviled" or "possessed" nature'.[89]

Ah Q emerges at a specific moment. The era between 1919 and 1922 witnessed the start of a contemporary Chinese cultural and political consciousness. In China this national consciousness took the form of Ah Q and generated a cultural discourse which, as Paul B. Foster argues, has maintained continual relevance throughout the twentieth century. In 1938 Mao Zedong called Lu Xun 'China's first-rate sage. Confucius was a sage of feudal society and Lu Xun is a sage of new China'.[90] But paradoxically, the modern 'new' of Ah Q represented a phenomenology of absence – a spectre – of moral-cultural order of imperial China as ruin.[91]

From spatial to temporal and cosmotechnical understandings of empire conflict and change

The May Fourth and New Culture Movements were concerned with a new relationship between technics, *Qi* (器 tools [literal translation]), and *Dao/Tao* (道 cosmological consciousness). As Yuk Hui argues, in Chinese philosophy, particularly in Confucianism, the highest standard is expressed as a unification between *Qi* and *Dao* (道 器 合 一). To Yuk Hui they embody a " 'moral cosmotechnics": a relational thinking of the cosmos, and human beings, where the relation between the two is mediated by technical beings'.[92] The May Fourth Movement concerned itself with Mr Science and Mr Democracy, wherein technology is integrated into the category of science. The result is a collapse of *Qi* and *Dao* and possibly even a reverse of the cosmotechnics – of using *Qi* to create *Dao*.[93] In this way *Li Qi* (禮器 vessel of rituals) expresses a Confucian rationalism which incorporated ghosts into a moral cosmology via ritual – an idea central to the hierarchical conceptualisation of ancestral rituals within the Confucian governance classic Zhou Li (周禮 Rites of the Zhou).[94] Ah Q bridges these concepts and temporality. With Ah Q, Lu Xun writes a politics of hauntological time, of cultural radicalism wherein Mao's permanent revolution is enabled through a new subject of history, who so enmeshed with the ghostly and old is paradoxically a guide to the new 'allegorical drama of forgetting, haunting, and mourning'.[95]

At the same time as the New Culture Movement, during the aftermath of the First World War, the British Empire also developed metropole/colony-unifying cultural memory tropes that would shape identity and civic participation for the next century. Like China these were a mix of the old and new.[96] Their peculiar modernity was a unifying 'real-time' quality. The commemorative practices of the Unknown Soldier, silence, poppies and poetic odes were invented and globally accepted between 1919 and 1922. Developed to cope with trauma, they have become forms of participative collective culture which pivot around memory.[97] New commemorative rituals were more than ways to link individuals' suffering and loss to a collective, democratic ideal: they were forms of 'social technology'. These commemorative technologies construct inter-subjectivity. 'Reflexive self-modification' and 'new modalities' of 'social remembering' are 'technologically mediated' forms of 'spectacle where participants are absorbed in their own enactment of empathy and sorrow'.[98]

Recursion, post-colonial paradox and the cryptosphere of eternity politics

Innovation in military technologies which mobilised bodies in the First World War also served metaphorically to integrate the subject within an apparatus of nationalism post-war. As Friedrich Kittler affirmed, paraphrasing Virilio: 'World War 1 perfected technical storage information.' These storage media were 'combined with early prototypes of transmission media'.[99] Equally, commemorative technologies, invented in aftermath, store an absence. 'No more arresting emblems of the modern culture of nationalism exist than cenotaphs and tombs of Unknown Soldiers,' asserted Anderson. The 'transmission media' for post First World War nationalism was an epistemological projection of the subject onto the void. Who else could the 'Unknown' occupant be but a national body?

Nationalist imagining is connected to religious imagination.[100] Nationalism's imaginary arose from larger cultural forms which dealt with eternal mystery of the Other and death's certainty, as the secular replaced the sacred in Western societies. In the British Empire the synchronicity of the moment's silence, for example, was a kind of telepathically connected empire. These psychic imaginings of empire invented through 1919–21 have proved remarkably resilient.[101] Post-war social technologies of 'ghostly national imaginings'[102] have proved adaptable, even to virtual technologies.[103]

Chinese culture has a long complex imaginary of ghosts,[104] but in 1976 the construction of Chairman Mao's mausoleum as China's national tomb at Tiananmen Square replaced looking into the void with viewing the communist materialism of Mao's body. More recently, a new form of national, equally hauntological, imaginary is recently emergent in China. Instead of mausoleum, the crypt in the nationalist imaginary of the CCP is now increasingly what Hillenbrand has termed the 'cryptosphere': a digital participatory, propaganda strategy which aims to 'create an emergent social space' where state secrecy is now 'every citizen's business'.[105] The CCP's recent adoption of sacralised, British Empire–originating commemorative practices and a Russo–British style veneration for the Second World War is, I argue, a component of this change. The mystery in this imaginary is not religious, however, it is a national secret which must be protected in an era of 'Eternity Politics'.[106]

Globalisation's post-truth theatre of apparitions, 'fake news', hidden conspiracy and mischievous trolls epitomise eternity politics. In the fog of 'infowar' a sense of facticity and historicity fades to impressionist flashes of memory. The 1919 moment of silence on Armistice Day in the British Empire was intended as a ritual to enable access to the past in the present and process it individually and collectively, clearing the path to the future. But past, present and future are beginning to blur in the uncanny historical consciousness of contemporary society, and this has significant ramifications in a world where memory is becoming a critical determinant of social identification and political action.

Election analysis and Brexit breakdowns in the United Kingdom signalled these new trends of a politics of temporality. People now define themselves and their politics in relation to 'pastness' in the present more strongly than any other measure. People's relationship to history is becoming a more significant frame for the future than class, gender or political party. Nearly 80 per cent of Britons who believed 'things were better in the past' voted to leave the European Union.[107] In non-cosmopolitan 'backwaters' a higher proportion supported 'turning the clock back to the way Britain was 20–30 years ago'.[108] Meanwhile, remnant rituals of commemoration like Remembrance Day are now deployed on the same digital technology that may have accelerated the 'Back to the Future' Brexit vote.[109]

Shanzhai: nationalism, noise, signal and the oscillations of origin

For the arc of the communist twentieth century, in China, nationalist commemoration of China's 1919 was future looking. Since 1939, 4 May has been recognised as 'Youth Day' (青年节 *Qīngnián jié*). In 1959 Qīngnián jié was celebrated as part of the Great Leap Forward.[110]

In reality, Ah Q and 4 May were always hauntological. Ah Q demonstrates how 4 May, while a complex, contradictory incorporation of Western modernity is also shanzhai (山寨).[111] Shanzhai is a Chinese neologism – which gained large currency from 2008 – which refers to fakes, but the 'genuine fake'.[112] Etymologically, the term derives from a 'mountain stronghold' where bandits elude a larger authority in the classical novel *Water Margin* (水浒传). In the present shanzhai refers to consumer items which are produced using stolen intellectual property. Copied mobile phones are the most obvious example of the genre. Philosopher Byung-Chul Han has developed the shanzhai concept as a heuristic for Chinese traditional thought. To Han, a negativity of 'decreation', 'absence' and 'desubstantized' *Being* accompanied with an 'essence which resists transformation' is what 'dominates the Chinese awareness of time and history'.[113] There is no identity to a 'unique event'. Chinese tradition has an alternate perception of originality than the Western model. Thought is pragmatic, and shanzhai objects are non-metaphysical with no first origin.[114] The original in classical Chinese aesthetics (真跡 *zhen ji*) – is a trace, via which processuality and continuous change does not condense in a *presence*. Rather, Han argues 'Far Eastern thought *begins with* deconstruction'.[115] Shanzhai is a form of deconstruction – from the outset, as a form of Confucian constant – transformation.[116] Han suggests 'Maoism was itself a kind shanzhai Marxism', which enables it to mutate without contradiction into a kind of hyper-capitalism though its continuous hybridity. So, I would suggest, the nationalism (爱国主义) and formation of the CCP that was emergent in 1919–23 was a form of *shanzhai nationalism*. In literature, shanzhai was evident in how Western modernism was adopted in characterisation and language via tradition. Ah Q's identity, focussed on decreation and return to the void, expressed the notion of the 'original' as a form of subjectivity. Equally, Lu Xun's use of vernacular Chinese undermined the classical 'dead literature' of elites, as it championed literature's traditional semantic function in education and examination.

Communications technology facilitated shanzhai in 1919. The technicity of the telegraph amplified the shanzhai form of 4 May. The role of the telegraph as a 'signal trace' pulsed with the processuality central to the idea of the 'original' in shanzhai conception. The 'time axis manipulation' of a telegraph message and the binary oscillation of an absence/presence state in the signal form, which provided the trigger of the revolutionary century in the May Fourth Movement, was indicative of a form of Chinese modernity that is accelerationist.[117] In addition, the May Fourth Movement is an original as a trace which both incorporates an integration of the Confucian rituals of *Qi* and *Dao* as unified in a cosmotechnics, which thereby accommodates the notion of culture across time and space.[118]

The more recent commemoration of the May Fourth Movement in China expressed the continuum and expression as a *shanzhai* (山寨) *nationalism* (中国民族主义). The CCP has adopted international memory forms with 'Chinese characteristics'. Britain and her former Dominions have also experienced a memory boom since 1990.[119] Just as nations of the former British Empire have recently seen an expansion of memory, so has China, albeit in an ambiguous way. The commemoration of 4 May has undergone a transformation under Chairman Xi Jinping. Like the so-called resurgence of Anzac in Australia, even the ritual of Qingming – largely banned in the Mao era – made a comeback in the 1990s. Since taking power as Communist Party General Secretary in 2012 and president in March 2013, Xi Jinping has accelerated a turn towards tradition. Facilitated by Wang Huning, Mr Xi has devised the notion of the 'China Dream' (中国梦).[120] Launched just ahead of 4 May 2013, 'China Dream' is number three of the

'Xi Thought' mind map.[121] The map is a visualisation of 'Xi Jinping Thought', the ideological document launched at the 19th Congress in October 2017.[122] 'China Dream' has a complex integration of Chinese history and memory into its formula. As Ian Johnson points out, the 'role of history in China during the CCP era is complex, paradoxical. At once integral, and sanitised, erased. Suppressed and recreated to serve the present'.[123]

For almost a century, 4 May and Ah Q were a uniquely Chinese take on the remembrance of the Armistice and aftermath of the Great War. But from 2007, Lu Xun and Ah Q were gradually removed from school textbooks.[124] Lu Xun has been replaced by other, more foreign memorial forms. Like Russia and the United Kingdom, the CCP has formally adopted the state-sponsored sacralisation of the Second World War. Equally, under Xi Jinping, China has adopted the nihilist populist politics of eternity.[125] Now, far from Ah Q's maudlin modernist individualism, the memory cultures of the CCP resemble the mass participative memory cultures the British Empire developed between 1919 and 1921, and the transnational technologies of commemoration which have dominated British Empire diaspora international memory cultures ever since.

The 100th anniversary of these events in Chinese history was marked on 4 May 2019. The centenary was commemorated in China within a new, and highly technological, conception of history and memory. Xi Jinping's speech for 4 May 2019 stated, 'in the new era, Chinese youth should establish their belief in Marxism, faith in socialism with Chinese characteristics, and the confidence of the great rejuvenation of the Chinese nation and the Chinese dream'.[126] The inherent ambiguity of 4 May for the current regime meant that centenary commemorative events were not heavily celebrated on Mainland PRC.[127] However, in the lead up, First World War remembrance activities were examined and British expertise drawn upon. Based upon reported observances of PRC groups in the United Kingdom alone, the CCP have been actively learning about British origin commemoration forms and the activities surrounding the centenary of the First World War.[128] To mark the centenary, memory culture experts, such as Jay Winter, were invited to the Beijing-based academic events associated with 4 May in 2019.[129]

Processing the ambiguities of 4 May via transnational forms[130] arises from commemorative convergence. The CCP values decennial anniversaries, 1919 and 1949 in particular. However, 2019 was also the 40th anniversary of the Tiananmen Square Protest of 1989. The students of 1989 had started their protest around 4 May that year and saw themselves as the natural bearers of the 'Spirit' of 4 May 1919.[131] The 1989 history of Tiananmen Square has been actively repressed and censored in the PRC.[132] Much of the flooding of PRC-based social media with nationalist messages on commemorative days is to prevent social cohesion erupting at these moments. Control of the internet and its development since 1989 has also been haunted by the trajectory of Tiananmen Square.[133] For almost 40 years the figure of the 1989 ghost has haunted the memory interstice of binaries within the state cryptosphere. A core crypto binary exists, for example, between a specific demographic of the people who possess a living memory of the Tiananmen incident and the state that seeks to repress that memory. This reflexive bind between living memory and the state is a kind of allegory for a subtle but important change in defining the 'original'. The shanzhai hauntological has transmuted through 4 May, and Ah Q has now become the 'core conceptual metaphor for public secrecy in China'.[134]

Centenaries are the focus of Xi Jinping's leadership: soon after becoming leader, Xi specified deadlines for meeting each of his 'Two Centennial Goals'. China will aim to double its 2010 per capita GDP by 2021, when it celebrates the 100th anniversary of the CCP.[135] Second, it will become a 'fully developed, rich, and powerful' nation by the 100th anniversary of the People's Republic in 2049.[136] Once again, a century later, the spectre of empire hegemony and competition is emergent, this time between the United States and China. In the months that Ah Q was serialised and the CCP formed in late 1921, the first Naval Conference in Washington was underway.[137]

The most striking thing about the subsequent Washington Naval Treaties of 1923, as Kori Schake has observed, was their purpose to 'prevent Anglo-American competition'.[138] Britain remained the world's greatest naval power, but its hegemony was evaporating. It was American power which most threatened the empire, not Japan's. Churchill stated of the conference that the United States would 'have a good chance of becoming the strongest Naval Power in the world and thus obtaining the complete mastery of the Pacific'.[139] At this conference China had laid out ten proposals for sovereignty: it was not to be. This contest for the naval power in the Pacific continues a century on.

Liquid modernity: from wetware soft machine photography to Stack shanzh-AI silicon Deep Fakes

In 1919 a telegram from Paris concerning Qingdao had ignited a revolution. Now Qingdao on the Shandong peninsula is a location of one of the seven internet submarine landing cable stations in China where, to seek an isolated internet, information is managed and controlled via a complex process of deep package inspection and VPN management.[140] In 2019 naval hegemony in the South China Sea is as much a competition of information as it is of naval power. Maps of an empire's naval hegemony are redrawn in children's movies such as *Abominable*, or in National Basketball Association (NBA) TV graphics and tweets as plotted on charts.[141]

If the hegemony of empire is the ability to frame the rules of international engagement and then use those rules to create order amongst other states, the Armistice and aftermath of 1919–23 did not ultimately create peaceful transition between British and US hegemony in the Asia-Pacific. The question remains how will this transition between 2019 and 2023 begin to work itself out between the United States and China? History, memory and new technological empires will all play a part.[142]

Now the mercantile *nomos* of empires has been replaced by the challenge of planetary geopolitics of internet Stacks.[143] The literature of the Chinese cybernetizen is more likely to be that of science-fiction than Lu Xun.[144] Perhaps, living in a digital surveillance state, thematically relevant fiction might increasingly imitate *Blade Runner* and its themes of posthuman policing and secrecy.[145] The original *Blade Runner* film had been set in an aesthetically Pan-Asian-Pacific US city in November 2019. Produced mid-way during the centenary, *Blade Runner 2049*, set it in its namesake year, was a sequel to the 1980s original. In *2049* the protagonist's angst is cryptospherical because the burden is his awareness that he is fake, and freedom is a choice of self-sacrifice uncannily similar to the self-sacrifice valorised in First World War commemoration.

In his 1925 published work 'On Photography and Related Matters' (論照相之類) Lu Xun used the idea of the photograph to represent the technology of the 'foreign devils'.[146] Most analysts of this text make much of the folk fears of photography Lu Xun depicts 'like witchcraft', stealing 'a person's spirit' and 'foreign devils' excising Chinese eyeballs, storing them in layers in jars, to transform them into photographs and wire. But these tropes are used by Lu Xun merely to introduce the 'body' of the text, which more centrally deals with execution, dissection and hearts torn out, with 'menstrual juices and semen', with 'blood; excrement and urine'. A 'body is rent in two', he writes, becoming a 'Picture of Two Selves'.[147] The photograph Lu Xun that suggests most represents China is that of a 'single man: the Peking opera star Mei Lanfang' playing the character of woman. 'In China,' Lu Xun emphatically concludes, 'the art that is the most noble, most eternal, and most universal in China is the art of men impersonating women'.[148] Lu Xun repeats a version of this phrase three times in the text. Connected with a capture and storage of photography, which eviscerates, dissects and divides, the technology of 'foreign devils' is akin to the fixation on the cuts and gore of Nanjing massacre photography commemoration in contemporary China.[149] However, in conclusion, Lu Xun emphasises the pinnacle of Chinese *techne* to be identity 'passing' to an audience.[150]

Reading Lu Xun's 'On Photography' in 2020, it is impossible not to think of Turing's 'The Imitation Game' of man/woman/machine – the Turing Test: 'to consider the question, "Can machines think?"' whereby the 'object of the game for the interrogator is to determine which of the other two is the man and which is the woman'.[151]

The Turing Test conjures the 'ghost in the machine' that often inhabits cultural representation of future AI. The People's Liberation Army (PLA) of the CCP envisages that the future metric of global planetary power for 2049 will be '"intelligentized" (智能化) warfare, in which AI will be as integral as information technology has been in today's "informatized" (信息化) warfare'.[152] The Washington Naval Conferences of 1921–23 were a table-top negotiation concerning naval power in the Pacific. Geopolitical relations in 2021–23 will involve leveraging AI in cyber operations negotiations over approaches to AI safety or security (人工智能安全). China's AI security concerns are the foundation of strategic future threat narratives of quantum supremacy and hegemony in computational applications of cryptography as a 'mountain fortress'.[153] Lu Xun wrote as Britain stood motionless in a moment of silence on Armistice Day in 1924. Lu Xun foresaw 'grabism' in a storage image which resembled the recursive layered infrastructure of Bratton's conception of the Stack:

> The use foreign devils had for pickled eyes, of course, lay elsewhere, only the preparation was influenced by S City's pickling of cabbage, which is sure proof of the saying that China has great power of assimilation over the West.[154]

Cabbage or computation, China's continuous shanzhai adaptation 'is not the inwardness of the essence but the outwardness of the tradition or the situation that drives change onward'.[155] The 'Neo-Confucian belief that "all the myriad things are within me" ' and which 'man is the "spirit of all things" '[156] is an immanence rather than a Western transcendence.

From social technology and the telegraph to the shanzhai fibre optic ouroboros of data souls

The Versailles Treaty of 1919 divided up borders and calculated a balance sheet for the costs of war, and technologies of commemoration were formalised across the British Empire over the next two years. Lu Xun finished his essay on photography on 11 November 1924.[157] At almost precisely that moment in London, well-known Spiritualist Ada Deane took a photograph of the silent crowd during the two-minute silence at the newly constructed Cenotaph, the peak of the 1924 Armistice Day ceremony. Deane claimed that, when the over-exposed photograph was developed, it showed faces of men hovering amidst the crowd, which she said were the spirits of dead soldiers of the Great War. A few days later, the newspaper the *Daily Sketch* exposed the image as fake. Deane had stolen and cut and pasted the images of the faces of the dead in a crude proto-photoshop manner.[158]

On 2 May 1919, as telegraphs pulsed from Paris to Beijing two days before the uprising in China, French poet Paul Valéry published 'Crisis of the Spirit' in English.[159] Empires, he wrote, were 'watching millions of ghosts . . . meditating on the life and death of truths; for ghosts'. Meanwhile, 'the exploitation of the globe, and the general spread of technology, all of which presage a *deminutio capitis* for Europe' led Valéry to ask 'must these be taken as absolute decisions of fate? Or have we some freedom against this threatening conspiracy of things?'[160]

In 2020, reflecting on Valéry, Yuk Hui points out, the year marks the centenary of 'Crisis of the Spirit' and of 100 years of crisis.[161] The start of this century from 2000 to 2020 is a recursive trace of the previous 100 years, as information wars disintegrate the borders of nation states just as they seek to close them and as climate change, coronaviruses and civil disorder start to create an economics of sacrifice and loss requiring instant commemoration.[162]

Now on the threshold of a new century, where both the 'West' and the 'East' are entangled within a planetary infosphere of spiralling deconstruction, there has been a post-colonial return: a 'Journey to the West' of 'Shanzhai 山寨 Nationalism 中国民族主义'. In empires experiencing crises of diffuse causality, conspiracy theories swarm on social media seeking a monotheist truth of definitive 'origins': whether of a singular 'Patient Zero' of zoonotic transmission of SARS-CoV-2, US or People's Liberation Army lab-created viruses on the loose, a lone wildfire arsonist or a 'Deep State' Galapagos of Gonkai (公开) 5G conspiracy. Return in eternal politics is a reflexive epistemological 'aesthetic of the original preserved through the copying (east) rather than the authenticity of the ruin (west)'. Shanzhai nationalism in the West expresses itself in the Anglophone sphere as the recursive paroxysm of stasis as it fails to resolve into one copied form or another nor acknowledge what is metonymic or metaphoric.[163] Equally, China is not immune in this reflexive entanglement. Mimesis is radically integrated within alterity.[164] China may, in pursuing the 'China Dream', experience oscillations of memory and amnesia as itself, a new enthusiastic coloniser of an Other within a new geopolitical internet hegemony. In such a metanarrative, the CCP and PLA are in the PRC, perpetually policing the mimesis machine – whether in a *Blade Runner* set in 2019 or 2049 – to ensure shanzhai nationalism's alterity may require suppressing that very identity which is key to shanzhai reproductive iteration.[165] Perhaps the future commemoration of a century of the CCP's rule in 2049 will be haunted by a century of Turing's 'Imitation Game' more than the ghost of Ah Q.

Notes

1 Sarah Fling, "Spanish Influenza in the President's Neighborhood," *The White House Historical Society*, October 2, 2019, https://www.whitehousehistory.org/spanish-influenza-in-the-presidents-neighborhood.
2 Ibid.
3 John M. Barry, *The Great Influenza: The Story of the Deadliest Pandemic in History* (New York: Penguin Books, 2005).
4 Anonymous, "Mind-Boggling," *The Economist*, November 10, 2018, 60–61.
5 "Breaking News, World News & Multimedia," *New York Times*, 2020, accessed June 1. https://www.nytimes.com.
6 "China Pays 'Virtual' Respects to Ancestors," *BBC World*, April 4, 2020, accessed May 27. https://www.bbc.com/news/world-asia-china-52157455.
7 Stephen McDonell, "China Stops for Three Minutes to Remember the Dead," *@BBCWorld*, www.bbc.com/news/av/world-asia-china-52161087/coronavirus-china-stops-for-three-minutes-to-remember-the-dead; "China Pauses to Honour Those Killed by COVID-19," *@SBSNews*, www.sbs.com.au/news/china-pauses-to-honour-those-killed-by-covid-19.
8 Cao Desheng, "Top Leaders Mourn Virus' Victims," *China Daily*, April 6, 2020, www.chinadailyhk.com/article/126767?showpdf=true.
9 James L. Watson and Evelyn Sakakida Rawski, *Death Ritual in Late Imperial and Modern China* (Berkeley: University of California Press, 1988), 270; Edoarda Masi, *China Winter: Workers, Mandarins, and the Purge of the Gang of Four*, 1st ed. (New York: Dutton, 1982), 98; David Biello, "In China: A Moment of Silence to Mourn Quake Victims," *Scientific American*, May 19, 2008, www.scientificamerican.com/article/in-china-a-moment-of-sile/; Madelein Schreiber, "Silence China Quake Victims," 2008, accessed April 14, 2020, http://noosphere.princeton.edu/china.silence.quake.html.

10 "China Honors Martyrs with Moment of Silence at Tian'anmen Square," *CGTN*, September 29, 2019, www.youtube.com/watch?v=Wc3HwvW_5cc&list=PLJeut_81i6KuXnX_Zw-i–wAHd7e2hAx4&index=3.
11 Tom Sear, "This Remembrance Day, Digital Commemoration Makes It Impossible to Forget," *The Conversation*, November 9, 2016, http://theconversation.com/this-remembrance-day-digital-commemoration-makes-it-impossible-to-forget-65560.
12 R. I. George, "The Glorious Dead," *Times*, November 7, 1919; Edward Honey, "Five Minutes Silence," *The Evening News*, May 8, 1919; Adrian Gregory, *The Silence of Memory: Armistice Day, 1919–1946* (Oxford: Berg Publishers, 1994).
13 Steven D. Brown, "Two Minutes of Silence: Social Technologies of Public Commemoration," *Theory and Psychology* 22, no. 2 (2012): 234–52, doi:10.1177/0959354311429031.
14 George, "The Glorious Dead"; Honey, "Five Minutes Silence"; Gregory, *The Silence of Memory*.
15 Gregory, *The Silence of Memory*.
16 Adrian Gregory, *The Last Great War: British Society and the First World War* (Cambridge, UK: Cambridge University Press, 2008), 112–51.
17 Brown, "Two Minutes of Silence," 234–52.
18 Margaret Hillenbrand, *Negative Exposures: Knowing What Not to Know in Contemporary China* (Durham, NC: Duke University Press, 2020); Margaret Hillenbrand, "Selling the Cryptosphere in China," *Cultural Studies* 34, no. 4 (October 2019): 625–55, doi:10.1080/09502386.2019.1671470.
19 Badiucao 巴丢草 (@badiucao), "#LiWenliang the Whistle Blower Doc Who Post About the #Coronavirus #Outbreak in China Passed Away Just Now," *Twitter*, February 6, 2020, 9:57 a.m., https://twitter.com/badiucao/status/1225433402788040705?s=20; Bill Bostock, "China Declared Whistleblower Doctor Li Wenliang a 'Martyr' Following a Local Campaign to Silence Him for Speaking Out About the Coronavirus," *BIAUS*, April 3, 2020, www.businessinsider.com.au/coronavirus-china-li-wenliang-whistleblower-doctor-martyr-2020-4.
20 Stephan Feuchtwang and Michael Rowlands, *Civilisation Recast: Theoretical and Historical Perspectives* (Cambridge: Cambridge University Press, 2019); David Wengrow, "Review of Civilisation Recast: Theoretical and Historical Perspectives," *Antiquity* 94 (2020): 275–77, doi:10.15184/aqy.2019.226.2020.
21 Hillenbrand, *Negative Exposures*.
22 Ian Johnson, "China's Great Awakening: How the People's Republic Got Religion," *Foreign Affairs* 96, no. 2 (2017): 83–95.
23 Paulin Batairwa Kubuya, *Meaning and Controversy Within Chinese Ancestor Religion* (Cham, Switzerland: Palgrave Macmillan, 2018), 148–49.
24 H. Li and Y. Cao, "Time Will Tell: Temporal Landmarks Influence Metaphorical Associations Between Space and Time," *Cognitive Linguistics* 29, no. 4 (2018): 677–701, doi:10.1515/cog-2017-0043.
25 Antonia Finnane, "Sweeping Graves," *Inside Story: International*, April 7, 2020, https://insidestory.org.au/sweeping-graves/.
26 Andrea Chen, "First National Martyrs' Day Remembers Those Who Sacrificed for China," *South China Morning Post*, September 30, 2014, www.scmp.com/news/china/article/1604473/first-national-martyrs-day-remembers-those-who-sacrificed-china; I. Johnson, "In Creating 'Martyrs' Day,' China Promotes a Vision of the Past," *New York Times*, September 29, 2014, www.nytimes.com/2014/09/30/world/asia/in-creating-martyrs-day-china-promotes-a-vision-of-the-past.html.
27 I. Johnson, "China's Memory Manipulators," *The Guardian*, June 8, 2016, www.theguardian.com/world/2016/jun/08/chinas-memory-manipulators; Johnson, "China's Great Awakening."

28 Jacob Pouster, "China Outpaces India in Internet Access, Smartphone Ownership," *Pew Research Center*, March 16, 2017, www.pewresearch.org/fact-tank/2017/03/16/china-outpaces-india-in-internet-access-smartphone-ownership/.
29 Nicole Jao, "WeChat Now Has Over 1 Billion Active Monthly Users Worldwide · TechNode," *Technodechina*, March 5, 2018, https://technode.com/2018/03/05/wechat-1-billion-users/.
30 Zhihua Liu, "Qingming Festival Traditions Go Digital in China," *asiaone.com*, April 3, 2015, www.asiaone.com/asia/qingming-festival-traditions-go-digital-china; "Ancient Chinese Tomb Festival Goes Hi-Tech," *BBC World*, April 4, 2017, www.bbc.com/news/world-asia-39487437; Wei Cang, "App Offers Live Streaming of Tomb Sweeping Service," *asiaone.com*, March 31, 2017, www.asiaone.com/asia/app-offers-live-streaming-tomb-sweeping-service; "China Pays 'Virtual' Respects to Ancestors," *BBC World*.
31 Zhihua Liu, "Qingming Festival Traditions"; "Ancient Chinese Tomb Festival," *BBC-World*; Cang, "App Offers Live Streaming"; "China Pays 'Virtual' Respects to Ancestors," *BBCWorld*.
32 Q. N. Jasonqng, "Blocked on Weibo," *Tumblr*, June 4, 2014, https://blockedonweibo.tumblr.com/ & https://web.archive.org/web/20200524085008/https://blockedonweibo.tumblr.com/.
33 Gary King, Jennifer Pan, and Margaret E. Roberts, "How the Chinese Government Fabricates Social Media Posts for Strategic Distraction, Not Engaged Argument," *American Political Science Review* 111, no. 3 (July 27, 2017): 484–501, doi:10.1017/S0003055417000144.
34 Ibid.
35 Kori N. Schake, *Safe Passage: The Transition from British to American Hegemony* (Cambridge, MA: Harvard University Press, 2017).
36 Jim Mattis, "Summary of the 2018 National Defense Strategy of the United States of America," January 20, 2018, https://dod.defense.gov/Portals/1/Documents/pubs/2018-National-Defense-Strategy-Summary.pdf.
37 Great Britain and Foreign Office and The National Archives (UK), *Foreign Office Files for China. 1919–1929: Kuomintang, CCP and the Third International, 1910–1933* (Marlborough, England: Adam Matthew Digital, 2013); Tony Saich and Bingzhang Yang, *The Rise to Power of the Chinese Communist Party: Documents and Analysis* (Armonk, NY: M. E. Sharpe, 1994).
38 Johnson, "China's Memory Manipulators."
39 Brendan Thomas-Noone, "Mapping the Third Offset: Australia, the United States and Future War in the Indo-Pacific – United States Studies Centre," *@USSC*, 2017, www.ussc.edu.au/analysis/mapping-the-third-offset-australia-the-united-states-and-future-war-in-the-indo-pacific.
40 Benjamin H. Bratton, *The Stack: On Software and Sovereignty* (Cambridge, MA: MIT Press, 2015).
41 Stephane Beaulac, "The Westphalian Model in Defining International Law: Challenging the Myth," *Australian Journal of Legal History* 8, no. 2 (2004): 181–213.
42 David Kilcullen, "David Kilcullen Discusses," *C-SPAN*, March 10, 2020, //www.c-span.org/video/?470042-1/david-kilcullen-discusses-the-dragons-snakes.
43 D. Kilcullen, *Blood Year: Islamic State and the Failures of the War on Terror* (Carlton, VIC, Australia: Australia Black Inc., 2016); an imprint of Schwartz Publishing Pty Ltd.
44 H. Streets-Salter, *World War One in Southeast Asia: Colonialism and Anticolonialism in an Era of Global Conflict* (Cambridge: Cambridge University Press, 2017).
45 McKenzie Wark and Petar Jandrić, "New Knowledge for a New Planet: Critical Pedagogy for the Anthropocene," *Open Review of Educational Research* 3, no. 1 (2016): 148–78. doi:10.1080/23265507.2016.1217165.

46 Rana Mitter, *A Bitter Revolution: China's Struggle with the Modern World* (Oxford: Oxford University Press, 2005), 65; Alan Hudson, "Mr Science and Mr Democracy: The Pursuit of Modernity in China," *City* 12, no. 2 (2008): 161–70, doi:10.1080/13604810802167002.
47 Hamid Molwana, "Roots of War: The Long Road to Intervention," in *Triumph of the Image: The Media's War in the Persian Gulf: A Global Perspective*, ed. Hamid Molwana, George Gerbner, and Herbert I. Schiller (Boulder, CO: Westview Press, 1992), 36.
48 Molwana, "Roots of War," 36; Great Britain and Foreign Office, *Foreign Office Files for China*.
49 Schake, *Safe Passage*.
50 Michael J. K. Walsh and Andrekos Varnava, "Introduction: 'Britannia Pacificatrix': Imagining a Post-Armistice Empire Through British Art," in *After the Armistice: Empire, Endgame and Aftermath*, ed. M. Walsh, A. Varnava and Margaret Hutchison (London: Routledge, 2021).
51 Holly Buck, "The Tragic Omissions of Governance by Curve," *Strelka*, May 15, 2020, https://strelkamag.com/en/article/the-tragic-omissions-of-governance-by-curve.
52 J. Adam Tooze, *The Deluge: The Great War, America and the Remaking of the Global Order, 1916–1931* (New York: Penguin Books, 2015), 13.
53 Schake, *Safe Passage*, 225.
54 Guoqi Xu, *Strangers on the Western Front: Chinese Workers in the Great War* (Cambridge, MA: Harvard University Press, 2011); Guoqi Xu, *Asia and the Great War: A Shared History*, 1st ed. (Oxford: Oxford University Press, 2016).
55 Jianlang Wang, *Unequal Treaties and China*, vol. 1 (Honolulu: Silkroad Press, 2016), 53.
56 Tooze, *The Deluge*, 327–28; Mitter, *A Bitter Revolution*, 3.
57 Erez Manela, *Wilsonian Moment: Self-Determination and the International Origins of Anticolonial Nationalism* (Cary, NC: Oxford University Press, 2007); Shakhar Rahav, "Beyond Beijing: May Fourth as a National and International Movement," *Journal of Modern Chinese History* 13, no. 2 (2019): 325–31, doi:10.1080/17535654.2019.1688982.
58 Rahav, "Beyond Beijing."
59 N. K. Lee, "How Is a Political Public Space Made? – The Birth of Tiananmen Square and the May Fourth Movement," *Political Geography* 28, no. 1 (2009): 32–43, doi:10.1016/j.polgeo.2008.05.003.
60 When this chapter was presented in November 2018, there was little scholarly discussion of the role of the telegraph in these events. Since that time, GUO Shuanglin (Renmin University) has explored source material in his presentation "Telegraphy and Political Time: Understanding the May Fourth Incident in 1919," Global May Fourth, CGC 10th Anniversary, Beijing Center, Columbia University, May 14, 2019, www.youtube.com/watch?v=bJJurn7Df40.
61 James W. Carey, *A Cultural Approach to Communication* (New York: Routledge, 2008); Friedrich A. Kittler, *Discourse Networks 1800/1900* (Stanford, CA: Stanford University Press, 1990).
62 Ralph Schroeder, Neus Rotger, Diana Roig-Sanz, and Marta Puxan-Oliva, "Historicizing Media, Globalizing Media Research: Infrastructures, Publics, and Everyday Life," *Journal of Global History* 14, no. 3 (2019): 437–53, doi:10.1017/S1740022819000202. William J. Phalen, *How the Telegraph Changed the World* (Jefferson, NC: McFarland & Company, Inc. Publishers, 2014); Simone M. Müller, *Wiring the World: The Social and Cultural Creation of Global Telegraph Networks* (New York: Columbia University Press, 2016).
63 Yongming Zhou, *Historicizing Online Politics: Telegraphy, the Internet, and Political Participation in China* (Stanford: Stanford University Press, 2006).

64 Wang, *Unequal Treaties and China.*
65 Jarkko Haapanen, "Chinese People and the Others: Notes on Contemporary Chinese Nationalism and the May Fourth Movement," *Journal of China and International Relations* (*JCIR*) 7, no. 1 (2019): 1–20.
66 Chen Zhongping, "The May Fourth Movement and Provincial Warlords: A Reexamination," *Modern China* 37, no. 2 (2011): 135–69, doi:10.1177/0097700410391964.
67 Ibid.
68 Robin Boast, *The Machine in the Ghost: Digitality and its Consequences* (London: Reaktion Books Ltd., 2017), 182, 89.
69 Ranjan Ghosh and Ethan Kleinberg, *Presence: Philosophy, History and Cultural Theory for the Twenty-First Century* (Ithaca, NY: Cornell University Press, 2013), 27.
70 Wark and Jandrić, "New Knowledge for a New Planet."
71 Mitter, *A Bitter Revolution*; Jinhuan Dai, "Culture," in *Afterlives of Chinese Communism: Political Concepts from Mao To Xi*, ed. Christian P. Sorace, Ivan Franceschini, and Nicholas Loubere (Acton, Australia: ANU Press, Verso, 2019), 49.
72 Martin Weizong Huang, "'The Inescapable Predicament: The Narrator and His Discourse' in the True Story of Ah Q," *Modern China* 16, no. 4 (1990): 430–49, doi:10.1177/009770049001600403.
73 Paul B. Foster, "Ah Q Genealogy: Ah Q, Miss Ah Q, National Character and the Construction of the Ah Q Discourse," *Asian Studies Review* 28, no. 3 (2004): 243–66, doi:10.1080/1037820420002910 88.
74 Ibid., 243.
75 Gloria Davies, "The Problematic Modernity of Ah Q," *Chinese Literature: Essays, Articles, Reviews (CLEAR)* 13 (1991): 57–76, doi:10.2307/495053.
76 Xudong Zhang, "The Will to Allegory and the Origin of Chinese Modernism: Rereading Lu Xun's Ah Q – The Real Story," in *The Oxford Handbook of Global Modernisms*, ed. Mark Wollaeger and Matt Eatough (Oxford: Oxford University Press, 2012), 173–201, esp. 183, 201.
77 Jacques Derrida, "Specters of Marx," *New Left Review* 205 (1994): 31–58; Francis Fukuyama, *Have We Reached the End of History* (Santa Monica, CA: Rand Corporation, 1989).
78 L. Perrott, "Time Is Out of Joint: The Transmedial Hauntology of David Bowie," *Celebrity Studies* 10, no. 1 (2019): 119–39, doi:10.1080/19392397.2018.1559125.
79 Mark Fisher, "What Is Hauntology?" *Film Quarterly* 66, no. 1 (2012): 16–24, doi:10.1525/fq.2012.66.1.16; Mark Fisher, "The Metaphysics of Crackle: Afrofuturism and Hauntology," *Dancecult: Journal of Electronic Dance Music Culture* 5, no. 2 (2013): 42–55, doi:10.12801/1947-5403.2013.05.02.03; Mark Fisher, *Ghosts of My Life: Writings on Depression, Hauntology and Lost Futures* (Winchester, UK: Zero Books, 2014).
80 Fisher, "What Is Hauntology?"
81 Ibid., 24; Perrott, "Time Is Out of Joint."
82 K. S. Inglis, *Sacred Places: War Memorials in the Australian Landscape* (Carlton, VIC: Melbourne University Publishing, 2005), 277.
83 Inglis, *Sacred Places*, 273; Australian War Memorial (AWM), "Menin Gate at Midnight," @AWMemorial, accessed June 4, 2020, www.awm.gov.au/collection/ART09807/.
84 "Menin Gate at Midnight," *@AWMemorial*, www.awm.gov.au/collection/ART09807/.
85 Inglis, *Sacred Places*, 274; AWM, accessed June 4, 2020.
86 "Anzac Spirit | The Australian War Memorial," *@AWMemorial*, accessed May 27, 2020, www.awm.gov.au/articles/encyclopedia/anzac/spirit.
87 Gloria Davies, *Lu Xun's Revolution: Writing in a Time of Violence* (Cambridge, MA: Harvard University Press, 2013).

88 Wang Hui, "Intuition, Repetition, and Revolution: Six Moments in the Life of Ah Q," in *The Oxford Handbook of Modern Chinese Literatures*, ed. Carlos Rojas and Andrea Bachner (Oxford: Oxford University Press, 2016).

89 Xudong Zhang, "The Will to Allegory and the Origin of Chinese Modernism: Rereading Lu Xun's Ah Q – The Real Story," in *The Oxford Handbook of Global Modernisms*, ed. Mark Wollaeger and Matt Eatough (Oxford: Oxford University Press, 2012), 173–201.

90 Paul B. Foster, *Ah Q Archaeology: Lu Xun, Ah Q, Ah Q Progeny and the National Character Discourse in Twentieth Century China* (Lanham, MD: Lexington Books, 2006), 246.

91 Zhang, "The Will to Allegory and the Origin of Chinese Modernism," 182–83.

92 Yuk Hui, *The Question Concerning Technology in China: An Essay in Cosmotechnics* (Falmouth: Urbanomic Media Ltd., 2016), 65.

93 Ibid., 158.

94 Ibid., 29, 109–10.

95 Zhang, "The Will to Allegory and the Origin of Chinese Modernism," 183.

96 Stefan Goebel, *The Great War and Medieval Memory: War, Remembrance and Medievalism in Britain and Germany, 1914–1940* (Cambridge, UK: Cambridge University Press, 2007).

97 Sear, "This Remembrance Day."

98 Brown, "Two Minutes of Silence."

99 F. Kittler, *Literature, Media, Information Systems: Essays*, ed. John Johnston (Amsterdam: GB Arts International, 1997), 122.

100 Benedict Anderson, *Imagined Communities: Reflections On the Origin and Spread of Nationalism*, rev ed. (London: Verso, 1991), 9–10.

101 Bruce Scates, Rae Frances, Keir Reeves, Frank Bongiorno, Martin Crotty, Gareth Knapman, Graham Seal, Annette Becker, Andrew Reeves, Tim Soutphommasane, Kevin Blackburn, Stephen J. Clarke, Peter Stanley, Andrew Hoskins, Jay Winter, Carl Bridge, Laura James, Rebecca Wheatley, Leah Riches, Alexandra McCosker, and Simon Sleight, "Anzac Day at Home and Abroad: Towards a History of Australia's National Day," *History Compass* 10, no. 7 (2012): 523–36, doi:10.1111/j.1478-0542.2012.00862.x; Inglis, *Sacred Places*.

102 Anderson, *Imagined Communities,* 9.

103 Tom Sear, "Dawn Servers: Anzac Day 2015 and Hyper-Connective Commemoration," in *WarMemoryandCommeration*(*MemoryStudies: GlobalConstellations*), ed. Brad West (Routledge, 2016), www.unsworks.unsw.edu.au/primo_library/libweb/action/dlDisplay.do?vid=UNSWORKS&docId=unsworks_modsunsworks_44440.

104 John Williams, "Superstition," in *Afterlives of Chinese Communism: Political Concepts from Mao To Xi*, ed. Christian P. Sorace, Ivan Franceschini, and Nicholas Loubere (Acton Australian Capital Territory, Australia: ANU Press, Verso, 2019), 271.

105 Hillenbrand, "Selling the Cryptosphere in China."

106 Timothy Snyder, *The Road to Unfreedom: Russia, Europe, America* (London: Vintage Digital, 2018).

107 BEST, "Brexit Britain: British Election Study Insights from the post-EU Referendum Wave of the BES Internet Panel – The British Election Study," *British Election Study*, June 10, 2016, accessed June 2, 2020, www.britishelectionstudy.com/bes-resources/brexit-britain-british-election-study-insights-from-the-post-eu-referendum-wave-of-the-bes-internet-panel/#.XtZA_sARW73.

108 Will Jennings and Gerry Stoker, "The Bifurcation of Politics: Two Englands," *Political Quarterly* 87, no. 3 (2016): 372–82, doi:10.1111/1467-923X.12228.

109 Carole Cadwalladr, "Facebook's Role in Brexit – and the Threat to Democracy," *Ted Talks*, April 16, 2019, www.ted.com/talks/carole_cadwalladr_facebook_s_role_in_brexit_and_the_threat_to_democracy.
110 Mitter, *A Bitter Revolution*, 198–99.
111 Ibid.
112 Bruce Sterling, "New Shanzhai 山寨 (shanzhai)," *Wired*, August 24, 2018, www.wired.com/beyond-the-beyond/2018/08/new-shanzhai-山寨-shanzhai/; Andrew Chubb, "China's Shanzhai Culture: 'Grabism' and the Politics of Hybridity," *Journal of Contemporary China* 24, no. 92 (2015): 260–79, doi:10.1080/10670564.2014.932159.
113 Byung-Chul Han, *Shanzhai: Deconstruction in Chinese* (Cambridge, MA: MIT Press, 2017), location 46–47.
114 Gregory Jones-Katz, "Where Is Deconstruction Today? On Jacques Derrida's 'Theory and Practice' and Byung-Chul Han's 'Shanzhai: Deconstruction in Chinese'," 2019, *Los Angeles Review of Books*, May 8, 2018, https://lareviewofbooks.org/article/where-is-deconstruction-today-on-jacques-derridas-theory-and-practice-and-byung-chul-hans-shanzhai-deconstruction-in-chinese/.
115 Han, *Shanzhai: Deconstruction in Chinese*.
116 Ibid., 24; M. Wenning, "Shanzhai: Deconstruction in Chinese," *Philosophy East and West* 64, no. 1 (January 2014): 264–66.
117 Kittler, *Literature, Media, Information Systems*; Sybille Krämer, "The Cultural Techniques of Time Axis Manipulation: On Friedrich Kittler's Conception of Media," *Theory, Culture & Society* 23, no. 7–8 (2006): 93–109, doi:10.1177/0263276406069885; Kate Maddalena and Jeremy Packer, "The Digital Body: Telegraphy as Discourse Network," *Theory, Culture & Society* 32, no. 1 (2015): 93–117, doi:10.1177/0263276413520620.
118 Hui, *The Question Concerning Technology in China*; Carey, *A Cultural Approach to Communication*, 1983.
119 Jay Winter, *Remembering War: The Great War Between Memory and History in the 20th Century* (n.p.: Yale University Press, 2008); Jenny Macleod, "The Fall and Rise of Anzac Day: 1965 and 1990 Compared," *War & Society* 20, no. 1 (2002): 149–68, doi:10.1179/072924702791201935; Daniel Todman, *The Great War: Myth and Memory* (London: Hambledon Continuum, 2005).
120 Lutgard Lams, "Examining Strategic Narratives in Chinese Official Discourse Under Xi Jinping," *Journal of Chinese Political Science* 23, no. 3 (2018): 387–411, doi:10.1007/s11366-018-9529-8; Ane Bislev, "The Chinese Dream: Imagining China," *Fudan Journal of the Humanities and Social Sciences* 8, no. 4 (2015): 585–95, doi:10.1007/s40647-015-0099-2.
121 Xi Xinping, "TE_ximindmap.pdf," *The Economist*, 2020, accessed May 21, 2020, https://cdn.static-economist.com/sites/default/files/pdfs/TE_ximindmap.pdf; "Mind-Boggling," *The Economist*, 60–61; Kirsty Needham, " 'Consciously Mystifying': Xi Jinping Thought Mapped for the Masses," *The Sydney Morning Herald*, October 19, 2018, www.smh.com.au/world/asia/consciously-mystifying-xi-jinping-thought-mapped-for-the-masses-20181018-p50aln.html.
122 Jinping Xi, *The Governance of China*, 1st ed. (Governance of China. Beijing: Foreign Languages Press, 2014); John Garrick and Yan Bennett, "Xi Jinping Thought," *China Perspectives* 1, no. 2 (2018): 99–105.
123 Johnson, "China's Memory Manipulators"; Johnson, "In Creating 'Martyrs' Day."
124 Liz Carter, "China's War on Deep Thinking," *The Atlantic*, September 5, 2013, accessed May 30, 2020, www.theatlantic.com/china/archive/2013/09/chinas-war-on-deep-thinking/279384/.
125 Snyder, *The Road to Unfreedom*.

126 Bang Xiao, "Xi Jinping Celebrates 1919 Students Protests While Sidestepping Tiananmen Massacre," *ABC News*, April 30, 2019, www.abc.net.au/news/2019-04-30/xi-jinping-100-years-since-student-protests-in-china/11059206.

127 Q. Edward Wang, "The May Fourth Movement: A Centennial Anniversary-Editor's Introduction," *Chinese Studies in History: The May Fourth Movement of 1919: A Centennial Anniversary* 52, no. 3–4: 183–87, doi:10.1080/00094633.2019.1675438.

128 Paul Huddie, "@TomSear Indeed & they Have Been Coming to the UK to Learn. I Taught a Local & Central Gov Delegation in 2016 #China," *Twitter* (tweet), April 26, 2017, https://twitter.com/PaulHuddie/status/857118295446695938?s=20.

129 Aimee Fox-Godden and David G. Morgan-Owen, "Conference Report: Commemorating the Centenary of the First World War," *Defence – In – Depth*, February 28, 2017, https://defenceindepth.co/2017/02/28/conference-report-commemoratin,g-the-centenary-of-the-first-world-war/.

130 Helen B. McCartney and David G. Morgan-Owen, "Commemorating the Centenary of the First World War: National and Trans-National Perspectives," *War & Society* 36, no. 4 (2017): 235–38, doi:10.1080/07292473.2017.1384136.

131 Wang, "The May Fourth Movement."

132 Bang Xiao, " 'Consternation, Fear and Disbelief': Chinese Soldier Remembers Tiananmen Square Massacre," *ABC News*, June 1, 2019, www.abc.net.au/news/2019-06-02/tiananmen-square-massacre-30-year-anniversary/11163332; Louisa Lim, *The People's Republic of Amnesia: Tiananmen Revisited* (New York: Oxford University Press, 2014).

133 James Griffiths, *The Great Firewall of China: How to Build and Control an Alternative Version of the Internet* (London: Zed Books, 2019).

134 Hillenbrand, *Negative Exposures*; Margaret Hillenbrand, "Remaking Tank Man, in China," *Journal of Visual Culture* 16, no. 2 (2017): 127–66, doi:10.1177/1470412917703154.

135 Philippe Le Corre, "China: Xi Jinping's 2021 Countdown," *Carnegie Endowment for International Peace*, December 18, 2017, https://carnegieendowment.org/2017/12/18/china-xi-jinping-s-2021-countdown-pub-75100.

136 Shannon Tiezzi, "Why 2020 Is a Make-or-Break Year for China," *The Diplomat*, February 13, 2014, https://thediplomat.com/2015/02/why-2020-is-a-make-or-break-year-for-china/; Robert Lawrence Kuhn, "Xi Jinping's Chinese Dream," *The New York Times*, June 4, 2013, www.nytimes.com/2013/06/05/opinion/global/xi-jinpings-chinese-dream.html; CCP 2014, https://web.archive.org/web/20150502113010if_/http://paper.people.com.cn/rmrb/html/2014-05/28/nw.D110000renmrb_20140528_1-01.htm.

137 Mitter, *A Bitter Revolution*, 138; Schake, *Safe Passage*, 238.

138 Schake, *Safe Passage*, 237.

139 Ibid.

140 Griffiths, *The Great Firewall of China*; Tom Sear, "网络主权 (wangluo zhuquan) and Multipolar Data Sovereignties in an Era of Cosmotechnic Conflict A Critical Geopolitics of Data? Territories, Topologies, Atmospherics?" August 29, 2018, www.youtube.com/watch?v=YK3pyVMXcbQ; Tom Sear and James Griffiths, "Password123 Podcast: James Griffiths," 2019, https://soundcloud.com/unsw-canberra-podcasts/s1e1.

141 Paul S. Lieber, "Rethinking Communication Influence from a Strategic Communication Approach," *NSI*, January 2020, https://nsiteam.com/rethinking-communication-influence-from-a-strategic-communication-approach/; Paul S. Lieber, "Strategic Communication," *JSOU Quick Look*, February 2020, https://jsou.libguides.com/ld.php?content_id=52541507.

142 Tom Sear, "Dawn Servers: Anzac Day 2015 and Hyper-Connective Commemoration," in *War Memory and Commemoration*, ed. Brad West (n.p.: Routledge,

2016), 66–88, www.unsworks.unsw.edu.au/primo_library/libweb/action/dlDisplay.do?vid=UNSWORKS&docId=unsworks_modsunsworks_44440; Tom Sear, "Uncanny Valleys and Anzac Avatars: Scaling a Postdigital Gallipoli," in *Beyond Gallipoli: New Perspectives on ANZAC*, ed. Frances R. Scates (Victoria, Australia: Monash University Press, 2016), 55–82, http://unsworks.unsw.edu.au/fapi/datastream/unsworks:44110/bin5e1185fd-daf1-4f54-a89b-79512f11a218?view=true; Tom Sear, "#Anzac: Cloud Commemoration and the Centenary of the First World War," August 24, 2017, www.youtube.com/watch?v=RoUOn_j1qcY; Tom Sear, " 'The True Story of Ah Q': British Decline, American Power, the Rise of Chinese Nationalism 1918–1923 – YouTube," November 29, 2018, www.youtube.com/watch?v=xqUKtAEAhLo.

143 Bratton, *The Stack*.

144 Song Mingwei, "Representations of the Invisible: Chinese Science Fiction in the Twenty-First Century," in *The Oxford Handbook of Modern Chinese Literatures*, ed. Carlos Rojas and Andrea Bachner (Oxford: Oxford University Press, 2016).

145 Denis Villeneuve, "Blade Runner 2049," *IMBd*, October 6, 2017, www.imdb.com/title/tt1856101/.

146 Lu Xun, *Jottings Under Lamplight* (Cambridge, MA: Harvard University Press, 2017).

147 Ibid., 265.

148 Ibid., 269.

149 Hillenbrand, *Negative Exposures*, 45–89.

150 Benjamin Bratton, "Benjamin Bratton. Design, Philosophy and A.I. 2016," September 26, 2016, accessed June 3, 2020, www.youtube.com/watch?v=4TIUVeOO5tk.

151 A. M. Turing, "Computing Machinery and Intelligence," *Mind* 59, no. 236 (1950): 433–60.

152 Elsa B. Kania, "Battlefield Singularity: Artificial Intelligence, Military Revolution, and China's Future Military Power," *Center for a New American Security*, November 28, 2017, 12, www.cnas.org/publications/reports/battlefield-singularity-artificial-intelligence-military-revolution-and-chinas-future-military-power; Elsa B. Kania and Andrew Imbrie, "AI Safety, Security, and Stability Among Great Powers Options, Challenges, and Lessons Learned for Pragmatic Engagement," *Center for Security and Emerging Technology*, December 2019, https://cset.georgetown.edu/wp-content/uploads/AI-Safety-Security-and-Stability-Among-the-Great-Powers.pdf.

153 Kania and Imbrie, "AI Safety, Security, and Stability"; Jon R. Lindsay, "Demystifying the Quantum Threat: Infrastructure, Institutions, and Intelligence Advantage," *Security Studies* 29, no. 2 (2020): 335–61, doi:10.1080/09636412.2020.1722853.

154 Xun, *Jottings Under Lamplight*, 262.

155 Han, *Shanzhai: Deconstruction in Chinese*.

156 Xun, *Jottings Under Lamplight*, 263–64.

157 Ibid., 269.

158 Martyn Jolly, *Faces of the Living Dead: The Belief in Spirit Photography* (Carlton, Victoria: Melbourne University Publishing, 2006), 128–30; Brown, "Two Minutes of Silence," 234–35.

159 Paul Valéry, 'The Crisis of the Spirit' was written at the request of John Middleton Murry. 'La Crise de l'esprit' originally appeared in English, in two parts, in *The Athenaeum* (London), April 11 and May 2, 1919. The French text was published the same year in the August number of *La Nouvelle Revue Française (From History and Politics*, trans. Denise Folliot and Jackson Mathews, vol. 10, 23–36).

160 Valéry, "La Crise de l'esprit," https://en.wikisource.org/wiki/Crisis_of_the_Mind.

161 Yuk Hui, "One Hundred Years of Crisis," *E – flux* 108 (April 2020), www.e-flux.com/journal/108/326411/one-hundred-years-of-crisis/.

162 Tom Sear, "Bushfires Are 'Australia's War' and That Means We Need a Battle Plan," *ABC News*, February 6, 2020, www.abc.net.au/news/2020-02-07/

australia-bushfires-adf-operation-bushfire-assist/11931704; Tom Sear, "Xenowar Dreams of Itself," *Digital War*, July 23, 2020, https://doi.org/10.1057/s42984-020-00019-6; Sear and Griffiths, "Password123 Podcast: James Griffiths."

163 McKenzie Wark, "Byung-Chul Han: Shanzhai Theory," *Verso* (blog), March 25, 2019, www.versobooks.com/blogs/4283-byung-chul-han-shanzhai-theory; bunnie, "From Gongkai to Open Source," *Bunnies: Studios* (bunnie's blog), 2014, www.bunniestudios.com/blog/?p=4297; bunnie, "The $12 'Gongkai' Phone," *Bunnies: Studios* (bunnie's blog), 2014, accessed June 1, 2020, www.bunniestudios.com/blog/?page_id=3107; Cheng'en Wu, *Journey to the West*, ed. W. J. F. Jenner, 2nd ed. (Beijing: Foreign Languages Press and Distributed by China International Book Trading Corp., 1990).

164 Michael T. Taussig, *Mimesis and Alterity: A Particular History of the Senses* (New York: Routledge, 1993).

165 Bratton, "Benjamin Bratton."

8 An empire man on the road to Dominion independence

Robert Randolph Garran and the Armistice 'blunder'[1]

Colin Milner

The political relationship of the self-governing Dominions of the British Empire with Britain itself was transformed during the Great War of 1914–18. The eminent Australian international lawyer, James Crawford – a Judge of the International Court of Justice since 2015[2] – has defined this transformation as follows:

> It was the events of 1914 to 1918. . . which brought about effective Dominion independence. Imperial federation, mooted on various occasions, proved completely unacceptable. . . . Rejection of the only alternative made rapid Dominion independence virtually certain. The question is at what point international practice accepted the implications of these events.[3]

This transformation did not emerge from a vacuum. For decades before the war, the organisation of the political relationship between Britain and its self-governing settler colonies – known overall to fervent imperialists as 'Greater Britain'[4] – had been a matter of considerable interest and serious debate for key political and intellectual elites. This was certainly so in the new federal Commonwealth of Australia, which had been formally established on 1 January 1901, under an act passed by the Imperial Parliament at Westminster the previous year.[5]

The challenges of the Great War brought this matter to a head, as the problem of how to make cooperation and coordination effective for the imperial war effort could not be ignored. Many, including in Australia, desired closer imperial unity and consultation as a means to solve this problem, and some were prepared to consider the possibilities of imperial federation to achieve these outcomes in the future. But the latter proved too difficult to establish in practice, due primarily to the strong centrifugal forces at work for all the national governments of the empire.

The events of 1918–19, particularly surrounding the Armistice, demonstrated the realities in a dramatic manner. The debate about the way ahead was largely settled, even though it took some years for the consequences to be fully accepted and implemented. As Crawford observed, Dominion independence (except for Newfoundland, which was a special case, eventually becoming a province of Canada in 1949) was quite clear by the outbreak of another great war in 1939.[6] Still, the desire for closer imperial unity and consultation, though not in the form of imperial federation, persisted for some and particularly for important political leaders in Australia.[7]

This chapter provides a distinctive perspective on this transformation through the personal experience and reflections of the distinguished Australian constitutional lawyer and civil (or public)[8] servant Robert Randolph Garran (1867–1957). It examines how imperial tensions during the Great War years led to Garran's experience of the Armistice 'blunder' (as he called it)[9] in 1918 and its aftermath. It seeks to demonstrate that these were crucial events influencing Garran's own developing views on imperial relations and guiding him to the path which would ultimately lead to Dominion independence.

Why Garran?

There are good reasons why Garran is an enlightening choice to study in this regard. As inaugural Secretary of the Attorney-General's Department (from 1901) and first Solicitor-General (from 1916) of the Commonwealth of Australia, he was a trusted adviser to successive federal governments of all types, until his formal retirement from the Commonwealth Public Service in 1932. During the Great War, he became personally engaged in Australia's unprecedented level of involvement in imperial and international diplomacy as an adviser in London and Paris to the then Prime Minister W. M. Hughes (who was also serving concurrently as Attorney-General at this time and thus was Garran's portfolio Minister as well).

Assisting Hughes for meetings of the Imperial War Cabinet and Conference in London during 1918, Garran directly experienced disappointment at Britain's failure to consult the Dominions (including Australia) on the terms of the Armistice, which highlighted the conflicts of interest that could exist within the empire. Then, and later at the Paris Peace Conference of 1919, he led an able group of officials, notably including John Latham[10] and Frederic Eggleston, who played pioneering diplomatic roles in supporting Australia's political leaders. The key politician was Hughes, who evidently respected Garran's administrative, intellectual and drafting abilities and appreciated his trustworthy character.

Specifically, Garran offers a valuable perspective because he was a career civil servant enjoying secure tenure over a long period of time, rather than a politician subject to the uncertain whims of the democratic electorate. Unlike Latham and Eggleston, who each entered politics, Garran was continuously involved in Australia's executive government at the highest bureaucratic level for decades, which gave his views considerable authority and influence. He was engaged, after all, in establishing and developing institutions of government and a body of practice designed to stand the test of time. The existing Australian historiography of this period, understandably in its earlier stages, has focussed much more on politicians and political developments than career civil servants and the agencies in which they served, though there have been welcome signs that the balance is gradually shifting towards a more comprehensive assessment.[11]

Fundamentally, Garran was an establishment Anglo-Australian figure and a committed empire loyalist in the Australia of this time. Although Australian-born,

Garran's recent family background and cultural affiliation were not only British in general terms but essentially English, and notably London-centred southern English at that. These attributes were, however, cast on a British imperial scale. Garran's maternal line went back to ancestors in colonial Virginia, similarly of largely southern English family background and cultural affiliation, the most recent of whom had remained Loyalists at the time of the American Revolution. Garran's Virginian great-grandmother was a Randolph, cousin to Thomas Jefferson, as well as other descendants of the Randolph family who were significant in the history of the United States of America.[12]

As the son of London-born Andrew Garran (an editor of the *Sydney Morning Herald*) and Suffolk-born Mary Isham Garran, née Sabine (who was prominent in charitable causes in Sydney), a Sydney Grammar School boy, a graduate in Classics of the University of Sydney, and a practising barrister of the Supreme Court of New South Wales, the young Garran was completely at home in Sydney's Anglophile elite.[13] He was culturally and emotionally tied to the heart of an empire centred in southern England on the great metropolis of London but which found a colonial outpost at the Antipodes.[14]

Imperial loyalty was not incompatible with an Australian nationalism. Garran's involvement as a young man in the popular federal movement of the 1890s associated him closely, indeed somewhat paradoxically, with others of a comparable background and bent. The movement's leader Edmund Barton (who would become the first Prime Minister of Australia in 1901) and younger supporters, such as Thomas Bavin, Atlee Hunt and John Peden, had similarly elite educational and professional backgrounds to Garran. Instinctively, like these colleagues, Garran was more than a nationalist who campaigned for the federation of Britain's Australian colonies; he was a committed empire man as well. This sentiment was clearly expressed in the classic work he co-wrote with a Cornish-born lawyer and politician from Victoria, John Quick, and published in 1901, *The Annotated Constitution of the Australian Commonwealth* (still well-known to the Australian legal profession by the shorthand of 'Quick and Garran').[15] Although Garran had been to Britain once prior to the Great War (in 1907, to appear for the Commonwealth of Australia in a case before the Judicial Committee of the Privy Council[16]), the truly international dimension to his career would result from that tragic conflict.

The debate on imperial federation

Garran's association with Lionel Curtis and the Round Table organisation demonstrated his genuine interest in imperial and international affairs. Curtis was sent out in 1910 by The Round Table in London to establish the organisation, not only in Australia but in other Dominions as well.

The Round Table had been formed in 1909, primarily by a group of men (including Curtis) who had served as civil servants under Lord Milner's leadership in South Africa, thus gaining the appellation of 'Milner's kindergarten'. The formation of groups of younger men as disciples around an older, distinguished man in public life whom they admired, often in pursuit of objectives they considered noble, was a feature of this period; Garran's own experience as one of Barton's young men in the popular federal movement in Australia was comparable.[17] Marc Girouard has explained this 'band of brothers' phenomenon (this quotation, favoured at the time, was taken from Shakespeare's history play *Henry V*) in terms of the philosophy of imperialism and the elitist, even if not always anti-democratic tendencies it encouraged.[18] The Round Table had attractions for scholarly and high-minded civil servants like Garran.

Curtis was a proponent of imperial federation, which The Round Table was essentially established to promote.[19] In later life, when the possibility of imperial federation had disappeared, he would go even further and articulate a concept for world government.[20] For his part, Garran had demonstrated at least an intellectual interest in exploring the possibilities of imperial federation as a 'leading member' of the Imperial Federation League, and he would have been well aware of Curtis's aims.[21] One of the distinguishing characteristics of the early Round Table members was their conviction that the Dominions would never achieve full national status until they had a voice in the determination of the empire's defence and foreign policy.[22] This conviction on its own may have been sufficient to unite Curtis and Garran in their commitment to The Round Table.

The two men had evidently met when Garran was overseas in 1907. Certainly, Curtis wrote to Garran the following year that he would 'look forward to coming to Australia and to renewing a friendship of which you have shown such signal proof'.[23] Garran had prepared a paper for Curtis on the Australian federation when Curtis was involved in efforts to create a new federal Dominion in South Africa.[24] By the time they were together in London and Paris during 1918–19, Curtis and Garran had become as close, as friends and as colleagues, as was possible given the distance which had separated them most of the time.[25]

In February 1915, Garran was involved in preparing a draft article for *The Round Table* journal, which canvassed the issue of whether an Imperial Conference should be held later that year to discuss, among other issues, the principles of peace. This does not necessarily mean that Garran was the chief writer of the draft, but he was clearly engaged in its preparation.[26] He sent the proof to his portfolio minister, Hughes, who was then attorney-general in the Labor Government led by Andrew Fisher which had returned to office in 1914, seeking his opinion.[27] Hughes had also encountered Curtis in Australia in 1910 and arranged for him to meet Fisher and other notable people.[28]

Hughes was not in favour of the suggestion that an Imperial Conference be held at that stage. He told Garran that the Dominions:

> ought to be and must be consulted when the terms of Peace are being considered. I do not believe that any good could come from anticipating the positions which will exist at the termination of the war and/or discussing the subject at large . . . some very plain speaking will be necessary. We may hurt the feelings of one or more of our present allies. It is conceivable, nay it is probable, that a settlement of say a Pacific policy which would be acceptable

> to Britain – might be most distasteful to us. And we should have a right to be heard – for we should be chiefly concerned.

Perhaps more clearly than Garran, Hughes was aware of the potential for conflicts of interest between Britain and Australia in these matters. He had a lingering suspicion that, notwithstanding the existence of good intentions at the imperial centre, Australia might end up being ignored. On future imperial relations, Hughes advised:

> as for a re-adjustment of our relations with Great Britian [sic], that can wait. We ought to approach this question in calmer mood: War is <u>not</u> the normal condition of civilization. But Imperial Federation <u>must</u> – if it is not to be either an empty pageant – deal with the normal prosaic requirements of a Government whose constituent parts are scattered all over the Earth. Let us deal with this matter when we are not obsessed with this one idea of War!

He added:

> I think it would be good to suggest however that arrangements should be made so that the representatives of the Oversea Dominions should be in London (or Paris, wherever it is) when Peace is being discussed. We ought to have a chance to argue questions, not merely to say Yes! or No![29]

Hughes had foreshadowed to Garran much that would come to pass. Ever the practical politician, Hughes was anticipating the possibility of difficulties about the disposal of Germany's Pacific possessions, as well as the intentions of Britain's ally, Japan. The immediate outcome was the following statement, which quoted from Hughes's letter to Garran and appeared soon afterwards in an issue of *The Round Table* journal:

> The question of summoning the Imperial Conference for its appointed meeting in 1915, discussed in the last number of *The Round Table*, has received some attention in Australia. . . . A leading politician in the Commonwealth, whose opinion will carry great weight whenever a decision comes to be taken, can see nothing but embarrassment and possible danger in the present discussion of the delicate questions arising out of the changed position in the Pacific. Ultimately, of course, there must be discussion and with it, doubtless, some plain speaking on matters wherein the Imperial Government and the Australian Governments may not readily be at one. For this reason, Dominion representatives should accompany the British delegates who attend the Peace Conference, when that stage is arrived at. But as yet the whole situation is too uncertain, the object of the war on our part not sufficiently near achievement, for it to be wise to enter upon discussions which must be based on conjectures and possibilities rather than on accomplished facts. Nor, in the

> opinion of the same statesman, is the present the time for 'the re-adjustment of our relations with Great Britain'.[30]

Hughes had set out in pragmatic terms the fundamental conflict of interest which perceptive observers already were sensing was at the heart of the political nationalism of Australia and the other Dominions. The classic statement of this position had been made by Richard Jebb in his 1905 book, *Studies in Colonial Nationalism*, in which he advocated a looser association than imperial federation – in effect, an alliance of Britain and the Dominions – to accommodate the political realities as he saw them.[31]

Like Garran, Latham and Eggleston were members of The Round Table. But Hughes – though sympathetic – did not join them, perhaps reflecting the greater scepticism of an elected politician in Australia about the popularity and thus likely viability of this objective.[32] Indeed, imperial federation would be abandoned as a policy by the Australian Round Table groups at the end of the Great War. But this did not lead them to disband, as other issues relevant to imperial relations still commanded their attention.[33] Garran remained a Round Table member in Melbourne until 1928, the year after he had moved with his department from this temporary seat of federal government to the permanent national capital of Canberra.[34]

By then, issues and organisations extending beyond imperial relations were engaging Round Table members, too. In Garran's case, he was a founding member of the British (later Royal) Institute of International Affairs, established after discussions held on the margins of the Paris Peace Conference, and attended the meeting convened by Latham in 1925 which led to the formation of a branch in Melbourne. Significantly, no Round Table group was set up in Canberra during Garran's lifetime,[35] but he did convene the meeting which led to the establishment in 1936 of a branch of the newly separate Australian Institute of International Affairs there.[36] Garran also became involved after the War with the League of Nations Union.[37] In short, the question of imperial federation as a viable governance option for the empire to pursue had been answered in the negative. This was made especially clear when those most likely to support it, like Garran, moved their focus on to other priorities.

The desire for consultation

No major politician in Australia questioned the British government's decisions leading to the declaration of war in 1914.[38] There was wide acceptance in Australia that, as part of the empire, the nation had to play its part in the wider imperial war effort. Even Hughes later acknowledged that, in the circumstances, it was difficult to see how the Dominions could have been consulted before war was declared.[39] An important shift in political and official attitudes which occurred in Australia's case during the Great War was from not really expecting consultations with the British government on such matters towards expecting them as a matter of course.

Australian leaders were aware that, like the other Dominions, the actual extent of their nation's military support to the empire was more within their control, although obviously tempered (in the absence of conscription for overseas service) by the willingness of Australians to enlist voluntarily. This had initially been enthusiastic, but the long conflict took its toll in casualties and inevitably affected ongoing political attitudes. These factors were reflected in the loss of two referendums on conscription which Hughes placed before the Australian electorate in 1916 and 1917. His advocacy of conscription led to Hughes's expulsion from the Labor Party, but he continued as Prime Minister with the support of his core followers and erstwhile political opponents, eventually in a new Nationalist Party.

Over 330,000 men and women from Australia served overseas during the Great War: 61,520 died, another 153,500 were wounded or gassed and over 3,600 were taken prisoner, at a time when Australia's population was fewer than 5 million.[40] The sombre, round figure of Australia's '60,000 dead', used by Hughes to address President Woodrow Wilson of the United States in a tense episode of negotiation at the Paris Peace Conference in 1919, has entered the folk memory of Australians and remains an inspiration to creative artists for elegiac remembrance in our own time.[41]

An apparent psychological impact of the Great War was to reduce the overall confidence of Dominion leaders, including Hughes, in the capacity of the authorities in Britain to handle matters of war and peace wisely and well on behalf of the British Empire as a whole.[42] Hence, their growing desire for meaningful consultation and cooperation by Britain with their governments. But it did not start out that way. H. H. Asquith, the British Prime Minister at the start of the war, was not well disposed towards giving the Dominions a voice in the making of policy. Hughes had encountered Asquith's attitude directly when he visited Europe in 1916 and attended the Allied conference in Paris to determine economic policies towards Germany. There he was part of the British Empire delegation and only won, with difficulty from Asquith, the right to speak independently for Australia.[43]

A similar attitude prevailed regarding the conduct of the war's military operations. The national government in Australia was not directly involved in preparations for the Gallipoli landings, for example, despite the substantial commitment of Australian forces. Indeed, this tendency continued throughout the war, even when Asquith was no longer British Prime Minister. Britain did not consult Australia about the intense discussions on Allied strategy for the Western Front during 1917, even though Australian forces were to be involved in the planned operations.[44]

Hughes visited Canada, on his way to London early in 1916, and discussed the conduct of the war and the need for the Dominions to develop a voice in imperial foreign policy with the Conservative (later Unionist) Canadian Prime Minister, Robert Borden.[45] He gained a sympathetic hearing.[46] Borden had already tangled with the Asquith government in requesting greater influence over imperial policy on the conduct of the war; indeed, he had advocated Dominion influence over Britain's foreign policy even before the war, when some Canadian leaders, such as the then Liberal Prime Minister Wilfrid Laurier, were less keen, fearful of the potential for their nation to be drawn into imperial entanglements.[47]

Some at the imperial centre were now coming to accept that a new approach to relations with the Dominions was needed, at least for the War's duration. Just how much of this shift was due to Hughes's own advocacy is difficult to determine. But there is no doubt that he made a strong connection with the British public on his 1916 visit through his speeches, in which he urged more co-operation with the Dominions. Hughes was helped in these activities by his publicist, the Australian journalist Keith Murdoch, who also edited a volume of Hughes's speeches, published that same year with an introduction by David Lloyd George.[48] Murdoch would continue in this public-relations role when Hughes visited Britain again in 1918, though, by the time of the Paris Peace Conference the following year, they had fallen out.[49] It is evident from his diaries that Garran had a fair amount of direct contact with Murdoch.

Lloyd George succeeded Asquith as British Prime Minister in December 1916. He was more willing than his predecessor to recognise that the Dominions had a role to play in decision-making due to their contributions to the imperial war effort.[50] Indeed, he signalled his intentions early by having invitations sent out to the Dominions to attend an Imperial War Conference in London in 1917. The conference duly met from March to May that year. But Australia was not represented due to the timing of the 1917 federal election. Hughes was unsuccessful in having the timing of the election changed, as he had wished, so that he could attend. Unlike his South African counterpart, General Louis Botha, who sent his deputy, General Jan Smuts,[51] Hughes did not appoint a representative in his place. His suspicious nature meant that not even the former Prime Minister, Andrew Fisher, by then Australia's High Commissioner in London, was allowed to attend.[52] Hughes's credibility would be damaged in London as a result of his – and Australia's – failure to attend.[53]

In Hughes's absence, Borden firmly took the lead and secured unanimous approval for Resolution IX of the Conference, which provided that any post-war readjustment of the constitutional relations of the component parts of the empire:

> should be based upon a full recognition of the Dominions as autonomous nations of an Imperial Commonwealth, and of India as an important portion of the same, should recognise the right of the Dominions and India to an adequate voice in foreign policy and in foreign relations, and should provide an effective arrangement for continuous consultation in all important matters of common Imperial concern and for such necessary concerted action, founded on consultation, as the several governments may determine.[54]

This Resolution was the basis on which Dominion leaders formed an expectation that they would be consulted on all important matters of imperial foreign policy, including the peace terms to end the war. Garran appears to have taken it to heart, but David Lee has suggested that Hughes would not have liked it.[55] Much later, Garran acknowledged its importance as containing 'the germ of the most quoted paragraph of the Balfour Report of 1926', adding that it 'thus negatived the idea of an Imperial Federation, as was pointed out by General Smuts at the time'.[56]

An Imperial War Cabinet also sat alternately with the 1917 Imperial Conference.[57] It continued, insofar as this was permitted by circumstances, until the Armistice. Consisting of the British War Cabinet and the Prime Minister of each of the Dominions, the inclusion of the term 'Cabinet' in its name was 'something of a misnomer', as Garran put it.[58] Some had hoped it would become a permanent part of the empire's constitutional organisation, as Lloyd George himself had formally proposed in 1917.[59] But this did not happen.[60] Nevertheless, as Garran acknowledged in his memoir, 'The existence of the Imperial War Cabinet . . . inevitably suggested consideration of how Imperial relations should be conducted after the war'.[61]

The Armistice 'blunder'

Hughes returned to London in 1918 and Garran was there, ready to assist – indeed, he arrived in London beforehand, on 8 June.[62] Garran was thus present at the 'first session' at 10 Downing Street on 11 June, managing to speak with Lloyd George both before and after lunch, as he noted in his diary, and met Hughes on his arrival at Euston Station on 15 June.[63] Hughes then began to attend meetings of the reassembled Imperial War Cabinet, later maintaining that he and other Dominion leaders were resolved that their nations must have the opportunity to express their views before being committed to any war in the future.[64] Garran's role, as one of the Dominion officials, was essentially to be present in rotation with others as an assistant secretary at the Cabinet meetings, where he saw Lloyd George and Arthur Balfour, amongst others, in action.[65] But his more important role was as adviser to Hughes.

Soon Hughes, Borden and the Prime Minister of New Zealand, William Massey, were expressing their rage against the incompetence of the British generals on the Western Front.[66] Although few would have predicted it just then, the tide would shortly turn decisively against Germany. The United States had entered the war in support of Britain and France and their Allies in 1917, and President Wilson seized the initiative with a speech to the US Congress in January 1918 containing his famous 'Fourteen Points'.[67] These included the proposed formation of what would become the League of Nations.

Active hostilities against Germany and its allies were now entering their final months. In October 1918, a new German Chancellor, Prince Max of Baden, was appointed, and an armistice leading to a peace based on Wilson's Fourteen Points was sought. So, it was that the war-weary German Empire approached the United States, not the British Empire or France, to end the conflict. This left the Wilson Administration with the lead, the Allies had to fall in behind, and, crucially, this meant the Armistice, and in large measure the terms of peace, were agreed to without Britain consulting the Dominions.[68]

The Australian officials in London were, unsurprisingly, angered by this omission. As early as 7 November 1918, Garran had written in his diary:

> At Versailles Conference – supposed to be to settle armistice conditions only – peace terms have been settled – Wilson's 14 points with modifications – without consulting Hughes or Dominions. This is breach of an obligation, & serious trouble is brewing. Lunch at Australasian Club. Hughes spoke strongly.[69]

The following day, Garran recorded that 'Hughes returned to the charge.'[70] He wrote in his journal-letter on 9 November about:

> the extraordinary blunder made by the British Government in not taking Hughes, and the Dominions generally, into consultation when they were settling the peace terms. The Versailles Conference that has just been sitting was supposed to be settling the terms of armistice – a purely military matter; when like a bolt from the blue came the announcement that they had also agreed on the terms of peace. Seeing that they had promised that the Dominions would be consulted as to the terms of peace – and also that they had earned the *right* to be consulted, Hughes is naturally wild, and is saying so in no uncertain voice. The official reply is very lame – to the effect that they had discussed peace terms with the Dominions in 1917, and had talked about them during the War Conference of 1918; but of course Hughes's smashing reply is that those were general talks about a remote possibility, whilst this is a decision of actual terms of peace – terms which had not been discussed with the Dominions in any way. It may do untold harm to the Empire, and is altogether inexcusable and damnable.[71]

This was strong language to use in describing the state of imperial relations in the moment of victory – even in private – by someone like Garran, although, long after the event, he would be content to include this extract in his memoir. The fear of being ignored on the peace terms, which had underlain Hughes's February 1915 letter to Garran on the draft article for *The Round Table*, had come to pass. It is not surprising that on 10 November (a Sunday), the day before the formal end of hostilities, Garran was in the 'office most of day', according to his diary.[72]

Hughes was indeed wild at what he saw as this betrayal of the promised new era of imperial relations and vented his anger in the public arena. Neville Meaney has made the point that Smuts, who was clearly regarded by the British leaders as the outstanding Dominion statesman, had been consulted and had attended all the relevant War Cabinet meetings which discussed Wilson's proposed armistice terms, suggesting that Lloyd George slighted Hughes because of the difficulties he had caused rather than the fact that he hailed from the colonies.[73] Hughes, of course, would not have seen the involvement of Smuts alone as meeting the requirement for consultation with the Dominions.

Garran, naturally, was also alert to the larger significance of the Armistice and connected with the rejoicing of the crowds in London after it was announced.[74] But soon he, like Hughes, returned to the serious issues at stake for Australia and the other Dominions in how the matter had been handled by the British government. On 14 November, his diary entry stated: 'Lunch at Brit. Empire Club with the Agents-General. Hughes spoke on non-consultation as to peace terms'.[75]

The key Australian officials in London – Garran, Latham and Eggleston – agreed with Hughes and similarly did not take this turn of events lightly. The best group of opinion-makers at the imperial centre to whom they had ready access was The Round Table, which provided an arena where civil servants like Garran could make a difference. He made an entry in his diary on 21 November as follows: 'Round Table at Curtis's house . . . Latham and I maintained the breach of faith in not consulting Dominions. Interesting discussion – resulting in a general admission that "some-one had bungled" '.[76]

A few days later, Garran wrote again about the same gathering:

> In the evening, Latham and I attended a Round Table meeting at Lionel Curtis's house, to affirm the wrongfulness of the British Government in not consulting Australia as to the peace terms . . . we sat round the fire and Latham pleaded our cause. Lord Selborne was in the chair; and among those present were F. S. Oliver (*Ordeal by Battle*), Zimmern (*Greek Commonwealth*), Sir Valentine Chirol (*Times* Indian correspondent), Dawson (Editor of *The Times*). We had quite a good hammer-and-tongs discussion; and though they were rather against us at first, they came round and admitted that there had been a bad blunder.[77]

Latham recorded his impression in similar terms to Garran, but the official minutes of this Round Table meeting suggest that their position was not supported in general.[78] Eggleston had been unable to attend the meeting in person, but there is no doubt about his sympathy with the views of his two close colleagues.[79] The day after the meeting, Garran took time off to relax and went with Latham and friends to dinner at a Pall Mall restaurant and then on to attend a performance of the hit musical *Chu Chin Chow*.[80] The show's book and lyrics were written by the acclaimed Australian actor Oscar Asche, who also directed and appeared in this original stage production.[81] Garran and Latham might have reflected on the fact that, while an Australian could triumph in London's West End, the Australian government had yet to secure in full measure what they saw as its rightful place in the counsels of the empire.

Less than a year later, Latham expressed dismay at the lack of response to Hughes's public campaign:

> It will be remembered that in November, 1918, as soon as the armistice was announced, Mr. Hughes addressed a meeting in London, at which he protested most vigorously against the action of the British Government in consenting to the armistice, including as it did the Fourteen Points, without consulting

> the Dominions. This protest gained little or no support at the time, either in Australia, the other Dominions, or in Great Britain. The complacency with which the people of the Dominions accepted the position was, I think, due to the common belief that the armistice dealt only with naval and military subjects, and had nothing to do with the final terms of peace.[82]

This suggests that the proximity of the Australian officials to Hughes and the broad sweep of events in London in 1918 gave an edge to their reactions on this issue.

Let it not be forgotten that, when it suited them, virtually all the key political leaders failed to consult appropriately. Hughes could ignore his Australian cabinet colleagues in Melbourne at times, just as Lloyd George had ignored him in relation to the Armistice and Wilson had initially gone ahead in the Armistice negotiations with Germany without the concurrence of George. There was an outbreak of lack of consultation among leaders ostensibly on the same side in the war, reflecting the power relativities at play, the time pressures of fast-moving events and presumably also a wish to avoid the complications that consultations might bring.

What matters for this chapter, though, is the Armistice blunder's effect on the attitudes of the Australians in London as they prepared for the Paris Peace Conference. The immediate response was that Hughes sought distinct representation at the conference for Australia; Borden had already done so on behalf of Canada. Though their motivations differed somewhat, neither leader was seeking Dominion independence as such. The Dominions eventually achieved distinct representation as part of the British Empire delegation, after Lloyd George persuaded the other Allied powers to accept this resolution of the matter.[83]

So, Garran, Latham and Eggleston went off to Paris in support of their political masters. Fortified by their experience of imperial relations during the war and chastened by the shock of Australia's total exclusion from the Armistice negotiations, they were determined that their nation should have an influence on the outcome, at least on the matters of most direct interest to it. In Paris, they would experience more imperial tensions. An example was Garran's involvement in the difficult negotiations between the then British Colonial Secretary Lord Milner, Hughes and Massey about the 'C' class League of Nations mandate for Nauru, which their nations shared, and the division of its phosphate resources between them.[84] Garran's diary entries for May and June 1919 reveal something of these tensions.[85]

At the Peace Conference, Eggleston evidently prepared an insightful memorandum[86] which began as follows:

> The claim of the Dominions to separate representation at the Peace Conference is the logical conclusion of Dominion policy for the last 50 years. It is the direct result of the protest made by the Prime Minister of Australia in November when the Peace terms were settled without any consultation whatever. The difference in the attitude of the British Government is somewhat remarkable. The position now occupied by the Dominions is quite new – they

> are in diplomatic touch for all purposes with foreign nations. Such a change in the situation must profoundly affect Australian national policy and one of the most urgent tasks is to work out the implications of the change and see what they lead to. It is an entirely worthy ambition to manage our own case before the Peace Conference.

Eggleston was careful to deal with the realities of relative power in the situation faced by Australia. He recognised the possibility of conflict developing between Australian and British objectives on defence issues, for example, and concluded:

> The increased liberty and discretion given to Dominion policy carries with it the obligation of always seeing that no real divergence arises between the actual policy acted on by each branch of the Empire. This obligation is not dictated merely by a feeling of duty or loyalty to England but by a commonsense view of our own interests.

In this conclusion that, in effect, Australia's pragmatic sense of its own national interest was the most relevant factor in its relationship with the empire as a whole, Eggleston was drawing much closer to Jebb's view of the future of imperial relations, rather than Curtis's.

In due course, the Dominions were able to sign the Treaty of Versailles individually and become founding members of the League of Nations. To his credit, Lloyd George – perhaps still mindful of the negative impact of the Armistice blunder on his ongoing relations with at least some of the Dominion leaders – supported these aspirations. The Australians who had laboured at the Paris Peace Conference could now enjoy the satisfaction of knowing that their nation had secured a place in the counsels not just of the British Empire but of the wider world.

And what of Garran? We can be confident that, as a conscientious civil servant leading a team of officials, he would have read Eggleston's memorandum in Paris. But what were his own views at that time? Where did he stand as a result of all that had happened during the war years, on the future organisation of the empire and Australia's place within it? Evidently before the end of the Great War, Garran was grappling with these issues. Indeed, he wrote some notes[87] contrasting the ideas which Curtis and Jebb had put forward:

> We must either come closer together, or drift further apart. The latter means eventual separation. Curtis has shown conclusively that Jebb's 'Co-operation' idea means, in the ultimate analysis, alliance between sovereign Dominions – i.e. political separation and international agreement. . . . If that is the only solution which proves ultimately attainable, it will be a confession of failure, to maintain the Empire as an international unit.

But on the issue of organic union, Garran realistically acknowledged that 'it does not appear at present that the people of either the U. K. or any of the Dominions are so prepared.'

There is a hint of wistful regret in Garran's tone here. He had been, after all, sympathetic to his friend Curtis's aims, keen for closer imperial unity and certainly not seeking formal Dominion independence. Yet, by 1919 Garran had perceived, dimly and reluctantly, what would prove to be the final resolution of this debate. Writing his memoir decades later, near the end of his long life, he was much more reconciled to the ultimate outcome of Dominion independence. He recalled that imperial federation 'had considerable support in England, but very little in Australia, where the emphasis was on autonomy without the complications of any implied legal obligations' and compared this with Jebb's advocacy of 'a looser form of union' in which the Dominions would be 'autonomous nations loosely linked by a common allegiance to the Crown'. Garran concluded: 'It was the looser form of association that the course of history ultimately followed, acting upon the sound principle that the larger the area the looser should be the union'.[88]

If someone like Garran, with his elite Anglo-Australian background, active Round Table membership and strong British imperial loyalty could reach this conclusion, it is not surprising that most fellow Australians agreed. As Meaney has written, despite the strong emotional appeal of 'British race patriotism', Australians 'unwaveringly insisted on maintaining an exclusive political control over their own affairs'.[89]

Conclusion

There was still a way to go after 1919, until the Balfour Declaration of 1926 and its effective enactment in the imperial Statute of Westminster[90] in 1931 laid down the formal basis for Dominion independence.[91] In the interim, Lloyd George would make a fine-sounding statement at the 1921 Imperial Conference committing Britain to equality of partnership with the Dominions,[92] only to ignore its practical implications when, once again, he was caught in the time pressure of events during the Chanak crisis in 1922. On this occasion, Britain almost went to war with Turkey on the assumption that it would have support from the Dominions.[93] Hughes protested to Lloyd George privately at this time that:

> The Empire ought not to be pushed into a war, the Dominions ought not to be asked whether they will associate themselves with Britain after Britain has in effect committed them', adding that 'above all they should not be asked to join in an unjust or unnecessary war.[94]

How different this was to 1914. Dominion consent to or acquiescence in British actions on matters involving war and peace – the gravest decisions that any sovereign nation makes in its external relations – could no longer simply be assumed. This lesson was eventually learnt and, for its part, the Australian government would be consulted by the British government throughout the crisis, which led to the declaration of war against Nazi Germany in 1939.[95] As part of this transformation, the experience of the Armistice blunder was a particularly significant milestone for Garran and his close Australian colleagues, guiding them towards the destination of Dominion independence. For Garran, and indeed for many Australians at that time, Australia's national interest and a primary concern for its welfare would end up trumping interests and sentiments shared more broadly with others in imperial and international affairs.

Notes

1 The author is grateful for the helpful comments made by Professor Frank Bongiorno AM on earlier drafts.
2 International Court of Justice, www.icj-cij.org/en/current-members.
3 James Crawford, *The Creation of States in International Law* (Oxford: Oxford University Press, 1979), 238. Crawford's views were confirmed in the second edition, published in 2006.
4 Richard Lehane, "A Military Mission for Greater Britain: Edward Hutton's 'A Co-Operative System for Defence of the Empire'," in *Australia and the World: A Festschrift for Neville Meaney*, ed. Joan Beaumont and Matthew Jordan (Sydney: Sydney University Press, 2013), 101–19 at 101–4.
5 *Commonwealth of Australia Constitution Act 1900* (Imp) 63 & 64 Vict, c 12.
6 Crawford, *The Creation of States*, 238–39, 245.
7 James Curran, *Curtin's Empire* (Port Melbourne, VIC: Cambridge University Press, 2011).
8 Civil servants are usually called 'public servants' in Australia, and the Commonwealth (now Australian) Public Service refers to the main bureaucratic arm of the national government.
9 Sir Robert Randolph Garran, *Prosper the Commonwealth* (Sydney: Angus and Robertson, 1958), 249; quoting from Garran's journal letter dated November 9, 1918.
10 Latham officially reported to Hughes's deputy, Joseph Cook, who was also in London and Paris during 1918–19.
11 See, for example, Neville Meaney, *Fears & Phobias: E.L. Piesse and the Problem of Japan, 1901–1939* (Canberra: National Library of Australia, 1996) and the earlier sections of Carmel Meiklejohn, ed., *Achieving a Just and Secure Society, Attorney-General's Department, 1901–2001* (Canberra: Attorney-General's Department, 2001) and Paul Tilley, *Changing Fortunes: A History of the Australian Treasury* (Carlton, VIC: Melbourne University Press, 2019).
12 Garran, *Prosper the Commonwealth*, 13–14; Colin Milner, "Robert Randolph Garran and the Creation of the Australian Commonwealth," in *Australia and the World: A Festschrift for Neville Meaney*, ed. Joan Beaumont and Matthew Jordan (Sydney: Sydney University Press, 2013), 121–44 at 131–34; and, on the settler culture of Tidewater Virginia, David Hackett Fischer, *Albion's Seed: Four British Folkways in America* (New York: Oxford University Press, 1989), 207–418.
13 Garran, *Prosper the Commonwealth*, 3, 12, 16–25, 65, 70–79.
14 James Belich, *Replenishing the Earth: The Settler Revolution and the Rise of the Anglo-World, 1783–1939* (Oxford: Oxford University Press, 2009), 460. A similar point could be made about Garran's Virginian ancestors prior to 1783; see Julie Flavell, *When London Was Capital of America* (New Haven: Yale University Press, 2011).
15 Michele Maslunka, "Sir John Quick (1852–1932)," in *Australian Dictionary of Biography (ADB)*, ed. Geoffrey Serle, vol. 11 (Melbourne: Melbourne University Press, 1988); John Quick and Robert Randolph Garran, *The Annotated Constitution of the Australian Commonwealth* (Sydney: Angus & Robertson, 1901), 34.
16 Garran, *Prosper the Commonwealth*, 171, 179.
17 Like Garran, Bavin and Peden (but not Hunt) also became members of The Round Table; see Leonie Foster, *High Hopes: The Men and Motives of the Australian Round Table* (Carlton, VIC: Melbourne University Press, 1986), 192, 229.

18 Marc Girouard, *The Return to Camelot: Chivalry and the English Gentleman* (New Haven and London: Yale University Press, 1981), 41, 224–25.
19 Foster, *High Hopes*, 12.
20 Lionel Curtis, *Civitas Dei: The Commonwealth of God* (London: Palgrave Macmillan, 1938).
21 Foster, *High Hopes*, 210.
22 J. F. Kendle, "Foreword," in Foster, *High Hopes*, vii; John Kendle, *Federal Britain: A History* (London: Routledge, 1997), 80.
23 Letter, Curtis to Garran, February 5, 1908, *Family Papers of Robert Garran*, National Library of Australia (NLA), MS 2001/10/1.
24 The paper was evidently published as R. R. Garran, "The Starting of a National Government in Australia," in *The Government of South Africa*, vol. 1 (South Africa: Central News Agency, 1908), 373–89, Chapter XX. The Union of South Africa was created in 1910 but on a more unitary model than the Australian federation.
25 This is clear from Garran's diaries covering 1918–19, in *Family Papers of Robert Garran*, NLA MS 2001/3/21–22, which mention Curtis with some regularity.
26 This article does not appear to have been published as such in *The Round Table* journal. The evident practice was for most Australian articles to be subjected to group criticism and possible amendment prior to submission to London for publication in the journal; see Foster, *High Hopes*, 3.
27 Fisher resigned as Prime Minister and Hughes succeeded him in October 1915, while still retaining (until December 1921) the attorney-general's portfolio.
28 Foster, *High Hopes*, 18–19.
29 Letter, Hughes to Garran, February 27, 1915, *Family Papers of Robert Garran*, NLA MS 2001/13/1, typescript copy of the original.
30 This quotation is taken from the section entitled "The Imperial Conference' in 'Australia'," *The Round Table* 5 (1914–1915): 670–71.
31 Richard Jebb, *Studies in Colonial Nationalism* (London: Edward Arnold, 1905); also see Neville Meaney, *The Search for Security in the Pacific, 1901–14, vol. 1 of a History of Australian Defence and Foreign Policy 1901–23* (Sydney: Sydney University Press, 1976), 5–7.
32 Foster, *High Hopes*, 207, 209–10, 219.
33 Ibid., 3.
34 Ibid., 210.
35 The Commonwealth Round Table in Australia (CRTA) was set up in Canberra, in association with The Round Table in London, in 2002 (well after other Round Table groups in Australia had ceased to function). A major activity is the annual Anthony Low Commonwealth Lecture, held in conjunction with the Australian National University. Personal knowledge of the author.
36 J. D. Legge, *Australian Outlook: A History of the Australian Institute of International Affairs* (St Leonards, NSW: Allen & Unwin, 1999), 23–24, 31, 37, 46.
37 Garran, *Prosper the Commonwealth*, 408–9.
38 Neville Meaney, *Australia and World Crisis, 1914–1923, vol. 2 of a History of Australian Defence and Foreign Policy, 1901–23* (Sydney: Sydney University Press, 2009), 6; also see Douglas Newton, *Hell-Bent: Australia's Leap into the Great War* (Melbourne: Scribe, 2014).
39 W. M. Hughes, *The Splendid Adventure: A Review of Empire Relations Within and Without the Commonwealth of Britannic Nations* (London: Ernest Benn, 1929), 35–36.
40 Joan Beaumont, *Broken Nation: Australians in the Great War* (Sydney: Allen & Unwin, 2013), 1. The statistics given by Professor Beaumont are those of the Australian War Memorial and include deaths from 4 August 1914 to 31 March 1921.
41 L. F. Fitzhardinge, "William Morris Hughes (1862–1952)," in *ADB*, ed. Bede Nairn and Geoffrey Serle, vol. 9 (Melbourne: Melbourne University Press, 1983), 398. The world premiere of '60,000 Bells – A Peal for the Fallen,' by the distinguished

Australian composer Ross Edwards, was a highlight of the 2014 Canberra International Music Festival; see www.australianmusiccentre.com.au/workversion/edwards-ross-60-000-bells-a-peal-for-the-fallen/28656.

42 Margaret MacMillan, "Australia and Canada from the Boer War to the Great War," in *Parties Long Estranged: Canada and Australia in the Twentieth Century*, ed. Margaret MacMillan and Francine McKenzie (Vancouver: UBC Press, 2003), 13–33 at 18–19, discusses the psychological impact of the war on Dominion leaders, especially Hughes, in somewhat similar terms.
43 Fitzhardinge, "William Morris Hughes," 396.
44 Beaumont, *Broken Nation*, 67, 267.
45 MacMillan, "Australia and Canada from the Boer War to the Great War," 19.
46 John Darwin, *The Empire Project: The Rise and Fall of the British World System, 1830–1970* (Cambridge: Cambridge University Press, 2009), 335.
47 Ibid., 334; also see Simon J. Potter, "Richard Jebb, John S. Ewart and the Round Table, 1898–1926," *English Historical Review* 133 (2007).
48 Keith A. Murdoch, ed. *'The Day' – and After: War Speeches of the Rt. Hon. W. M. Hughes* (London: Cassell, 1916).
49 Geoffrey Serle, "Sir Keith Arthur Murdoch (1885–1952)," in *ADB*, vol. 10 (Melbourne: Melbourne University Press, 1986).
50 Beaumont, *Broken Nation*, 269, 272.
51 Darwin, *The Empire Project*, 335.
52 E. M. Andrews, *The Anzac Illusion: Anglo-Australian Relations During World War I* (Cambridge: Cambridge University Press, 1993), 132.
53 Beaumont, *Broken Nation*, 449.
54 Quoted in Garran, *Prosper the Commonwealth*, 299–300.
55 Foster, *High Hopes*, 83–84; David Lee, *Australia and the British Empire Between the Wars,* The Trevor Reese Memorial Lecture 2004 (London: Menzies Centre for Australian Studies, 2004), 10.
56 Garran, *Prosper the Commonwealth*, 299–300.
57 A. D. Ellis, *Australia and the League of Nations* (Melbourne: Palgrave Macmillan, 1922), 11.
58 Garran, *Prosper the Commonwealth*, 298.
59 Neville Meaney, *Australia and the World: A Documentary History from the 1870s to the 1970s* (Melbourne: Longman Cheshire, 1985), document 137 at 252–53.
60 Keith Hancock, *Problems of Nationality 1918–1936, vol. 1 of Survey of British Commonwealth Affairs* (London: Oxford University Press, 1937), 51.
61 Garran, *Prosper the Commonwealth*, 298.
62 Diary entry by Garran for June 8, 1918, *Family Papers of Robert Garran,* NLA MS 2001/3/21.
63 Diary entries by Garran for June 11 and 15, 1918, *Family Papers of Robert Garran,* NLA MS 2001/3/21.
64 Hughes, *The Splendid Adventure*, 51–52.
65 Garran, *Prosper the Commonwealth*, 155–56.
66 Darwin, *The Empire Project*, 336.
67 Meaney, *Australia and the World*, document 140, 254–56.
68 Meaney, *Australia and World Crisis*, 280–309; Christoph Mick, "1918: Endgame," in *The Cambridge History of the First World War*, ed. Jay Winter and The Editorial Committee of the International Research Centre of the Historial de la Grande Guerre (Cambridge: Cambridge University Press, 2014), 133–71 at 162–64.
69 Diary entry by Garran for November 7, 1918, *Family Papers of Robert Garran,* NLA MS 2001/3/21.
70 Diary entry by Garran for November 8, 1918, *Family papers of Robert Garran,* NLA MS 2001/3/21.

71 As quoted in Garran, *Prosper the Commonwealth*, 249–50.
72 Diary entry by Garran for November 10, 1918, *Family Papers of Robert Garran*, NLA MS 2001/3/21.
73 Meaney, *Australia and World Crisis*, 293–94.
74 Diary entries by Garran for November 11 and 12, 1918, *Family Papers of Robert Garran*, NLA MS 2001/3/21.
75 Diary entry by Garran for November 14, 1918, *Family Papers of Robert Garran*, NLA MS 2001/3/21.
76 Diary entry by Garran for November 21, 1918, *Family Papers of Robert Garran*, NLA MS 2001/3/21. Additional people mentioned in this entry as being present at this occasion (beyond those recorded in the quotation from Garran's memoir, referenced in the next footnote) were Coupland, Brand, Malcolm and Hitchins, as well as Christie of Canada.
77 Garran, *Prosper the Commonwealth*, 253.
78 See Meaney, *Australia and World Crisis*, 301–2 and also Foster, *High Hopes*, 84–85.
79 The author's reference to this occasion in an earlier publication suggests that Eggleston actually attended, too, which was not the case; see Milner, "Robert Randolph Garran and the Creation of the Australian Commonwealth," 140. Instead, Eggleston registered his views, which supported those expressed by Garran and Latham, in writing; see Foster, *High Hopes*, 84.
80 Diary entry by Garran for November 22, 1918, *Family Papers of Robert Garran*, NLA MS 2001/3/21.
81 L. J. Blake, "Thomas Strange Heiss Oscar Asche (1871–1936)," in *ADB*, ed. Bede Nairn and Geoffrey Serle, vol. 7 (Melbourne: Melbourne University Press, 1979).
82 J. G. Latham, *The Significance of the Peace Conference from an Australian Point of View* (n. p.: Melville and Mullen, 1920), 4. This is the published text of an address delivered on 23 October 1919 by Latham before the Melbourne University Association.
83 Meaney, *Australia and World Crisis*, 302–9.
84 Nancy Viviani, *Nauru: Phosphate and Political Progress* (Canberra: Australian National University Press, 1970), 42–43.
85 Diary entries by Garran for May and June 1919, *Family Papers of Robert Garran*, NLA MS 2001/3/22.
86 See Memorandum on the "National Policy of Australia," *Papers of Frederic William Eggleston*, NLA MS 423/6/386-407.
87 Notes by Garran, *Family Papers of Robert Garran*, NLA MS 2001/13/18. This document is undated, but it is clear from the text that it was written during the Great War.
88 Garran, *Prosper the Commonwealth*, 298–99.
89 Meaney, *The Search for Security in the Pacific*, 5.
90 *Statute of Westminster 1931* (Imp), 22 Geo 5, c 4.
91 But also note the comment in relation to Australia in Andrews, *The Anzac Illusion*, 224–25.
92 Quoted in Ellis, *Australia and the League of Nations*, app. A, 56.
93 Paul R. Bartrop, *Bolt from the Blue: Australia, Britain and the Chanak Crisis* (Rushcutters Bay, NSW: Halstead Press, 2011).
94 Meaney, *Australia and the World: A Documentary History*, document 177, 336.
95 Stuart Macintyre, *Australia's Boldest Experiment: War and Reconstruction in the 1940s* (Sydney: NewSouth Publishing, 2015), 18–20.

Part II

Cultural aftermaths

9 'The threshold of the British Empire'

Accommodation, coercion and the commemoration of a national Australian narrative of war at an imperial site of memory

Matthew Haultain-Gall

At the unveiling of the Imperial War Graves Commission's Menin Gate Memorial to the Missing, King Albert of the Belgians declared that Ypres was 'the threshold of the British Empire. Its name will stand for ever as a symbol of British courage and endurance'.[1] Some 90 years later, Ypres remains a significant British site of memory with thousands crossing the Channel every year to visit the town.[2] However, Ypres' place within the Great War narratives of other countries that constituted the empire has never quite been so assured, often overshadowed by sites of national – as opposed to imperial – significance. For instance, the selection of Vimy Ridge as the site for the Canadians most impressive war memorial has served to channel most of Canada's commemorative attention towards this site in France as opposed to the Ypres salient, while Gallipoli has long dominated the memory of the war in the 'Anzac' nations, Australia and New Zealand.[3] As one Australian ex-serviceman wrote in the Returned Sailors and Soldiers' Imperial League magazine *Reveille*, just a year after the Menin Gate's well-publicised unveiling:

> For Australia and Australians, Gallipoli symbolises many things which Ypres does not, though the toll of our dead and wounded in 'the immortal salient' was infinitely greater than the Peninsula demanded. Gallipoli occupies its pre-eminence in the national conscience because it provided for the sons of Australia the first actual test under conditions of modern warfare, and conditions the nature of which were immeasurably intensified by the character of the terrain. No trial of a more drastic order could have been made.[4]

For those familiar with the history of Australian First World War commemoration, this statement is not all that surprising; Gallipoli has always been the focal point of antipodean remembrance. However, other Great War engagements – notably Fromelles, Pozieres, Bullecourt, Le Hamel and Villers-Bretonneux – have all benefitted from concerted Australian commemorative efforts, particularly in recent years. Interest in the third battle of Ypres (commonly known as Passchendaele), on the other hand, is far more ambiguous.[5] This ambiguity is somewhat surprising, given the extent of the Australian Imperial Force's (AIF) involvement in the fighting in that 'immortal salient', where all five infantry divisions of the AIF were engaged in the same battle for the first time in the war. Moreover, by the time the AIF's main contribution to the offensive had ended, the Australians had suffered over 38,000 casualties, including 10,000 dead, far outweighing the Force's losses in any other campaign of the Great War.

One of the key reasons why Australians have not paid quite as much attention to the 1917 campaigns is due to Australia's rather limited memorial presence, or 'memory footprint', in Belgium when compared to other locations in France.[6] To understand how this has come to be, we must consider the legacy of Australia's wave of memorial building on the Western Front soon after the war had ended, as well as the Ypres Salient's status as both an imperial and a multinational site of memory. Australians alone have certainly not been responsible for these developments. During the interwar years, the Battle Exploit Memorials Committee[7] and the Imperial War Graves Commission (IWGC) were also key agencies in shaping Australia's memorial presence in the salient. More recently, this British influence over Australian commemorative activity has waned, and local Belgian agents have come to play an increasingly significant role in the development of AIF remembrance projects. The aim of this chapter is to reflect on how the interactions between Australian, imperial and Belgian agents have left Australia with a relatively shallow memorial footprint in Flanders, which has helped maintain third Ypres on the periphery of Australian First World War memory for much of the last century.

Treading lightly: establishing Australia's memory footprint in Belgium

While we can trace the origin of Australia's limited memorial presence in Belgium primarily back to Prime Minister William Hughes (see next paragraph), it is essential not to overlook the impact of British officials on Australian memorial schemes. Throughout the interwar years, the burial of the Australian dead and the erection of numerous monuments were carried out within a broader imperial project principally managed by the IWGC, which strived for a message of equality of sacrifice throughout the empire. The Commission's policies concerning the burial of Australian soldiers on Great War battlefields and the tensions they caused in the Commonwealth have already been explored by historians, most notably by Bart Ziino.[8] However, not quite as much attention has been paid to the relationship the IWGC and the Battle Exploit Memorials Committee (before the Commission took over its responsibilities) fostered with Australian officials as the latter planned to erect several memorials on the Western Front. This relationship was both accommodating and coercive, allowing Australian bureaucrats a certain freedom to commemorate the AIF's feats of arms, while pushing for the dominion's participation in the Commission's broader imperial project. In the case of Australian commemorative activity in Belgium, the Commission's strategies of accommodation and coercion can be clearly seen in two major memorial projects in the salient: the 5th Division's memorial at Polygon Wood and the Menin Gate Memorial to the Missing.

Of these two monuments, the Polygon Wood obelisk was the first to be completed. It was Prime Minister Hughes who first suggested in 1919 that each of the AIF's five infantry divisions raise a memorial at a site in either France or Belgium 'to mark the spot where it considers it made itself most famous'.[9] The divisional memorials, paid for by the government, were very different from those erected by local communities throughout Australia. Erected in locations that dominated the landscape around them, they were dedicated to the men 'who fought in France and Belgium'.[10] As Ken Inglis has noted, these monuments were 'the 1914–18 equivalent of regimental memorials raised on sites of earlier wars'.[11] In other words, they were not specifically conceived as 'sites of mourning', rather they celebrated the battle prowess of a specific division and the military heroism of its men.[12] Crucially, the prime minister also proposed that another 'memorial for the whole of the AIF', which was soon cast as a national memorial, be erected in France'.[13] As with the divisional memorials, this national monument was meant to be triumphalist in nature.

On the whole, the commanders of the infantry divisions agreed with Hughes's proposals for the memorials on the Western Front. The next step was to select the most fitting sites for the divisional monuments. To do this, General Talbot Hobbs, ex-commander of the 5th Division and chairman of the Australian Battle Memorials and Soldiers' Graves Committee,[14] held a conference with the AIF's division and brigade commanders. Of the five sites they earmarked for monuments, only the 5th Division's memorial at Polygon Wood would be located in Belgium.[15] As for the proposed AIF memorial, the prime minister, aided by Hobbs, selected Villers-Bretonneux as the most appropriate site because, as the *Sydney Morning Herald* informed its readers, this was where 'the Australian Divisions stamped their influence upon the war . . . in the hours of highest critical importance to the Allies'.[16] However, the commanders were concerned that of the 'two fronts' on which the Australians had fought in Western Europe, the Belgian front – where the AIF had 'lost as many men . . . as anywhere' – was being overlooked. A solitary divisional memorial would not be enough because, as the officers accurately predicted, 'the next generation will have forgotten the separate divisions and think only of Australia'. They therefore declared, in a motion that was carried unanimously, that 'a single memorial for the whole of the AIF . . . is not adequate' and instead they suggested that 'an Australian memorial, similar to that proposed for Villers-Bretonneux, should also be erected in the Ypres area'.[17] In keeping with the Australians' aim to erect memorials in surroundings they would dominate, the Broodseinde crossroads was eventually selected as the most appropriate site. Here it was envisaged that the completed monument would 'be sufficiently high to tower over any buildings that are likely to be built on the corners of the cross roads'.[18] The only voice missing at the meeting when plans for this second national memorial were put in motion was that of the Prime Minister.

Having obtained provisional agreement from its members, the Australians then sought permission from the British to erect the memorials. At this stage, it was not the IWGC that directly approved the Australians' applications but the British Battle Exploit Memorials Committee, which had been formed 'to consider claims made by units to erect permanent memorials of their exploits on battlefields'.[19] Normally, it was 'not the general policy of the Battle Exploit Memorials Committee to approve of any proposed site for a memorial submitted by a unit until the Committee has had an opportunity of reviewing and co-ordinating claims from all units'.[20] However, with the Australians pressing for a response 'so that men of the AIF may be involved in the memorials' erection for both 'commercial and sentimental reasons, before they leave for home', the Committee acceded to the demand for special consideration.[21] In doing so, it afforded a certain leeway to the Australians by adjudicating on the claims 'as they are received and without waiting for all other claims'.[22] In short, Australia (and the other dominions) received the first pick of memorial sites, without having to wait for other British units to submit their claims and, with one exception, the Committee quickly approved all the sites, including Broodseinde. The lone site whose fate hung in the balance was that of the 5th Division, as another British unit had managed to submit an early claim for the butte. Nevertheless, for reasons that are not quite clear in the Commonwealth War Graves Commission (CWGC) archives, the British chose to accommodate the Australians and gave the greenlight for the 5th Division's memorial. This decision, as it turned out, was a double-edged sword. The Australians may have gained a prime location, but the butte – 'honey-combed with tunnels and dug-outs' – was not properly filled in, leaving the obelisk at risk of sinking into the earth.[23] It would take officials several more years and further expenditure to stabilise the mound. Of arguably even greater consequence was the fact the erection of the memorial at Polygon Wood was fatal to plans for a national Australian memorial in Belgium.

When the Australian Battle Memorials Committee met again the following month, the British had finally confirmed the 5th Division's claim to Polygon Wood would be upheld. During the same meeting, Hobbs informed the committee that he had approached Hughes about the proposed second AIF memorial at Ypres and received a negative response: 'Mr Hughes did not think the monument at Broodseinde Ridge was necessary as the monument at Polygon Butte would be less than a mile away'.[24] However, the proximity of the 5th Division's memorial may not have been the only element that swayed Hughes's decision on this matter. The fact that the preliminary design of the Broodseinde memorial was based on the divisional memorial obelisks – albeit one of considerably larger dimensions – probably did little to convince Hughes of the project's importance. Moreover, there are indications that Hughes did not feel that the third Ypres campaign was particularly worthy of national attention and remembrance. Several years after the divisional memorials had been erected in Europe, he penned his book *The Splendid Adventure*, in which he branded the campaign as 'the most useless, bloody and deplorable battle of the whole war, which swept away the flower of the British Army, left the troops utterly worn out, their morale seriously impaired, and won nothing'. With no grand design, facing competition from a near identical memorial within a mile of its proposed location and referring to 'a most useless battle', Hughes's objection to a national monument in the salient is hardly surprising.[25] Nevertheless, his rejection of the proposal denied Australia a stronger memorial presence in Belgium, especially when compared to the concentration of structures built in the vicinity of Péronne in the Somme region of France. This not only included the National Memorial at Villers-Bretonneux but four out of the five divisional memorials *and* a section of Australia's 'most sacred acre' around the Pozières windmill site, purchased by the government in 1932 and upon which a commemorative tablet and fence were erected in the following years.[26]

Hughes's rejection of a national memorial at the Broodseinde crossroads meant there would be only two Australian-specific monuments in Belgium: the official battle exploit memorial at Polygon Wood and a smaller obelisk erected by the 1st Australian Tunnelling Company at Hill 60 (Zillebeke). Perhaps aware that the shelving of the national memorial left Australians with a fairly minimal memorial presence at Ypres, officials working at Australia House in London requested the IWGC change the layout of the Buttes New British Cemetery next to which the 5th Division memorial had been erected. While the monument itself, located on top of the Polygon Wood Butte, was already visible from a good distance and dominated the surrounding area, the Australians wished to extend the cemetery and lay out the grave plots in a manner that evoked the rising sun of the AIF, all at the expense of the Commission.[27] Naturally, this idea was less impressive than a national memorial and also a little perplexing, given that less than half of the identified graves in the cemetery actually belonged to men who had fought in the AIF. Nevertheless, the plan to stamp the symbol of the Australian forces into Belgian soil could be read as an oblique way of commemorating all five AIF infantry divisions' involvement in fighting around the region.

This time round the British were not quite so willing to indulge Australian plans. The IWGC's Director of Works was far from enamoured with the proposal and raised his concerns with the Commission's Land and Legal advisor, pointing out 'there would be very serious objections to graves being set out in a formal garden design. . . . It appears to me a very incongruous suggestion'.[28] In the end the idea was dispensed with when an officer from the Australian Graves Services (AGS) reported that the scheme was 'not practicable, for the ground in question is an absolute swamp'.[29] Withdrawing the plan avoided potential conflict with the IWGC, but the AGS officer's evaluation of the terrain was undoubtedly short-sighted as not only did the wood eventually grow back, but New Zealand also erected one of its seven monuments to the missing on the Western Front in approximately the same position as the proposed rising sun. Over the following years, the IWGC did react more favourably to other Australian demands at Polygon Wood, but these were rather more superficial in nature. For example, the Commission was at pains to find a way to beautify the stark butte, which was covered in thin, patchy grass that was prone to wash away. They believed that gorse bush might be a solution but had to backtrack when they learned that the plant was 'considered a pest in Australia', and its presence on the mound had 'offended the susceptibilities' of a group of Australians visiting the site.[30] Still, the Commission's resistance to the grander horticultural initiative proposed in 1920 ensured that an opportunity for the Australians to stake a stronger and more visible claim on the Belgian landscape had been passed up.

If the IWGC had somewhat curtailed the Australian memorial presence in Belgium by refusing to entertain a rising sun layout at Polygon Wood, several years later it coerced the reluctant Prime Minister Stanley Bruce to include Australian names on the Menin Gate Memorial to the Missing. Initially, the gate had been conceived as a monument to British military exploits, and both the Australian High Commissioner in London and Australian Battle Memorials and Soldiers Graves Committee recommended that the 'Commonwealth Government should participate in the scheme'.[31] The government, however, led by a man who did not consider the fighting around Ypres central to the AIF's experience of the war – and probably baulking at the approximately 15,000-pound participation fee[32] – showed little interest in the project. Even when the monument's scope was broadened to include names of the missing, Australian officials had originally shown a preference for inscribing the names of the missing on nearby cemetery walls.[33] Eventually swayed by forecasts of cheaper costs and the Menin Gate's favourable location in Ypres itself, the government agreed to cooperate with the IWGC's plan in 1922.

This decision was nearly reversed again two years later when the Bruce government decided that the National Memorial at Villers-Bretonneux would include the names of Australian missing on its walls. As Bruce wrote to the Commission's director, Fabian Ware, '[we] consider essential that names of all Australian missing both in France and Belgium should be recorded there (Villers-Bretonneux)'.[34] This would mean either inscribing the names on the Menin Gate and the National Memorial, the cost of which the IWGC was not willing to pay, or having the Australians withdraw from the Menin Gate project altogether. As Philip Longworth has pointed out, an Australian withdrawal would have threatened the Commission's 'spirit of imperial co-operation'.[35] His vision under threat, Ware quickly wrote back to Bruce informing him that work had already begun on the memorial and that the Commission would be 'seriously embarrassed' by any Australian reversal. Moreover, he claimed – without any hard evidence, it would appear – that the move might also upset the Belgians, who would be 'undoubtedly disappointed if these (Australian names) transferred to a monument in France'.[36] The ruse worked, and Australian officials, once again, acceded to the wishes of the Commission. The names of some 6,200 of the Commonwealth's men lost to the fighting in the salient, along with others from all other corners of the British Empire, with the exception of New Zealand, were inscribed on the monument.[37] Fortunately for the Australian government, the popular reaction to the memorial in the Commonwealth, later distilled in the tour of Will Longstaff's evocative painting *Menin Gate at Midnight* vindicated the decision to bend to the will of the IWGC.[38] Still, despite the inclusion of Australian names on the Menin Gate, the dominion's memorial presence in Flanders remained rather weak. After all, not only were the names of the Commonwealth's missing vastly outnumbered on the

Menin Gate, but Australian graves were a minority in many cemeteries around Ypres as well. Australian sacrifice was thus subsumed within a landscape of generalised British sacrifice. The 'Immortal Salient of Ypres' was a site of British or imperial memory first, an Australian site second.

During the interwar years, this lack of a strong monumental presence in Flanders ultimately had a limited impact in shaping the collective memory of the war back in Australia. As long-distance travel was beyond the means of most Australians at the time, the closest many would come to seeing any of the AIF or IWGC memorials and cemeteries in Belgium was through photos or paintings, such as *Menin Gate at Midnight*. More importantly, for those who did manage to head abroad, their journeys were not shaped by an abstract narrative of national military triumph, which memorials like Polygon Wood represented. Admittedly, battlefield tourists were drawn out of curiosity to places 'whose names are imperishable consequent on their connection with the Great War', but bereaved pilgrims and ex-servicemen travelled to the battlefields for more personal reasons.[39] The bereaved went in search of the final resting places of loved ones or to see their names engraved on memorials to the missing. The chance to pay respects to old mates and nostalgia motivated ex-servicemen to return to sites with which they had become familiar during the turbulent years of their war service.[40]

Putting Ypres on the map: the Australian remembrance trail

Nowadays, Australians' understanding of the First World War is no longer based on individual memories of lived experience, or 'living memory'. Instead, the conflict has passed into what Jan Assmann and Aleida Assmann term 'cultural memory', which they distinguish from living memory by generational distance and from cold, hard, 'objective' history by its emotional appeal to contemporaries.[41] In this transition from living to cultural memory, the meaning of the First World War in Australia has shifted; the dominant narrative, the Anzac legend, no longer focuses as intensely on glorious martial triumphs, which was clearly exemplified by the process behind the selection of the sites for the national and divisional memorials discussed earlier. Instead, the discourse surrounding Anzac is considerably more tragic, traumatic and anti-imperialist in tenor.[42] Nevertheless, as cultural memory is 'founded on durable carriers of external symbols and material representations', including sites and monuments, many contemporary acts of 'collective remembrance' have grown out of decisions taken during the interwar period.[43]

The revival of Villers-Bretonneux in Australian memory over the last few years is a good example of this. As Linda Wade's and Romain Fathi's studies tracing Australia's relationship with the French town have shown, Villers-Bretonneux, along with other sites intimately linked to the AIF's struggles on the Western Front, was forgotten in the years following the Second World War.[44] But as Australians have gradually 'rediscovered' these European battlefields in recent years, it has been the national, as opposed to divisional or imperial, dimension of the memorial at Villers-Bretonneux that has helped channel renewed interest in the commemoration of the AIF's 1916–18 battles. Since its establishment in 2008, the Anzac Day dawn service at the memorial has attracted thousands of attendees, and even outside this significant date in the Australian commemorative calendar, tens of thousands of Australians visit the French town annually.[45] Judging from visitor numbers to sites just across the Franco–Belgian border, the Polygon Wood monument and even the Menin Gate do not hold quite the same appeal for Australian visitors.[46]

Evidently, the legacy of Australia's interwar memory work has been incredibly influential in shaping the nation's present-day memory footprint in both northern France and Belgium. Yet this legacy alone does not sufficiently explain why other previously neglected sites – Fromelles, Bullecourt and Le Hamel – have garnered considerable attention and new, costly monuments in the past few years. Therefore, it is also important to consider another crucial difference between Australian sites in Belgium and those in France that have witnessed an explosion of Australian commemorative activity: Ypres and its surrounds are *multinational* sites of memory. This distinction between the multinational nature of commemoration around Ypres and the more concentrated commemorative focus on Australian exploits in certain French villages is evident when analysing the Department of Veterans' Affair's (DVA) Australian Remembrance Trail (ART) on the Western Front. Along with the multimillion-dollar Sir John Monash Centre, which opened at Villers-Bretonneux in 2018, the ART was one of the department's two major centenary projects on the former Western Front. Unlike the interwar years, when officials worked with and through the IWGC, this project has been built on relationships established directly with local agents in France and Belgium. The ART has centred on 12 principal sites, three of which are located in Belgium: Ypres, Zonnebeke (Polygon Wood) and Ploegsteert (known as 'Plugstreet' to British troops). While the first two sites are predictable inclusions, Ploegsteert is perhaps a little more surprising, given that, with the exception of Australians buried in nearby CWGC cemeteries, there is not much of a visible Commonwealth memorial presence in the area. However, as Joan Beaumont has noted, not only does each site have some 'intrinsic historical importance' related to the AIF's 1917 battles in Flanders, 'their inclusion owes something to the fact that they have established local museums on the First World War'.[47] These museums are the In Flanders Fields Museum (IFFM) in Ypres, Memorial Museum Passchendaele 1917 (MMP 1917) in Zonnebeke and the newly opened Plugstreet Experience 14–18 Interpretation Centre in Ploegsteert (Comines-Warneton).[48] None of these institutions are privately owned; they are overseen by the tourism departments of the Belgian *communes* in which they are located.

On the surface it might appear that inclusion in the ART could be seen as a significant step towards recovering the AIF's struggles in Belgium from the margins of the Anzac legend. As Stephen Miles has argued, in drawing travellers to particular locations, remembrance trails such as the ART serve to 'elevate' and 'enshrine' specific sites above others.[49] However, these developments in Belgium need to be put into perspective. According to DVA figures, not even a tenth of the ART's 10 million dollars' worth of funding has gone to the Belgian sites, which make up a quarter of the Trail.[50] Nor is it simply a question of how much money has been spent on each site but *what* the money has gone towards. In France, a large portion of the ART funds have been used to carry out extensive renovations on and create displays in the Bullecourt 1917 – Jean and Denise Letaille Museum, the Museum of the Battle of Fromelles and the Franco-Australian Museum in Villers-Bretonneux. While each of these institutions does not ignore the experiences of men and women of different nationalities in their exhibitions, a considerable amount of space is dedicated to telling 'the story of the Australian soldiers who fought' at Bullecourt, Fromelles and Villers-Bretonneux.[51] In Belgium, on the other hand, locals responsible for the IFFM, MMP1917 and Plugstreet speak highly of their relationship with the DVA and are keen to attract Australian visitors, but antipodean tourists are not their primary target audience.[52] As a consequence, Australian elements in displays are not as integral to the Belgian ART sites as they are in their Gallic counterparts.

At least in the case of Plugstreet and MMP1917, both of which have received sums of approximately $370,000 and $270,000 (AUD) respectively, Australian officials and local curators have worked together to install Australian exhibits in each institution.[53] In the smaller Plugstreet Interpretation Centre, an interactive display draws specific attention to the AIF's presence in Comines-Warneton in 1917 and early 1918. Made up of several touchscreens, the display contains some 200 photos and short videos that cover a vast array of subjects, including the establishment of trenches in the sector, logistics, mining operations, artillery bombardments and the battle of Messines, which was a prelude to the larger third battle of Ypres. It therefore offers visitors patient enough to browse the numerous images and films a relatively comprehensive visual overview of the time the AIF spent in the vicinity of Ploegsteert Wood and of the Messines engagement in particular. However, in aiming to tell 'the visitor about [the war's] effects in the area of Comines-Warneton, which was devastated by four years of bloody fighting and deprivations', Plugstreet's scope extends well beyond this 1917 battle.[54] The presence of the AIF was not a constant in the region throughout the war; therefore, it is hardly surprising the centre includes numerous additional exhibits that focus on the experiences of civilians and soldiers of all nationalities who spent time in the sector. The story of the Australians occupies a significant position, but it is not dominant within the centre. Ultimately it is just one of many that Plugstreet Experience 1914–18 introduces to visitors.

Like Plugstreet, an Australian presence at the MMP1917 is visible, but nonetheless subsumed within the broader narrative of the Passchendaele campaign, as recounted in a museum that concentrates on the military history of the war and on the third battle of Ypres in particular.[55] The original iteration of the MMP1917 did not have any distinct national displays amongst its exhibits. Yet, as with many other Great War–related sites in Flanders, it underwent an expansion in the lead up to the centenary and added sections with a specific national focus, and Australia has been one of the nations to benefit from this extra attention. Each section includes explanatory panels that give a brief overview of a particular nation's involvement in the 1917 Flanders campaign, various objects related to that country's experience of war and, in some cases, an interactive display. In the Australian section, an eclectic assortment of equipment, clothing, photos and community honour boards, amongst other objects, portrays 'an Australian story' that is related to the nation's experience of the First World War in general but has little to say about the AIF's experience of fighting in the salient.[56] Those few objects that do refer explicitly to third Ypres reflect the modern Anzac narrative, with its emphasis on tragedy, futility and human frailty. These include the death plaques of the three Seabrook brothers killed during the battle of Menin Road and a short, looped video of aged veteran Frank MacDonald describing the chaos of a battle that had been fought over ground that was 'all mud and water'. The interactive display, which provides curious visitors with very short accounts of the AIF's third Ypres battle, also highlights Australian sacrifices 'in terrible conditions which made the fighting men reach the lowest possible depths of human misery'. Yet, although this section serves to present a somewhat distinctive Australian perspective on the Great War and at third Ypres in the MMP1917, the AIF's history in Belgium does not receive any particularly special treatment from the museum either. The other nation-specific sections are based on the same layout and made up of similar objects. Moreover, given that the description of the general military history of third Ypres comes earlier on in the exhibition, these sections can hardly be considered central to the museum's main narrative.

The third Belgian museum on the Remembrance Trail, the IFFM in Ypres, aims to present a much wider history of the First World War in Flanders than either the Plugstreet Centre or the MMP1917, and does not attempt to distinguish between the involvement of particular nations. Instead, its focus on the 'broad story' and its underlying message of peace aim to highlight the commonalities of experience and suffering between the belligerents.[57] Inclusion in the ART has not seen the IFFM deviate from its decidedly internationalist objectives, nor does it appear that the institution has received any publicity-worthy sum of ART money, although Australian officials were reportedly involved in developing some content following its refurbishment in 2012.[58] At this museum, one is hard-pressed to find anything at all that acknowledges the Australians specifically. Observant visitors to the IFFM may notice a Brodie helmet bearing the colours of the 2nd Anzac Mounted Regiment or an Australian correspondence set, which are displayed alongside other objects that refer to the 'multicultural' nature of war in the salient. Those who 'log in' with the IFFM's electronic poppy bracelet at several points in the museum may also learn about the experiences of individual Australians, such as Fanny Seabrook, mother of the Seabrook brothers, whose death plaques are on display in the MMP1917. Still, these are only fleeting allusions to the Australians compared to more sustained Anzac references in other locations, especially France.

Looking for an Australian corner of Belgium

The commemoration of the AIF's exploits on the Western Front has accelerated in recent years, and although third Ypres has not been entirely overlooked, it still remains on the fringes of major commemorative projects. The most significant developments encouraging Australians to commemorate the sacrifices and achievements of their countrymen and women on the Western Front have been reserved for French villages. This situation has its roots in the interwar years and the outcome of Australian and British exchanges over memorial plans. Were it not for the Commission asserting greater dominion participation in its imperial project, Australia's memory footprint in Belgium would be even more shallow than it is today. As the imperial elements of Australia's First World War narrative have been toned down, Hughes's rejection of the proposal to erect a national memorial in the former salient ensured the Somme would become the centre of renewed commemoration on the Western Front. Yet, this is not the sole reason why Australian initiatives have been concentrated elsewhere. It is hard to see Ypres, Zonnebeke or Comines-Warneton claiming to be 'a corner of Australia' in Belgium, like Villers-Bretonneux does in France. After all, while isolated villages on the Somme and French Flanders have become specifically associated with Australia, these Belgian localities are studded with numerous memorials from other countries. The former Ypres salient is a truly multinational site of memory, and this is not only reflected in its monuments but also in the institutions that make up the Belgian ART sites, where the Australians are far from central to the IFFM, MMP1917 or Plugstreet exhibitions. Given that the Anzac legend elevates the Australian experience of the Great War above all others, it is not unexpected that the Australian commemorative turn to the Western Front has centred on particular French townships, while less has been done to build on the Australian presence that has existed in the salient since the interwar years. In Belgium, antipodean travellers have to look much harder for traces of the AIF than in a handful of French villages.

Notes

1 *Sydney Morning Herald*, July 26, 1927.

2 M. Connelly and S. Goebel, *Ypres: Great Battles* (Oxford: Oxford University Press, 2019), 180–87.

3 J. F. Vance, *Death So Noble: Memory, Meaning and the First World War* (Vancouver: UBC Press, 1997), 60; G. R. Bird, "Landscape, Soundscape and Youth: Memorable Moments at the 90th Commemoration of the Battle of Vimy Ridge, 2007," in *Battlefield Events: Landscape, Commemoration and Heritage*, ed. K. Reeves, G. R. Bird, L. James, B. Stichelbaut, and J. Bourgeois (Abingdon: Routledge, 2016), 52–53, 57; J. Phillips, "Passchendaele: Remembering and Forgetting in New Zealand," in *The Myriad Legacies of 1917: A Year of War and Revolution*, ed. M. Abbenhuis, N. Atkinson, K. Baird, and G. Romano (Basingstoke: Palgrave Macmillan, 2018), 252–54, doi:10.1007/978-3-319-73685-3.

4 "Observer", "Gallipoli on the Film," *Reveille*, July 31, 1928.

5 J. Beaumont, *Broken Nation: Australians in the Great War* (Crows Nest, NSW: Allen & Unwin, 2013), 391.

6 J. Beaumont, "Australia's Global Memory Footprint: Memorial Building on the Western Front, 1916–2015," *Australian Historical Studies* 46, no. 1 (2013): 45–63, doi:10.1080/1031461X.2014.998246.

7 This committee was sometimes referred to as the 'Battle Memorials Committee' in Australian sources. See National Archives of Australia (NAA) A2909 AGS1/2/1, Minutes April 29.

8 B. Ziino, *A Distant Grief: Australians, War Graves and the Great War* (Crawley, WA: University of Western Australia, 2007).
9 *Australian War Memorial* (AWM) 27 623/3, Extracts from Report of Conference held by G.O.C Australian Corps, Ham-sur-Heure, March 14, 1919.
10 5th Divisional Memorial Plaque inscription, Polygon Wood, Zonnebeke, Belgium.
11 K. S. Inglis, *Sacred Places: War Memorials in the Australian Landscape*, 3rd ed. (Carlton, VIC: Melbourne University Press, 2008), 247.
12 Jay Winter, *Sites of Memory, Sites of Mourning: The Great War in European Cultural History* (Cambridge: Cambridge University Press, 1995).
13 AWM27 623/3, Report Extract March 14, 1919.
14 Committee members included former Prime Minister Andrew Fisher, who was currently High Commissioner for Australia in London and leading AIF officers, such as General Birdwood and Major General White.
15 The 1st Division's memorial was erected at Pozières; the 2nd Division memorial at Mt St Quentin; the 3rd Division memorial at Sailly-le-Sec and the 4th Division memorial at Bellenglise.
16 *Sydney Morning Herald*, July 22, 1938. It should be noted that Hobbs was not an entirely neutral adviser on this matter. It was his division that had helped hold the line on April 24 and then recapture the town on the following day. According to Joan Beaumont, he felt that his division had not been given enough credit for the action. Beaumont, *Broken Nation*.
17 AWM27 623/3, Report Extract, March 14, 1919.
18 NAA: A2909 AGS6/1/5 PART1, Keesing, "Particulars of Australian War Memorials," April 10, 1919 and Consulting Engineer to AIF HQ London, March 25, 1920, Memorials – Western Theatre General.
19 AWM27 623/9, Army Order, April 12, 1919.
20 Commonwealth War Graves Commission (CWGC) WG857/3 Pt. 1, War Office to Ware, April 25, 1919.
21 CWGC: WG857/3 Pt. 1, Australia House to Anglo-French Mixed Committee, April 20, 1919.
22 CWGC: WG857/3 Pt. 1, War Office to Ware, April 25, 1919.
23 NAA: MP367/1, Extract from Seccombe Report, January 19, 1922.
24 NAA: A2909 AGS1/2/1, Minutes May 29, 1919.
25 W. M. Hughes, *The Splendid Adventure: A Review of Empire Relations Within and Without the Commonwealth of Britannic Nations* (London: Ernest Benn, 1929), 62–65.
26 Australia's official war correspondent and official historian C. E. W. Bean was the first to raise the idea of purchasing a block of land at Pozières during third Ypres, and he remained instrumental in ensuring the plan came to fruition. AWM38 3DRL 6673 403, Bean and Treloar, 1930–1935.
27 CWGC: WG 857/3/1, Ingpen to IWGC, October 4, 1919 and Hogben to Ware, February 3, 1920.
28 CWGC: WG 857/3/1, Director of Works to Land and Legal Adviser, February 24, 1920.
29 NAA: A2909 AGS6/1/5 PART 1, Consulting Engineer to AIF HQ London, March 25, 1920.
30 NAA: WG 857/3/1, Parker 5th Australian Divisional Memorial Report April 6, 1925.
31 NAA: A6006, Cabinet paper March 15, 1921.
32 NAA: A461 K370/1/15, High Commissioner to Prime Minister's Department, January 13, 1921.
33 Ziino, *A Distant Grief*, 105.
34 CWGC: WG 219/2/1 Pt. 2, Bruce cited in Hogben to Ridger, May 3, 1924.
35 P. Longworth, *The Unending Vigil: A History of the Commonwealth War Graves Commission 1917–1967* (London: Constable & Company, 1967), 92.

36 CWGC: WG 219/2/1 Pt. 2, Ware to Bruce, May 8, 1924.

37 For more on the separate path New Zealand took to the commemoration of its missing soldiers, see C. Pugsley, "Breaking Ranks with Empire: New Zealand's Gallipoli Graves," *Griffith Review* 48 (2015): 45–54.

38 J. Stephens, "'The Ghosts of Menin Gate': Art, Architecture and Commemoration," *Journal of Contemporary History* 44 (2009): 21–23, doi:10.1177/0022009408098644.

39 *Mercury*, November 6, 1929.

40 B. Scates, *Return to Gallipoli: Walking the Battlefields of the Great War* (Cambridge: Cambridge University Press, 2006), 67–84, 145–47.

41 J. Assmann and J. Czaplicka, "Collective Memory and Cultural Identity," *New German Critique* 65 (1995): 130–31; A. Assmann, "Memory, Individual and Collective," in *The Oxford Handbook of Contextual Political Analysis*, ed. Robert E. Goodin and Charles Tilly (Oxford: Oxford University Press, 2006), 215–17, doi:10.1093/oxfordhb/9780199270439.003.0011; K. L. Klein, "On the Emergence of Memory in Historical Discourse," *Representations* 69 (2000): 130.

42 C. Twomey, "Trauma and the Reinvigoration of Anzac: An Argument," *History Australia* 10, no. 3 (2013): 85–108, doi:10.1080/14490854.2013.11668482; M. Haultain-Gall, "Same Old Relics, Same Old Story? Displaying the Third Battle of Ypres at the Australian War Memorial, Past and Present," *History Australia* 14, no. 3 (2017): 451–54, doi:10.1080/14490854.2017.1359076.

43 Assmann, "Memory, Individual and Collective," 215; J. Winter and E. Sivan Sivan, "Setting the Framework," in *War and Remembrance in the Twentieth Century*, ed. J. Winter and E. Sivan (Cambridge: Cambridge University Press, 1999), 6.

44 Romain Fathi, *Our Corner of the Somme: Australia at Villers-Bretonneux* (Cambridge: Cambridge University Press, 2019), doi:10.1017/9781108558884; Linda Wade, "'By Diggers Defended, by Victorians Mended': Searching for Villers Bretonneux" (PhD diss., University of Wollongong, Wollongong, 2008).

45 Fathi, *Our Corner of the Somme*, 144–48; Department of Veterans' Affairs Annual Reports 2008–2019; Observatoire de Tourisme Westtoer, "Tourisme de Mémoire – Great War: Départements Nord, Pas-de-Calais, Somme," 2015, https://www.entreprises.gouv.fr/files/files/directions_services/tourisme/territoires/img/tourisme_de_memoire/TR1_Quel_impact_des_commemorations_sur_l%27economie_touristique_des_territoires.pdf.

46 Kenniscentrum Westtoer, "Wereldoorlog I Herdenkinstoerisme in de Westhoek: Volumes en evoluties 2013–2018," 2019, https://corporate.westtoer.be/sites/westtoer_2015/files/westtoer_corporate/kenniscentrum/ra-woi-herdenkingstoerisme_wh_volumes_evoluties_2013-2018.pdf.

47 Beaumont, "Australia's Global Memory Footprint," 62.

48 The ART sites in France are Fromelles, Bullecourt, Thiepval, Pozières (1st Australian Division Memorial and the Windmill), Villers-Bretonneux, Le Hamel, Mont St Quentin and Bellenglise.

49 S. Miles, "Remembrance Trails of the Great War on the Western Front: Routes of Heritage and Memory," *Journal of Heritage Tourism* 12, no. 5 (2017): 447, doi:10.1080/1743873X.2016.1242589.

50 Fromelles ($1 million), Bullecourt ($540,000) and Villers-Bretonneux ($2.1million) have all received considerably more funding than Ploegsteert ($370,000), MMP1917 ($270,000) and IFFM (amount not disclosed by DVA).

51 "Explore Arras – Remembrance," *Arras Tourisme*, 2015, www.explorearras.com/en/visit/remembrance.html.

52 Toerisme Vlaanderen and Kenniscentrum Westtoer, "Toeristisch marketingplan 100 jaar Groote Oorlog," June 2012, www.toerismevlaanderen.be/sites/toerismevlaanderen.be/files/assets/documents_PROMOTIE/20120919_1418_MKT_Def.pdf; Peter Slosse (business director of IFFM and head of tourism for Ieper), interview with

author, September 30, 2015; Steven Vandenbussche (curator of MMP 1917 and tourism officer for Zonnebeke), interview with author Zonnbeke, September 30, 2015; François Maekelberg (President of Local Returned Services Associations in Comines-Warneton and founding member of Plugstreet 14–18) and Anny Beauprez (founding member of Plugstreet 14–18 and former president of tourism for Comines-Warneton), interview with author, Ploegsteert, October 2, 2015.

53 "Australians on the Western Front 1914–1918," *Department of Veterans' Affairs*, 2015, https://webarchive.nla.gov.au/awa/20140801013844/www.ww1westernfront.gov.au/.

54 "Presentation," *Plugstreet 14–18 Experience*, www.plugstreet1418.be/en/presentation.

55 "Mission and Vission," *Memorial Museum Passchendaele 1917*, December 4, 2017, www.passchendaele.be/en/About_us/Mission_and_Vission.

56 Steven Vandenbussche interview.

57 Peter Slosse interview.

58 "Australians on the Western Front 1914–1918."

10 'A deathless monument of valour'

Memorialising Anzacs as ancient Greek citizen-soldiers from the war's aftermath to Julia Gillard's 2012 Gallipoli Dawn Service speech

Sarah Midford

> We come back. As we will always come back. To give the best and only gift that can matter anymore – our remembrance. We remember . . . what they did to shape our nation in peace. . . . This is the legend of Anzac, and it belongs to every Australian. Not just those who trace their origins to the early settlers but those like me who are migrants and who freely embrace the whole of the Australian story as their own. For Indigenous Australians, whose own wartime valour was a profound expression of the love they felt for the ancient land. And for Turkish-Australians who have not one but two heroic stories to tell their children. All of us remember, because all of us inhabit the freedom the Anzacs won for us. These citizen-soldiers, who came here untested and unknown, and who 'founded a deathless monument of valour' through the immensity of their sacrifice. This dawn will turn to darkness at the ending of today. But the sun will never set on the story of their deeds. Now and for all time, we will remember them. Lest We Forget.[1]

On Anzac Day 2012, Prime Minister Julia Gillard delivered the Dawn Service speech at Gallipoli, Turkey. In this speech, she quoted a fifth-century BCE Athenian inscription commemorating the sacrifice of a group of ancient Greek warriors who died fighting in the Dardanelles. She also paraphrased the words of the First World War correspondent and official historian C. E. W. Bean who had, in turn, paraphrased the ancient Greek historian Thucydides recording a speech delivered by the Athenian statesman Pericles in 431 BCE. In doing so, Gillard's words connected Australian democratic ideals to those held by fifth-century Athenians through Bean's commemorative efforts. Although Gillard and her audience were unlikely to have made the connection between her words and Athenian democracy, particularly because each reference has been filtered through Bean's and others' First World War commemorative efforts, their inclusion can still offer insight into the nature of Australian war commemoration and its connection to Athenian precedents. This chapter traces the ancient Athenian references evident in Gillard's speech back to their original sources to demonstrate the centrality of ancient Greek democratic ideals to Australian war commemoration from its aftermath to the speech's delivery in 2012. It argues that because Bean strategically included references to fifth-century Athens in the Anzac commemorative projects with which he was involved, a legacy that is imbued with references to ancient Greek democratic ideals continues to exist at the centre of Australian First World War commemoration more than a century after the Gallipoli landing.

During and after the First World War, Bean dedicated his professional life to the commemoration of the Anzac soldiers with whom he served at Gallipoli and on the Western Front. From the first anniversary of the Anzac landing at Gallipoli, Bean cultivated the notion that the Anzac soldier was exemplary, saying '[a] year ago Australians made a world name and the word "Anzac" became a synonym for every desirable human quality'.[2] In every major commemorative project with which he was involved, Bean embedded some aspect of classical myth, history, ritual practice or architecture, and the result is an Anzac narrative replete with veiled classical allusions.[3] For Bean, the First World War was an opportunity for the Australian nation to demonstrate its potential. Not content to leave this to chance, he evoked ancient models in his commemorative efforts so that Australians were guided appropriately as they reflected on their involvement in the war and performed their duty to make the Australian nation great. Bean was not alone in drawing on the classics for commemorative inspiration. Others who also drew parallels between Anzac deeds and those of ancient ancestor and warrior heroes from historical and mythological texts were crafting a venerable legacy for the young nation that positioned Australia as the next great democratic civilisation. After the war, the classics were used to situate Australia's experience in a meaningful context from which commemoration that ameliorated the trauma of war could emerge. There was a movement away from the Homeric and mythical references that had been popular during the war, toward fifth-century Athenian literary and historical references in the war's aftermath. Commemorative efforts that idealised ancient Greek values offered grieving Australians a retrospective cause for which the Anzacs fought and justified the large-scale loss of life for a grieving nation using well-established and familiar methods.[4]

This chapter investigates the modification and reconfiguration of ancient Greek words repurposed in Australian First World War commemorative contexts. This is evident in the carefully chosen words included in Gillard's 2012 Dawn Service speech and their relationship to Bean's commemorative efforts, ancient Athenian funerary practices and the promotion of democratic ideals. By focussing closely on a few key words in a section of Gillard's speech (quoted earlier), the chapter demonstrates the importance of ancient Greek culture to Anzac commemoration in the immediate aftermath of the First World War, as well as its ongoing role in contemporary commemorative practice. To achieve this, it is important to understand how the references to ancient Greece in Gillard's speech reconfigure meaning. One way to demonstrate this is through an example eloquently made by another scholar. In the very first words of the introduction to *Bereavement and Commemoration: An Archaeology of Mortality*, Sarah Tarlow elucidates the epigraph with which she prefaces her book: 'what will survive of us is love'. Tarlow re-contextualises this single line into the last stanza of Philip Larkin's 1964 poem 'An Arundel Tomb' to demonstrate her manipulation of the quotation to suit her own end. In doing so, she reveals the differences between the contextualised words' original and less-suitable meaning concerning love and fidelity. She confirms that her intended meaning for the short and specifically chosen extract was as a reference to the archaeological remains that commemorate the dead beyond living memory and not to the broader meaning of the original poem. Tarlow's decision to take only the words that suited her purpose is explained as a 'manipulation and reconfiguration of meaning'; something that 'occurs when words or things, or sounds, smells, colours, ideas or textures, are taken across contexts'.[5] Although the words take on new meaning in their new context, their original meaning in their original context does not cease to be. It is, therefore, important to understand both contexts to comprehend a more complete meaning of Tarlow's newly employed words. In the same way, Gillard's manipulation of Bean's words, originally from ancient Athenian contexts, reconfigures their meaning to suit her purpose as Prime Minister and generates new meaning for Australian First World War commemoration in the process.

Democratic commemoration of citizen-soldiers

Gillard's reference to 'a deathless monument of valour' is a direct quotation of Bean's translation of an ancient Greek inscription commemorating the sacrifice of a group of Athenian warriors who died fighting in the Dardanelles in 440 BCE. In 1935, the Director of the Australian War Memorial, John Treloar, acting on advice from Bean, commissioned a cast of this inscription. The cast was featured in the memorial's Hall of Valour from 1954, although it is no longer on display. Bean's translation of the inscription is as follows:

> These by the Dardanelles laid down their shining youth in battle; and won great glory for their land so that their foemen groaned carrying war's harvest from the field; but for themselves they founded deathless memorial of valour.[6]

Accompanying the original inscription were the names of 28 Athenian soldiers, listed by tribe, who died at the site of the monument.[7] The Athenian casualty list was not cast for the memorial. However, the placement of this inscription in the Hall of Valour figuratively included the names of the 28 Athenian dead among the most decorated Australian soldiers, who, through the inclusion of the inscription, were venerated in the manner of ancient Greek warriors. Making this association in the Hall of Valour equated its purpose with the state memorials erected in Athens, where the immortal deeds of dead warriors were venerated as heroic expressions of democratic duty.

The number of Australian casualties who fell in the same landscape in 1915 far exceeded the 28 Athenians who died at the Dardanelles in 440 BCE. However, just as it was important to mark the sacrifice made by those who died in service to

Athens, so too was it important to mark the deaths of each Australian citizen who died in service to their nation. To do this, ancient Greek casualty lists were used as a commemorative model for Australian commemorative practices. Central to the design of the Australian War Memorial was the list of Australian casualties, which would come to be known as the Roll of Honour. 'I strongly felt', Bean wrote about his vision for the memorial, 'that in the great hall surrounded by the 80,000 names, Australians would feel almost the presence of the fallen – as though these themselves lay there with the great record, which they had created, lying around them'.[8] This list, wrapped around the memorial's central courtyard and overlooking the Pool of Reflection, includes the name of every Australian who has died in military service to the nation.[9]

The names are arranged by conflict, then unit, with each individual listed alphabetically by surname. From the outset, it was agreed that the Roll of Honour would not show a soldier's rank or military honours.[10] Bean's reason for the omission of rank was presented to the Parliamentary Standing Committee on Public Works on 23 March 1928:

> It was suggested from the very first that no ranks should be shown. It was thought that would be altogether in line with the Australian attitude during the war, and my own opinion is that, far from such a course detracting from the honor of such men as General Bridges and General Holmes, the fact that their names are recorded simply in the same way as those of the men with whom they fought, will add to the honor in which they are held.[11]

Athenian casualty lists – which were traditionally erected after state funerals and recorded the location of the battle as well as the name of each individual under the heading of their tribe on stone *stelai* – were clearly a strong influence on Bean as he considered the order and placement of Australia's Roll of Honour in the war's aftermath. Crucial to Bean's interest in the ancient commemorative practice was that, regardless of wealth or status, a soldier who died in service to the Athenian state received the same commemorative space as any other, so that the equal sacrifice of each citizen-soldier was equivalently honoured.[12] Names were arranged by tribe and tribal affiliation, rather than in alphabetical order, to de-emphasise each soldier's individual identity and recognise the people and community who were most affected by the loss, without detracting from the worthiness of the individual's sacrifice.[13] It also allowed descendants to look up the names of their ancestral heroes centuries later.

Three options were discussed when deciding how Australian names would be ordered on the Roll of Honour: by unit, by time, or by locale. Bean favoured categorising the names by locale because it would allow people from the same city or town to locate the names of 'relatives and ancestors', '[e]ven after the lapse of three or four hundred years'.[14] Bean believed that 'this is the only way to preserve local tradition based on the sacrifices made by the AIF'.[15] Notably, this mimicked ancient Greek practice. His vision of the Roll's enduring importance to the Australian people indicates that he saw it as a point of connection between future

Australian citizens and their national ancestors, and Bean's hope for an ancestral legacy maintained by the Roll of Honour links its function to the ancient Greek casualty lists – both were erected to commemorate the deeds of soldiers as exemplary models of citizenship to be emulated in the present and the future.

In ancient Greece, the practice of erecting casualty lists coincided with the emergence of democracy, and in this context, it is clear why all citizen-soldiers needed to be commemorated equally for their sacrifice to the preservation of the state.[16] Like ancient casualty lists, the Australian Roll of Honour is a democratic means of commemoration.[17] By venerating all men equally and not singling out individuals, it eliminates reliance on class or status to determine esteem. Bean wished to venerate the deeds of the Anzac soldiers who died in service to his state as the ultimate expression of democracy. Like the state memorials that recognised the deeds of Athenians who died so their state could prosper, the Roll commemorated Australians who died so their nation might flourish. The equal honour paid to each soldier produced an anonymous ideal of Australian character to which others could aspire. By modelling Australian commemoration upon that of ancient Hellenic soldiers who died in service to their state, Bean established a strong connection between a citizen's duty and the construction and preservation of a glorious and successful Australian nation.

The inclusion of a reference to this inscription in Gillard's speech conjures a connotation with the soldiers remembered on the Roll of Honour in Canberra, who were figuratively transported back to the Dardanelles, where many of them 'la[id] down their shining youth'. Uttering the ancient Athenian words in their original landscape elides the deaths of those for whom the inscription was written and the Australian First World War dead. This elision of words and battlefield landscapes also connects the ideologies of ancient Athens and contemporary Australia. Each state had been a youthful democracy at the time of the conflict being commemorated, and the civic identities of both Athens and Australia were shaped by their participation in wars fought by volunteer citizens driven to preserve the best of their homelands. In the Athenian inscription and Gillard's speech, it is the most noble citizen-soldier that is remembered, and, more importantly, venerated, so that pride in the state would prevail and potentially even drive others to serve and protect it as dutiful citizens. In ancient Athens, this service was intended to be military in nature, but in the Australian context, the nationalism engendered could also serve a less overtly military purpose. This is emphasised in Gillard's framing of the Anzac's deeds in terms of shaping a peaceful nation.

War commemoration and civic pride

To understand the extent to which ancient Greek war commemoration is evident in Australia's First World War commemorative practices, it is necessary to outline ancient Athenian funerary ritual in some detail. In the winter following a military campaign, bones of unknown fallen Athenian soldiers from each tribe were returned to Athens, where the community commemorated its war dead with a public ceremony. The select dead soldiers represented all those who sacrificed their liberty to fulfil their democratic duty to the state. By approximately the late 470s BCE, responsibility for their burial, which traditionally had been the duty of the deceased's family, transferred to the state so their sacrifice could be publicly acknowledged.[18] The rise of state expenditure on funerals coincided with the raising of Athenian war casualties to heroic status, and the transition from private to state burial also coincided with the rise of Athenian democracy.[19]

By the end of the fifth century, funeral orations were delivered after a procession of coffins holding the bones of the unknown soldiers through the city's streets had concluded.[20] These orations were designed to simplify the traumatic elements of mass death and encourage its acceptance among the mourners. Honours were bestowed collectively because every soldier had given the equivalent gift of their life to the state and were therefore worthy of equal commemoration. State funerals satisfied the ritual mourning needs of the bereaved families and publicly thanked them for their sacrifice without naming any individual or singling out a particular soldier for special praise.[21] The commemorative funerary ritual venerated the deeds of citizen-soldiers who died upholding the democratic principles that were understood to have made Athens great. They also served the purpose of giving meaning to the deaths of so many citizens by highlighting the continued greatness of Athens.[22]

Politicians used orations to express Athenian democratic ideals by following a formula designed to perpetuate collective feeling and promote Athenian strengths and virtues, including democracy.[23] The most famous extant funerary oration from this time is that of the Athenian statesman Pericles, recorded by the historian Thucydides. In his public oration for the Athenian soldiers who had died during the Peloponnesian War, fought between 431 and 404 BCE, Pericles emphasised that the deeds and virtues of the dead would live forever in the glory it bestowed on their families and the state.[24] According to his oration, 'it is from the greatest dangers that the greatest honours accrue to the state as well as to an individual'.[25] He explicitly linked the esteem of the city to that of the individual, and therefore the sacrifice of an individual in service to Athens acted to preserve the memory of the dead while justifying their deaths.[26] In turn, the deaths of Athenian soldiers were transformed into a reason for Athens' greatness.[27] Superficially, Pericles' oration was a eulogy for those who had died in service to Athens; however, it also served the more complex purpose of praising the Athenian *polis* as an expression of the valorous deeds of the dead.[28] By explicitly linking the esteem of the city to that of the citizen-soldier, the sacrifice of a citizen in service to Athens acted to preserve the memory of the dead while justifying their deaths.[29]

In funeral orations of this period, myth and history were combined to generate a timeless expression of Athenian prowess and excellence; and to this end, historical details were sometimes altered to better align with the sentiment being promoted.[30] James Porter has argued that Pericles' oration constructed an illusion of fifth-century Athens designed for future consumption.[31] The ageless vitality in Athenian funerary speeches that Porter identified is reflected in the ritualised refrains used in ceremonies commemorating the soldiers of the First World War.

The 'Ode to Remembrance', recited regularly at commemorative ceremonies, includes the line: 'they shall not grow old, as we are left to grow old', which echoes the same sentiment evident in Pericles' commemoration of Athenian citizen-soldiers.[32] The late first-/early second-century CE Greek biographical historian Plutarch recognised that Pericles' words were *arkhaîos* (antique) from the moment they were uttered.[33] In his biography of Pericles, Plutarch wondered at the greatness and complexity of his protagonist's works:

> They were created in a short time for much time. Each one of them, in its beauty, was from the very first already then antique; but in the freshness of its vigour it is, even to the present day, recent and newly wrought. Such is, as it were, the bloom of perpetual newness upon these works of his, which makes them ever look untouched by time, as though the unfaltering breath of an ageless vitality had been infused into them.[34]

The ageless vitality identified here is reflected in the ritualised refrains used in ceremonies commemorating the First World War and employed in Gillard's speech. The 'Ode to Remembrance' comes from the fourth stanza of a longer poem, 'For the Fallen' (1914), written by the classically educated English poet Laurence Binyon. The poem as a whole, like Pericles' funeral oration, glorifies war, praises the nation and is full of pro-imperial sentiment, and – also like Pericles' funeral oration – the 'Ode' is part of a ritual that asks participants to remember historical events collectively and in so doing binds them together.[35] The separation of a single stanza for use in ceremonies commemorating the horror of war demonstrates Tarlow's point about the reconfiguration of meaning when words are taken out of context.

Anzac Day is Australia's main annual commemorative event, and, as Tom Clark argues, it employs ceremonial aspects, including the use of poetic refrains like the 'Ode of Remembrance' and 'Lest We Forget', which creates a sense of timelessness that bonds participants over geographical and chronological spaces.[36] The timelessness of commemorative words monumentalises their meaning in the same manner the timeless language of Pericles' funeral oration connects the deceased to the collective strength and beauty of Athens.[37] Because of its preoccupation with presenting an idealised version of Athens, the funeral oration invented Athens as much as Athens invented the funeral oration.[38] The dead offered their lives to the state, and the state celebrated those lives by honouring the sacrifice of its citizens. This acted to bind Athenians together as a people: by asserting the greatness of Athens and venerating the deeds of its citizenry, those Athenians who remained were bonded, and a sense of what it meant to be Athenian was created. Likewise, the words 'lest we forget', the last words of Gillard's speech, bind those remembering fallen service people to those who served. The refrain, used across Britain, Canada, New Zealand and Australia, also connects Australian remembrance more broadly to the British Empire and the greater Commonwealth experience.

The timelessness of the Anzac legacy is further emphasised by Gillard's reworking of the final paragraph of Bean's contribution to the *Official History of Australia in the War of 1914–1918*:

> What these men did nothing can alter now. The good and the bad, the greatness and smallness of their story will stand. . . . It rises, as it will always rise, above the mist of ages, a monument to great-hearted men; and, for their nation, a possession forever.[39]

Bean's construction of these words would have been laborious, compacting references to the epic poet Homer, the historian Herodotus and the words of Pericles (through the historian Thucydides) into just a few lines.[40] But the effort was worth it because their impact has been significant. Over the years, this paragraph has become part of Australia's commemorative vocabulary and can be found across several commemorative contexts.[41] These words are connected not just with the memory of Anzac deeds but also with the landing at Anzac Cove in 1915. This is evident in the Australian War Memorial, where they are inscribed underneath a boat that conveyed Anzac troops to shore at dawn on 25 April, positioned so they are the first words visitors read as they enter the memorial.

Gillard's speech alludes to this paragraph, rephrasing it without obscuring the reference to Bean's original: 'We come back. As we will always come back. To give the best and only gift that can matter anymore – our remembrance. We remember . . . what they did to shape our nation in peace'. Her shift from 'it rises' to 'we come back' is discernible in the sentence construction, but the reworking of the actual words reflects the outcomes of Bean's original hope for the Anzac legacy. The national monument to great-hearted men he had imagined, in Gillard's speech, is Australia's continued remembrance of their deeds. The perennial return to which Gillard refers is to Gallipoli – the site of the historic landing that sparked the Anzac legend – and her delivery of the speech occurred upon a monument raised to those who died in service to the nation on that very spot. The story of the Anzacs, to whom she refers, had risen sufficiently across the ages such that annual pilgrimage to Gallipoli was then (and still is) a common undertaking of the Australian people.[42] The Australian Commemorative Site, from where Gillard spoke these words, was constructed above North Beach in 1999 to accommodate the ever-increasing number of Australian and New Zealand tourists who 'came back' to Gallipoli in remembrance of the Anzac soldiers.[43] The link between this monument, the peace Gillard speaks of, and the references to Athenian democratic war commemoration embedded in Bean's original paragraph, to which her speech owes a debt, is evident in the plaque unveiled by Australian Prime Minister John Howard, New Zealand Prime Minister Helen Clark and the Turkish Minister of Forestry Nami Çağan upon the site's dedication in April 2000: 'The Gallipoli Peninsula Peace Park is dedicated to the pursuit of peace, harmony, freedom and understanding. In establishing this site within the park, Australia and New Zealand demonstrate they share these ideals with Turkey and with all democratic nations.' Gillard too, as a successive Prime Minister, had also 'come back' to

Gallipoli to pay her respects to the citizen-soldiers who had died protecting Australia's democracy. Her presence represented the legacy of their acts and acted as a tribute. As the democratically elected leader of the Australian people, she too owed a debt for the sacrifice made in the Gallipoli landscape to which she had returned and to which all prime ministers since her tenure concluded have also returned.[44]

Gillard's reference to Bean conveys ideas of the citizen-soldier's democratic duty to the state being worthy of eternal preservation. Much of the passage, upon which Gillard's speech draws, is inspired by Thucydides' account of Pericles' funeral oration.[45] This passage, in particular, is evident in Bean's final paragraph and therefore in Gillard's speech:

> For Athens . . . the admiration of the present and succeeding ages will be ours, since we have not left our power without witness, but have shown it by mighty proofs . . . we have forced every sea and land to be the highway of our daring, and everywhere, whether for evil or for good, have left imperishable monuments behind us. Such is the Athens for which these men, in the assertion of their resolve not to lose her, nobly fought and died.[46]

Here, Thucydides conveys the idea that, as long as the deeds undertaken during war are remembered, the deaths of those who undertook them remains meaningful. In his hope that Australia might become one of the greatest countries in the world, Bean drew on Pericles' proclamation that Athens was the greatest city-state in all of Greece and therefore a society worthy of emulation. Moreover, honouring the soldiers and eliciting pride in their communal sacrifice helped citizens overcome their grief and loss, which readied the bereaved for future losses while justifying those that had already occurred.[47] Since future conflicts would inevitably need to be fought, the reason for participation (a more beautiful, better, greater and happier state) needed to be established.[48] Gillard's speech, too, references the debt contemporary Australians had to the Anzacs who 'shape[d] our nation', and who now 'inhabit the freedom the Anzacs won for us'. Just as Pericles' Athenians had fought to preserve the greatness of Athens into the future, so too did Gillard's Anzacs.

Both Gillard and Pericles, through their respective speeches, express democratic ideals by following a formula designed to perpetuate collective feeling and promote civic strengths and virtues, including democracy.[49] Superficially, Pericles' oration was a eulogy for those who had died in service to Athens; however, it also served the more complex purpose of praising the Athenian state as an expression of the valorous deeds of the dead.[50] Myth and history were combined to generate a timeless expression of Athenian prowess and excellence; and historical details were glossed over to better align with the sentiment being promoted.[51] In the same way, Gillard's speech employs familiar and powerful formulaic language to express Australian values and promote a feeling of collective strength that celebrated the Australian nation. By using the words of Pericles and those from an Athenian war memorial, Gillard's speech is itself Periclean – using democratic ideologies to engender pride in the state and foster a strong collective identity aligned with nationalistic sentiment. The insertion of herself (a female), migrants and indigenous Australians into her version of the Anzac narrative is designed to be inclusive and to make the otherwise very white, very masculine event more relevant to contemporary Australian people – privileging myth over history and reconfiguring meaning. The timelessness of Bean's words, taken from ancient Greek sources, facilitates a mythologisation of the Gallipoli campaign that promotes a popular understanding of events rather than an historical account. The result is a familiar and comforting representation of Anzac sacrifice as a core component of Australian democracy and national identity, reconfigured to appeal to a contemporary audience. Recognising that ancient Greek democratic values and civic understanding has shaped this familiar Australian rhetoric gives us greater insight into Bean's continued influence on expressions of national values, identity and conceptions of democracy. Bean had intended to construct a legacy for Australians based on ancient Greek democratic ideals that would persevere into the nation's future, and Gillard's speech is evidence of his success in this endeavour.

Notes

1 Julia Gillard, "Dawn Service, Gallipoli," *Transcripts from the Prime Ministers of Australia*, April 25, 2012, Transcript ID 18532, https://pmtranscripts.pmc.gov.au/release/transcript-18532.
2 C. E. W. Bean, "Anniversary of the Anzac Landing," *Argus*, April 26, 1916.
3 Sarah Midford, "Revealing Homer, Herodotus and Thucydides in CEW Bean's Official History," in *Australia and the Great War: Identity, Memory and Mythology*, ed. Michael J. K. Walsh and Andrekos Varnava (Melbourne: Melbourne University Press, 2016), 193–94.
4 Ana Carden-Coyne, *Reconstructing the Body: Classicism, Modernism, and the First World War* (Oxford: Oxford University Press, 2009), 28.
5 Sarah Tarlow, *Bereavement and Commemoration: An Archaeology of Mortality* (Oxford: Blackwell, 1999), xi–xii.
6 Plaster cast of a Greek inscription: Australia War Memorial (AWM), RELAWM 12276, Hellespont [Dardanelles], 5th century BC. The official AWM translation is: 'Doing battle beside the Hellespont these men lost their shining youth. They brought honour to their homeland, so that the enemy groaned as it carried off the harvest of war, and for themselves they set up a deathless memorial of their courage'. On Bean's translation, see Fiona J. Nicholl, *From Diggers to Drag Queens: Configurations of Australian National Identity* (Sydney: Pluto Press, 2001), 24; Christopher Brennan translates the inscription as: 'These by the Dardanelles laid down their shining youth/In battle and won fair renown for their native land,/So that their enemy groaned carrying war's harvest from the field – /But for themselves they founded deathless monument of valour,' quoted in C. E. W. Bean, "Appendix VII," in *Gallipoli Mission* (Canberra: Australian War Memorial, 1952), 389–90.
7 The Athenian soldiers died in a revolt of the people of Samos, who rose against the Athenian state. Bean, "Appendix VII," 389.
8 AWM 38, 3DRL 6673, item 619, 36/1, Typescript, "The Beginnings of the Australian War Memorial," with notes by Arthur Bazley, *c.* 1959.
9 The list also retrospectively included the names of those who died in military service to Australian colonies before federation in 1901.

10 Treloar did not agree to the omission of military honours from the Roll of Honour until 1928. Bean objected to their inclusion on the basis that the process by which military honours were conferred was fundamentally flawed and that those who should have earned recognition were often overlooked. Although Bean did not disagree that those who were honoured deserved to be so, he was fearful that individuals with awards listed next to their name would be considered 'braver' than their peers and that this would affect the equality of their sacrifice. Eventually Treloar agreed to the Roll including only the name of the deceased. Treloar to Bean, February 27, 1928; AWM 93, 746/1/2 pt. 1, Bean to Treloar, February 28, 1928.

11 C. E. W. Bean, "Report Together with Minutes of Evidence Relating to the Proposed Australian War Memorial, Canberra," in *Parliamentary Standing Committee on Public Works* (Canberra: The Parliament of the Commonwealth of Australia, 1928), 6.

12 Judson Herrmann, *Athenian Funeral Orations* (Newburyport, MA: Focus Publishing, 2004), 1.

13 Polly Low, "Remembering War in Fifth-Century Greece: Ideologies, Societies, and Commemoration Beyond Democratic Athens," *World Archaeology* 35, no. 1 (2003): 99.

14 Bean, "Report Together with Minutes of Evidence Relating to the Proposed Australian War Memorial," 6.

15 Ibid.

16 When Pausanias visited Marathon in the second century CE, a list of Athenian war dead was located on the plain. On the veneration of those who died at the battle of Marathon, see Pausanuis, *Descriptions of Greece*, 1.32.3–4 and *IG* II, 471 (= *IG* II², 1006). On the monument to the Battle of Marathon being located at the site of the conflict and not in Athens with all other commemorative monuments, see Pausanuis, *Descriptions of Greece*, 1.29.7. However, several monuments to those who died at Marathon were erected throughout Greece, including a five-metre-long base for a monument at Athens, *IG* I³ 503/4. On monuments dedicated to those who died at Marathon, see Nathan T. Arrington, "Inscribing Defeat: The Commemorative Dynamics of the Athenian Casualty Lists," *Classical Antiquity* 30, no. 2 (2011): 194–95, 199, 204. An epigram for those who died at Marathon c. 447 BCE reads: 'These men by the Hellespont lost their brilliant youth fighting', *IG* I³ 1162, ll. 45–46. On inscriptions commemorating the dead at Marathon focusing on the courage of the soldiers who fought to the bitter end and in the manner of epic warriors, see Arrington, "Inscribing Defeat," 188. Marathon was remembered as a clash of civilisation and barbarism during the Great War and became emblematic of the defence of liberty; Elizabeth Vandiver, *Stand in the Trench, Achilles: Classical Reception in British Poetry of the Great War* (Oxford: Oxford University Press, 2010), 172–73; James Whitley, "The Monuments That Stood Before Marathon: Tomb Cult and Hero Cult in Archaic Attica," *American Journal of Archaeology* 98, no. 2 (1994): 213. The earliest known list of Athenian war casualties is that from Marathon, which points to the practice of state burial on the outskirts of Athens coinciding with the beginning of Athenian democracy. Mary Ebbott, "The List of the War Dead in Aeschylus' 'Persians'," *Harvard Studies in Classical Philology* 100 (2000): 92.

17 Ana Carden-Coyne, "Gendering Death and Renewal: Classical Monuments of the First World War," *Humanities Research* 10, no. 2 (2003): 41.

18 By approximately 430 BCE, private memorials began to be erected, pointing to a new practice of both public and private memorialisation of the dead. Private commemorations, in addition to public commemorations and the listing of war casualties on cenotaphs, continued in the fourth century; Christopher W. Clairmont, "Patrios Nomos: Public Burial in Athens During the Fifth and Fourth Centuries B. C. The Archaeological, Epigraphic-Literary and Historical Evidence," *BAR International Series* 161, no. 1 (1983): 15.

19 Low, "Remembering War in Fifth-Century Greece," 109; Clairmont, "Patrios Nomos," 12, 14–15.

20 Processions ceased to be annual by the time of the rhetorician Isocrates (c. 355 BCE).

21 It was very unusual to name an individual soldier in a funeral oration, although occasionally it did occur; see Low, "Remembering War in Fifth-Century Greece," 109; Herrmann, *Athenian Funeral Orations*, 2.

22 On the commemoration of war dead in their home *polis* in the ancient Greek world, see Low, "Remembering War in Fifth-Century Greece," 99.

23 Ibid., 100; K. R. Walters suggests that funeral orations strongly asserted Athenian virtues and the city's superiority because of a deep-seated fear of isolation and alienation from the rest of Greece, K. R. Walters, "Rhetoric as Ritual: The Semiotics of the Attic Funeral Oration," *Florilegium* 2 (1980): 2–3, 7–8.

24 On the iconography associated with Athenian dead, see Reinhard Stupperich, "The Iconography of Athenian State Burials in the Classical Period," in *The Archaeology of Athens and Attica Under the Democracy*, ed. W. Coulson (Oxford: Oxbow Monograph, 1994), 100. On the lack of details as a feature of funeral orations in the Periclean style, see Simon Stow, "Pericles at Gettysburg and Ground Zero: Tragedy, Patriotism, and Public Mourning," *The American Political Science Review* 101, no. 2 (2007): 202.

25 Thucydides, *The History of the Peloponnesian War*, trans. C. F. Smith, 1.144.3, https://thegreatthinkers.org/thucydides/featured-editions/.

26 Julia L. Shear, "'Their Memories Will Never Grow Old': The Politics of Remembrance in the Athenian Funeral Orations," *The Classical Quarterly* 63, no. 2 (2013): 513.

27 Thucydides, *The History of the Peloponnesian War*, 2.42.1. See also, Michael Palmer, "Love of Glory and the Common Good," *The American Political Science Review* 76, no. 4 (1982): 825.

28 Walters, "Rhetoric as Ritual," 1. For an extensive account of the *epitaphios* as a genre as well as a list of examples from antiquity, see Katharine Derderian, *Leaving Words to Remember: Greek Mourning and the Advent of Literacy* (Leiden: Brill, 2001), 161–88.

29 Shear, "'Their Memories Will Never Grow Old'," 513.

30 Walters, "Rhetoric as Ritual," 10, 18.

31 J. I. Porter, "What Is Classical About Classical Antiquity? Eight Propositions," *Anon* 13, no. 1 (2005): 51.

32 'They shall not grow old, as we that are left to grow old' is a line from the 'Ode of Remembrance', taken from Laurence Binyon's poem 'For the Fallen' and first published in the London *Times* in September 1914. Binyon studied Classics at Trinity College, Oxford and would have been was familiar with Pericles' funeral oration.

33 Plutarch became a Roman citizen during his life but was ethnically Greek. He was born in Boeotia just east of Delphi.

34 Plutarch, *Life of Pericles*, trans. B. Perrin (Cmbridge, MA: Harvard University Press, 1916), 13.3.

35 Shear, "'Their Memories Will Never Grow Old'," 515.

36 Tom Clark, "Public Poiesis: Theorising Contemporary Civic Uses of Poetry in Australia and the United States," *Social Science Research Network* (October 2011): 4.

37 On the endurance of collective memory being bound to space, see B. S. Osbourne, "Landscape, Memory, Monuments, Commemoration: Putting Identity in Its Place," *Department of Canadian Heritage for the Ethnocultural, Racial, Religious and Linguistic Diversity and Identity Seminar Proceedings, Halifax, Nova Scotia* (November 1–2, 2001): 3.

38 Nicole Loraux, *The Invention of Athens: The Funeral Oration in the Classical City*, trans. Alan Sheridan (Cambridge, MA: Harvard University Press, 1986), 1.

39 C. E. W. Bean, *Official History of Australia in the War of 1914–1918, vol. 6., in the Australian Imperial Force in France During the Allied Offensive, 1918* (Sydney: Angus and Robertson, 1942), 1096.

40 This chapter will only examine the Thucydidian elements in this paragraph. For a full analysis of the classical references, see Midford, "Revealing Homer, Herodotus and Thucydides," 188–203.

41 A simple Google search demonstrates this point. In the top ten search results, the following diverse examples of this paragraph being employed for commemorative purposes can be found (NB. examples in academic scholarship have been excluded): opening quotation on the Australian War Memorial's "Anzac Voices – Remembering Them," page, www.awm.gov.au/visit/exhibitions/anzac-voices/remembering-them; opening quotation on the UNSW AIF Project page, www.aif.adfa.edu.au/disclaimer.html; quoted in Brendan Nelson's Geoffrey Bolton Lecture, "'Here Is Their Spirit' – The ANZAC Centenary and the Generation That Gave a Nation Its Story," delivered at Government House in Perth, Western Australia, November 3, 2014, www.sro.wa.gov.au/sites/default/files/2014_geoffrey_bolton_lecture_by_dr_brendan_nelson_3_nov_2014.pdf; commemorative plaque on the 90th Anniversary of the Armistice monument, Esk Highway, St. Marys, Tasmania, https://monumentaustralia.org.au/themes/conflict/ww1/display/108340-90th-anniversary-of-the-armistice; reproduced as 'eloquent words' in the 'Items of human interest about people and events noted in the rotary field' section of *The Rotarian: An International Magazine* 80, no. 4 (April 1952): 38.

42 On Australian and New Zealand pilgrimage to Gallipoli from the war's aftermath until the centenary of the Anzac landing, see Richard Reid, Ian McGibbon, and Sarah Midford, "Remembering Gallipoli," in *Anzac Battlefield: A Gallipoli Landscape of War and Memory*, ed. Antonio Sagona, Mithat Atabay, C. J. Mackie, Ian McGibbon, and Richard Reid (Melbourne: Cambridge University Press, 2016), 216–20.

43 "The Significance of the Gallipoli Peninsula," *Inquiry into Matters Relating to the Gallipoli Peninsula*, Parliament of Australia, October 12, 2005, 4, www.aph.gov.au/Parliamentary_Business/Committees/Senate/Finance_and_Public_Administration/Completed_inquiries/2004-07/gallipoli/report/index.

44 One exception to this is the current Prime Minister Scott Morrison. Morrison remains in office and still has the opportunity to attend a Gallipoli Dawn Service before his tenure ends.

45 Thucydides provides a detailed account of this conflict and records Pericles' funeral oration, Thucydides, *History of the Peloponnesian War*, 2.34–46.

46 Ibid., 2.41.

47 K. A. Raaflaub, J. Ober, R. W. Wallace, P. Cartledge, and C. Farrar, eds., *Origins Democracy in Ancient Greece* (Berkeley: University of California Press, 2007), 113.

48 Although the Great War was thought of as the 'war to end all wars', it is clear from Bean's commemorative works that he did not fully believe this would be the case. As Bean was writing his Official History, the Second World War became increasingly inevitable, and the need for a complete record of the First World War was justified. On the pervasive idea that the Great War was the 'war to end all wars', see Hew Strachan, "Introduction," in *The Oxford Illustrated History of the First World War*, ed. Hew Strachen (Oxford: Oxford University Press, 2014), 7–8.

49 Low, "Remembering War in Fifth-Century Greece," 100; Walters suggests that funeral orations strongly asserted Athenian virtues and the city's superiority because of a deep-seated fear of isolation and alienation from the rest of Greece: Walters, "Rhetoric as Ritual," 2–3, 7–8.

50 Walters, "Rhetoric as Ritual," 1. For an extensive account of the *epitaphios* as a genre as well as a list of examples from antiquity, see Derderian, *Leaving Words to Remember*, 161–88.

51 Walters, "Rhetoric as Ritual," 10, 18.

11 *If Not In This World*

Memorialising the personal narrative of war and its aftermath with music

Andrew C. B. Harrison

The horror of the Great War elicited significant musical responses from some of the twentieth century's great composers. For example, French composer Maurice Ravel's seminal piano work *Le Tombeau de Couperin*, written during the years of the conflict, honoured the lives of friends of the musician who had died in battle. At a similar time, England's Edward Elgar produced his orchestral piece *Le Drapeau Belge*, a composition from 1917 about the wartime significance of the Belgian flag, featuring text from poet Émile Cammaerts. A few years later, British composer Ralph Vaughan Williams conceived of his *Pastoral Symphony*, written in 1922, as a musical antidote to the horrors he experienced as an ambulance driver on the Western Front[1] whilst William Bliss dedicated his oratorio *Morning Heroes*, which premiered in 1930 and was a reflection upon his military service, to his brother who died on the Western Front.[2]

However, despite the First World War's acknowledged influence upon post-bellum Australian society,[3] in the early decades after the Armistice there was minimal engagement from Australian composers with the war as a point of cultural and creative inspiration. Indeed, at the time English composer Benjamin Britten's landmark *War Requiem* premiered at the Coventry Cathedral in 1962, in Australia, it had been the Anzac Fellowship of Women – an organisation founded in Sydney by Dr Mary Booth – which had generated most of Australia's post-war musical reflections through their regular Anzac Eve Festival competitions. (Three early Australian works not associated with these competitions also need mentioning; Henry Tate's 1929 solo piano work *The Australian*, which includes movements with titles *The Mother*, *Youth's Unrest* and *Gallipoli Threnody*; Miriam Hyde's 1934 orchestral work *Heroic Elegy*, honouring the life of a First World War veteran who later died in a car accident and Roy Agnew's *Anzac Symphony*, which remained unfinished at his death in 1944.)[4]

We can only speculate why early Australian composers did not seek inspiration from World War I. Perhaps the dark shadow of the conflict left too many scars on composers and they simply chose to forget? Or, was it that, with the state-sponsored construction of war monuments, these artists felt enough memorialisation of the war had occurred, making the need to participate in the public discourse unnecessary? It is always difficult to really know motivations, or the lack thereof, behind creative endeavours. Nevertheless, questions about interpreting and understanding the Great War from a cultural perspective have continued into present-day Australia. In 2014, the documentary series *The War That Changed Us*, directed by Don Featherstone and produced by Electric Pictures, proffered answers to this conundrum by closely exploring the lives of six different Australians and their transformation by the war.[5] Moreover, noting the intimate approach adopted within the show, Australian historian Tanja Luckins suggested that the First World War may be 'understood best not from historians' blow-by-blow accounts of battles . . . but individual points of view'.[6]

Aspects of Luckins's observation have resonated with my own artistic practice. Indeed, the notion of creatively exploring the life of one person to gain a better understanding of a broader event has guided much of my research. Granted, Luckins's contention presents an oversimplified and, in some ways, outdated understanding of the difference between broad narrative and individual stories; Bill Gammage's book *The Broken Years* and Ken Burns's television series *The Civil War* both combine individual narratives and larger historical observations in a compelling manner.[7] Nonetheless, the idea of asking 'large questions in small places'[8] – to use the words of Charles Joyner – has played a significant role in shaping my recent compositions, from both a musical and historical perspective.

My 2018 composition, *If Not In This World*, highlights this.[9] It demonstrates my ongoing desire to find musical inspiration in my own family's connection to the First World War. The work's narrative explores the relationship between my great-great uncle Leslie Robins, who died on the Western Front, and his mother, Emma Elizabeth Robins, who had to pick up the pieces of her life following the death of her son. This chapter presents an overview of Leslie Robins's all-too-brief life and describes my process for researching and compiling his story. Finally, it considers how this historical research informed and shaped the compositional decisions I made to creatively memorialise the legacy that Leslie and Emma left my family, and the small but significant contribution they both made to our national narrative of war.

'My dear loving son': a snapshot of Leslie Robins's life[10]

Leslie Robins was born in Melbourne on 28 June 1897 to Emma Elizabeth Robins (née Webster) and William Charles Robins. Although Leslie was Emma's seventh pregnancy, he was only the family's third child to survive beyond the age of five.[11] Subsequently, Emma and William had seven more children, bringing their brood to a total of ten. After spending time in Myrtle Creek and Ballarat, the Robins family settled in Bendigo in central Victoria during the first decade of the 1900s, where Leslie spent most of his childhood.[12]

On 16 July 1915 – almost a year after the outbreak of World War I – Robins enlisted in the Australian Imperial Forces in Melbourne. He was just nineteen years old. Attached to the 10th Reinforcements of the 14th Battalion, Robins completed basic training in Melbourne before embarking for Egypt aboard *HMAS Port Lincoln* on 16 October 1915.[13] Following a period of training with his unit at the Tell El Kebir camp between January and May 1916, Robins shipped out to the European battlefields with his battalion in early June. As such, Robins and his comrades arrived in France in time for the commencement of the Somme Offensive in the summer of 1916.[14] Initially, between 1 and 3 July, the men of the 14th Battalion were involved in trench raids that saw fighting at close quarters. However, these skirmishes proved to be a minor prelude compared to the unit's next and more significant role within the Somme campaign; the Battle for Pozieres Ridge.[15]

On 6 August, the 14th Battalion moved into the front line at Pozieres Ridge, relieving the 26th and 28th Battalions. During the evening, the Germans unleashed an eight-hour, full-frontal artillery assault that wrought havoc on the area. Indeed, war historian Newton Wanliss, who wrote the official history of the 14th Battalion, noted that soldiers 'who experienced this [bombardment] always recalled it as surpassing anything that they ever faced, both in its fury and continuity'.[16] Subsequently, after surviving a German counter-attack upon the trenches on 7 August, Robins sustained gunshot wounds to his left leg and arm on 8 August, resulting in his repatriation to England to recuperate. His discharge from hospital occurred on 24 August 1916. Robins returned to his unit; however, over the next couple of months, he found himself attached intermittently to the 4th Australian Division Base Depot and 1st Canadian Tunnelling Company. Sometime towards the end of 1916, he became reattached to the 14th Battalion and settled in for the winter of 1916–17.[17]

After spending much of January assisting in the reconstruction and repair of roads to facilitate the movement of war traffic around Bazentin and Mametz, the 14th Battalion took part in a fateful exercise at the beginning of February: a raid on the sector near the village of Gueudecourt that centred around Stormy Trench.[18] It was to be Leslie Robins's last action on the Western Front. In the first phase of the operation, commencing on 1 February, men from the 15th Battalion attempted an unsuccessful raid on Stormy Trench; the Germans managed to hold on to their position. Three days later, the 13th Battalion received instructions to mount another assault on Stormy Trench, this time with men of the 14th Battalion's C Company, including Robins, providing support. Their role was straightforward: assist the 13th Battalion in any way necessary. At 7:30 p.m. on 4 February 1917, as the 13th Battalion moved stealthily across no man's land to begin their attack, Robins's C Company occupied a trench known as Shine Trench, which was further back from the German lines. At 10 p.m., the British guns opened fire, and the raid by the 13th Battalion soldiers achieved its aim in capturing some enemy territory. However, soon the German artillery responded, and the full force of its anger rained down upon C Company in Shine Trench as well as the communication trench. Describing the carnage, Newtown Wanliss writes:

> Shrine [sic] Trench[19] was well known to the enemy, and it received the full blast of the storm. Missiles of every description rained upon it. . . . There was little shelter: men hugged the bottom of the trench for some protection. . . . The trench soon became a shambles, from which few expected to escape

Figure 11.1 Private Leslie Robins, ca. 1916, photo taken at an unknown location. Private collection of the Robins family.

> alive. There was no excitement of action; it was a continual passive expectation of death or mutilation.[20]

This artillery fire abruptly brought the life of Leslie Robins to a terrible end, along with numerous others from the 14th Battalion's C Company. He was not yet twenty-one years old.

Researching and establishing family connections

While throughout my life, numerous family members have spoken to me about the death of my great-great uncle Leslie Robins in World War I, my formal research into his wartime service commenced in 2012 upon receiving a commission to compose a solo work for British-based Australian pianist Zubin Kanga.

During initial discussions with Kanga about the piece, I indicated my desire to explore the wartime experiences of my forebears through music. This was something I had been considering for some time; with the centenary of the beginning of the First World War a couple years away, I was contemplating writing a piece (or pieces) that reflected upon my family's involvement in the Great War. (As well as being interested in Leslie Robins's war service, I was also keen to explore the service of my maternal grandfather, Andrew Maddocks.)[21] Zubin Kanga was very much in favour of me writing a composition inspired by Robins. Nonetheless, once we agreed upon the concept of my composition and the trajectory it would take, I knew my previous knowledge of Robins's life – which up to that point was quite vague – would not provide me with enough substance to create a work that allowed me to explore my artistic intentions whilst also staying true to my great-great uncle's historical narrative. I realised I needed to delve deeper into his story and gather evidence about his war experiences, such as the nature and timing of his wounding, the period of his recovery and how and when he died. I also needed to establish some sense of his character. Thus, before commencing any creative work, I spent a significant amount of time studying Robins's war record in detail.[22] I consulted other primary sources, including the unit diaries of Leslie's 14th Battalion and other AIF records, and read numerous historical accounts of the battles where Robins was a combatant. Lastly, I spoke with my father and his sister to ascertain their anecdotal knowledge of Leslie.

Ultimately, the piece I wrote in 2012 creatively reflected upon Robins's experiences at the Battle of Pozieres, where he sustained wounds from gunfire. I particularly chose as a compositional focus the unrelenting artillery bombardment that Robins and his unit endured during their period on the front line in early August 1916. Moreover, Newton Wanliss's description of the German shelling at Pozieres on the night of Robins's wounding provided the title for my composition *The drumfire was incessant, and continued all night with unabated fury*.[23] The drama implied by Wanliss's words, when combined with historical research, inspired me to consider how I could creatively engage with issues like the disconnection between the British High Command's notion of formulating a plan for the battle and the actuality of what occurred once soldiers went over the top into no man's land. (In this case, I used improvisation – an important part of my compositional *modus* operandi – to infer the dynamic and unpredictable nature of battle.)

As well as providing vital historical information and creative impetus for my composition, the process of researching Robins's military service also facilitated new and welcome connections with members of my extended family. Following Zubin Kanga's premiere of *The drumfire* at the Melbourne Recital Centre on 11 August 2012, I had the pleasure of meeting my distant relative Bette Paynting for the first time. Bette is the granddaughter of Leslie Robins's youngest sister, Violet. During our conversation, Bette piqued my interest when she described a letter Leslie wrote to his mother, Emma – my great-great grandmother – whilst recovering from his wounds in England in mid-August 1916. Robins penned it a little less than seven months before his death. Naturally, I immediately expressed my enthusiasm to see the letter, and Bette soon forwarded a copy to me.

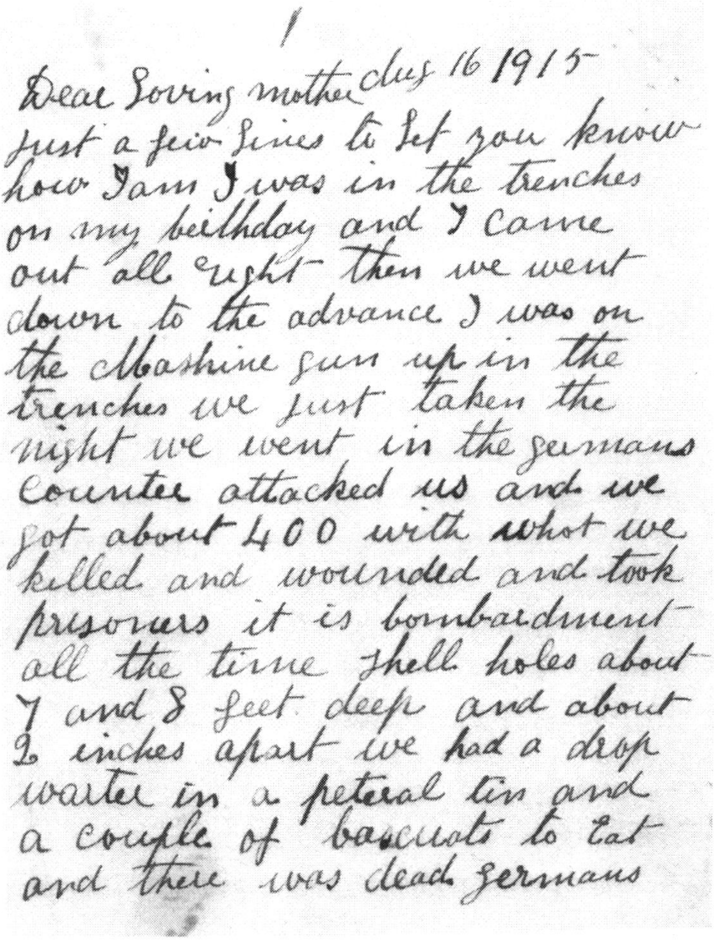
1

Dear Loving mother Aug 16 1915
just a few lines to let you know
how I am I was in the trenches
on my birthday and I came
out all right then we went
down to the advance I was on
the Machine gun up in the
trenches we just taken the
night we went in the germans
Counter attacked us and we
got about 400 with what we
killed and wounded and took
prisoners it is bombardment
all the time shell holes about
7 and 8 feet deep and about
2 inches apart we had a drop
water in a peteral tin and
a couple of bascuits to eat
and there was dead germans

Figure 11.2 First page of Leslie Robins's letter to his mother, Emma, 16 August 1916. Private collection of the Robins family.

My initial impression of Robins's letter was how ordinary and matter of fact it was. He writes:

August 16th [1916][24]

Dear loving mother

Just a few lines to let you know how I am[.] I was in the trenches on my birthday and I came out all right[.] [T]hen we went down to the advance[.] I was on the Machine gun up in the trenches we had just taken[.] [T]he night

> we went in the germans [sic] counter attacked us and we got about 400 with what we killed and wounded and took prisoners [sic][.] [I]t is bombardment all the time shell holes about 7 and 8 feet deep and about 2 inches apart[.] [W]e had a drop of water in a peterol [sic] tin and a couple of bascuits [sic] to eat and there was dead germans [sic] and our fellows all around and [the] smell [was] pretty high[.] [W]e used german flears [sic] and pistols through the night and the second morning there was only about 4 of us on the gun[.] [T]he others had been wounded and our cobber got nocked [sic] in the back[.] [W]e was bandaging him up and the 2 of us got nocked [sic] with shrapnel[.] I got a little bit in the leg and blew a revolver pouch off my arm and only scratched it[.] [T]hen we met the rest of our cobbers of the gun coming down in the train so they knocked 12 of us out on 2 guns[.] I got the boate [sic] to France and went to England in the hospital[.] I will be out in a few days and be ready to go back for some more[.] [T]his is all I can say at present[.] [L]ove to all dear mother, brothers and sister[.] [T]ill we meet again, if not in this wourld [sic] in the next.[25]

At first glance, Robins seems to speak of the war with an air of detachment. Other scholars have noted a sense of nonchalance and antipathy towards war by those actively serving; historian Joy Damousi states that 'writers and soldiers alike have emphasised the inadequacy of language to convey the experience of trench warfare'.[26] This observation connects with the tone of Robins's letter. Leslie – a young farm labourer from regional Victoria – plainly describes his experience of being in the trenches on his nineteenth birthday, killing Germans whilst manning the machine gun, and the gunfire wounds he sustained at Pozieres. The straightforward style of his narration appears to deemphasise the gravity and horror of his surroundings.

However, Robins's minimisation of his situation throughout the letter links directly with his attempts to reassure his mother about his health. As such, the honesty and candour of the soldier's written accounts of his frontline experiences – despite the horrific imagery – has the inadvertent effect of shielding and protecting Emma from the full scope of Robins's predicament. Thus, anticipating her inevitable anxiety about his wounding, Robins seeks to placate his mother by insisting that he 'came out all right' from the trenches, that he only got 'a little bit' of shrapnel in the leg and that his arm had a revolver pouch blown off it and, as a result, was 'only scratched'.[27] Again, Damousi highlights the desire of soldiers to calm their mothers and notes how this often brought them closer together: 'Soldiers addressed their mothers in loving terms. A son who enlisted could create anguish for his mother.'[28] Damousi also notes that, in their absence, some soldiers allowed their mothers to 'infantilise' them in their correspondence, thus strengthening the mother–son relationship.[29] This sort of language is not evident in the correspondence between Emma and AIF headquarters, and, unfortunately, I do not have any letters written by Emma to Leslie. Nonetheless Emma's depth of love for Leslie, concerns for his welfare and final grief are on full display through her desperation to stay connected to his memory by obtaining some of the possessions he left at the front line.

Whilst Robins's frank descriptions of his time on Pozieres Ridge captured my imagination and helped me craft a mental picture of the chaos that ensued during the battle, ultimately it was the poignancy of the letter's final line – 'till we meet again, if not in this world, in the next' – that left a lasting impression after my first encounter with the text. (This same line also attracted the most media attention years later during the promotion of the premiere performance of *If Not In This World.*) In the final stages of the letter, Robins acknowledges the reality that will inevitably confront him once he returns to the front line. Realising the inescapability of his situation, he speculates about the chances of seeing his mother once more. Again, in this moment, he conveys his sentiments with direct, unsentimental language; however, here the pretence of his mortality becomes exposed. Whilst Robins may have 'come out all right' from his Pozieres experience, he concedes there are no guarantees that he will be able to repeat the same feat twice. In fact, given the exposure to death he had already seen, Robins begins preparing his mother in anticipation of his possible demise. As such, he was giving her the opportunity to come to terms with the price they would both finally pay; he as a gallant young man fighting for his country and she – again, in the words of Damousi – as a 'sacrificial mother'; a mother 'whose sacrifice was deemed to be the most worthy amongst the living'.[30] Tragically, Emma came to embody this role when Robins's prediction came true after he was killed by German artillery fire at Gueudecourt in February 1917.

After reading Robins's letter in the days following the premiere of *The drumfire* in August 2012, I realised my musical exploration of my great-great uncle's story was not over. Instinctively, I knew it was incumbent on me to give his letter to Emma a musical setting. However, I also felt it was essential to create the optimal artistic environment for this prospective work; I did not want to compromise the integrity and emotional depth of his text nor his sentiments towards Emma. At the time, I did not have any creative options on the horizon that I believed would be suitable. As a result, my strong desire to do justice to Robins's narrative – in combination with other commitments arising from my recent enrolment in a doctoral program – meant that, in late 2012, I filed the letter away and decided to revisit it at another time.

If Not In This World: using historical research to memorialise war and its aftermath

The opportunity to return to Leslie Robins's letter and use it as the basis of a composition came five years later, when, in mid-2017, the Melbourne-based Arcko Symphonic Ensemble, led by artistic director Timothy Phillips, commissioned a new work called *If Not In This World*, composed for soprano, tenor and chamber orchestra. The piece would form a significant component of a concert scheduled for November 2018 commemorating the centenary of the First World War Armistice.

In the intervening years since first encountering Robins's letter, I had written two pieces that further explored my interest in using music as a way of understanding historical events. Indeed, these compositions – *Gassed Shell (Severe)*, written about my grandfather's experiences as a gunner at the Battle of Passchendaele in 1917, where he was gassed, and *Hum*, a collaborative piece written with Detroit-based poet Jamaal May that creatively reflected upon the emerging post-industrial narrative of the Motor City – consolidated my belief that research-informed musical works could shine a light on aspects of an historical narrative that might not be apparent through text alone. Moreover, in September 2015, I visited the battlefields of northern France and walked around the approximate location of Shine Trench where Robins had perished ninety-nine years earlier. This decision to follow R. H. Tawney's maxim of 'lay[ing] aside my books in favour of . . . boots',[31] afforded me the opportunity to experience first-hand the ground that Robins might have seen in his final hours (albeit much less churned over and damaged). In this moment – standing alone on farmland in the rural village of Gueudecourt – my thoughts turned to my great-great grandmother. Would she have wanted to see where her son died? Would doing so have provided closure or, rather, exacerbated the emptiness in her life following Leslie's death? Such ponderings highlighted the emotional and visceral nature of my 'footstepping' journey to the area of Robins's death.[32] Furthermore, they reinforced the value of such sensory experiences, as observed by historian Emily Robinson. She states, 'an encounter with *the actual place* where something happened can produce intellectual insights, allowing us to join up the dots and make connections which may not have been possible in the abstract.'[33]

Later, these factors informed and shaped my approach to the historical research I conducted and the compositional process I employed for *If Not In This World*. Through planning the composition in the year of the Armistice centenary, I came to understand the work was as much about Emma as it was Leslie. (In fact, the level of media interest in Leslie's letter reinforced the importance of allowing *If Not In This World* to present Leslie's narrative from multiple perspectives.) When the Armistice came on 11 November 1918, Leslie was gone, and like so many millions of mothers around the world, Emma had to find a way to continue living without him. Consequently, in the Robins family, as with so many others, the end of the war did not bring solace but revealed a gaping wound that tore at the internal fabric of society for a generation through the presence of damaged returned soldiers and their brutalised loved ones. Martin Crotty and Marina Larsson summarise this well: 'the ends of war are never . . . clean cut.'[34]

In the initial phase of getting reacquainted with Robins's text for my pre-compositional process, I sensed *If Not In This World* needed another viewpoint, a different perspective to counter the horrendous brutality outlined in a matter-of-fact fashion in his letter. In short, a *sotto voce* tone imbued with the emotion of those left behind. I recalled that Robins's official war record had retained all correspondence between Emma and AIF headquarters. Upon reading these official communications, it struck me that they would fulfil this function with depth and pathos. Including Emma's letters thus enabled me to infuse the work with

Figure 11.3 Leslie and Emma Elizabeth Robins, ca. 1910–15, photo taken at a family wedding. Private collection of the Robins family.

humanity and the despair that mothers and families faced on the home front as they sought to stay connected to their boys serving overseas.

Within the work, the written exchanges between Emma Elizabeth Robins and the AIF administration cover a six-year period.[35] The communications consist of four of her letters and two official responses from the Officer in Charge of Records. I decided to use Emma's enquiry about her son's wounding at Pozieres in August 1916 as her opening statement, as it establishes the tone for her frame of mind at the outset of the piece. As such, she is polite, despite her obvious distress. She begins with a simple request:

> September 12th, 1916
>
> Dear Sir,
>
> Will you be so kind to let me know what hospitable (sic) . . . my son is in . . . and be so kind to let me know how he is wounded.
>
> From an anxious mother.

The official reply that came back from Base Records goes some way to assuaging Emma's fears about Leslie's condition. It reads:

September 28th, 1916

Dear Madam,

> [Your son] . . . is not reported as seriously wounded . . . and in the absence of further particulars, it is to be assumed he is making satisfactory progress towards recovery.

Emma wrote the second letter used in the work one month after Robins's death on 5 February 1917 and six months after his letter home. Inevitably, Emma's tone within this correspondence has become more pronounced with the passing of her son. She is full of sorrow and despair and is desperately trying to maintain her relationship with Leslie despite his death. This is evident in her unusual and highly implausible request that the Australian military authorities locate a tiny 'Good Luck' heirloom ring that she gave Robins before he left Australia for the war.[36] The pathos of this impossible task highlights Emma's emotional state as she struggles to clutch to the memory of her boy.

March 20th, 1917

Dear Sir,

> In regard to my son . . . killed in action on 5th February 1917. . . I would like you to try and get . . . my dear son's personal effects. I would like the kit bag if possible, and anything that belongs to my dear son Leslie. I would like you to get the gold ring. . . . I gave it to my boy when I said our last goodbye.

Emma's third communication with AIF headquarters comes nearly twelve months later, on 21 March 1918. From the outset, it is apparent there has been little action on her petition of the AIF to find Robins's ring, outlined in her previous letter. In this moment, she pleads with the authorities to try harder to locate it; her sense of frustration and despair is palpable.

March 1st, 1918

Dear Sir,

> I do so wish you would try and find my dear loving son's . . . ring that I gave him when he went away. . . . It had a horseshoe and 'Good Luck' on it . . . and my dear son just adored it. As far as I know he . . . put it in some place to be [kept safe] when he was in the firing line. Hoping you will do your best.

From a lonely mother.

Emphasising her point, Emma invokes the memory of Leslie and her sense of loneliness to cajole the authorities into action. However, despite the war still being an ongoing concern – every day, mothers and families continued sending their sons off to the slaughter – Emma's language suggests she feels ignored, or worse still, she is becoming forgotten. In the aftermath of war, especially post-bellum Australian society, families of dead soldiers often wanted their grief vindicated and acknowledged. Yet, over time, the recognition of the sacrifices of families changed. Damousi observes that mothers of deceased soldiers came to feel overlooked and rejected by broader society as the immediate traumas of war faded from public view. She writes, 'motherhood had attained a prize status during the war, but the eulogy of the "sacrificial" mother did not endure in the collective memory.'[37] In Emma Robins's case, she possibly felt that the effects of the war's aftermath – the cloak of invisibility that gradually came over the families of the dead – had already been visited upon her by the time of the Armistice in November 1918.

Notwithstanding Emma's sentiments, an official reply from AIF headquarters came ten days later. This response – Emma's fifth statement in *If Not In This World* – confirms the inevitable truth. Unsurprisingly, Leslie's ring is not retrievable, and Emma ultimately remains a broken-hearted 'lonely mother'.[38]

March 11th, 1918

Dear Madam,

No trace can be found of the ring . . . and as no information is available as to where the late Private Robins placed it . . . prior to entering the firing line, no hope can be entertained that it will be recovered at a later date.

Written in December 1922, Emma's letter to AIF headquarters requesting Leslie's Victory Medal comes four years after the Armistice. This text serves as the final words of *If Not In This World.*

December 1st, 1922

Dear Sir,

Would you be so kind as to forward the Victory Medal to me due to my late son Private Leslie Robins, Number 3127 14th Battalion C Company, killed in action. By doing so you will greatly oblige me.

Mrs E. E. Robins

In 1919, the Australian government publicly honoured mothers of sons who died in battle with a badge bearing a star to remember their sacrifice. Given her previous correspondence, we can only speculate as to whether Emma felt spared of the ignominy of becoming what historian Marina Larsson describes as a 'disenfranchised griever',[39] someone whose loss went unrecognised. Perhaps she saw the irony in the mother of a dead soldier writing to the government to request a medal ostensibly celebrating a win for the nation. Regardless, the country's official acknowledgement simply could not make up for Leslie's ongoing absence. To this end, Emma's final words appear bittersweet and imbued with a sense of defeat.

After choosing the text I felt would best convey the drama and emotion inherent to the narrative of Leslie and Emma Robins's relationship, I focussed my attention on the form of the piece. Several questions about the work's structural design quickly came to mind. How should I present Leslie's letter? Should it unfold progressively in small stanzas, or, rather, would it function better as a large block of text? Should I give all of Emma's correspondence to the soprano, or should I get the male voice to sing the responses from AIF headquarters? What role would the chamber orchestra take within the piece? Would there be any sections that featured the instruments only?

Considering these questions, I realised it made compositional sense to alternate back and forth between Leslie and Emma, given the amount of text that each singer needed to perform and interpret. This enabled me to explore the depth of each protagonist's story, focussing in turn on the horror and acquiescence of fate contained in Robins's letter and the pathos and desperation of Emma's enforced continuity of a lonely life.[40] Thus, utilising a formal design based around two parallel stories meant I could control the ebb and flow of the drama, allowing the intensity of the piece to shift back and forth, guided by the textual instalments of each character. On the other hand, whilst the continual shifts between Leslie and Emma propel the trajectory of the work's narrative, I felt it was also important to be clear from the outset that they are never in dialogue within the piece. Rather, Leslie and his world are frozen in a state of temporal stasis – the day of 16 August 1916 – whilst Emma moves through time, providing us with an insight into her unfolding grief as she travels forward. From a compositional viewpoint, the identification of this dichotomy – the friction between a moment suspended in time and a life moving forward by necessity – provided me with options on how to approach the relationship between each of the voices and between the voices and the ensemble. As such, it became a central theme within my compositional process, influencing my creative decisions at both a broad and smaller scale.

An example of this can be found in the melodic material of the tenor, who presents Robins's words across six discrete sections within *If Not In This World*. His first entry comes at bar 27, when he announces the date of the letter – 'August 16th, 1916' – in a speaking voice, before changing to a singing voice for the letter's opening sentences – 'Dear loving mother, Just a few lines to let you know how I am' – one bar later.

Figure 11.4 Andrew C. B. Harrison, *If Not In This World*, bars 28–32, tenor.

As well as indicating Robins's close emotional bond with his mother, the opening phrase from bars 28 to 29 – a five-note setting of 'Dear loving mother' – outlines a short melodic sequence that subsequently plays an integral role within the work's compositional material. At bar 28, the tenor begins on middle C, then ascends a major sixth to A, followed immediately by a semitone up to B flat; it moves up again by a perfect fourth to E flat before descending by a major third (spelt in this example as a diminished fourth), coming to rest briefly on B natural.

This fleeting gesture then becomes the starting point for some of Robins's later entries. Reiterating the same pitches, the five-note phrase next appears at the beginning of Robins's second entry, accompanying the text 'It is bombardment.'

Figure 11.5 Harrison, *If Not In This World*, bars 28–29, tenor.

Figure 11.6 Harrison, *If Not In This World*, bars 81–83, tenor.

Figure 11.7 Harrison, *If Not In This World*, bars 140–41, tenor.

Figure 11.8 Harrison, *If Not In This World*, bars 8–24, cello.

Similarly, at bar 140, the tenor's third entry, with the text 'We used German flares,' takes the five-note phrase as its starting point. On this occasion, the phrase is in intervallic inversion, with all five pitches presented a semitone above those heard in the opening of the second tenor entry. The phrase of the tenor's third entry begins thus: D flat, down a minor third to B flat, up a semitone to B natural, down a perfect fifth to E and then up a minor sixth to C.

Employing this intervallic sequence at the beginning of these tenor entries enabled me to create continuity and unity across the piece. Moreover, returning to the gesture in entries two and three helped subtly reinforce the notion that time in Robins's world is inert.

Time also played an important role in my creative process for other sections of the work. In addition to the six alternating instalments of Emma's correspondence with AIF headquarters that move forward and act as a temporal counterbalance to Leslie's static letter context, the concept of temporality influenced my construction of the three short instrumental episodes that frame the work's text at various points of the piece. I want the musical material of these episodes – a slow, mournful melodic passage labelled 'lament' – to remind us of the endless grieving of those left behind, the family members of soldiers and other loved ones.[41]

The first presentation of the 'lament', played by the solo cello beginning at bar 8, captures the sense that, in the case of those mourning dead soldiers, the passage of time will not heal their wounds.

Subsequent iterations of the 'lament' – heard in the B flat clarinet at bar 122 and the trombone at bar 219 – infer a similar interpretation of time as a continuum that unceasingly churns on without resolution.

Also reinforced in the piece is the idea of two discrete and disconnected temporal spaces between Leslie and Emma, through my choices about orchestration. As such, I divided the ensemble forces into different instrumental groupings, aligning them with the text of Leslie or Emma. The musical accompaniment for the six instalments of Robins's letter varies throughout the piece. When the tenor describes the brutality of trench warfare in sections 1–3 of Robins's narrative, the orchestration draws upon the power of the entire ensemble playing *tutti*. Using the full capacity of the ensemble in these moments enabled me to provide weight and timbral density to the horrors depicted by Robins. Conversely, later in the work – during the fifth instalment of the letter and at the beginning of the sixth – the musical accompaniment becomes suddenly stark and sparse. Beginning at bar 263, Leslie contemplates his fate and metaphorically reaches out to his family, articulated by his words 'This is all I can say at present. Love to all dear mother, brother and sister. 'Til we meet again, if not in this world, in the next.' To underscore the poignancy of this moment, I scaled back the musical accompaniment to solo chordal figures provided by the piano, vibraphone and electric guitar.

In contrast to the fuller orchestration accompanying much of Leslie's letter, I allocated small groups of instrumental forces to underpin Emma's musical settings, highlighting the fraught nature of her communications with AIF headquarters.

For example, I decided to make the vibraphone, playing a slow-moving harmonic sequence, a constant instrumental companion for each of Emma's four

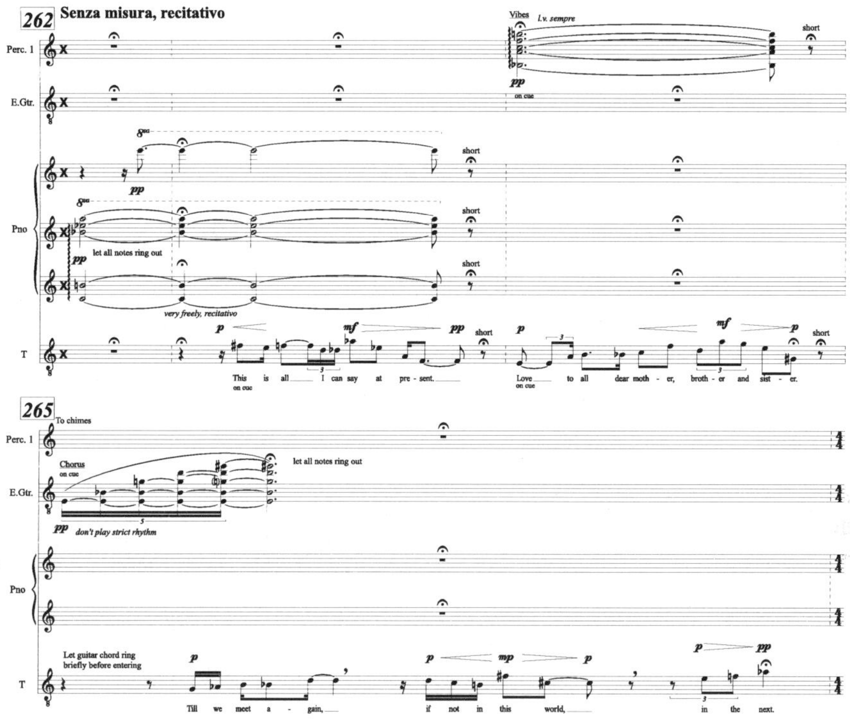

Figure 11.9 Harrison, *If Not In This World*, bars 262–65, tenor, piano, vibraphone and electric guitar.

letters written to the AIF. I felt that using the vibraphone for harmonic accompaniment in this way enabled me to convey an ethereal sense of floating, heightening the uncertainty of Emma's words as she seeks to discover further information about her son and his condition. This is evident between bars 65 and 80, during the soprano's presentation of Emma's first letter. As the music unfolds, other instruments join in, contributing to the texture of the sonic landscape. The strings draw upon the vibraphone's harmonic sequence in their accompanying role, whilst the clarinet and flute provide intermittent interplay with the melodic material, occasionally imitating and responding to some of Emma's phrases. Lastly, the percussion provides occasional rhythmic reinforcement of the music underneath the soprano; these sporadic gestures contribute a shimmering effect to the overall sound.

Likewise, I chose a smaller section of ensemble forces to accompany the two official responses from the AIF to Emma. For these moments, I engaged the orchestra's brass section. On each occasion, I instructed the players to perform the music in a *quasi chorale* manner. By requesting the musicians to play in this particular style, I intended to link these parts of *If Not In This World* to the brass band

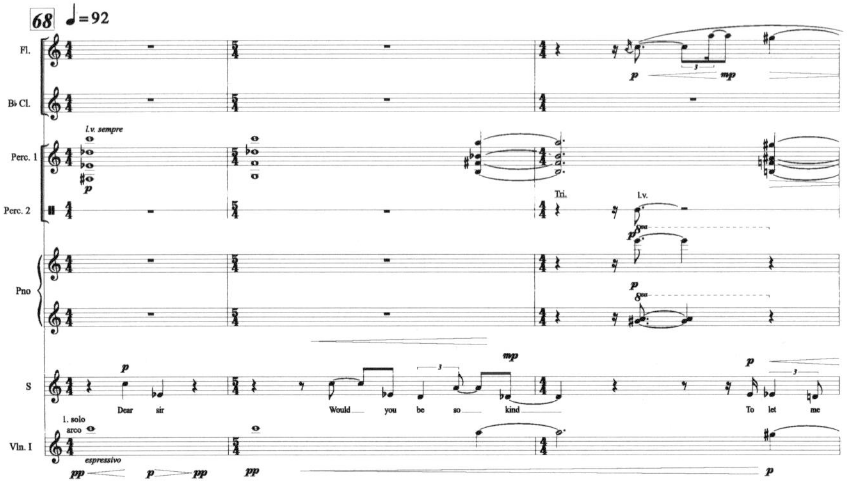

Figure 11.10 Harrison, *If Not In This World*, bars 68–73, flute, B flat clarinet, vibraphone, triangle, piano, soprano and strings.

Figure 11.11 Harrison, *If Not In This World*, bars 242–46, horn, B flat trumpet, trombone, tuba and soprano.

Section	Lament One: melody w. solo cello	Leslie's letter – instalment 1	Emma's first letter to AIF	Leslie's letter – instalment 2	Emma's first response from AIF
Tempo (BPM)	48	112	92	112	92
Section	Lament Two: melody w. clarinet	Leslie's letter – instalment 3	Emma's second letter to AIF	Leslie's letter – instalment 4	Emma's third letter to AIF
Tempo (BPM)	48	112	76	112	76
Section	Lament Three: melody w. trombone	Leslie's letter – instalment 5	Emma's second response from AIF	Leslie's letter – instalment 6 (duet with Emma)	Emma's fourth letter to AIF (spoken)
Tempo (BPM)	48	40 (*tempo rubato*)	66	*senza misura,* then 66	*senza misura,* very slow and still

Figure 11.12 Harrison, *If Not In This World*, tempo map.

tradition, often associated with the military. Simultaneously, I was also indicating that the sombre nature of Emma's text required an interpretation of the musical accompaniment centred upon a slow, hymnal style.

Finally, I also used tempo as an active element for creating a sense of disparity between the temporal worlds of Robins and his mother. The tempo of the first four instalments of Leslie's letter remains fixed at ♩ = 112, taking the listener constantly back to the unrelenting drudgery and terror of the trenches – something Robins describes in his letter with 'it is bombardment all the time.' The constancy of the tempo in the sections also implies an environment where the individual is helpless and unable to change their situation. Contrasting the constraints on tempo for Leslie's letter, the pacing of Emma's sections changes to emphasise her growing anxiety. Thus, her first entry, where she enquires about her son's wounding, has the metronome marking ♩ = 92; however, as the piece unfolds and her despair builds, the tempo of her sections slows significantly. Thus, her final sung entry (the second response from AIF headquarters) occurs at ♩ = 66, and her final letter – delivered in a speaking voice – carries the tempo instruction *senza misura* (without measure or time).

If Not In This World is the third piece about my family's connection to the Great War.

It adds to a growing number of new Australian works that creatively reflect upon the First World War and its impact upon Australian society. Before I started composing *If Not In This World*, I was asked why I needed to write another piece about the Great War. The pejorative undertone of this question initially irked me;

nonetheless, it did push me to reflect upon my motivations. What did I hope to achieve with this piece? A hundred years on, why would expressing Leslie and Emma Robins's story through music – a tragedy visited upon countless Australian families – make any difference to our understanding of World War I and the way it shaped the world? Ultimately, I believe Timothy Phillips, the Arcko Symphonic Ensemble's artistic director, answered this question with substantial clarity when he stated, 'remembering will help foster peace in the future.'[42]

Notes

1 Eric Saylor, " 'It's Not Lambkins Frisking at All': English Pastoral Music and the Great War," *The Musical Quarterly* 91, no. 1–2 (2008): 48–49, doi:10.1093/musqtl/gdn030.

2 Glenn Watkins, *Proof Through the Night: Music and the Great War* (Berkeley: University of California Press, 2002). Glenn Watkins's study of music from World War I is comprehensive and detailed.

3 Bill Gammage, *The Broken Years: Australian Soldiers in the Great War* (Canberra: The Australian National University Press, 1974), 279. Bill Gammage describes 'how great was the impact of the war on Australia – on the lives and hopes of individuals, on the direction and cohesion of society and on the assumptions and opinions of the nation'. He illustrates his point with a short quote from the diary of an unnamed Australian soldier, written in September 1917; 'Adieu, the years are a broken song, And the right grows weak in the strife with wrong, The lilies of love have a crimson stain, And the old days never will come again.'

4 Andrew C. B. Harrison, "Sounding Out the Past" (PhD diss., The Australian National University, Canberra, 2020), 25–30.

5 Don Featherstone, *The War That Changed Us* (Perth, Western Australia: Electric Pictures, 2014).

6 Tanja Luckins, " 'To Make the Past Present, to Bring the Distant Near': Affective History and Historical Distance in the War That Changed Us," *Australian Historical Studies* 46, no. 3 (2015): 474, doi:10.1080/1031461X.2015.1074592.

7 Gammage, *The Broken Years*; Ken Burns, *The Civil War*, vol. 1–3 (Brisbane: Magna Pacifica, 1990), DVD, DBX03020.

8 Charles Joyner, *Shared Traditions: Southern History and Folk Culture* (Urbana: The University of Illinois Press, 1999), 1.

9 A video of the Melbourne premiere of *If Not in This World* on 11 November 2018 can be viewed at https://vimeo.com/326116908. The performers are the Arcko Symphonic Ensemble, featuring Timothy Phillips (conductor), Robert Latham (tenor) and Justine Anderson (soprano).

10 'My dear loving son' is how Emma Robins, Leslie's mother, referred to him in the letters that she sent to AIF headquarters between 1916 and 1922.

11 Leslie Robins, "Birth Registration," in *Registration no. 19051* (District of North Fitzroy, Colony of Victoria: Births, Deaths and Marriages (Victoria), 1897). In the Robins family, four boys passed away prior to Leslie's birth. Firstly, in 1891, Robert died at the age of five months. The following year, the family lost James, aged five, and Thomas, aged three. Within another twelve months, they had buried another boy, Albert, who was three months old.

12 Bendigo is a regional city about 150 kilometres northwest of Melbourne. The city rose to prominence as an important Australian geographical location due to the discovery of gold in the region in the 1850s.

13 The Australian War Memorial, "Leslie Robins," *Darge Photographic Company Collection of Negatives*, studio portrait, ca. October 1915, www.awm.gov.au/collection/C1003803.

14 Newton Wanliss, *The History of the Fourteenth Battalion, A. I. F.* (London: Naval and Military Press & Imperial War Museum, 1929; repr., 2010), 110–23.
15 C. E. W. Bean, "The Arrival of II Anzac," in *The Official History of Australia in the War of 1914–1918, vol. 3: The Australian Imperial Force in France, 1916* (Sydney, NSW: Angus and Robertson, 1941), 300–4.
16 Wanliss, *The History of the Fourteenth Battalion, A. I. F.*, 138.
17 The exact date of his return to his unit is not clear from the details provided in his war record.
18 Wanliss, *The History of the Fourteenth Battalion, A. I. F.*, 174.
19 Newton Wanliss mistakenly labels Shine Trench as 'Shrine' Trench. Both Charles Bean and the 14th Battalion's unit diary refer to the trench as Shine Trench.
20 Wanliss, *The History of the Fourteenth Battalion, A. I. F.*, 177.
21 I later wrote a composition entitled *Gassed Shell (Severe)* about Andrew Maddocks's experiences as a gunner at the Battle of Passchendaele. The Monash Art Ensemble commissioned the work in 2014.
22 This process proved to be fruitful almost immediately, as it enabled me to establish that Robins's death occurred in 1917; some family members had previously thought Robins perished at the Somme in 1916.
23 Wanliss, *The History of the Fourteenth Battalion, A.I.F.*, 138.
24 The year written on the letter – '1915' – is incorrect, as Robins enlisted in 1915 and was on the Western Front in 1916. I suspect that a member of the Robins family added the incorrect date sometime after Leslie's death.
25 Leslie Robins, "Unpublished Letter to Emma Elizabeth Robins" (August 16, 1916, private collection of the Robins family). Leslie's letter has no punctuation at all. When preparing and editing the letter for its incorporation into *If Not In This World*, I added in punctuation and corrected spelling mistakes to give the text a sense of logic, flow and clarity. I have included the original version of the letter for this chapter.
26 Joy Damousi, *The Labour of Loss: Mourning, Memory and Wartime Bereavement in Australia* (Cambridge: Cambridge University Press, 1999), 11.
27 Robins, "Unpublished Letter to Emma Elizabeth Robins."
28 Damousi, *The Labour of Loss*, 28.
29 Ibid., 27.
30 Ibid., 26.
31 Eric Kerridge, "Ridge and Furrow and Agrarian History," *The Economic History Review, New Series* 4, no. 1 (1951): 14.
32 Richard Holmes, *Footsteps: Adventures of a Romantic Biographer* (London: Hodder and Stoughton, 1985), 67, 136. Foot stepping is an approach to historical research that involves travelling to a location to experience it much in the same way as the subject or person under examination. Foot stepping takes its name from the book *Footsteps*, written by the biographer Richard Holmes. Whilst constructing biographies about some well-known Romantic writers, Holmes realised he had to resist the influence of previous scholarly interpretations; he needed to formulate his opinions based upon his own detailed research. Hence, to get as close to his subjects as possible, Holmes attempted to travel in their footsteps whenever he could.
33 Emily Robinson, "Touching the Void: Affective History and the Impossible," *Rethinking History: The Journal of Theory and Practice* 14, no. 4 (2010): 506, doi:10.1080/13642529.2010.515806.
34 Martin Crotty and Marina Larsson, "Introduction: The Many Faces of Return," in *Anzac Legacies: Australians and the Aftermath of War*, ed. Martin Crotty and Marina Larsson (North Melbourne: Australian Scholarly Publishing, 2010), 2.
35 NAA: B2455, "Various Correspondence Between Emma Elizabeth Robins and A.I.F. Headquarters," Service record of Leslie Robins, No. 3127, A. I. F., 1916–1922; as indicated, Leslie's service record contains all six letters between Emma Robins and A. I. F. Headquarters.

36 In her letter dated 1 March 1918, Emma indicates that the ring belonged to her great-great grandmother.

37 Damousi, *The Labour of Loss*, 30.

38 NAA: B2455, Emma Elizabeth Robins, "Letter to A.I.F. Headquarters, March 1, 1918," Service record of Leslie Robins, No. 3127, A.I.F., 1916–22.

39 Marina Larsson, "A Disenfranchised Grief: Post-War Death and Memorialisation in Australia After the First World War," *Australian Historical Studies* 40, no. 1 (2009): 82, doi:10.1080/10314610802663035.

40 In purely practical terms, alternating between the tenor and the soprano also allowed each of the singers to have a short break.

41 James Porter, "Lament," in *Grove Music Online* (Oxford: Oxford University Press, 2001), doi:10.1093/gmo/9781561592630.article.15902. Porter notes that the term 'lament' is 'associated not only with mourning rites for the dead but also with ritual leave-as in the case of . . . a mother's farewell to a son recruited by war service'.

42 Arcko Symphonic Ensemble, "Remembering Will Help Foster Peace in the Future," *CutCommon Mag*, October 29, 2018, www.cutcommonmag.com/remembering-will-help-foster-peace-in-the-future/.

12 Pleasant remembrances and foreboding futures

Glorifying representations of empire and their opposition within Britain's national cinema during the 1930s

Ellen Whitton

In his 1969 memoir, *Michael Balcon Presents . . . a Lifetime of Films*, the famed British producer reflected upon his executive influence and efforts at Gaumont British Picture Corporation during the 1930s. Overall, his account regarding the healthiness of Britain's studios and trade, its notable figures, and its popular films was fairly positive; however, there was one aspect from this period that nagged at his conscience long after the decade had concluded. He wrote,

> I realise that the preceding chapters of this story have played against a shadowy background of world events – some world-shattering . . . now that events can be seen in their historical perspective, one cannot escape the conclusion that in our own work, we could have been more profitably engaged. Hardly a single film of the period reflects the agony of those times.[1]

Balcon's comments invite the critique of Britain's film catalogue during the interwar period and prompt questions that specifically address narrative content. If films produced during the 1930s avoided contemporary politics and critical social commentary in their narratives, then what were the primary themes or messages being conveyed through cinema screens? Who vetted the industry's scripts to ensure such themes were cut, and what were their specifications for this process? Did any filmmakers endeavour to circumnavigate these censors and their parameters, or were they, as Balcon said, disengaged from the agony of the times? The following chapter considers a selection of popular British films – across the 1930s – and argues that there were two primary styles of narrative that graced the silver screen during this time. Furthermore, it argues that some productions challenged this norm by alluding to – or by directly commenting upon – reality's topical issues despite the threat of criticism and the ire of industry censors. Before delving into narrative themes, it is pertinent to outline censorship and its influence in Britain's industry after the Great War, as it greatly impacted the creative parameters of filmmakers at this time.[2]

The powerful reign of the British Board of Film Censors, 1912–39

Understanding the influence of the British Board of Film Censors (BBFC) is paramount when considering British cinema during the 1930s because this group had the power to approve or reject studio projects. Prior to this decade, some censorship guidelines had been established in both Britain and Hollywood; however, the authority of the BBFC grew exponentially during the interwar years and successfully stifled the activities of many filmmakers. Officially established in 1913 as a reaction to the Cinematograph Act of 1909, the BBFC was initially tasked with policing the new regulations put in place for exhibitors. The act itself had little to do with the censorship of cinema content, and its set of provisions, ten in total, were actually produced to combat the fears regarding the health and safety of audience members. Principally, the act focused on reducing the amount of fire risks at movie theatres. Exhibitors were required to apply for a license that confirmed their adherence to new safety laws – a process that was facilitated through designated local councillors.[3] According to James C. Robertson's analysis in *The Hidden Cinema: British Film Censorship in Action, 1913–1975*, the phrasing of this bill was somewhat vague, and local councillors took it upon themselves to also act as censors for film content as well as safety officers.[4] This alarmed a number of industry groups – studio producers, filmmakers, and exhibitors – and their concerns prompted Reginald McKenna, the British Home Secretary, to officially establish the BBFC as the industry's 'self-censorship body'.[5] As of 1 March 1913, the BBFC were tasked with the classification (A = Adult, U = Universal) or rejection of submitted films.

To properly classify films, the BBFC's examiners were equipped with a list of scenarios and behaviours that were deemed inappropriate for the screen. Some were defined by morals, others by politics. Films containing any of the following 'immoral' scenes were subject to rejection if filmmakers refused to act on the recommendations made by examiners. They included cruelty to animals, drunken scenes, the irreverent treatment of sacred subjects, the modus operandi of criminals, indelicate sexual situations, cruelty to young infants, indecorous dancing, outrages on women, confinements, executions, gruesome murders, suicides, scenes laid in disorderly houses, and vulgarity and impropriety in conduct and dress.[6] This list developed incrementally over the years and often took changing social/political issues into account. For instance, during the Great War, caveats directly concerned with warfare were added. Films depicting 'realistic horrors of warfare, incidents tending to scare the public, scenes depicting the movement or disposition of troops, incidents calculated to afford information to the enemy, etc.' were scrupulously vetted by censors.[7]

Throughout the 1920s, censorship continued; however, filmmakers concerned with the aftermath of the Great War were provided leniency in their work. Oftentimes, the war films produced after the Armistice were overshadowed by other industry issues, like the influx of American films and the slump in Britain's production, but their existence in cinema during this decade suggests that the BBFC was somewhat flexible with war-based content.[8] This would have been influenced by the filmmakers' approach to their decided issue as well as the subject's position as a past event. In this case, military intel, the horrors of warfare, or panic-inducing events could affect the wartime morale of the nation. After the Armistice, British filmmakers focused the 'digestion' of the conflict and often shied away from glorification. Film studies specialist Lawrence Napper suggested three different categories for this type of cinematic therapy: 'remembrance', 're-membering', and 'recollection'.

Remembrance: Encompassed scenarios that contained public acts of remembrance and the linkage of private loss with the 'public discourse of meaning, a discourse about sacrifice, honour and moral debt'.

Re-membering: Films that take the 'fragmented and chaotic personal experiences of wartime service' and put them together in a comprehensible historical narrative.

Recollection: Stories that recall the 'visceral sense of being in the trenches' and the re-experience of the death, destruction, and helplessness found there – common features in the personal reminiscences of returned servicemen.[9]

While films like *Ypres: The Story of the Immortal Salient* (1925), *Remembrance* (1927), and *Dawn* (1928) addressed concerns directly within wartime settings, others did not. Other features considered the emotional and physical consequences of its aftermath.

According to Christine Glendhill, many films contained the 'war touch' without directly depicting military campaigns. In her essay 'Remembering the War in 1920s British Cinema', she listed four major motifs that signified the 'war touch':

1. Uncertainty towards traditional masculinity and the presence of a tortured anti-hero. A film's hero often suffered, both mentally and physically, as they navigated society's new norms after the mechanised mass destruction of the Great War.
2. Scenarios questioning the ideals surrounding the Victorian 'true woman'. During the conflict, the movement of middle-class women from the home to the workplace was necessary; however, after the conflict ended there was conjecture about women and their position in public spaces.
3. The bonds between men are challenged and undermined through rivalry.
4. A child is present and acts as a signifier for regeneration. They often test the role and power of the film's dysfunctional anti-hero, which may result in the man's restoration or exit within the narrative.[10]

While features containing such elements were released during the 1920s, censors tightened their hold after the decade concluded, and Great War content lessened considerably. This reduction also coincided with the appointment of new, liberal-aligned, BBFC presidents.

During the 1930s, the BBFC had two presidents. The first, Rt Hon. Edward Shortt, began his tenure in 1929 and remained with the board until his death in 1935. He was a lawyer, member of the Liberal Party, and a staunch believer in the upkeep of good morals on screen. During his time as president, the industry faced some criticism; however, American productions drew the ire of censors more than British productions. In particular, Shortt protested against Hollywood's gangster films, stating to the Exhibitors Association how 'the whole of the gangster's gamut of crime, murder, kidnapping, robbery with violence, arson, etc.' was 'highly undesirable' and 'unwholesome'.[11] Alongside this, Shortt highlighted his concerns regarding horror films, animals on screen, and religious films but failed to mention the portrayal of contemporary issues pertinent to the security of the British Empire. After his death in November 1935, Lord Tyrrell filled the position, and the BBFC, almost unfathomably, tightened their censorship guidelines. Examiners became more vigilant towards the depiction of foreign countries and their politics, and according to historian Jeffrey Richards:

> The Board's attitude to the depiction of all foreign countries, Fascist and non-Fascist alike, was one of appeasement, the avoidance of offence by the elimination of any criticism or hostility. . . . It became standard for censors to suggest that any film with a foreign setting be submitted to the relevant embassy for clearance.[12]

With such processes in place, it is unsurprising that filmmakers were discouraged, and at one stage, the number of films addressing topical issues was low enough for Tyrrell to boast about. In his 1937 address to the Exhibitors' Association, he made it abundantly clear that the BBFC's decisions were driven predominantly by the politics of the day. 'We may', he said, 'take pride in observing that there is not a single film in London today which deals with any burning questions of the day'.[13]

The decisions made by the BBFC effectively created a microcosm within British cinema and led to the dominance of two particular narrative types over the course of the decade. They can be aptly described as follows:

Complaisant Dreamscape: Scenarios that advocate class harmony and reiterate the significance of one's social status in Britain. They often contain the notion that any issues, like industrial unrest or unemployment, can be overcome with respect, good cheer, and honesty.

Empire Films: Patriotic films that hark back to Britain's imperial expansion and administration during the Victorian Era, honour is highly prized, 'Red Coats' are abundant, and British methods of rule usurp the traditions employed by local communities.

Such films were unconcerned with the representation of the trials and tribulations of contemporary politics and promoted a nostalgia towards the British Empire's traditions prior to 1914. The following sections will explore these overarching narrative types in greater depth to highlight how integral they were within

Britain's industry and to further demonstrate how such stories distracted contemporary audiences away from the topical issues they faced in the interwar years.

The 'Complaisant Dreamscape' and the 'All is Well' attitude in cinema

In a 1937 piece for *Kinematograph Weekly*, Arthur Dent, a key distributor and figure within Britain's film industry, had this to say about audiences: 'The masses do not change: they still go to the kinema [sic] for relaxation. A picture which demands too much mental exertion does not give them the relaxation and is, therefore, a failure'.[14] The comment was pointed and did two things: Firstly, it suggested that trade leaders viewed audiences as little more than escapist drones; Secondly, it advocated the production of frivolous films that did little to challenge creative practices within the industry or encourage critical thinking amongst viewers. Unfortunately, Dent's comment does describe a significant number of British films distributed during the 1930s.

The birth of the British 'B' film, also known as the 'Quota Quickies', occurred during this early period, and it can be said that their narratives did not prompt any form of 'mental exertion' from cinemagoers. Such productions emerged in response to legislation outlined in the Cinematograph Films Act of 1927, which was a protectionist act passed to ensure the longevity of the national industry. According to Steve Chibnall, the act 'required that a certain proportion of films distributed and exhibited in Britain had to be British in origin . . . to promote . . . economic and cultural interests, at home and abroad'.[15] Overall, the act was successful. The industry in Britain survived, and early career filmmakers, like Michael Powell and Alfred Hitchcock, were able to hone their directorial skills without fear of financial loss or scathing criticism. They were invaluable films for testing technical developments and filmmaking practices; however, their narratives were simplistic and industry workers, as well as audience members, were well aware of their shortcomings. For example, in 1935, Joan Lappa recounted one of her experiences for *Picturegoer* magazine:

> Upon entering one of the best-known kinemas [sic] in Manchester, I was amazed to see flashed upon the screen a lengthy apology for a British quota film which had been shown the week before . . . the manager apologised for inflicting upon the public a British film of that calibre. . . . 'We know that you cannot enjoy such films, but for the sake of patriotism we crave your indulgence for them'.[16]

Lappa went on to say that appealing to patriotism could not sustain the trade indefinitely and implored the community to 'make use of such stars as Noel Coward, Gertrude Lawrence and Conrad Veidt' in a bid to create 'more worthy productions in the future'.[17] Unfortunately for Lappa, sub-par pictures continued to be produced until the 1938 Films Act introduced a new 'grading' framework for British B films.

Therefore, how did such films help to create the 'Complaisant Dreamscape'? They did this through their generic and simplistic plots. As noted earlier, the 'Complaisant Dreamscape' was filled with innocuous stories that did little to challenge Britons. Movies that promoted good cheer and avoided conflict, sex, social unrest, and the shaming of state institutions were swiftly passed by BBFC censors and screened to the masses (both nationally and internationally). They were also unencumbered by the parameters of a single genre. Data compiled by Chibnall shows that between 1928 and 1937 Quota Quickies came in various guises. Comedies had the highest production rate (37.2 per cent), followed by crime films (26.7 per cent), dramas (12.5 per cent), musicals/revues (9.9 per cent), romances (6.7 per cent), and those defined as 'other' (7 per cent).[18] In some instances, films aligned with genre expectations; however, realism or naturalism was generally absent.[19] This lack of realism is extremely noticeable when examining the film synopsis listed in Denis Gifford's comprehensive *British Film Catalogue 1895–1970*. In some instances, his summation of a film's narrative seems downright bizarre – almost absurd – but these productions existed and conveyed the notion that anything could be resolved with the 'right' attitude (predominantly the 'stiff-upper-lip' British attitude). The following examples are a small selection from those listed in Gifford's publication:

Birds of a Feather (1931) – Romance: Bohemian reforms for love of widowed artist's daughter.
Verdict of the Sea (1932) – Adventure: Ex-doctor joins tramp steamer crew and thwarts mutiny.
Guest of Honour (1934) – Comedy: Lord posing as professional dinner guest unmasks blackmailer.
The Last Journey (1935) – Drama: Express train driver goes mad thinking his fireman is having affair with his wife.
Patricia Gets Her Man (1937) – Comedy: Girl tries to make star jealous by hiring gigolo who is really a count.
Thistledown (1938) – Musical: Scotland. Laird believes continental wife is unfaithful.[20]

Even in this brief list of examples, it is clear that topical issues were not at the forefront of the British B reel. Insipid cases of blackmail and paranoid spouses dominated the catalogue, effectively distracting – in some cases boring – audiences with trite scenarios. B-grade films also reiterated Britain's traditional beliefs and encouraged the preservation of the rigid class system. Scenarios that contained cases of mistaken identity or deliberate disguise hardly ever concluded with the shift of a character's social position. With such films in place, alongside the staunch guidelines of the BBFC, the 'Complaisant Dreamscape' thrived throughout the decade. As already mentioned, this was not the only narrative type to divert audiences away from the struggles of reality.

Love for the glorious empire: from adventures in the exotic East to hagiographic monarchs at home

Patriotism and honour were strong themes in the industry's higher-end cinematic projects. They encouraged escapism in a manner that Quota Quickies simply could not, and audiences flocked to see them. Two sets of pro-empire films were particularly popular:

1 Alexander Korda's 'Empire' films: *Sanders of the River* (1935), *Elephant Boy* (1937), *The Drum* (1938), and, most famously, *The Four Feathers* (1939)
2 Herbert Wilcox's monarchical biopics: *Victoria the Great* (1937) and its sequel *Sixty Glorious Years* (1938)

Both series of films hark back to a period in Britain's history that had been somewhat mythicised after the events of the Great War. Set during the Victorian era, each narrative within this category celebrates the triumphs of British tradition, law, and order over the underdeveloped and uncivilised world. Described by Professor Marcia Landy as Britain's 'counterpart to the western genre', such films appealed to audiences because they: a) were exotic and adventurous, b) were conservative despite the rising radicalism elsewhere, and c) promoted nineteenth-century ideals and beliefs of national destiny and identity.[21] The films' celebration of such elements was striking, and even though the representation of the nation's health was outdated, the pro-empire message was always present. Korda's films, in particular, utilised a number of tropes and scenarios to allow for the, as BFI curator Mark Duguid described it, 'unrelenting pro-Empire flag-waving' and 'assumptions of British superiority over 'primitive' or untrustworthy natives' that often sits poorly with audiences nowadays.[22]

Traditionally hailing from the small town of Túrkeve, Hungary, Alexander Korda and his brothers, Zoltan and Vincent, arrived in Britain in the early 1930s after refining their trades (all film- and art-related) in the European and Hollywood circuits. The British industry at this time was struggling to produce films that could keep up with their Hollywood counterparts and, as mentioned in the previous section, was relying heavily on Quota Quickies to sustain the industry. The arrival of the Kordas and the subsequent establishment of Alexander's *London Films* production studio in 1932 marked the start of a new chapter in the British context and acted as a beacon for several Continental émigré artists. While B films continued to be made as supporting features for the industry, Alexander and his 'group of polyglot Continentals' brought a sense of exoticness and excitement to the 'glamourless and rather parochial' British scene.[23] By 1933 the group proved their abilities as excellent filmmakers and provided Britain with its first feature film to attract Academy Award nominations. *The Private Life of Henry VIII* (1933) was, in a sense, a miracle film. According to screenwriter Lajos Biro – a key member of Korda's circle – it was the production that 'Korda had put his shirt, coat, hat and everything on', and had it failed,

Korda and his associates would have struggled to survive.[24] After its success, Korda, his brothers, and his colleagues began to expand the London Films catalogue and its studio spaces.

An array of films followed – each with their own unique narrative, budget, cast, and crew, but it is the adventurous pro-empire films that stand out most within London Films' catalogue. Each film in the empire series was based off already acclaimed novels (which guaranteed an interested audience prior to cinematic release) and every story heavily emphasised British expansionism and rule during the Victorian era. Briefly summarised next, the motifs, themes, and tropes present within Korda's pictures promoted the nation in a manner that encouraged nostalgia and escapism.

Sanders of the River

Original source material: Edgar Wallace's novel *Sanders of the River*, published in 1911.

Synopsis: Set in N'Gombi, Nigeria, a British Commissioner, R. G. Sanders (Leslie Banks), successfully supervises several local tribes within the region, preventing power struggles and violence. After learning that an unauthorised native has taken on the role of chief in one of the tribes under his supervision, Sanders investigates the matter. He learns that Bosambo (Paul Robeson) is a fair leader and sympathetic to the British cause, so he allows Bosambo to remain in the tribe as chief. When Sanders travels back to London to marry, Bosambo defends his tribe and the wider river region against the rebellious King Mofolaba. Sanders returns to the region to restore the peace, and Bosambo kills Mofolaba after rescuing his kidnapped wife. Later, Bosambo is dubbed the King of the Peoples of the River.

Elephant Boy

Original source material: Rudyard Kipling's short story 'Toomai of the Elephants', published in 1893 and within *The Jungle Book* collection.

Synopsis: A young boy in India, Toomai (Sabu), dreams to be a great hunter but is content to help his father, a *mahout* (elephant driver) with their family's elephants. Their most prized elephant, Kala Nag, is chosen for an expedition by a local British official, Peterson (Walter Hudd), as he wishes to explore the northern hills and locate the elusive wild elephants. A hunting incident leaves Toomai orphaned, and Peterson assigns another handler to Kala Nag, Rham Lahl (Bruce Gordon), but he is cruel and beats the elephant. In response, Nag tramples and injures Lahl. In accordance with the law the elephant must be killed, but Sabu escapes with Nag. Peterson and his servants follow. The missing herd of wild elephants is located, and Kala Nag's violence is swiftly forgotten. The elephants are captured, and Toomai is dubbed 'Toomai of the Elephants'.

The Drum

Original source material: A. E. W. Mason's novel *The Drum*, published in 1937.

Synopsis: Set in India, a British Captain, Capt. Carruthers (Roger Livesey), discovers the trade and transport of illegal firearms to a restless part of the local region. Concerned about the possibility of a violent rebellion, Carruthers informs high command, and the British governor (Francis L. Sullivan) organises a treaty with a neighbouring kingdom, Tokot, in an attempt to waylay the violence. The Khan's son, Prince Azim (Sabu), befriends Carruthers and the British; however, the Khan's brother, Prince Ghul (Raymond Massey), rebuffs their presence. Ghul assassinates his brother and attempts to kill his nephew, too, but Azim escapes and finds sanctuary with Carruthers's wife (Valerie Hobson). He leaves after a short time to hide amongst his people. Whilst in hiding, Azim learns that his uncle is behind the weapons trade and is also the mastermind of a plot to kill Carruthers and his British detachment. Azim warns Carruthers by tapping out a message on his drum; his uncle is then overthrown by the British.

The Four Feathers

Original source material: A. E. W Mason's novel *The Four Feathers*, published in 1902.

Synopsis: In 1895 Lieutenant Harry Faversham (John Clements) and his comrades in the Royal North Surrey Regiment are called to active service in the Mahdist War (1881–99). Faversham joined the Army due to familial pressures, and his dislike of warfare comes to the forefront when he resigns his commission. He is then shunned by his friends and former comrades – Capt. John Durrance (Ralph Richardson), Lt Burroughs (Donald Gray), and Willoughby (Jack Allen) – and receives a white feather from each of them for his cowardice. When his fiancée Ethne (June Duprez) agrees with their actions, Faversham leaves. He realises that his actions were cowardly and departs for Egypt. Disguised as a mute Sangali slave, Faversham locates and assists his former comrades in an effort to redeem himself and in one instance helps to overrun the Khalifa's stronghold and hold it until Kitchener's army arrives. Redeemed, Faversham returns home, and Ethne agrees to his courtship as she has learnt about his deeds.

While each film contains fairly different storylines, the tropes they share are strikingly similar and, according to Marcia Landy, were common in all empire films.[25] For example, each film contains the notion of 'savagery vs. civilisation' or 'the British vs. the barbaric'. This is represented in a variety of ways throughout the films' narratives and *mise en scènes*. To illustrate, British officials' actions are dictated by the framework of 'the law', and they will not resort to unmitigated violence before attempting to reason, for example, Sanders learns of Bosambo's self-appointment to the position of Chief, so he investigates the matter before passing judgement. In a similar vein, Ferguson tries to persuade Rham Lahl against the execution of the elephant Kala Nag; however, the injured man will not budge, and Ferguson accepts his responsibility as the upholder of the law. Within the *mise en scène*, costumes are utilised to contrast British 'civility' against native 'savagery'. Sabu and Bosambo were half-clothed, Bosambo sported feathers and animal skins, the Khalifia donned a turban, and various extras wore non-descript shabby ensembles. In comparison, British subjects were highly manicured and clean. Their uniforms were impeccably neat, and any female characters were dressed in the popular fashions of the day. Furthermore, the British presence in these 'uncivilised' places is depicted as a positive patriarchal presence: Sanders is well known for his just leadership, Ferguson is well-respected and upholds the law, Carruthers is attempting to halt violence, and Faversham's regiment is able to quell the dangerous Khalifa. The local populations (filled with 'blacked up' British extras) were either depicted as childlike people, easily led astray by the plots and false promises of those attempting to oust the British, or as loyalists to the British regime. Overall, this main theme – savagery vs. civilisation – and all the tropes it entailed actively portrayed the wider empire in a manner that suggested good health. In reality, India was establishing its foundations for independence, elite leaders in Africa had begun to study self-determination, and Egypt was in flux until the Anglo-Egyptian treaty of 1936 provided them with a form of independence. As historian Jeffrey Richards once stated: 'There is no reflection of the fact that the Empire was in a constant state of flux during the interwar years, evolving towards something quite different'.[26]

While Korda displayed England's prowess on a global stage, director and producer Herbert Wilcox chose a subject set squarely within the United Kingdom for his patriotic feature films. Wilcox had been a solid figure within Britain's industry, being one of the limited number of filmmakers to produce films that dealt with the events of the Great War and its aftermath. He was incredibly skilled at reading the public's mood and was particularly artful when meeting their needs, whilst also falling within the parameters set by the BBFC. Although a busy filmmaker throughout the 1930s, his historical projects that centred on the life of Queen Victoria – *Victoria the Great* and *Sixty Glorious Years* – are particularly interesting when considering how Britons were handling national events and global politics during the interwar period.

Victoria the Great was a well-timed release for several reasons. Firstly, it was one of the first major pictures to depict a British monarch on screen. According to Jeffrey Richards, there had been a ban in place within the industry preventing filmmakers from depicting or directly referring to the royal family on screen.[27] This ban was lifted in time for the 100th anniversary of Queen Victoria's accession to the throne, and Wilcox made sure to avoid the image of a 'little old lady, potato-like in appearance, dressed in everlasting black'.[28] Instead, his Victoria was youthful, passionate, strong-willed, and saint-like – a hagiographic figure in a tumultuous time. Portrayed by popular actress Anna Neagle (later Wilcox's third wife), the film focused primarily on the love story between the young Queen and

Albert of Saxe-Coburg and Gotha (Anton Walbrook). The portrayal of a strong and happy marriage within the royal family was especially poignant at this time, as the House of Windsor had just experienced one of its largest scandals, Edward VIII's abdication crisis. After Edward VIII's abdication, the image of a united and steadfast royal family was in flux, and re-establishing this perception was paramount. Brian McFarlane highlighted how this 'wholesome image' was, most likely, assisted by Wilcox's film: '[*Victoria the Great*] may be seen to reinforce the role of the monarchy in the troubling wake of Edward VIII's abdication, with the film "celebrat[ing] a perfect marriage and a dedicated partnership in the service of the nation" '.[29]

This is a fair assessment, as advertisements and critiques at the time actively linked the film's narrative to the activities of the current royals. For example, *Film Weekly* magazine highlighted how 'Anna Neagle's coronation as Queen Victoria will be taking place at Denham at almost the same time as the coronation of George VI and Queen Elizabeth'.[30] Meanwhile, US magazine *Variety* believed the film would appease the 'deeper interest in the British monarchy evinced by Americans since the Windsor-Warfield [Wallis Simpson] page-one smear'.[31] Overall, the first film was a resounding success and was praised for its style, cast, cinematography, and historicity.

The formula for the first film did not really leave room for a sequel, as it concluded with Queen Victoria's Diamond Jubilee in 1897, but nevertheless, spurred on by the success of the first film, Wilcox created the second, *Sixty Glorious Years*. It adopted a similar approach with its narrative and continued to use the same themes/motifs: a saint-like monarch, a healthy marriage, political intrigues, international disputes, and their conclusion, the implementation of positive social changes, etc. It was received warmly, and 'Queen Anna' was given the seal of approval from fan magazines like *Picturegoer*.[32] Both films reflected Britain's history within a 'nostalgic bubble', and Balcon's comment, 'hardly a single film of the period reflects the agony of those times', seems dishearteningly true. After considering Korda and Wilcox's film, it is difficult to comprehend how any filmmakers could compete with such successful narratives. Patriotism, in both cases, sold well – so how did filmmakers convey their unease about the future without attracting the ire of BBFC censors or alienating an audience that clearly loved pro-empire stories? Put simply, they disguised their messages within other genre films.

The subtlety of disguised criticisms in British cinema

In a 1938 interview for *Film Weekly*, Alfred Hitchcock neatly outlined the necessity of subterfuge when presenting politicised stories to the BBFC. He said:

> If you imply 'It can't happen here' – if you set your story in central Europe or even make your villain a foreigner – officialdom raises no objections. But if your picture is too obviously a criticism of the social system, Whitehall shakes its head.[33]

This comment does two things. Firstly, it demonstrates how some filmmakers were frustrated with their inability to incorporate contemporary politics into their projects. Secondly, it reveals that there was a method for inadvertently conveying criticism through cinema – which suggests that there is an indeterminate number of pictures within Britain's catalogue that did evaluate contemporary politics in a meaningful way. Jeffrey Richards once described such projects as 'disguised criticisms', and they are, arguably, the third style of narrative present within cinema during the interwar years. While Quota Quickies and pro-empire dramas dominated the landscape, 'disguised criticisms' emerged sporadically to test audiences in new ways.

It is only right to begin this section with the film that prompted Balcon's lamentations. *Jew Süss* (1934), produced by Balcon and directed by Lothar Mendes, was adapted from the 1925 historical novel *Jud Süß* and submitted to the BBFC for approval in 1933.[34] Set during the eighteenth century, the story follows Joseph Süss Oppenheimer (Conrad Veidt), a wealthy and ambitious Jew, as he climbs to one of the highest offices he can occupy within the court of the Duchy of Württemberg. Whilst acting as the sole financial advisor to Duke Karl Alexander (Frank Vosper), Süss uses his authority to heavily tax the region in the hopes of prompting a rebellion. This scheme is incited after the death of his daughter, who was killed whilst attempting to escape the Duke's lecherous advances. Süss's plan is barely in motion when the Duke, Süss's only defender in Württemberg's antisemitic court, has a heart attack and dies. Subsequently, Süss is arrested, and the community demands that he convert to Christianity. Süss refuses to deny his Jewish faith. He is subsequently blamed for the Duke's death and is executed.

The scenario clearly contains messages about anti-Semitism and the violence it incites; however, the BBFC censor's report made no mention of the issue and was primarily concerned with the depictions of violence and sexual scenes.[35] James Robertson suggests that this was a deliberate moment of 'turning a blind eye to attacks upon Nazi anti-Semitism'.[36] *Jew Süss* contained distinct moments that alluded to the persecution of contemporary European Jews. For example:

1. The opening title card reads 'it was a time of universal intolerance and the Jews above all suffered oppression and boycott' – the Nazi boycott of Jewish businesses began in earnest during 1933 and received significant press coverage in the UK.[37]
2. Other title cards contain comments like 'his story lives', which signals the continuance of persecution.[38]
3. Most damningly, when discussing the ill-treatment of the Jewish community, a secondary character announces, 'They can do it in 1730, they can do it in 1830, they can do it in 1930!'[39]

Determining whether such connections were made by everyday viewers is difficult to discover; however, some critics at the time did note the film's relationship to contemporary issues. One such critic was the prominent C. A. Lejeune. In her column for *The Observer*, she commented upon the lengthy delay between the purchase of the novel's rights and the film's release: 'The film was never made, and no more was heard of the project until the Spring of this year, when Gaumont-British apparently saw in the present political situation in Germany and excellent reason for taking over the production rights'.[40]

Lejeune's overall review was disparaging – she believed the production cost was too high – but nevertheless, her ability to identify the picture's links to contemporary politics shows that the filmmakers' criticisms were identifiable within the project's historical setting.

Another type of film that was remarkably well-placed for the disguise of political commentaries was the 'thriller/espionage' film. As noted by Marcia Landy, 'films of espionage began to address foreign threats to national security and the need for preparedness . . . [they] capitalize on an atmosphere of uncertainty, paranoia, and physical and verbal belligerence'.[41] Such pictures had the ability to 'hint' towards particular foreign powers (mostly Germany) as the enemy; however, as mentioned earlier, BBFC guidelines dictated that the adversary, 'Fascist and non-Fascist alike', had to remain unnamed. Those within the industry had found ways to work around this restriction, though. Although dependent on the audience's prior knowledge of topical issues, filmmakers used 'clues' to suggest the identity of foreign threats. These clues included:

The use of 'foreign' accents that → sounded decidedly German.	Émigré artists, like Conrad Veidt and Lucie Mannheim, leant a genuine air when cast in such roles, due to their natural German accents.
The discussion/inclusion of → technological advancements that coincided with developments in reality.	For example, rearmament begins in Germany (1933), Hitler announces his German air force (1935), and Richard Hannay (Robert Donat) foils the plans of a spy ring as they attempt to send the formula for a silent engine to a foreign power in *The Thirty-Nine Steps*.
The presence of physical traits/items → of clothing that was synonymous with threatening foreign powers.	The uncomplicated inclusion of a toothbrush moustache and a lengthy leather coat could represent a Nazi Party member/affiliate.

More often than not, clues inferred a German enemy, but in one instance, *East Meets West* (1936), the antagonist had Asian features and was required to commit suicide if he failed in his political mission. Robertson noted that the allusion towards Japan as a rival was rare in British cinema.[42] By the end of the decade, espionage films began to dominate the new release list, and in 1939 filmmakers began to directly name the enemy, especially after the disintegration of European relations and the subsequent declarations of war. Cinema's 'disguised criticisms' could never stop the oncoming conflict; however, it is arguable that their indirect criticisms prevented true escapism within the cinema.

Naming the enemy and the acceptance of inevitable conflict

It is abundantly clear that throughout the entirety of the decade there was a significant effort to stifle any productions that tested the boundaries of acceptable moral behaviours (as perceived by the BBFC), as well as those that addressed state/international affairs. Some features had managed to sneak their way through as 'disguised criticisms', but as the tenuous interwar relationship between Britain and Germany began to deteriorate, filmmakers became more confident when labelling the enemy on screen. One of the few films to actively label a German enemy during this decade was Michael Powell and Emeric Pressburger's first collaborative piece, *The Spy in Black* (1939) – *U-Boat 29* for US audiences.

Released in August, *The Spy in Black* was a topical and well-timed production. Endorsed by Alexander Korda and produced at Denham Studios, the project initially began as the adaptation of John Buchan's spy novel but quickly morphed into something new. Set during 1917 (but lacking any historical embellishments), the film's plot focused on a German U-boat commander, Captain Hardt (Conrad Veidt), as he infiltrated the Orkney Islands to collect vital information regarding the British Grand Fleet's manoeuvres within the Scapa Flow region. Hardt's efforts were thwarted by British double agents, 'Commander Ashington' (Sebastian Shaw) and 'Fräulein Tiel' (Valerie Hobson), and his escape from the area ultimately failed, leading to his death. The British retained their secrets, and the Germans lost an experienced Captain. Emeric Pressburger's characters were well-developed, and the German enemy was written in a manner that encouraged empathy and sympathy, rather than hatred or bitterness. Captain Hardt openly showed his disdain for spying, he was proud to wear his uniform, he showed his humanity through the good treatment of enemy civilians, and ultimately he demonstrated his honourable character by following the maritime tradition that 'the Captain goes down with the ship'. He was Pressburger's first 'Good German', and audiences responded positively to his character despite his position as the enemy.

As a whole, the film was received well, and Powell claimed that this was due to its narrative: 'it didn't matter that it was the 1914–18 war. . . . It was a war picture, all about submarines and spies, full of action and suspense. The British Navy triumphs in the end and it was all lovely!'[43] Various reviews from newspapers support his comment, and *Mass Observation* findings also provide insight into audience response. Some focused primarily on performance, particularly from the film's expatriate German lead: 'I doff the monocle to Conrad Veidt. After eighteen years he is still the best spy in the business', Guy Morgan wrote for *The Daily Express*.[44] Other reviews claimed that it had 'more downright good acting' than a 'dozen epics'.[45] While such reviews focused on talent and star power, others considered the film a cautionary tale for the future and linked its scenario to contemporary topical issues.

Powell and Pressburger's decision to avoid elaborate historical settings and costumes emphasised the topicality of film's major themes/motifs, which made it impossible for viewers (both then and now) to truly believe such dangers depicted were only applicable to the First World War period. By the time *The Spy in Black* reached cinema screens in August 1939, the relationship between Britain and Germany could only be described as 'dire'. Negotiations regarding appeasement had broken down, and the Munich Agreement had only briefly appeased Hitler's ambitions concerning territorial expansion. War was imminent, and although *The Spy in Black* was set during the Great War, some shrewd critics and exhibitors were quick to link the film to the present. For instance, the vendor for the Granada cinema in Tooting, London, displayed posters that read 'The Spy in Black – The Story the Papers Didn't Dare to Print'.[46] In a similar vein, the *Liverpool Echo* described the film as follows: 'now . . . this sensational story can be told . . . of enemy menace in its grimmest form . . . of U-boat 29. . . Lurking, waiting . . . The British Fleet in Peril . . . See and thrill to a terrific drama as topical as todays headlines!'[47] In other instances, the links made between the film and reality lacked such sensationalism. At times, viewers wrote to newspapers or magazines to share their thoughts with others. For example, an unnamed contributor to the *Yorkshire Post*'s opinion column believed the film's naval blockade was particularly poignant:

> This film holds a lesson for the citizens of this country. And that lesson is, 'GROW MORE FOOD AT HOME.' We need to grow sufficient food in Britain to remove forever the danger of starvation by blockade. Blockade which might be imposed on our food ships, either from above the earth by airplanes or from beneath the seas by submarines, whose sinister courses you follow in 'The Spy in Black'.[48]

It was an astute observation because the picture's commentary upon food shortages was primarily in the opening sequences before becoming embedded within the script as an 'in-joke' amongst the German characters. In the wider scope of the film's narrative, the issue actually lingers behind the threat of espionage and the theft of military intelligence. The contribution in the *Yorkshire Post* exhibits genuine concern about food shortages and an overall irritation at the lack of agricultural development. Such links, both the sensational and the collected, were prominent after the film's release; however, a later incident would cement its reputation as one of the most perceptive pre-war films produced by the British industry.

Britain's declaration of war in September reiterated the prophetic nature of the film but did not mark the end of its predictions. Eerily, on October 13 – only ten weeks after *The Spy in Black*'s release – a German U-boat, *U-boat 47*, entered the Scapa Flow anchorage and destroyed the Revenge-class battleship the HMS *Royal Oak*. The reputation that the well-fortified region received during the Great War splintered, and its moniker 'the Impregnable Scapa' was immediately forgotten as news of the attack spread.[49] Columnists began connecting the attack to the film almost immediately, which then prompted the second wave of screenings within the cinema circuit. Sensationalist column titles like 'Nazis Made Film of "U-Boat Raid" True' began to emerge, and a general sense of bewilderment at the film's anticipation of future events was reported in the media.[50] Internationally, the links between *The Spy in Black* and reality's events were featured in the press as well. For example, Queensland's *Evening News* described the *Royal Oak*'s destruction as 'a truly amazing coincidence of fiction and fact'.[51] On the other side of the world, an exhibitor in Winnipeg, Canada, 'carried copies of the headlines from two local dailies telling of the Royal Oak sinking' and displayed them in the lobby while the film was showing.[52] Evidently, the days of subtle criticism were truly over.

To conclude

The films discussed in this chapter were selected to demonstrate a series of key points about the overarching narrative themes within Britain's catalogue during the interwar years. Firstly, after the Armistice, there was a legitimate attempt made by filmmakers to assist society with the comprehension of the emotional and physical aftermath of the Great War. Cinema was able to incorporate individual experiences into the conflict's wider narrative, which acted as a form of 'cinematic therapy' for returned servicemen and their families. Some features explicitly dealt with issues on the battlefield; however, others opted for the 'war touch' and were able to demonstrate the after-effects of violence and their impact within household settings. Over time, the popularity of such topics in cinema began to dwindle, and the rising influence of the BBFC ultimately impacted upon filmmakers' ability to produce such violent scenarios on screen.

Secondly, as the 1920s came to a close, the BBFC effectively 'tightened' its hold on cinematic content. Any films containing depictions of violence, mockery of state officials and institutions, union strikes, sex, and indecorous situations were immediately shortlisted for deletion, but such edits could drastically alter the overall composition and aim of a project. This inherently created the 'Complaisant Dreamscape' within Britain's catalogue. Filled with British B films, also known as Quota Quickies, those within this category did little to challenge audience members. The plots were often innocuous and concerned with the same recycled issues – unfaithful spouses and cases of blackmail were particularly common – and, overall, they reiterated the notion that all dilemmas could be solved by clear reasoning. All was well within this dreamscape, and topical issues, like the rise of threatening foreign powers or industrial action at home, were either far off concerns or manageable with a jaunty song. While this category helped to sustain the industry and assist with its technological advancements, another prominent theme began to dominate Britain's cinematic catalogue – 'pro-empire'.

Thirdly, pro-empire films (predominantly produced by Alexander Korda) began to emerge in greater numbers after the release of *Sanders of the River*. Such films harked back to Britain's dominance as an imperial power and celebrated their governance of 'uncivilised' territories. Set in exotic locales, such as India, Africa, and Sudan, and filled with exceptional talent, these films would have appeased any Anglophile. Similarly, Herbert Wilcox's films struck a patriotic chord and reminded viewers of the strength of the monarchy, and in the wake of Edward VIII's abdication, the projection of a strong royal family was paramount for repairing reputations. Both types of pro-empire film presented a strong and healthy Britain on screen, which was somewhat misleading, as the empire was beginning to splinter after the strain of the Great War. Nevertheless, the nostalgic microcosm was established, and cinematically the health of the empire was splendid.

The final point in this chapter investigated how combatting nostalgia and questioning the vitality of British governing processes, at home and overseas, was a difficult task for filmmakers; however, it was feasible. As Hitchcock said, subterfuge was necessary if one wanted to slip any topical critiques past censors. Aptly categorised as 'disguised criticisms', these types of films hid their political commentaries with historical characters/settings and attempted to combat the safe messages disseminated by the 'Complaisant Dreamscape' and pro-empire films. Alongside them, espionage/thriller films also prompted the need for preparedness in the face of another global conflict. To work around BBFC guidelines, directors/producers 'dropped' clues within a production's dialogue and mise en scène.

Overall, Balcon's comment, 'hardly a single film of the period reflects the agony of those times', is a fair criticism. The dominance of the 'Complaisant Dreamscape' and the popularity of epic pro-empire films left little room for the meaningful critique of contemporary politics. In addition to this, the sharp eye of the BBFC prevented any taboo scenarios reaching audiences, so they were effectively ensconced in a bubble of safety and nostalgia. In spite of this, some filmmakers actively worked around censorship guidelines to incorporate political critiques into their projects, and they managed with moderate successes. The number of disguised criticisms within Britain's catalogue may be small; however, it is likely that there are more than Balcon assumed, and they are worth further investigation.

Notes

1 M. Balcon, *Michael Balcon Presents . . . A Lifetime of Films* (London: Hutchinson & Co Ltd., 1969), 99.

2 It is somewhat difficult to obtain a full picture of British censors and their decisions during this time due to a gap within the BBFC's official records. According to James Robertson, the BBFC's premises, Carlisle House (Soho), was destroyed during the Blitz – on the night of 10–11 of May 1941; J. C. Robertson, *The Hidden Cinema: British Film Censorship in Action, 1913–1975* (London and New York: Routledge, 1993), 165.

3 His Majesty's Government of the United Kingdom and Great Britain, "Cinematograph Act, 1909," *The National Archives: Legislation*, November 25, 1909.

4 Robertson, *The Hidden Cinema*, 1.

5 Ibid.

6 The British Board of Film Censors, "Annual Report," December 31, 1914, https://bbfc.co.uk/sites/default/files/attachments/BBFC%20From%20The%20Archive%20Annual%20Reports.pdf.

7 Ibid.
8 L. Napper, "Remembrance, Re-Membering and Recollection: Walter Summers and the British War Film of the 1920s'," in *British Silent Cinema and the Great War*, ed. M. Hammond and M. Williams (London: Palgrave Macmillan, 2011), 109–17.
9 Ibid.
10 C. Gledhill, "Remembering the War in 1920s British Cinema," in *British Silent Cinema and the Great War* (London: Palgrave Macmillan, 2011), 94–108.
11 E. Shortt, "Problems of Censorship," Summer Conference of the Cinematograph Exhibitors' Association of Great Britain and Ireland, June 27, 1935, 8.
12 J. Richards, "Controlling the Screen: The British Cinema in the 1930s," *History Today* 33, no. 3 (March 1, 1983): 16–17.
13 M. Brooke, "Social Problem Films," *BFI Screenonline*, www.screenonline.org.uk/film/id/1074067/index.html.
14 A. Dent, "Appealing to the Ninepennies," *Kinematograph Weekly*, January 14, 1937.
15 S. Chibnall, *Quota Quickies: The Birth of the British 'B' Film* (London: BFI Publishing, 2007), 1.
16 J. Lappa, "Apologies for British Films: Quota Quickies Denounced," *Picturegoer Weekly*, August 17, 1935.
17 Ibid.
18 Chibnall, *Quota Quickies*, 94.
19 Ibid., 96.
20 D. Gifford, *The British Film Catalogue 1895–1970: A Guide to Entertainment Films* (Great Britain: David & Charles Ltd., 1973).
21 M. Landy, *British Genres: Cinema and Society, 1930–1960* (Princeton, NJ: Princeton University Press, 1991), 98.
22 M. Duguid, "Korda and Empire," *BFI Sreenonline*, www.screenonline.org.uk/film/id/445836/index.html.
23 K. Kulik, *Alexander Korda: The Man Who Could Work Miracles* (Great Britain: Virgin Books, 1990), 83.
24 Ibid., 95.
25 Landy, *British Genres*, 98.
26 Ibid., 100.
27 Richards, "Controlling the Screen," 15.
28 L. Worsley, *Queen Victoria: Daughter, Wife, Mother, Widow* (Great Britain: Hodder & Stoughton, 2019), 1.
29 B. McFarlane, "Royal Parade: The Young Victorian and Its Antecedents," *Metro Magazine* 163 (2009): 114.
30 "Victoria Comes to the Screen," *Film Weekly Magazine*, May 1, 1937, 4–5.
31 "Film Reviews: Victoria the Great," *Variety*, August 25, 1937, 17.
32 " 'Queen Anna' Receives Our Medal," *Picturegoer Magazine*, June 18, 1938, 20–21.
33 J. Danvers William, "The Censors Wouldn't Pass It, Says Hitchcock," *Film Weekly*, November 5, 1938.
34 Robertson, *The Hidden Cinema*, 60.
35 G. Toffell, *Jews, Cinema and Public Life in Interwar Britain* (London: Palgrave Macmillan, 2018), 160.
36 Robertson, *The Hidden Cinema*, 62.
37 Toffell, *Jews, Cinema and Public Life*, 161.
38 Ibid.
39 Ibid.
40 C. A. Lejuene, " 'Jew Suss': A Costly Experiment in Horror," *The Observer*, October 7, 1934.
41 Landy, *British Genres*, 124.

42 J. C. Robertson, "British Film Censorship Goes to War," *Historical Journal of Film, Radio and Television* 2, no. 1 (1982): 49–64.
43 M. Powell, *A Life in Movies* (Great Britain: Methuen, 1986), 335–36.
44 G. Morgan, "First Responses to Cinema Releases," *The Daily Express*, July 28, 1939.
45 Columbia Pictures Distribution, Panel Advertisement for *The Spy in Black*, *The Daily Express*, August 7, 1939.
46 Mass Observation Report, "The Cinema in the First Three Months of the War (September to November 1939)," *Mass Observation Archive*, January 1940, 12.
47 Ibid., 13.
48 Unknown, "Film with a Lesson," *The Daily Express*, August 1, 1939.
49 A. McKee, *Black Saturday: The Tragedy of the Royal Oak* (London: Souvenir Press, 1959), 14.
50 R. Whitley, "Nazis Made Film of 'U-Boat Raid' True," *The Daily Mirror*, October 19, 1939.
51 Unknown, "Cashing in: Topics and Gossip of the Day," *The Evening New*, Rockhampton, November 9, 1939.
52 C. Drazin, "The Distribution of Powell and Pressburger's Films in the United States, 1939–1949," *Historical Journal of Film, Radio and Television* 33, no. 1 (2013): 57.

13 Reconciliation through commemoration

Ireland, empire, and the 1987 Enniskillen Armistice Day bombing

Murphy Temple

Used with the wisdom which is sown in tears and blood, this tragedy of Europe may be and must be the prologue to . . . the reconciliation of Protestant Ulster with Ireland and the reconciliation of Ireland with Great Britain.[1]

On the morning of 8 November 1987, Protestant communities across Northern Ireland gathered to commemorate their military dead on Remembrance Sunday, just as they had done since the end of the First World War. The events in Enniskillen, a fairly small town in County Fermanagh just north of the border separating Northern Ireland from the Republic of Ireland, were typical: civilians holding poppy wreaths milled about near the town's war memorial, awaiting the start of the service at 11 a.m. Meanwhile, soldiers, veterans, police, firefighters, local dignitaries, and a regimental band were getting into formation for the march that would commence the ceremony.[2] At 10:43 a.m., however, an unexpected blast interrupted the calm scene. Explosives planted by the Provisional Irish Republic Army (IRA) detonated, destroying a nearby building and pinning many civilians under the rubble.[3] Eleven people, including three married couples, died at the scene.[4] They ranged in age from twenty to seventy-three and included Presbyterians, Methodists, and members of the Church of Ireland.[5] More than sixty others, including children as young as two months, were wounded, and in 2000, a twelfth victim died after thirteen years in a coma.[6]

The attack was part of the Troubles, a politico-religious conflict that plagued the six counties of Northern Ireland with paramilitary violence for three decades between 1968 and 1998. While the bombing demonstrates the consequences of political and sectarian division in Ireland, it also highlights the emotive significance of First World War commemoration in Irish culture. Ian McBride suggests that 'the interpretation of the past has always been at the heart of national conflict' in Ireland, where nationalist and unionist identities have focused on a series of dates – such as the rebellion of 1641, the signing of the Ulster Covenant in 1912, and the Armistice – that recall inter-Irish conflict. Enniskillen keenly demonstrates his observation that Irish anniversaries, 'not content merely to remind us of ancient quarrels, . . . have an uncanny way of making history themselves'.[7]

The outbreak of war in 1914 had come during a protracted struggle for home rule. The Third Home Rule Bill, meant to bring self-government to Ireland, was introduced in 1912 (it passed but was never enacted due to wartime delays), and in the same year, 500,000 unionists signed the Ulster Covenant in protest against home rule.[8] Despite these political tensions, as many as 206,000 Irishmen from both the Catholic nationalist and Protestant unionist communities volunteered for the war effort. Though the conflict would become associated almost exclusively with the Protestant community, Catholics represented a larger percentage of Ireland's volunteers – 56.6 per cent – and a larger percent of its casualties.[9]

While some volunteers were motivated by a paycheck or lust for adventure, many justified their participation in political terms. For unionists, enlistment demonstrated loyalty to the United Kingdom. As a piece of unionist propaganda from October 1914 announced:

> And wherever the fight is hottest,
> And the sorest task is set,
> ULSTER WILL STRIKE FOR ENGLAND –
> AND ENGLAND WILL NOT FORGET.[10]

For nationalists, enlistment was more contentious. John Redmond, leader of the Irish Parliamentary Party, encouraged Irishmen to stand up for the rights of small nations like Belgium and Serbia. He also argued that the aspiring Irish nation needed a trial by fire, that 'no people can be said to have rightly proved their nationhood and their power to maintain it until they have demonstrated their military prowess'.[11] Though most nationalists sided with Redmond, a vocal minority – most notably those associated with the militant party Sinn Féin – condemned Irish participation in the war. Enlistment, they said, was a betrayal of Ireland. Their real fight was at home, against British imperialism.[12] Sinn Féin demonstrated the full measure of its opposition to imperialism with the 1916 Easter Rising, when over 1,000 nationalists seized strongholds in Dublin and proclaimed an Irish Republic. The British Army quashed the rebellion, and the subsequent execution of fourteen leaders of the Rising, combined with the threat of British conscription in 1918, cemented widespread popular opposition to the war in the south.

Jay Winter has emphasised the difficulty of finding an 'appropriate language of loss' for a war that many saw as wasteful and meaningless.[13] In Ireland, however, argues James Loughlin, this was not a problem because the meaning of the conflict was obvious: 'As both the dominant unionist and republican movements framed the war experience according to their own political agendas, Ireland, unlike Britain, was less affected by the traumatic question of what the war was fought for.'[14] In the north, commemoration was not only a way of mourning the dead, but it also advanced political priorities as an annual reminder of Northern Ireland's loyalty to the United Kingdom. In the south, by contrast, parades, ceremonies, and symbols of remembrance, such as the poppy, were controversial as early as 1919. At Dublin's Peace Day parade in July 1919, Sinn Féiners sang republican songs, flew republican flags, and attacked soldiers returning to their barracks.[15] After the party's victory in the election of December 1918, its disapproval of Irish participation became the dominant strain of nationalist opinion on the First World War. Though an Irish National War Memorial was completed in Dublin in 1939, it was not unveiled until 1994, and the Irish Free State was the only dominion that did not pay the Imperial War Graves Commission for the burial of its dead.[16]

Despite the war's divisive place in twentieth-century Irish history, Catholics and Protestants alike widely decried the Enniskillen bombing in the domestic and international media. The public was outraged that civilians had been killed, that children had been present, and that the explosion had disrupted a solemn day set aside for remembrance of the dead. The attack and the public conversations that followed prompted reflections on violence on both sides of the border – not only on the contemporary violence of the Troubles but also on the historic violence of the First World War. Since the signing of the Belfast Agreement and the formal end of the Troubles in April 1998, attendance at Remembrance Day services in the Republic has grown, and some southern communities have even unveiled new war memorials. This increased republican interest in the war, however, is not simply a reflection of improved relations among Northern Ireland, the Republic, and the United Kingdom; it has itself been a tool for reconciliation. Initiatives such as the Island of Ireland Peace Park, unveiled in Messines, Belgium, in 1998, have united republicans and unionists seeking to honour the dead, acknowledge Irish participation in the war, and work towards harmony after decades of conflict. This unified commemoration has required compromise: as they re-write a shared history of the First World War, unionists and republicans have had to face not only the discord of Ireland's recent past but also the violence of the distant past and their divergent relationships with Britain and the empire.

Attack and aftermath

Although Enniskillen is a fairly small and quiet town (its population was about 11,500 in the 1991 census), it was a likely target for a Remembrance Day attack.[17] It has a long military history, and its infantry regiment, the Royal Inniskilling Fusiliers, was part of the 36th Ulster Division, which later became renowned for its Protestant identity and heroism at the Battle of the Somme. Enniskillen had also asserted its unionist identity in the Williamite War, the Seven Years' War, the Napoleonic Wars, the Boer War, and the Second World War.[18] The town's cenotaph, built in 1922, bears witness to County Fermanagh's contribution to the 1914–18 war effort: the names of 622 dead are inscribed there, and over 300 of these are from Enniskillen. Despite the fact that the monument honours both Protestants and Catholics, commemoration in Enniskillen, as in the rest of Northern Ireland, became a unionist affair. A few years before the bombing, the town's residents had spent £15,000 on paper poppies. Although Protestants, the primary poppy-buying demographic, only constituted about half of Enniskillen's population, this figure was the highest of any branch of the Royal British Legion and almost double the per capita poppy sales in Britain itself.[19]

The bombing came two decades into the Troubles and two years after the signing of the November 1985 Anglo–Irish Agreement, which stated that 'if in the future a majority of the people of Northern Ireland clearly wish for and formally consent to the establishment of a united Ireland, they [would] introduce and support in the respective Parliaments legislation to give effect to that wish.'[20] Loyalists saw the document as an act of abandonment by the British government and a threat to Northern Ireland's future within the United Kingdom, and killings by loyalist paramilitary groups increased in the Agreement's aftermath.[21] In response, the IRA intensified its bombing campaign but claimed that civilians would not be harmed. Instead, their targets were members of the 'British war machine'.[22] Against this backdrop, Enniskillen, with its connections to the British military, was an appealing target for an IRA looking to justify its violence as being directed towards an oppressive military enemy.

The guerrillas, however, had grossly miscalculated the attack's impact. A revolted public immediately decried the bombing, mourned its human cost, and criticised the IRA for targeting a Remembrance Day service. A statement from the Royal Ulster Constabulary headquarters in Belfast, for instance, declared: 'Words are inadequate to describe the scenes of carnage and distress which resulted. . . . No condemnation is adequate to describe the sheer barbarity meted out to fellow human beings.'[23] Church of Ireland Archbishop Robin Eames lamented, 'it is unbelievable [that] at the moment [the victims] prepared to lay wreaths and have a moment of silent remembrance such a thing could happen.'[24] In Britain, the queen reportedly called the attack 'an atrocity', while Margaret Thatcher expressed shock at its 'appalling depth [of] callousness and inhumanity'.[25]

Republicans, too, were outraged. On the day of the bombing, Fine Gael senator Maurice Manning asserted that few events from the Troubles' 'long catalogue of horror' had 'generated such total revulsion as the massacre of innocent, decent Irish people, gathered to solemnly honour their dead'.[26] During mass a week after the bombing, Catholic priests across the Republic denounced paramilitary violence and declared that supporting the IRA was a sin. A statement from the Standing Committee of Irish Bishops of the Roman Catholic Church asserted: 'There is no room for ambivalence. In the face of the present campaigns of republican violence the choice of all Catholics is clear. It is a choice between good and evil.'[27]

Many politicians used the attack as an opportunity to call for peace and cooperation among republicans, unionists, and the British government. Because the attackers had targeted a Remembrance Sunday ceremony, and because First World War commemoration had been such a source of tension in Ireland, the war became an integral part of political efforts at reconciliation. This began as early as the day of the bombing in the Seanad, where John Robb, a Northern Irish Protestant senator, asked forgiveness for his role – and the role of all Protestants – in perpetuating the resentment and bitterness that had fuelled the Troubles. He expressed hope that Remembrance Day could become 'an opportunity for healing' rather than a source of resentment. He then offered a poppy to Fine Gael senator and deputy chairman of the Seanad Charles McDonald, who, despite traditional republican disdain for the paper flower as a symbol of British imperialism, pinned it to his lapel.[28] This act of cross-border commemoration foreshadowed the efforts at unified remembrance that would emerge in the years following the Enniskillen bombing, and it demonstrates the way in which traditional symbols – including symbols of imperialism – would be adapted and negotiated for the purposes of modern political reconciliation.

Remembering the First World War in the Republic

The revival of First World War commemoration in Ireland began with the Republic rediscovering and reclaiming its role in the conflict. While the Enniskillen bombing planted the seeds of reconciliation by prompting introspection and sympathy from many Catholics and republicans, serious republican dialogue about the war and its legacy did not begin in earnest until several years later, after the 1998 Belfast Agreement officially ended the Troubles and most of the violence. Since then, republican interest in the war has increased, with individuals and organisations researching family history, commemorating the dead with new services and monuments, and reinterpreting the war in the framework of republican history.

Modern republican interest in the war began publicly in the Seanad. On 12 November 1998, the day after Remembrance Day, senators spoke at length about the war. Fianna Fáil politician Daniel Cassidy opened the discussion by asserting that 'Ireland's Great War dead should be cherished alongside all patriots who struggled and suffered.' Although the soldiers who died in 1914–18, he said, deserved to be revered like republican freedom-fighters and mourned like those killed in the Troubles, 'their memory [had instead fallen] victim to a war of independence at home.' Recovering their stories, he suggested, would advance the peace process, and commemoration of the war would be a powerful statement about the wastefulness of war and a reminder of a time when Irishmen of all creeds fought side by side. Fianna Fáil senator Paschal Mooney agreed, arguing that nationalism had eclipsed the memory of republican soldiers, but he also suggested that Ulster had contributed to republican amnesia by '[claiming] almost exclusive right to this sacred memory'. Renewed remembrance of the First World War, then, would be a way for 'Nationalist Ireland' to '[reclaim] its birthright'.[29]

Many of the senators who voiced their support for republican commemoration emphasised that southern remembrance would need to assume a distinctly republican tone to differentiate it from its unionist counterpart. Fine Gael senator Maurice Manning, for example, evoked Tom Kettle, a poet and Irish Parliamentary Party MP killed on the Western Front who feared that while the rebels of the Easter Rising would 'go down in history as heroes and martyrs', he would go down 'as a bloody British officer'.[30] Manning noted that while many Ulstermen fought for empire, republicans fought for other reasons, and he read his colleagues a few lines of Kettle's poem 'To My Daughter Betty, the Gift of God':

> Know that we fools, now with the foolish dead,
> Died not for flag, not king, nor Emperor,

But for a dream, born in a herdsman's shed,
And for the Secret Scripture of the poor.[31]

Labour Party senator Joe Costello spoke more explicitly about the political motivations of nationalist soldiers, asserting that 'they did not fight for the extension of the empire, they fought so that Home Rule would be established in Ireland' and 'for the freedom of small nations'.[32]

In its most essential form, commemoration of the war was and is about individuals: it was a way for the living to come to terms with and draw meaning from the deaths of friends and family members. In the Republic, however, political upheaval, as Progressive Democrat John Dardis put it, 'reduced . . . the survivors and families of the fallen . . . to a silent and lonely commemoration'.[33] Then, as time went on, later generations 'tucked away . . . memorabilia such as old medals, ribbons, documents and letters relating to World War I in cigarette tins' and forgot that chapter of their family history alongside their national history.[34] Beginning in the 1990s, however, amidst growing interest in the Republic's part in the war, many individuals began to reassess their family histories. In 1998, Mooney encouraged members of the public to consult the Commonwealth War Graves Commission online database to learn more about where their ancestors died and were buried, and in March 2012, over 600 people attended a 'World War One Family History Roadshow' in Dublin to share family mementos for inclusion in a 'pan-European virtual archive of World War One'.[35] Others have connected with their ancestors by visiting the Western Front to retrace their footsteps or visit their graves. For instance, in 2012, one Enniscorthy woman who had visited the Somme, where her father had fought, told a reporter that she hoped republicans would 'never forget those unsung heroes, a noble, brave and unselfish generation of men who left homes and loved ones in a quest for peace and everlasting justice for all'.[36]

The war affected entire communities as well as individuals and families. Following the armistice, many republican towns constructed memorials in honour of local soldiers who had died in battle. These monuments were the centrepieces of Remembrance Day services and parades, but as commemoration became politically unsavoury, remembrance services were marginalised or ended entirely.[37] Just as republican individuals have become increasingly interested in their familial connections to the First World War, however, so too have local governments and organisations begun to embrace their communities' involvement in the conflict through research initiatives, monument unveilings, and Armistice Day ceremonies. In 2007, for example, the Byrne/Perry Summer School, an annual history conference held in County Wexford, focused on the county's experience of the war.[38] Attendance at the conference, which was founded in 1995, was the highest it had ever been.[39] In the last few decades, many republican towns, including Wexford, have also published reference books of their war dead.[40]

Nearly a century after the conflict, several republican towns built their first memorials to their war dead. In Fermoy, County Cork, for example, the 'Friends of Fermoy's Forgotten' committee spearheaded a door-to-door funding campaign to build a memorial for the town's 131 lost soldiers. The statue was unveiled on

8 October 2006 in a ceremony attended by veterans, RBL representatives, members of the Irish Guards and the Royal Naval Association, and Taoiseach Bertie Ahern.[41] Similarly, towns across Ireland – including Limerick, Enniscorthy, and Portlaoise – have observed Remembrance Day with increasing enthusiasm over the last two decades.[42] Although these republican ceremonies, with their military marches, prayers, and readings, are quite similar to their unionist counterparts, they differ in one significant way – while Ulster services proudly fly the Union Jack and praise those who sacrificed 'for King and Country', empire has no place in republican commemoration. Many towns instead focus on the local character of the war and remembrance. A 2012 Remembrance Day service in Longford, for example, seemed to be as much a celebration of the town's ability to band together to finance the memorial as it was a recognition of its part in the war. When Michael Fitzpatrick, a veteran who marched in the parade, was asked about the war's imperialist associations, he replied: 'At the end of the day, we're honouring Longford men. This monument was built by Longford money [and] raised by Longford people. . . . It was built by a Longford company, and it was for Longford men who died in the Great War.'[43]

Despite its association with imperialism, some republicans have also embraced the poppy as a symbol of remembrance and reconciliation. In 2012, a reporter surveyed popular opinion on the poppy in Sligo. Although there was no mention of the interviewees' political or religious views, it is safe to assume that many of them were Catholic republicans, and their responses were overwhelmingly in favour of the poppy. One respondent observed, for instance, 'a lot of Irish people died in that war, it wasn't just British people. By wearing the poppy, we are commemorating our own.'[44] Out of twelve respondents, only one person was opposed to the poppy, and this opposition was grounded in the misconception that Ireland had been neutral during the war. Since 2017, when grassroots organisation Anti-Imperialist Action Ireland launched a 'poppy patrol' to oppose 'Poppy Fascism in support of British Imperialism', social media users and republican politicians decried the campaign. Fine Gael TD Neale Richmond pointed out that 'the vast majority of [poppy] sellers are elderly men and women with family connections [to the war] seeking to raise money, that stays in Ireland, for good causes and commemorations,' and many Twitter users from the Republic noted that they wore the poppy not to support imperialism, but to remember family members who had died in the war.[45] This republican support for the poppy is an astounding reversal, for the poppy had quickly become the object of political and sectarian conflict in the post-war years. In 1918, nationalists ripped paper poppies from the lapels of ex-servicemen, who in turn escalated tensions by hiding razors underneath their pins.[46] After the War of Independence, poppy-wearers became the targets of IRA violence, and nationalists raided RBL sales booths.[47] The Troubles had further compounded opposition to the flower in the south of Ireland, where the annual Poppy Appeal was seen as support for the army that had 'wreaked murder on the streets of Northern Ireland'.[48]

Despite historic opposition to First World War commemoration on the part of republican politicians, remembrance has become a national affair as well as a personal and local one. Presidential participation in commemoration began in 1993, when Mary Robinson became the first Irish president to observe Remembrance Sunday in St Patrick's Cathedral.[49] Robinson's successor, Mary McAleese, also publicly participated in commemoration, with an emphasis on peace and cooperation. The war was a central theme of her political rhetoric from her inauguration on Remembrance Day 1997, when she honoured the republicans and loyalists 'who fought and died together. . ., the differences which separated them at home fading into insignificance as the bond of their common humanity forged friendships as intense as love can make them'.[50] She also attended several memorial services and monument unveilings, including the 1998 opening of the Island of Ireland Peace Park (discussed in detail later) and a 2007 exhibition on the 16th (Irish) Division at the Somme Heritage Centre, where she praised the

> courage and generosity of so many young Irish men, from every background and belief, from Antrim to Cork, whose sacrifice forged our shared history, our shared memory. They showed us that there is no contradiction between working together collegially, in friendship and good neighbourliness on missions of common concern and interest while continuing to hold differing views and identities.[51]

Ahern, who served as taoiseach from 1997 to 2008, was similarly outspoken about the importance of recovering the Republic's part in the conflict. Speaking at the 2006 Fermoy memorial unveiling, for instance, he asserted:

> As a country, we owe it to the many Irish men who fought and died in that war to remember the part that they played. The men who enlisted early had been sent off with public honour and celebration. Those that survived came back to a very changed Ireland that did not value their sacrifice. Those that died in the battlefield came close to being completely forgotten by the following generations.[52]

Ahern's recognition of these men is particularly striking, as he comes from a staunchly republican background – the type of family that would have been opposed to the war in 1914–18. In his autobiography, he recalls his father's IRA activities during the civil war and his mother's hatred of the Black and Tans. Stronger than Ahern's devotion to the canon of republican history, however, was his belief that traditions and narratives had to be 'rescue[d] from the extremists, and then celebrate[d] and stud[ied] for what they really are'.[53]

As demonstrated by the poppy patrols of Anti-Imperialist Action Ireland, this renewed interest in the Republic's role in the First World War has had its critics. One year after the Fermoy war memorial was unveiled, for example, the *Avondhu Press* reported that it had been vandalised with industrial acid.[54] In 2008, a letter to *The Irish Times* from a Dublin reader described renewed commemoration as 'a trend which aims to associate Ireland more closely with former colonial powers, particularly Britain, and conveniently to gloss over their murky deeds'.

He disagreed with the notion that 'all Irishmen who died in wars are heroic and deserve to be publicly commemorated while moral arguments must be cast aside for the sake of "reconciliation".'[55] Such criticisms, however, are uncommon, and public support for recognition of the Republic's part in the war has been widespread.

The commemorative gestures that have resulted from renewed interest in the Republic's part in the war have been distinctly republican, and the republican soldiers honoured on Remembrance Day and immortalised on memorials have joined the canon of republican dead alongside the leaders of the Easter Rising, soldiers of the War of Independence, and victims of the Troubles. The affiliation of the men who died in 1914–18 with these other republican dead rests on the assumption that their motivations for enlistment were different from those of their loyalist counterparts: modern republican commemoration honours men who fought for the freedom of small nations, an anti-imperialist cause that clearly echoed Ireland's own fight for independence. But renewed remembrance has also come in the wake of the peace process, as well as decades of paramilitary violence and sectarian hostility. Many instances of modern commemoration have thus centred on the need for cross-border reconciliation.

Unified remembrance and the peace process

The signing of the Belfast Agreement ushered in an era of historical revisionism based on a desire to forge shared narratives to promote the peace process. McAleese proclaimed that the agreement offered 'an opportunity to build bridges and partnerships based on mutual respect for all traditions, cultures and creeds on this island'.[56] Fianna Fáil politician Dermot Ahern echoed this sentiment in a 2005 *Irish Times* column, declaring that Ireland could 'no longer have two histories, separate and in conflict', and that it should acknowledge that the experiences of people on both sides of the border had, 'in some way, defined what it is . . . to be Irish'.[57] Because the First World War, as a central part of Northern Ireland's British identity, had been such a target of republican disdain and violence, it has been a focus of Ireland's new shared historical narrative. This narrative has focused on cooperation across political and sectarian lines, shared sacrifice, and the futility of war.

Writing a shared Irish history is particularly challenging because, as McBride suggests, each region has defined itself through its narrative of conflict with the other side.[58] While the spectre of partition prompted a 'historiography, [both] scholarly and non-scholarly, that would justify the apartness of Ulster', history had an equally significant role in forging the Republic's identity and establishing its sense of national otherness.[59] As Richard English notes, 'a vital strain within the appeal of nationalist culture has been nationalists' attachment to and reading of history' as a series of 'imaginative raids', '[e]pisodes of past suffering', and 'cults around great leaders such as O'Connell, Parnell or de Valera'.[60] The fact that republican politicians like McAleese and Dermot Ahern sought to establish a more unified understanding of Ireland's past constituted a notable break with historical – and historiographical – precedent.

The centrepiece of this revised narrative of the First World War was the Island of Ireland Peace Park, unveiled in Messines in 1998. From its inception, the hope of reconciliation has defined the Peace Park, which was spearheaded by Paddy Harte, a former Fine Gael TD from Donegal, a republican border county, and Glen Barr, a former spokesman for the Ulster Defence Association, which was responsible for many paramilitary killings during the Troubles.[61] The park's goal, according to Harte, was to unite the two sides of the border in their shared 'sadness and grief over what happened in the First World War'.[62] In 1996, after receiving support from Presbyterian, Methodist, and Church of Ireland clergy and lay Protestants in Northern Ireland, Harte and Barr announced the project from the steps of the Ulster Tower in Thiepval, declaring: 'As Protestants and Catholics, we apologise for the terrible deeds we have done to each other, and ask forgiveness.'[63] Their statement would later be immortalised as part of a 'peace pledge' inscribed on a plaque at the park. The project received popular support in the Republic, and the government contributed £200,000 towards its construction. After the monument's completion in 2001, the Northern Irish and republican governments agreed to jointly share financial responsibility for the maintenance of the park.[64]

The Peace Park's message of reconciliation was also reflected in its design. It is modelled after the Irish round tower, a medieval style that predates the Protestant Reformation and the Anglo-Norman Invasion, and it includes stones from every Irish county.[65] Harte noted that no party or religion could claim ownership of the design; it was a 'true symbol of ancient Ireland that the people of Ireland had no reason to dispute'. Four garden plots representing the four provinces of Connacht, Leinster, Munster, and Ulster further emphasised the park's statement of Irish unity.[66] The location of the memorial, too, was appropriate for its message of reunion, as both the 16th (Irish) Division and the 36th (Ulster) Division had fought together at the 1917 Battle of Messines.

The memorial's construction, which was carried out by thirty-six young people between the ages of eighteen and thirty-four from both sides of the border, was also meant to be a lesson in cooperation. One participant from Bray was shocked by the 'normality' of life in Belfast, where the group stopped on the way to Belgium, explaining that 'it always seemed so far away and it's only two hours from home.' After returning home, a Derry participant reflected that the project had demonstrated that 'everybody is really the same, no matter what religion they are', and a worker from Clonakilty, County Cork, observed, 'the peace process would have a good chance of working if [politicians] could take a leaf out of our book. We are all getting on fine and I don't see why other people can't do it.'[67]

In 1998, in another gesture of reunion that involved not only both sides of the border, but also Britain, McAleese and Queen Elizabeth jointly inaugurated the Peace Park before an audience of 140 politicians, business leaders, and church officials from every county in Ireland, along with approximately 1,000 additional pilgrims.[68] The DUP, Fianna Fáil, and Fine Gael, among other parties, were represented, as were the Church of Ireland, the Catholic Church, the UDF, the British and Irish armies, and the Northern Irish Civil Service.[69] At the beginning of the ceremony, Barr and Harte read the peace pledge, and McAleese unveiled the plaque inscribed with the pledge. Then, the two leaders laid wreaths – poppies from the queen, laurel from McAleese – and buglers from the Republic and Northern Ireland joined together to play the 'Last Post' and the 'Reveille'.[70]

Other cross-border commemorations have followed the Peace Park unveiling. The Farset/Inishowen & Border Counties Initiative, for instance, organised battlefield tours to unite people from both sides of the border. The initiative was a rare exception to typical cooperative commemoration, as its first tour was in 1983, before even the Enniskillen bombing. Although many participants set out with deeply ingrained prejudices about people from across the border, the tours helped to break down those biases. As one participant observed, his trip was an opportunity to meet people with 'differing historical interpretations' that he 'once might have simply dismissed as "untrue"'. Another participant, a nationalist, reflected that 'it is only by being put in close proximity to people and spending time with them that you start to see their humanity.' A group facilitator from the International School for Peace Studies reported that 'questions such as "Are you a Protestant? Are you a Catholic?" go out the window very quickly' on cross-border tours. The facilitator hypothesised that the emotional gravitas of the battlefields, combined with the fact that the Western Front was 'neutral territory', fostered vulnerability among participants.[71]

Unified remembrance has not been restricted to the 'neutral territory' of the Western Front, however. In 1999, the cross-border group of workers who had helped to build the Peace Park travelled to Derry in Northern Ireland to lay poppy wreaths at an Armistice ceremony. The city's SDLP mayor, Pat Ramsey, also attended the service, despite the fact that his party had traditionally avoided events at the city's cenotaph.[72] The Farset/Inishowen & Border Counties Initiative has also been instrumental in organising commemorative services in border towns. In July 2004, one such ceremony in Dunree, County Donegal, attracted over 500 attendees. Approximately 80 per cent of the crowd was from Northern Ireland, and many had never before crossed the border.[73] Similarly, an article in the *Drogheda Independent* marvelled at the sight of nationalists standing side by side with members of the Orange Order under the Union Jack at a 2011 Remembrance Day ceremony in County Louth, on the republican side of the border.[74] In each year of his term, Enda Kenny, who served as taoiseach from 2011 to 2017, laid a laurel wreath at Enniskillen's annual Remembrance Day service alongside Northern Ireland's first minister. Kenny's successor, Leo Varadkar, who served from 2017 to 2020, continued the tradition.[75]

Just as a changed political environment has enabled unified commemoration, so too has that commemoration been used to further the political aspects of the peace process – not only between the Republic and Northern Ireland but also between the Republic and Great Britain. In May 2007, when Ahern became the first taoiseach to address the British parliament, he acknowledged that the 'intertwined history of Ireland and Britain was . . . a story of division and conflict, of conquest, suppression and resistance', but he also noted that the Belfast Agreement had allowed the Republic, 'still conscious of [its] history but not captured by it, to build a new and lasting partnership of common interest that fully respects identity and sovereignty' with Britain. To illustrate this new relationship, he evoked the cooperation demonstrated by McAleese and the queen at the Peace Park unveiling, which he called a 'groundbreaking act of recognition of our shared journey'.[76] When Elizabeth in turn became the first British monarch to visit the Republic, she laid a wreath at the Islandbridge Garden of Remembrance, Dublin's war memorial, which, as noted earlier, was completed in 1939 but never officially unveiled due to political tensions. In May 2012, Downing Street issued a joint statement from British Prime Minister David Cameron and Kenny announcing the 'Decade of Centenaries', a programme of commemorations of the events of 1912 to 1922 that would offer the people of the Republic and the United Kingdom 'an opportunity to explore and reflect on key episodes of [their] past . . . in a spirit of historical accuracy, mutual respect, inclusiveness and reconciliation'.[77] The Decade of Centenaries embraces events as diverse as the sinking of the Titanic, the signing of the Ulster Covenant, and the founding of the Irish Volunteers, but the calendar focuses on the First World War era, with the events of 1916 as its centrepiece.[78]

It is notable that while the republican interest in the First World War discussed in the previous section was motivated largely by a desire to reclaim forgotten family, community, and national histories, unified remembrance has been a more political phenomenon. Because violence long dominated the relationship between the two regions, reclaiming an instance of military cooperation as shared history is a political gesture that renounces violence and celebrates diplomatic progress. Although contemporary political events like the Enniskillen bombing and the Belfast Agreement renewed republican interest in the war, that interest has involved digging through old shoeboxes, polishing tarnished medals, and reclaiming forgotten stories and denied identities; it is a process rooted in and focused on the past. Unified remembrance, on the other hand, is an act firmly situated in the present: it is about erasing disagreements, looking towards the future, and advancing the peace process.

The validity of unified remembrance

Although projects like the Island of Ireland Peace Park and cross-border battlefield tours have generally been successful and enjoyed widespread support, it is unlikely that the Republic and Northern Ireland can ever achieve a truly shared memory of the First World War. The most fundamental obstacle is the fact that, for the better part of a century, Northern Ireland's commemoration of the war was defined by assertions of and allusions to its unionist identity. Even if remembrance in Ulster was not explicitly intended to exclude republicans or Catholics, the presence of the Union Jack, the UDF, and Orangemen at Remembrance Day services was repellent to anti-imperialists, while the juxtaposition of scenes from the Battle of the Somme with images of loyalist paramilitaries on Troubles-era murals served to associate First World War soldiers with paramilitary troops and further cement the idea that the memory of the war belonged solely to Ulster.[79] Although unified remembrance ceremonies have certainly incorporated elements of loyalist symbolism alongside elements of republican martial tradition – take, for example, the presence of army buglers from both sides of the border at the Peace Park unveiling – some defining elements of loyalist commemoration have been absent. It is not this absence, however, that creates tension; it is the fact that instances of more traditional, exclusively unionist remembrance continue to occur. When McAleese travelled to Belgium to open the Peace Park, for example, the Irish government forbade her from placing a laurel wreath at the Menin Gate in Ypres because the service, which would incorporate the Union Jack and other symbols of Britain and its army, would be too imperial.

Another difficulty lies in the fact that the bulk of unified remembrance has taken place on the Western Front. As the tour facilitator for the International School for Peace Studies noted, the battlefields of Belgium and France are 'neutral ground', where people are sheltered from the tensions of the island. While this shared space helps pilgrims to set aside their political and sectarian differences, it also obscures the goal of unified commemoration: truly unified remembrance must occur in the Northern Irish cities where the First World War was claimed as exclusively unionist history or in the republican towns where nationalists once snatched poppies from the lapels of soldiers and Protestant civilians. Many of those who have travelled to the Western Front acknowledged this necessity; as one cross-border tour participant put it: 'Everyone goes over to Belgium and has a great experience there. But it's how to follow up when we get back home that we should now be focusing on.'[80]

While some cross-community remembrance services – like the 1999 Remembrance Day service in Derry and the July 2004 ceremony in Dunree – have taken place back on the island, it is notable that many of the attendees at these services had been on previous battlefield tours and had travelled from their own hometowns to attend the domestic ceremonies. These were people, then, with an established interest in cross-border commemoration, and they had already experienced the vulnerability and camaraderie of a battlefield tour. Queen Elizabeth's May 2011 visit to the Republic, which included a wreath-laying at the Irish National War Memorial in Dublin, might also be interpreted as an instance of domestic cross-border commemoration. The service included the Union Jack alongside the Republican tricolour; 'God save the Queen' along with 'Amhrán na bhFiann', the Irish national anthem; and politicians, veterans, and church officials from both sides of the border. All 500 attendees, however, had been hand-picked to receive invitations, and the ceremony was closer to choreographed political pageantry than organic cross-border remembrance.[81]

Perhaps the most difficult issue to negotiate is the connection between history and memory and the intermediary role that commemoration plays in that relationship. As Rebecca Lynn Graff-McRae notes, in Ireland 'commemoration is constructed as a site in which opposed groups seek to legitimise their territorial, social and political aspirations through competing claims to the past'. Through shared commemoration, then, these competing claims to legitimacy and ownership of history are smoothed over and simplified, a process that requires the erasure of past tensions. Graff-McRae suggests that shared commemoration, rather than forcing competing groups to confront their differences through 'contentious remembrance', actually involves 'constructive forgetting' and the rewriting of the past, and it thus 'serves to depoliticise and neutralise remembrance without addressing the actual sources of division'.[82] In the case of Ireland and First World War remembrance, however, what is being forgotten is not the war itself but, rather, the history of twentieth-century sectarian conflict. While contemporary politics and the 'actual sources of division' can be addressed through parliamentary debates and legislative referenda, perhaps commemoration-based reconciliation does inherently require a measure of forgetting. As Pierre Nora suggests, 'memory is always a phenomenon of the present', accommodating 'only those facts that suit it'. It involves 'appropriation', 'manipulation', and the discarding of inconvenient narratives – such as the history of British imperialism and inter-Irish conflict – in favour of more palatable ones – such as tales of Protestant and Catholic forces fighting side by side.[83] In a sense, unified commemoration of the First World War turns Maurice Halbwachs's theory of collective memory on its head; rather than using memory as a means of reinforcing an existing social group, shared commemoration uses remembrance – and a measure of 'constructive forgetting' – to create a new social group that unites people from both sides of Ireland's political, religious, and geographic divide.[84]

Notes

1 Tom Kettle, *The Ways of War* (New York: Scribner, 1917), 71.
2 *The Times*, November 9, 1987.
3 *BBC News Online*, November 8, 2012, www.bbc.com/news/uk-northern-ireland-20245311.
4 *The Times*, November 9, 1987.
5 Ibid.; Denzil McDaniel, *Enniskillen: The Remembrance Day Sunday Bombing* (Dublin: Irish American Book Co., 1997), 47.
6 *Belfast Telegraph*, November 9, 1987; *BBC News Online*, December 30, 2000.
7 Ian McBride, "Introduction: Memory and National Identity in Modern Ireland," in *History and Memory in Modern Ireland*, ed. Ian McBride (Cambridge: Cambridge University Press, 2001), 1, 4, 15.
8 Pat Coogan, *Ireland in the Twentieth Century* (London: Hutchinson, 2003), 22, 29.
9 David Fitzpatrick, "The Logic of Collective Sacrifice: Ireland and the British Army, 1914–1918," *The Historical Journal* 38, no. 4 (1995): 1017–18, 1024; Catherine Switzer, *Unionists and Great War Commemoration in the North of Ireland* (Dublin: Irish Academic Press, 2007), 55.
10 Keith Jeffery, *Ireland and the Great War* (Cambridge: Cambridge University Press, 2000), 15.
11 John Redmond, quoted by D. G. Boyce, " 'That Party Politics Should Divide Our Tents': Nationalism, Unionism and the First World War," in *Ireland and the Great War: 'A War to Unite Us All'?*, ed. Adrian Gregory and Senia Paseta (Manchester: Manchester University Press, 2002), 196.
12 David Fitzpatrick, "Commemoration in the Irish Free State: A Chronicle of Embarrassment," in *History and Memory in Modern Ireland*, ed. McBride, 191.
13 Jay Winter, *Sites of Memory, Sites of Mourning: The Great War in European Cultural History* (New York: Cambridge University Press, 1995), 5.

14 James Loughlin, "Mobilising the Sacred Dead: Ulster Unionism, the Great War and the Politics of Remembrance," in *Ireland and the Great War*, ed. Gregory and Paseta, 136–37.
15 Nuala Johnson, "The Spectacle of Memory: Ireland's Remembrance of the Great War, 1919," *Journal of Historical Geography* 25, no. 1 (1999): 51.
16 Ann Rigney, "Divided Pasts: A Premature Memorial and the Dynamics of Collective Remembrance," *Memory Studies* 1, no. 89 (2008): 90, 92; Fitzpatrick, "Commemoration in the Irish Free State," 191.
17 Northern Ireland Statistics and Research Agency, "1991 Towns and Villages Booklet," Belfast, 1991, www.nisra.gov.uk/sites/nisra.gov.uk/files/publications/1991-census-towns-villages-booklet.pdf.
18 Frank Fox, *The Royal Inniskilling Fusiliers in the Second World War: A record of the war as seen by the Royal Inniskilling Fusiliers, three battalions of which served* (Aldershot: Gale & Polden, 1951), 1.
19 McDaniel, *Enniskillen*, 113–16.
20 *Anglo – Irish Agreement 1985 Between the Government of Ireland and the Government of the United Kingdom*, November 15, 1985. A treaty signed by Thatcher and Fitzgerald, UK and Ireland, respectively.
21 Eamonn Mallie and David McKittrick, *The Fight for Peace: The Secret Story Behind the Irish Peace Process* (London: Random House, 1996), 29–30.
22 David McKittrick and David McVea, *Making Sense of the Troubles: A History of the Northern Ireland Conflict* (London: Viking, 2012), 205.
23 *Belfast Telegraph*, November 9, 1987.
24 House of Commons, Hansard Report, November 9, 1987, cols. 19–35.
25 *The Times*, November 9, 1987.
26 Seanad Éireann, "Debate," November 11, 1987, 117, 12, www.oireachtas.ie/en/debates/debate/seanad/1987-11-11/.
27 *The Times*, November 14, 1987.
28 Éireann, "Debate," November 11, 1987.
29 Seanad Éireann, "Debate," November 12, 1987, www.oireachtas.ie/en/debates/debate/seanad/1987-11-12/.
30 Kettle, quoted by Johnson, "Spectacle of Memory," 53.
31 Kettle, "To My Daughter Betty," quoted by Manning, Éireann, "Debate," November 12, 1987.
32 Éireann, "Debate," November 12, 1987.
33 Ibid.
34 Seanad Éireann, "Debate," November 12, 1998, https://www.oireachtas.ie/en/debates/debate/seanad/1998-11-12/1/.
35 Europeana, "World War One 1914–1918," press release, Hunt Museum, October 2012, www.europeana.eu/en/collections/topic/83-1914-1918.
36 *Enniscorthy Echo*, November 15, 2007.
37 Tom Burke, "'Poppy Day' in the Irish Free State," *Studies: An Irish Quarterly Review* 92, no. 368 (2003): 349.
38 *Leitrim Observer*, July 5, 2012; *Enniscorthy Guardian*, July 4, 2007.
39 *Enniscorthy Guardian*, July 4, 2007.
40 Tom Burnell and Margaret Gilbert, *The Wexford War Dead* (Dublin: Nonsuch Publishing, 2009).
41 *The Corkman*, October 12, 2006.
42 *Limerick Leader*, November 13, 2012; *Enniscorthy Echo*, November 15, 2007; *Offaly Express*, November 13, 2009.
43 "Armistice Day Commemoration," *Longford Leader*, video, 6, no. 23, November 12, 2012, www.longfordleader.ie/video/180973/Video–Armistice-Day-commemora tion-.html.
44 *Sligo Champion*, November 20, 2012.

45 *The Express*, October 29, 2019.
46 Jane Leonard, "Facing the 'Finger of Scorn': Veterans' Memories of Ireland After the Great War," in *War and Memory in the Twentieth Century*, ed. Martin Evans and Kenneth Lunn (Oxford: Berg Publishers, 1997), 66.
47 Burke, "'Poppy Day'," 352–53.
48 *Derry Journal*, November 12, 2007.
49 Richard Grayson, *Belfast Boys: How Unionists and Nationalists Fought and Died Together in the First World War* (London: Continuum, 2009), 179.
50 President Mary McAleese, *Building Bridges: Selected Speeches and Statements* (Dublin: The History Press, 2011), 20.
51 Ibid., 262.
52 *Irish Independent*, October 9, 2006.
53 Bertie Ahern and Richard Aldous, *Bertie Ahern: The Autobiography* (London: Arrows Books Ltd., 2010), 2, 295.
54 *Avondhu Press*, November 22, 2007.
55 *The Irish Times*, September 24, 2008.
56 McAleese, *Building Bridges*, 253–54.
57 *The Irish Times*, November 11, 2005.
58 McBride, "Introduction," 1.
59 Richard Vincent Comerford, *Ireland: Inventing the Nation* (London: Irish Academic Press, 2010), 79.
60 Richard English, *Irish Freedom: The History of Nationalism in Ireland* (London: Palgrave Macmillan, 2006), 446.
61 *The Irish Times*, November 25, 1997.
62 *The Irish Times*, July 2, 1998.
63 Ibid.; Paddy Harte, *Young Tigers and Mongrel Foxes: A Life in Politics* (Dublin: O'Brien Press, 2005), 324.
64 *The Irish Times*, November 25, 1997, June 20, 2001, June 7, 2004, November 11, 2005.
65 Ibid.
66 Harte, *Young Tigers*, 328, 335.
67 *The Irish Times*, July 2, 1998, November 12, 1998.
68 Ibid.; Harte, *Young Tigers*, 335.
69 *The Irish Times*, November 12, 1998.
70 Ibid.; Harte, *Young Tigers*, 334.
71 Michael Hall, ed., *A Shared Sacrifice for Peace* (Belfast: Island Publications, 2007), 14, 21–23.
72 *Belfast Newsletter*, November 10, 1999.
73 Hall, *Shared Sacrifice*, 21.
74 *Drogheda Independent*, November 9, 2011.
75 *Fermanagh Herald*, November 11, 2019.
76 *The Irish Times*, May 16, 2007.
77 David Cameron and Enda Kenny, "British Irish Relations, the Next Decade," joint statement, March 12, 2012.
78 For a scholarly analysis of the Decade of Centenaries, see Catriona Pennell, "'Choreographed by the Angels?': Ireland and the Centenary of the First World War," *War and Society* 36, no. 4 (2017): 256–75.
79 Switzer, *Unionists and Commemoration*, 152–53; Helen Robinson, "Remembering War in the Midst of Conflict: First World War Commemorations in the Northern Irish Troubles," *Twentieth Century British History* 21, no. 1 (2010): 94.
80 Hall, *Shared Sacrifice*, 24.
81 *The Irish Times*, May 19, 2011.
82 Rebecca Lynn Graff-McRae, "Forget Politics!: Theorising the Political Dynamics of Commemoration and Conflict," in *1916 in 1966: Commemorating the Easter*

Rising, ed. Mary Daly and Margaret O'Callaghan (Dublin: Royal Irish Academy, 2007), 227.

83 Pierra Nora, "Between Memory and History," in *Realms of Memory: Rethinking the French Past*, ed. Pierra Nora and trans. Arthur Goldhammer, vol. 1, 3 (New York: Columbia University Press, 1996), 3.

84 Maurice Halbwachs, *On Collective Memory*, ed. and trans. Lewis A. Coser (Chicago: University of Chicago Press, 1992).

14 *We're here because we're here*

Participatory art and the mobilisation of First World War memory in post-Brexit Britain

Kristin O'Donnell

Foregrounding questions of belonging and national identity, this chapter examines the role of the arts in constructing cultural imaginaries of the First World War that aimed to function as unifying acts in an increasingly divided Britain. By unpacking the way these seemingly inclusive events obscure difficult histories associated with Britain's Empire and mask a divided present, this chapter demonstrates how cultural memory is mobilised to act as a vehicle for protest and critique of contemporary political events. Through a focus on a national mass-participatory commemorative artwork commissioned to mark the 100th anniversary of the Battle of the Somme, *We're here because we're here*, this chapter examines the emotive power of the dominant cultural imaginary of the First World War soldier just days after Britain voted narrowly to leave the European Union (EU) in 2016. The name of the artwork, derived from a song sung by soldiers to emphasise the futility of trench warfare, was chosen by the artist behind the project, Jeremey Deller, because 'it explains nothing, it's pointless and repetitive, a little like the fate of a foot soldier or even the nature of man's addiction to conflict'.[1] The piece reinforced the dominant narrative of the Great War as a moment of tragedy. In contrast with popular perceptions of the Second World War, this was not 'Britain's finest hour'; it was 'lions led by donkeys' and 'mud, blood and futility'.[2] Despite various recent attempts by some politicians and historians to reconceptualise the conflict as a just, necessary, and well-fought war, the dominant representation is that Britain was drawn into a conflict for reasons most did not understand, where brave men were led by incompetent officers, and many men were left with physical and mental scars.[3]

We're here because we're here was one of the highest-profile commemorative events produced during the centenary in Britain. In addition to the approximately two million people who encountered the live artwork on the day, an estimated thirty million people came into contact with the project through both social media and traditional media outlets.[4] Deller's modern memorial has won widespread acclaim and received numerous awards, including the National Lottery Awards in the Best Heritage category (decided by public vote) and the Social Buzz award for Best Social Media Campaign in the Charity/Not for Profit Sector.[5] Newspapers commended the artwork for its ability to move 'even the toughest soul . . . to tears', 'sparking cherished memories', and stirring the emotions of passers-by.[6] I argue that the artwork was so popular through its clear use of recognisable imagery, combined with its ability to accommodate contradictory interpretations of recent events, namely the referendum to leave the EU.[7] This chapter situates the artwork within a broader centenary agenda of nation-making and social cohesion while problematising notions that military commemoration provides an ideal platform for bringing the nation together. It simultaneously charts some of the varied ways the British public used the artwork to inform their understanding of the results of the referendum on Britain's membership in the EU and the broader anxieties surrounding citizenship in twenty-first-century multicultural Britain. By employing participatory aesthetics, this chapter highlights how the metrics of the impact agenda in public art commissioning masks the limits of the artform promoting greater social cohesion.

Centenary context: 'a truly national commemoration'?

When British Prime Minister David Cameron announced the government's plans for the centenary of the First World War in 2012, he spoke about the ambition to create:

> a truly national commemoration . . . that captures our national spirit in every corner of the country, from our schools to our workplaces, to our town halls and local communities. A commemoration that . . . says something about who we are as a people.[8]

Thus, from the outset, the centenary commemorations were to be an exercise in shaping and rehearsing national identity.[9] Despite the highly politicised debates between historians and individual politicians about how the war should be commemorated playing out in the media at the onset of the centenary, the government aimed to resist politicising the centenary and instead aimed to 'relate the conflict to contemporary forms of citizenship and patriotism'.[10] Andrew Mycock highlighted the role of the government in setting the parameters through which the centenary should be understood, despite protestations that 'it would be wrong for the government to insist on a particular narrative'.[11] In addition to the official ceremonial aspects of national British remembrance culture, during the centenary, the Department of Digital, Media, Culture and Sport (DCMS) established a dedicated centenary arts programme, 14–18 NOW, which would play a central role in commemorative culture. The organisation's status as independent but largely funded by the central government presents an intriguing case study to examine the relationship between governments, extra-governmental organisations, artists, and individuals in the negotiation of war memory and its effect on national identity. Reflecting on the aims given to the organisation by the DCMS, 14–18 NOW Director Jenny Waldman cited two key aims. Firstly, to reach members of the public less likely to engage in official ceremonial aspects of the centenary and, secondly, to reach young people.[12] Understanding these aims in relation to concerns surrounding youth disaffection in Britain, particularly in relation to minority ethnic groups, provides insight into the mobilisation of the centenary commemoration in broader agendas to foster national cohesion.

There has been considerable anxiety in Britain surrounding multiculturalism, highlighted in the then-prime minister's speech at the Munich Security Conference in 2011. Cameron argued that multicultural Britain was failing to 'provide a vision of society to which [young British Muslims] feel they want to belong'.[13] He claimed the biggest threat facing the UK 'comes from terrorist attacks, some of which are, sadly, carried out by our own citizens . . . overwhelmingly from young men who follow a completely perverse, warped interpretation of Islam'.[14] He also argued that the reason so many young British Muslims are drawn to radicalised versions of Islam 'comes down to a question of identity. . . . [W]e need a clear sense of shared national identity that is open to everyone'.[15] At the outset of the centenary, foregrounding the British 'Commonwealth's' contributions to the allied war effort was presented as a means of fostering a greater sense of national identity amongst disaffected youth. Baroness Sayeeda Warsi, at that time senior minister at the British Foreign and Commonwealth Office and Minister for Faith and Communities, acknowledged that 'when we come to commemorate the centenary in 2014, people from ethnic minority backgrounds may wonder what it all has to do with them'.[16] Advocating for an increased awareness of the participation of 'the Commonwealth' not only as the right thing to do because 'this generation of brave soldiers deserves to be remembered' but also because knowledge that 'your ancestors played a part in British history, even if they weren't from this country' provides a powerful sense of belonging.[17] Vron Ware has demonstrated how the history of the First World War has been mobilised in attempts to 'bind the scattered stories of heroism during the course of a brutal global war into an inclusive narrative about contemporary national identity in Britain', resulting in 'configurations of identity that are both racialized and militarized'.[18] However, as demonstrated next, such low-context commemorative events have the potential to serve those with exclusionary conceptions of race and belonging. As Mycock reminds us, ' "collective" national forms of memory are intimately connected with the present, they are susceptible to instrumentalisation, manipulation and politicisation'.[19]

Early analysis of the centenary by Lucy Noakes has noted that although the scope of the commemorations overall had broadened out to include 'a much wider recognition of the contribution and experience of troops and labourers from around the Empire, of women on the Home Front, and of the impact of the conflict on displaced refugee populations', many of the dominant understandings of the war have remained unchanged.[20] The centenary undoubtedly provided space for lesser-known narratives of the war to emerge – such as those acknowledging the roles played by women and participants from around the globe – but the central stage was still occupied by familiar narratives, such as the British soldier on the Western Front, as epitomised by the visibility of high-profile commemorative events evoking that imagery such as *Blood Red Skies and Seas of Red*,[21] at which a ceramic poppy was planted in the moat of the Tower of London to commemorate the death of every soldier from Britain and the empire, and *We're here because we're here*, which foregrounded the high death toll on the first day of the Battle of the Somme. Where colonial soldiers have been included, representations often offered a redemptive narrative eschewing the more uncomfortable aspects of this history.[22] Drawing attention to the contributions of colonial soldiers is undoubtedly valuable for historical understanding and is often linked to identity formation in a positive way, with one young Muslim participant claiming a workshop on Muslim participation 'can help you find your identity because you find out that your family was in the World War'.[23] However, it often avoids confronting some of the more difficult aspects of colonial involvement in the war and poses difficult questions about constructing a shared sense of belonging for immigrants who do not share Britain's martial past. Although *We're here because we're here*, with its focus on fighting on the Western Front, doesn't appear to speak to issues surrounding empire or contemporary citizenship, a closer analysis of public responses to the artwork in the context of the political climate leading up to it are revealing.

The cultural terrain in which the centenary took place is further enriched by consideration of public investment in the arts. Participatory art, with its emphasis on agency and social connections provides an excellent platform for examining the negotiation of public memory, which has not been thoroughly addressed in relation to war commemoration. As Clare Bishop notes, one of the main motivating drivers behind the turn towards participatory art has been 'a restoration of the social bond through a collective elaboration of meaning'.[24] However, Bishop is rightly critical of the theoretical position that participatory art is emancipatory, arguing that the artform is susceptible to instrumentalisation and neoliberal agendas which demand measurable impact.[25] Combined with the turn towards participatory art in a political culture that increasingly demands quantifiable metrics of impact to justify funding, viewing *We're here because we're here* through the lens of participatory art allows for a consideration which draws together policy imperatives, artistic intensions, and individual agency.[26]

We're here because we're here

On 1 July 2016, First World War 'soldiers' appeared unannounced in shopping centres, train stations, beaches, and high streets across Britain as part of a nationwide mass-participatory artwork marking the centenary of the first day of the Battle of the Somme.[27] They loitered around casually, and when approached by the public, they did not speak; instead, they handed out business-sized cards to curious bystanders which included the sparse details of a single British soldier who had died on the first day of the Battle of the Somme: name, regiment, age, 'died at the Somme 1st July 1916', and the hashtag '#wearehere'. These unexpected and fleeting exchanges often resulted in highly emotional responses, with many members of the public photographed visibly moved. The piece generated a flurry of interest on social media, which the artist behind the piece, Jeremy Deller, viewed as an integral part of this mass-participation artwork. Deller spoke of wanting to create a 'living memorial', one that 'avoid[ed] sentimentality', and took commemoration to people on the streets that might not otherwise engage in commemorative activity. He stated:

> I really wanted to make a human memorial, something that was not comforting, had a random quality to it and was de-centralized. A memorial that travelled around the country, not one that you had to travel to and would then find the audience, it wouldn't wait for an audience. I think it was important that even if people didn't really want to see, they would have to see it. It had to be a different kind of commemoration.[28]

For Deller, the aesthetic power behind the piece rested on the unexpected, the uncanny, and the uncomfortable. He even wrote in his notebook that he wanted to make children cry,: '[he] thought it was important to upset and even frighten children because you should be frightened of war'.[29] But when faced with thousands of young men dressed in the uniforms of the First World War, the responses were largely emotive and positive. In a time where traditional sculptural war memorials are so ubiquitous in everyday life as to become almost invisible, this artwork captured the public imagination due in large part to its innovative form as a living memorial. The unexpected encounter with the symbolically loaded image of the First World War soldier drew on a vast repertoire of representation and meaning associated with the soldier and remembrance culture, what I refer to as the 'dominant cultural imaginary of the soldier'. This pre-existing cultural store influenced the public's responses to artwork, but it did so in tension with the political climate of multicultural Britain, as this case study reveals.

Although Deller insisted on keeping his name out of the public sphere on the day of the event, until the evening news, to allow space for individual interpretation and to create a certain level of intentional confusion, *We're here because we're here* was a highly authored piece with a distinct performance language imposed on the 'soldier'-participants, designed to disrupt the everyday spaces of the viewer-participants. The artwork offered virtually no historical context to understand either the causes of the battle, nor did it strive to contextualise it within the wider war. The social aspect of the work is underscored by the moment of encounter in which shared meaning was created. The 'soldiers' were activated by the exchange of the card with the social media hashtag, informing the viewer that the artwork was a memorial act for those that died on the first day of the Battle of the Somme and encouraging them to share their experience online. *We're here because we're here* undoubtedly takes moments of social interaction as its central premise. How are we to read the public reaction versus the authorial intent? Deller himself stated that he thought the piece might be provocative:

> We were worried that the public would react badly to it. We had all these scenarios where 'what if someone comes up to you and takes your hat? What if somebody starts abusing you? What if someone wants to have a fight? What if'. . . . [I]n the end what we should have planned for was 'what if someone comes up to you and you give them a card and they start crying in front of

> you?' And the public really reacted in a way that I was very impressed by but wasn't expecting or wasn't necessarily even wanting in a way. It was quite overwhelming.[30]

Through a deliberate strategy of avoiding linking the artwork to the artist until it was over, *We're here because we're here* resisted the fetishisation of the individual artist, relying instead on the power of the central image of the soldier. The ambiguity around the producers of the artwork also allowed it to resist didactic instruction and immediate straightforward interpretation. Instead of the viewer being given immediate narrative closure when coming into contact with the 'soldiers', the paucity of information encouraged extended reflection, akin to what Michael J. Shapiro describes as 'slow looking': 'resonating with embodied memories and encouraging public reflection and negotiation over the meanings and significance of what they reveal'.[31] And yet, through its use of the familiar image of the young British soldier seemingly heading off to war and their certain death, the artwork prompted interpretations which conform to the dominant cultural imaginary of the soldier on the Western Front – lions led by donkeys and mud, blood and futility. The political utility of the image of the soldier-victim over time has been well-documented in relation to pacifist movements in the interwar years, the anti-war movement surrounding both the war in Vietnam and the threats of the Cold War, and more recently in light of British involvement in controversial wars in Iraq and Afghanistan, demonstrating how narratives of futility surrounding the war are mobilised to serve contemporary societal concerns.[32] The anxieties presented by new models of ideological warfare which are not confined by the political borders of the nation-state, such as the 'war on terror', combined with anxiety surrounding multicultural Britain and immigration, provide new insight into the malleability of First World War memory. Rather than looking to authorial intention, we need to ask: What sort of narrative is being constructed by the viewer, and what this can tell us about the relationship between participatory art as a form of memorialisation and how it intersects with issues surrounding war commemoration and contemporary politics? To address this question, we must also look beyond the aesthetic qualities to the broader narratives linking the First World War and the European Union that circulated in the public sphere leading up to the piece.

Brexit and 'Our Brave Boys'

Many reactions to the 'soldiers' on social media rehearsed the familiar narratives surrounding the dominant cultural imaginary of the soldier; the so-called 'lost generation' of young men, often referred to as 'our boys', as Cameron did in his speech launching the centenary programme.[33] Referring to the 'soldiers' continuously as 'boys', 'baby-faced', or 'brave boys', as many did on social media, has the effect of framing the soldiers as children, subtly infantilising them. This has the effect of diminishing the agency of the individuals that chose to fight, thereby deflecting critique of individual agency within military intervention and avoiding consideration of the complex factors which motivated pre-conscription war service.[34] However, the use of 'boys' when referring to the soldiers goes much further than evoking sympathy for so many lives cut short. This evocation of familial language draws the nation together in the unifying narrative of a motherland with a symbolic royal family at its centre, reinforcing the 'imagined community' at the heart of the nation.[35] The idea of fighting for king (or queen) and country is a familiar British refrain. The family becomes a metonym for the nation with powerful effects. As Walker Conner notes, 'the core of the nation has been reached and triggered through the use of familial metaphors which can magically transform the mundanely tangible into emotion-laden phantasma'.[36] The notion of imagined kinship has a powerful emotional pull. Given the levels of historical involvement in the First World War, it is likely that many Britons *do* have a familial connection to the war, although as Dan Todman notes, 'in practice nearly half the male population did not serve in the armed forces, even if the contribution of civilian workers was as important in time of "total war" as those of the soldiers'.[37] Indeed, during the centenary many initiatives at a grassroots level have focused on finding familial, or community-based, connections to the war.[38] Many of these community-based projects required individuals to seek out engagement with them, but as Maggie Andrews, drawing on Michael Skey, notes, 'feeling entitled to construct the past, to write history, rests on both access to resources and a sense of cultural belonging' that is often lacking in communities where hostile attitudes towards immigration means they 'no longer feel "at home" in what they consider to be "their" country'.[39] *We're here because we're here* took the commemoration to the streets, and an awareness of a direct familial link to the First World War was not a necessary precursor to an emotional engagement with the artwork, but in many cases it did play a role.

On an intimate level, Todman suggests Marianne Hirsch's concept of 'postmemory', the intergenerational transmission of trauma, may explain the strong emotional attachment many Briton's feel to the First World War.[40] However, for some viewers of the artwork, concrete familial links to the Great War weren't as powerful as the dominant cultural imagery of the soldier. For example, part of the media strategy for *We're here because we're here* was to invite social media influencers to a space where they would encounter the 'soldiers', one of which was the broadcaster and journalist Jon Snow. Snow reflected on his inability to connect with the memory and experience of his own grandfather, a 'general, so he survived of course'.[41] It seems that for Snow, the archetypal uncaring general was such a difficult character that he could not identify with his own familial link. He reflected:

> I tried to connect with him; I tried to think about what he would have been dealing with. I couldn't get there at all – I was only able really to identify with who [I] was seeing that day and to think merely that they were bound for something terrible.[42]

For Snow it was more powerful to evoke the myth of lions led by donkeys than it was to connect with his own familial ties to the Great War. According to David

Morley and Kevin Robins, the return to 'family values' has accompanied the 'profound cultural anxiety' that has coincided with 'the loosening of personal identities from their traditional anchorages' associated with globalisation, postmodernism, and, arguably, immigration.[43] Viewed in this light, the appeal to familial connections and kinship ties in relation to the First World War suggests more than just a connection to the imagined kinship of the nation but a reaction against the uncertainties associated with anxious political times for the nation-state.

Brexit: lions led by donkeys?

During the planning stages of *We're here because we're here*, no one involved could have foreseen the fact that Britain would narrowly vote to leave the European Union just one week before. However, Deller's work gained emotional power from unintentionally coinciding with the Brexit vote. In the week that followed the referendum, political chaos ensued. Although he promised to stay in office no matter the outcome of the vote, then-Prime Minister Cameron unexpectedly stood down, triggering a leadership contest and political backstabbing amongst prominent Leave campaigners such as Michael Gove and Boris Johnson.[44] Deller observed the parallels between the view that the First World War was a political blunder, a politicians' war, and that, likewise, the EU referendum was a political manoeuvre gone terribly wrong:

> It was the week after the Brexit vote. After the vote, people saw politicians killing each other for their own careers, and then had a reminder of young men who had actually sacrificed their life for their country – quite the opposite. People understood that instinctively. Instead the politicians now were prepared to tear the country apart for their own vanity and survival. People were fed up with that.[45]

The notion of sacrifice was a key point here in this interpretation of *We're here because we're here*. It used the familiar symbol of the soldier on the Western Front, but it is asking 'what are we willing to sacrifice now and who is doing the sacrificing?' For Deller, the polarisation evoked by the divisive campaign and its likely disruptive repercussions were akin to war, and the idea of the noble sacrifice of the soldier was problematised by what he viewed as a country being sacrificed for political ambitions.[46] For Deller the commemoration thus became an outlet for present-day grief and a vehicle for finding meaning in a situation many found incomprehensible. For those with Remain sympathies the piece became a metaphor for a crisis in leadership and a warning against European disintegration. However, for those that sided with the Leave campaign it encapsulated the British underdog spirit and served as a warning to an EU perceived as being dominated by German hegemony.[47]

Deller wasn't alone in his interpretation of events, with many people taking to social media to share their views. Although this is a self-selecting audience of individuals that found the work meaningful and engaging enough to post about it online, their responses are revealing. Some people hinted at the relationship between the present political crisis and the emotive power of the artwork, with one politician observing that the 'moving . . . images of . . . soldiers around the UK . . . [seem] to put everything else into perspective'.[48] For others the link was much more explicit. One user commented, '[W]hat a beautiful & impressive art project to remember all those young lads we lost. Another colossal scaled tragedy caused by ill informed [sic] idiots in charge', to which another user replied, 'and the eu [sic] was set up to avoid these things happening again'.[49] The combination of familiar narratives with present politics is apparent in the response of one commentator, with the 'lions led by donkeys' narrative clearly influencing their interpretation of *We're here because we're here*:

> Thinking about how all those young men (some only a few years older than my 14 yr old son) went off to war to fight for our country and never came home. In utter contrast to all the self serving, shameful political manoeuvrings [sic] we have witnessed the past week. This picture makes me proud of our country and everything we stand for. The other stuff, thats [sic] not us. #strongertogether[50]

In this example, the Great War fought one hundred years ago between present-day allies is repurposed as an integrationist narrative to serve their pro-EU view. The past is reinterpreted and recycled selectively for present-day political realities.

While many observers drew links between *We're here because we're here* and the referendum, they were not all united in their interpretation of the decision to leave the EU as a mistake. For some it was ambiguous whether they supported the referendum result or wanted Britain to remain in the EU, but it was clear to one individual respondent on social media that regardless of whether one voted to leave or remain, war commemoration should function as a unifying act for the divided nation. Commenting on the fact that the soldiers had 'died for our freedom', which 'we take for granted', and 'for Great Britain, which is in disarray at the moment', they argued that 'we owe it to these soldiers of the past to unite'.[51] Others adopted a more threatening tone: 'Let's hope that a divided Europe doesn't forget what can happen when individual countries try to force their views on the rest!'[52] In the context of the First World War, it is likely that the commenter is referring to Germany, or the EU more widely, which for some, as David Reynolds points out, German dominance has become a proxy.[53]

This link between the First World War, and particularly the first day of the Battle of the Somme and the EU, were not only made because of the serendipity of timing, which was enhanced by the referendum results and the ensuing political turmoil taking place just one week apart. As noted by Reynolds, Britain's relationship with the EU is one that has long been underpinned by the cultural memory of two world wars.[54] Although the First World War and the Battle of the Somme, in particular, are viewed as failures, the use of such narratives in the present can actually have surprising effects. According to Fintan O'Toole, the allure of Brexit for some is rooted in the appeal of heroic failure. For instance, he argues that a heady mixture of colonial guilt and post–Second World War loss of global status has resulted in many people in Britain (although O'Toole does provide a caveat that it is mostly England he is referring to as the original coloniser and the nation with the highest Leave vote during the referendum) viewing the EU as a coloniser mega-state with Britain as the colonised victim.[55] For O'Toole this is compounded by the cultural memory of the Second World War and a strange transference of anti-Nazi sentiment onto an EU which some Britons view as uncomfortably dominated by Germany. Although O'Toole focuses his argument on how the cultural memory of the Second World War has influenced English sentiment towards the EU, he highlights the ways in which military failures are transmogrified in the British psyche into moments of heroism, ennobling victimhood and positioning the former coloniser as the colonised. According to O'Toole, military disasters such as Dunkirk, the Charge of the Light Brigade, and the Somme all form part of a catalogue of failures suitable for this victim identification.[56] He observes, 'if the British Army on the Western Front were lions led by donkeys, Brexit is those that feel they have nothing to lose led by those who will lose nothing either way'.[57]

Race: 'we are here because you were there'[58]

Many scholars have foregrounded the role of commemorative events as a response to personal grief. However, as the war has moved out of living memory, bereavement becomes a less-convincing explanation for such extensive engagement with commemorative activities. If we can no longer speak about direct grief as a primary motivation, as leading historians on the cultural memory of the First World War have done, what sort of losses do these new rituals of remembrance mark?[59] Britain's increasingly unstable status as a global leader, with its roots in the decline of empire in the post-war period, has come under renewed scrutiny in light of the vote to leave the EU. The run up to the EU referendum occurred alongside a period of intense debate surrounding questions of citizenship and immigration.

By turning to Paul Gilroy's concept of post-colonial melancholia, a deeper understanding of the utility of the narratives surrounding the First World War in Britain can be gleaned. Gilroy argues that Britain's obsession with constructing its national identity through the two world wars:

> reveals a desire to find a way back to the point where the national culture – operating on a more manageable scale of community and social life – was, irrespective of the suffering involved in the conflict, both comprehensible and habit-able. . . . That process is driven by the need to get back to the place or moment before the country lost its moral and cultural bearings.[60]

Considering the anxieties surrounding multiculturalism, particularly the influx of immigrants from the former colonies after the end of the Second World War, the image of the British 'Tommy' serves another function, constructing exclusive notions of citizenship and belonging. As Victoria Basham highlights, this figure is highly racialised and gendered.[61] This is not only historically inaccurate, overlooking the role of ethnic-minority participants, as Baroness Warsi points out, 'it wasn't just Brits who fought for our King and country in the conflict – our boys weren't just Tommies, they were Tariqs and Tajinders too'.[62] Indeed, as Santanu Das notes, an estimated 'four million non-white men were recruited into European and American armies during the First World War'.[63] This racially constructed understanding has potentially divisive consequences when individuals are viewed as not belonging due to race or ethnicity.

Perceptions surrounding race and national identity were at the heart of the few reports of situations where the 'soldiers' were not well received, highlighting how, for some, race constitutes a boundary for national identity. Several surveys of the British public at the onset of the centenary have highlighted a general lack of historical awareness of the contributions of non-white British and colonial troops and non-combatants.[64] The official meta-evaluation of the centenary programme commissioned by the DCMS noted that amongst black and minority ethnic groups, engagement with the centenary was 'low, despite an increased focus on uncovering significant contributions from the Commonwealth . . . partners aimed to address this problem and to demonstrate how the FWW was a truly global event and relevant to all ethnic groups'.[65] This is not surprising, given 'the lingering narrative that Britain only sent young, white men to fight – a narrative that could have left BME individuals feeling excluded from the history of the FWW'.[66] Although contributions from the Commonwealth have functioned to create shared bonds through transnational memory networks and practices, as Andrew Mycock notes, these networks have functioned through hierarchies of remembrance with race at the core. The contributions of the so-called 'White Dominions' of Canada, Australia, and New Zealand are often foregrounded at the exclusion of others.[67] By focusing on the benign-sounding 'Commonwealth' instead of the British Empire, difficult colonial histories are side-lined at the expense of a positive integrationist narrative that has failed to reach many.

However, as Anne Bostanci and John Dubber note, 'the First World War was a significant moment of interracial encounter. For the first time, for example, a man from Cornwall could find himself in a trench with a Punjabi Muslim man'.[68] The overlooking of contributions from ethnic minority communities in Britain has deep historical roots (with non-white colonial soldiers who were deliberately excluded from commemorative events), as a 'racial hierarchy of remembrance' emerged as early as the Peace Day Parade of 1919.[69] This deliberate 'eras[ure of] the memory of African and Caribbean service in the war' during the Peace Day Parade was an important element in the post-war construction of 'war service as white', albeit 'with a loyal Asiatic element'.[70] This extended through to the fiftieth anniversary, with the contributions of 'African Caribbean servicemen and the British West Indies Regiment' overlooked in the BBC's ground-breaking twenty-six-part series *The Great War*.[71] Although significant attention has been given to remedying this throughout the centenary, as John Siblon notes:

> British political and public discourse is shaped by what Kapoor terms a 'racial amnesia', what Joseph-Salisbury refers to as 'White amnesia', or what

> Stuart Hall simply calls a 'profound historical forgetfulness'.[72] The relative absence of BAME contributions from the public sphere can also be understood as 'structural amnesia', described by Paul Connerton as the tendency to only remember links to the past considered socially important to one's own pedigree.[73]

Returning to *We're here because we're here*, these selective visions of the British soldier as white had concrete consequences for non-white 'soldiers'. While most 'soldier'-participants reported overwhelmingly positive experiences, there were some negative reactions which are directly linked to questions of race. In one case a 'soldier' was 'repeatedly asked if they were born in the country by a member of the public'.[74] This selective understanding that Britishness equates to whiteness highlights how war commemoration can lead to divisive understandings of national identity, with the British soldier on the Western Front continuously represented in popular culture as white. Deller's insistence that 'it wasn't just exclusively white males. That was really important' suggests an attempt to broaden perceptions of participation during the Great War and break down racial constructions of difference and Britishness.[75] The inclusion of non-white soldiers with very little context with the expectation that it will support policies of social cohesion is problematic. It elides many of the difficult aspects associated with recruitment from the empire – such as racist recruitment policies based on a 'racialised hierarchy of Empire' as noted by Richard Smith.[76] This understanding can have serious consequences. Incidents of racially motivated hate crimes have increased dramatically since the referendum, as some individuals appear emboldened by the rhetoric of 'taking our country back'.[77] As Vron Ware has noted, linking conceptions of citizenship to military service has become a coded practice employed by groups such as the 'British National Party (BNP) and UK Independence Party (UKIP) to halt all immigration, stigmatize foreigners as invaders and return the country to its rightful indigenous inhabitants'.[78] Furthermore, it sets increasingly stringent demands for non-white Britons, who must demonstrate a shared militarised past to be considered worthy of citizenship, what Ware refers to as a promoting a 'militarised multiculture'.[79] Deller's comment suggests that through the inclusion of non-white participants, a sort of historical recovery validates the blood sacrifice paid by non-white soldiers.

Conclusion

Although *We're here because we're here* is admirable in its ethnically diverse portrayal of the British soldier, I argue that the dominant cultural imaginary of the Tommy is so deeply ingrained in Britain as white that this form of low-context representation aids neither historical understanding nor national unity. The question of whether these attempts to broaden public understandings of the contribution of non-white soldiers has had a large impact on the British public's understanding of the war was brought into sharp relief by the recent controversy sparked by the British actor Laurence Fox, who criticised the inclusion of a Sikh soldier in Sam Mendes's movie *1917* as distracting to the story, referring to the 'oddness in the casting'.[80] The backlash that ensued saw Fox issue an apology; however, the incident demonstrates that there is some way to go in the public's attitude and knowledge regarding the participation of non-white soldiers fighting in and with the British Army. Indeed, the racial abuse suffered by the 'soldier' in question demonstrates the limitation of the form of participatory art in achieving such seemingly laudable aims, masked behind metrics of success measured through engagement figures. Furthermore, while this recognition of the historical contributions of black and minority ethnic soldiers provides a visible presence where there has long been blindness, the question remains whether the sort of narratives we should be striving towards to bind us together should be based on a military legacy at all.

Notes

1 Jeremy Deller, *We're Here Because We're Here* (London: Culture Shock Media on Behalf of 14–18 NOW, 2017), 61, 128.
2 "War Situation," *HC Deb*, June 18, 1940, vol. 362, cc51–64, House of Commons, https://api.parliament.uk/historic-hansard/commons/1940/jun/18/war-situation; Alan Clark, *The Donkeys* (London: Hutchingson, 1961, repr. 2006); Peter Parker, *The Last Veteran: Harry Patch and the Legacy of War* (London: Fourth Estate, 2009), 19.
3 Dan Todman, *The Great War: Myth and Memory* (London: Hambledon, 2005). On attempts to correct the historical inaccuracies, see Brian Bond, *The Unquiet Western Front: Britain' s Role in Literature and History* (Cambridge: Cambridge University Press, 2002); Gary Sheffield, *Forgotten Victory, the First World War – Myths and Realities* (London: Review, 2002); Gordon Corrigan, *Mud, Blood and Poppycock* (London: Cassel, 2004); On contemporary understandings of the First World War, see: British Future, *Do Mention the War: Will 1914 Matter in 2014?* (London: British Future, Imperial War Museums, 2013), www.britishfuture.org/wp-content/uploads/2013/08/BRF_Declaration-of-war-report_P2_Web-1.pdf; Andrew Mycock, "The First World War Centenary in the UK: 'A Truly National Commemoration'?," *The Round Table* 103, no. 2 (2014), doi:10.1080/00358533.2014.898489.
4 Morris Hargreaves McIntyre, *A Contemporary Memorial: Breaking New Ground. An Evaluation of We're Here Because We're Here* (London, 2017), 12, https://mhminsight.com/articles/engaging-30-million-people-with-heritage-in-a-single-day-we-re-here-because-we-re-here-8009.
5 Morris Hargreaves McIntyre, *14–18 NOW Evaluation Report: 2016 Season Executive Summary* (London, 2017), 35, https://issuu.com/1418now/docs/14-18_now_evaluation_report_2016_-_.
6 Robert Mendick, "Ghosts of the Somme Bring Home Memories of Britain's Bloodiest Day," *The Daily Telegraph* (London), July 2, 2016; Kaya Burgess, "Silent Soldiers Fill Stations to Remember 19,000 Dead," *The Times* (London), July 2, 2016; David Young, "How Ghost Soldiers Brought Haunting Images to Belfast," *Belfast Telegraph* (Belfast), July 2, 2016.
7 For a much more in-depth analysis of the artwork, see Kristin O'Donnell, "The Cultural Politics of Commemoration: Participatory Art and Britain's Great War During the Centenary Moment" (PhD thesis, University of Brighton, Brighton, forthcoming).
8 David Cameron, "Speech at Imperial War Museum on First World War Centenary Plans," website of the Britsh government (gov.uk), October 11, 2012, www.gov.uk/government/speeches/speech-at-imperial-war-museum-on-first-world-war-centenary-plans.
9 Mycock, "The First World War Centenary in the UK."

10 Ibid., 157.
11 Andrew Murrison cited in Mycock, "The First World War Centenary in the UK."
12 Jenny Waldman, interview with author at the Imperial War Museum, February 14, 2019.
13 David Cameron, "PM's Speech at Munich Security Conference," website of the British government (gov.uk), 2011, www.gov.uk/government/speeches/pms-speech-at-munich-security-conference.
14 Ibid.
15 Ibid.
16 Baroness Warsi in British Future, *Do Mention the War*, 7.
17 Ibid.
18 Vron Ware, "From War Grave to Peace Garden: Muslim Soldiers, Militarized Multiculture, and Cultural Heritage," *Journal of War & Culture Studies* 10, no. 4 (2017): 292, doi:10.1080/17526272.2017.1396069; Vron Ware, "Whiteness in the Glare of War: Soldiers, Migrants and Citizenship," *Ethnicities* 10, no. 3 (September 1, 2010): 314, doi:10.1177/1468796810372297.
19 Mycock, "The First World War Centenary in the UK."
20 Lucy Noakes, "Centenary (United Kingdom)," *1914–1918 Online: International Encyclopedia of the First World War* (2019), https://encyclopedia.1914-1918-online.net/article/centenary_united_kingdom.
21 Although the artwork claims to represent soldiers from across the British Empire, its use of poppy imagery reinforces cultural imaginaries of the Western Front. Piper and Cummings, *Blood Red Skies and Seas of Red* (London: Tower of London, 2014).
22 Ware, "From War Grave to Peace Garden."; John Siblon, "Negotiating Hierarchy and Memory: African and Caribbean Troops from Former British Colonies in London's Imperial Spaces," *The London Journal* 41, no. 3 (2016), doi:10.1080/03058034.2016.1213548; Richard Smith, "The Multicultural First World War: Memories of the West Indian Contribution in Contemporary Britain," *Journal of European Studies* 45, no. 4 (2015), doi:10.1177/0047244115599147.
23 Michael Hough, Steve Ballinger, and Sunder Katwala, "A Centenary Shared: Tracking Public Attitudes to the First World War Centenary 2013–16," *British Future*, November 2016, www.britishfuture.org/publication/a-centenary-shared-ww1-tracker/.
24 Claire Bishop, *Participation* (London: Whitechapel, 2006), 12.
25 Ibid., 12–13.
26 Eleonora Belfiore and Oliver Bennett, *The Social Impact of the Arts: An Intellectual History* (Basingstoke: Palgrave Macmillan, 2008).
27 When referring to 'soldiers' throughout this chapter, I am referring to the participants representing historic individual soldiers that died on the first day of the Battle of the Somme, "We're Here Because We're Here: About," November 14–18, 2018, https://becausewearehere.co.uk/we-are-here-about/.
28 Jeremy Deller and Kate Church, "Jeremy Deller: We're Here Because We're Here – BBC Four," *BBC*, 2016, Television Programme, www.bbc.co.uk/programmes/b083bk7n.
29 Ibid.
30 Ibid.
31 Michael J. Shapiro, "Slow Looking: The Ethics and Politics of Aesthetics," *Millennium: Journal of International Studies* 37, no. 1 (2008): 182–83, doi:10.1177/0305829808093770.
32 Todman, *The Great War*; Helen B. McCartney, "The First World War Soldier and His Contemporary Image in Britain," *International Affairs* 90, no. 2 (2014), doi:10.1111/1468-2346.12110.
33 Cameron, "Speech at Imperial War Museum on First World War Centenary Plans."

34 For an excellent exploration of these issues, see: Adrian Gregory, *The Last Great War: British Society and the First World War* (Cambridge: Cambridge University Press, 2008).
35 Benedict Anderson, *Imagined Communities: Reflections on the Origin and Spread of Nationalism*, rev. ed. (London: Verso, 2006).
36 Walker Connor, "Beyond Reason: The Nature of the Ethnonational Bond," *Ethnic and Racial Studies* 16, no. 3 (1993): 385, doi:10.1080/01419870.1993.9993788.
37 Dan Todman, "The Ninetieth Anniversary of the Battle of the Somme," in *War Memory and Popular Culture: Essays on Modes of Remembrance and Commemoration*, ed. Michael Keren and Holger H. Herwig (London: McFarland, 2009), 31.
38 Noakes, "Centenary (United Kingdom)."
39 Maggie Andrews, "Entitlement and the Shaping of First World War Commemorative Histories," *Cultural Trends* 27, no. 2 (March 15, 2018): 63, doi:10.1080/09548963.2018.1453446.
40 Todman, "The Ninetieth Anniversary of the Battle of the Somme," 27.
41 Deller, *We're Here Because We're Here*, 63.
42 Ibid.
43 Krishan Kumar, "'Englishness' and English National Identity," in *British Cultural Studies: Geography, Nationality, and Identity*, ed. Dave Morley and Kevin Robins (Oxford: Oxford University Press, 2001), 10–11.
44 Lizzie Dearden, "Boris Johnson Responds to Michael Gove 'Betrayal' after Dramatically Dropping Out of Tory Leadership Race," *The Independent*, July 1, 2016, www.independent.co.uk/news/uk/politics/boris-johnson-michael-gove-betrayal-conservative-party-tory-leadership-prime-minister-brexit-eu-a7113946.html.
45 McIntyre, *A Contemporary Memorial*, 10.
46 Jeremy Deller, interviewed by author, November 26, 2018.
47 David Reynolds, "Britain, the Two World Wars, and the Problem of Narrative," *The Historical Journal* 60, no. 1 (2017): 225, https://doi.org/10.1017/S0018246X000509.
48 ColinGlover2, "Moving to See Images of #Somme100 #wearehere Soldiers," *Twitter*, July 2, 2016, https://twitter.com/ColinGlover2/status/749334896859111424/photo/1.
49 Landygrint, "What a Beautiful & Impressive Art Project to Remember All Those Young Lads We Lost," *Instagram*, July 2, 2016, www.instagram.com/p/BHWuQbgjAbx/.
50 a_m_c, "#wearehere Did Not See This Today but What a Brilliant and Deeply Moving Way to Mark the Centenary of the Somme," *Instagram*, July 1, 2016, www.instagram.com/p/BHVALXkjBtL/.
51 Mjriggers, "Today Is the 100 Year Anniversary of the Battle of the Somme," July 1, 2016, www.instagram.com/p/BHVC0E9B67S/.
52 Spencer Dunn, "Let's Hope That a Divided Europe Doesn't Forget," *Facebook*, July 1, 2016, www.facebook.com/BBCBerkshire/videos/10154162623772936/.
53 Reynolds, "Britain, the Two World Wars, and the Problem of Narrative."
54 Ibid.
55 Fintan O'Toole, *Heroic Failure: Brexit and the Politics of Pain* (London: Head of Zeus, 2018).
56 Ibid., 69.
57 Ibid., 142.
58 Kobena Mercer, *Welcome to the Jungle: New Positions in Black Cultural Studies* (New York and London: Routledge, 1994).
59 For histories of varying Great War commemorative practices, see: Alex King, *Memorials of the Great War in Britain: The Symbolism and Politics of Remembrance* (Oxford: Berg, 1998); David Lloyd, *Battlefield Tourism: Pilgrimage and the Commemoration of the Great War in Britain, Australia and Canada, 1919–1939* (Oxford: Berg, 1998); Catherine Moriarty, "Private Grief and Public Remembrance: British First World War

Memorials," in *War and Memory in the Twentieth Century*, ed. Martin Evans and Kenneth Lunn (Oxford: Berg, 1997); Adrian Gregory, *The Silence of Memory: Armistice Day 1919–1946* (Oxford: Berg, 1994); Jay Winter, *Sites of Memory, Sites of Mourning: The Great War in European Cultural History* (Cambridge: Cambridge University Press, 1998).

60 Paul Gilroy, *Postcolonial Melancholia* (New York and Chichester: Columbia University Press, 2005), 89–90.

61 Victoria M. Basham, "Gender, Race, Militarism and Remembrance: The Everyday Geopolitics of the Poppy," *Gender, Place & Culture* 23, no. 6 (June 2, 2015), https://doi.org/10.1080/0966369x.2015.1090406; Siblon, "Negotiating Hierarchy and Memory."

62 Warsi in British Future, *Do Mention the War*, 6.

63 Santanu Das, *India, Empire, and First World War Culture: Writings, Images, and Songs* (Cambridge: Cambridge University Press, 2018), 26.

64 Anne Bostanci and John Dubber, "Remember the World as Well as the War: Why the Global Reach and Enduring Legacy of the First World War Still Matter Today," *British Council*, 2014, www.britishcouncil.org/organisation/policy-insight-research/research/remember-the-world; British Future, *Do Mention the War*.

65 Jack Malan, Eugénie Lale-Demoz, and Michaela Brady, *First World War Centenary Programme: Legacy Evaluation*, Centre for Strategy & Evaluation Services (Department for Digital Culture Media & Sport, September 2019), 19, https://assets.publishing.service.gov.uk/government/uploads/system/uploads/attachment_data/file/832231/DCMS_FWWC_Legacy_Evaluation_Report__CSES_17_Sept_2019___1_.pdf.

66 Ibid.

67 Mycock, "The First World War Centenary in the UK," 160.

68 Bostanci and Dubber, *Remember the World as Well as the War*, 23.

69 Siblon, "Negotiating Hierarchy and Memory," 4–8.

70 Ibid.

71 Stephen Bourne, *Black Poppies: Britain's Black Community and the Great War* (Stroud, GL: The History Press, 2014).

72 " 'The sugar at the bottom of the English cup of tea': Centering race-critical studies in Brexit Britain," *British Sociological Association*, 2019, www.britsoc.co.uk/about/latest-news/2019/march/the-sugar-at-the-bottom-of-the-english-cup-of-tea-centering-race-critical-studies-in-brexit-britain/?fbclid=IwAR0hn27VKe3tNmlhha5HWOKDnX1PQTeINqtbM5RHujXF1oGACPXgmge3C-Q.

73 Paul Connerton, "Seven Types of Forgetting," *Memory Studies* 1, no. 1 (2008): 64, doi:10.1177/1750698007083889.

74 McIntyre, *A Contemporary Memorial*, 81.

75 Deller, interview.

76 Smith, "The Multicultural First World War," 348.

77 Claudio Schilter, *Hate Crime After the Brexit Vote: Heterogeneity Analysis Based on a Universal Treatment* (London: London School of Economics, December 22, 2018). www.dropbox.com/s/3e7j9vluti0822w/JMP_claudioschilter.pdf?dl=0.

78 Ware, "Whiteness in the Glare of War: Soldiers, Migrants and Citizenship," 319.

79 Ware, "From War Grave to Peace Garden," 301.

80 "Laurence Fox Apologises to Sikhs for 'Clumsy' 1917 Comments," 2020, www.bbc.co.uk/news/entertainment-arts-51233734.

Part III

Coda

15 The Hall of Remembrance

Richard Cork

With eyes and lungs damaged by German mustard gas, ten blindfolded soldiers struggle towards a dressing station. One of them, the fourth from the left, cannot stop himself twisting round and vomiting. Although an orderly tries to keep the others in a straight line, their progress is painful. Leaning on each other's shoulders for guidance and support, they are barely capable of staying on the narrow wooden pathway. But adhere to it they must. The ground at either side is clogged with the bodies of other blindfolded young men, slumped together like corpses waiting for burial in a mass grave.

John Singer Sargent's *Gassed*, painted in 1918–19 soon after he witnessed just such a harrowing scene on the Western Front, is moving enough when encountered at the Imperial War Museum in London. But the extraordinary cinematic width of this canvas was originally commissioned as the climax of a monumental building: the Hall of Remembrance. Intended to house an outstanding and powerful collection of paintings responding to the conflict, it would undoubtedly be cherished today as a profound memorial to the tragedy of the First World War. The Hall of Remembrance was never erected, however, and its absence can be felt even more acutely after our thoughts were focused recently on the centenary of the Great War's outbreak.

The Hall was conceived early in 1918 by the British War Memorials Committee, headed by Lord Beaverbrook and Arnold Bennett. As the Minister responsible for Information, Beaverbrook was an immensely ambitious supporter of the government's patronage of war artists. His enlightened Committee won agreement for a major building, designed by the adventurous architect Charles Holden, who had already worked with Jacob Epstein on the controversial headquarters of the British Medical Association in the Strand. A wide range of artists, from senior practitioners to youthful rebels like Wyndham Lewis, Paul Nash, C. R. W. Nevinson and William Roberts, were invited to produce images for the Hall of Remembrance. Many of these paintings were exactly the same size as Paolo Uccello's revered *Battle of San Romano* series, one of which had been on display in London since its acquisition by the National Gallery in 1857. But Sargent was commissioned to paint an even larger 'super-picture' – a colossal canvas called

Gassed, which focused, very movingly, on the helpless young soldiers whom the artist had watched as they struggled in the aftermath of their blinding.

Sargent had probably been haunted by human vulnerability ever since his younger sister, Emily, suffered a tragic accident which left her, at the age of only four, with a deformed spine. But the mood in the well-heeled society portraits that made his reputation is, above all, celebratory: he dotes on his own skilful ability to paint the splash of sunlight on his clients' privileged, carefully preserved faces. That is why the arrival of *Gassed* delivers such a shock. After painting so many flattering effigies of imperial grandees, all revelling in their peacock finery and a manicured opulence that seemed destined to last forever, Sargent finally allows himself to confront transience, suffering and extinction. He had recently been devastated by the death of his favourite niece, Rose-Marie, killed in a French church that was hit by German shells. 'I can't tell you how sorry I am for you, and you all', he wrote to his sister, 'and how I feel the loss of the most charming girl who ever lived'.

Commissioned to execute an immense canvas for the Hall of Remembrance, he went over to France in July 1918 with his old friend Henry Tonks. One month later, at le-Bac-du-Sud, they came across what Sargent described as 'a harrowing sight, a field full of gassed and blindfolded men'. Tonks later recalled that the two artists had set out on the road to Doullens, searching for the advance of the Guards Division, and encountered towards evening a thoroughly shocking scene. 'The Dressing Station was situated on the road', Tonks remembered,

> and consisted of a number of huts and a few tents. Gassed cases kept coming in, led along . . . by an orderly. They sat or lay down on the grass, there must have been several hundred, evidently suffering a great deal chiefly I fancy from their eyes which were covered up by a piece of lint. . . . Sargent was very struck by the scene and immediately made a lot of notes. It was a very fine evening and the sun toward setting.

The line of soldiers who shuffle across his elegiac *Gassed*, like the blind leading the blind in a medieval allegory, prove that the swagger in Sargent's pre-1914 figures had now come to a brutal termination. A football match is still being played by diminutive participants near the horizon, but their energy serves only to accentuate the exhaustion of the young men's broken bodies. A bleached sun descends in a sky punctured by distant aircrafts as tiny as gnats, and nothing is on hand to alleviate the imminent onset of darkness. Loss of sight, an affliction Sargent must have particularly feared as an artist so reliant on keen, first-hand scrutiny, reduces the principal figures in his mournful frieze to stumbling helplessness. Struck down before they had a chance to grow from manhood to full maturity, these stooped victims bear out all the forebodings that Sargent had managed for so many years to suppress within his imagination.

The plan for the Hall of Remembrance stated that Sargent's haunting masterpiece would be flanked by two epic 'Uccello-sized' landscapes: David Young Cameron's melancholy *The Battlefield of Ypres*, and Charles Sims's *The Old*

German Front Line, Arras, 1916. Although both these artists travelled over to see for themselves the landscape of the Western Front, the war had finished by the time they made the journey. Even so, Sims was himself struggling to cope with the traumatic loss of his own eldest son in the conflict. And Paul Nash, who painted another 'Uccello' canvas, felt profoundly disturbed by his visit in the winter of 1917 to the area where the Passchendaele campaign had just been fought. A commissioned war artist, he was appalled not only by the grievous loss of human life but also by the damage inflicted on the natural world. So, he transformed *The Menin Road* into a powerful, uncompromising vision of utter devastation. 'It is unspeakable, godless, hopeless', wrote Nash after he was sent to Passchendaele.

> I am no longer an artist interested and curious, I am a messenger who will bring back word from the men who are fighting to those who want the war to go on for ever. Feeble, inarticulate, will be my message, but it will have a bitter truth, and may it burn their lousy souls.

A few figures can be seen in *The Menin Road*, making their way along an artery leading towards the German lines. Most of this battered terrain testifies, nevertheless, to the wasteland left behind by war, with waterlogged shell craters, rubble and tree trunks stripped of everything which had once enhanced them. Nash, passionately involved in landscape painting, was horrified by this traumatic vision of hell. He saw the mutilated trees, essentially, as people. And after starting work on *The Menin Road* in 1919, sharing a rural shed at Chalfont St Giles with his brother John, he was determined to 'brood on those wastes in Flanders, the torments, the cruelty & terror of this war'. He stressed that 'it is on these I brood for it seems the only justification of what I do now – if I can rob the war of the last shred of glory, the last shine of glamour'.

As for Nevinson, his grim painting *The Harvest of Battle* is dominated by the corpse of a young soldier prostrate on the mud with his mouth gaping in a silent yell. Other dead infantrymen lie nearby, their helmets and equipment having failed to protect them from the onslaught of weaponry invented for the most mechanised war ever witnessed anywhere in the world. Earlier in the conflict, Nevinson had served in the Red Cross. He quickly felt overwhelmed by the sheer multitude of injured and dying soldiers who desperately needed medical attention. His first war paintings were executed in an avant-garde style influenced by futurism and vorticism, but by the time he addressed himself to *The Harvest of Battle*, Nevinson had decided to work with a more figurative idiom. Although it lacks the arresting, instantaneous impact of his early images, this 'Uccello' picture conveys an immense amount of tragic awareness. The stunned and wounded figures stumbling across this waterlogged landscape, many of them struggling to carry hapless comrades away from the inferno, are depicted with great compassion. Nevinson had decided to reject the enthusiasm for war voiced by Marinetti and the Italian futurists, whose aggressive movement he had once embraced. Instead, he emphasises here the victims of war, and the fires flaring on the horizon prove that the conflagration is still bent on destroying even more young lives.

Some of the large Hall of Remembrance paintings concentrate on the courage of servicemen at work during this nightmarish conflict. In *Heavy Artillery*, Colin Gill reveals the weary stoicism of hard-pressed gunners surrounded by death and devastation. William Roberts, who had suffered first-hand the horrors of war as a gunner, painted *A Shell Dump, France*. It emphasises the spirit of brotherly co-operation between young men almost overwhelmed by the weight of the shells they are endlessly passing to each other. Wyndham Lewis, who narrowly escaped death on many occasions during his war service with the Royal Artillery, showed the aftermath of disaster in *A Battery Shelled*. Most of the picture surface is dominated by the jagged remnants of a shattered battery, and mechanised figures reminiscent of Epstein's *Rock Drill* search for fellow soldiers in the fiercely gouged mud left behind by enemy attack. On the left of this impressive painting, three larger figures gravely contemplate the catastrophic damage inflicted during severe German bombardment. They seem to be positioned in front of the painting, like survivors who look back at their torment on the Western Front and wonder how anyone managed to return from such a horrifying apocalypse.

Four other remarkable paintings, less wide than the others, were made for the Hall of Remembrance. The greatest of them, by Stanley Spencer, was *Travoys arriving with Wounded at a Dressing-Station at Smol, Macedonia*. Concentrating on Spencer's own memories as a medical orderly in the Macedonian field of conflict, it shows soldiers taken with compassionate care on stretchers to an old Greek church used as an operating theatre. He later described how there 'were these rows of travoys with wounded and limbers crammed full of wounded men. One would have thought that the scene was a sordid one, a terrible scene'. But Spencer always searched for the redemptive element in even the most gruelling ordeal. 'I felt there was a grandeur about it', he continued, and the most moving part of his painting focuses on the tenderness of a Red Cross orderly, who, positioned near the centre, places his right hand comfortingly on the face of the injured soldier sheltering beneath an ample blanket. 'All these wounded men were calm and at peace with everything'. Spencer recalled, 'so that pain seemed a small thing with them. I felt there was a spiritual ascendancy over everything'.

By extreme contrast, Henry Lamb's dramatic painting is far more violent: with extraordinary skill, it shows *Irish Troops in the Judaean Hills Surprised by a Turkish Bombardment*. But Henry Tonks's contribution, *An Advanced Dressing-Station in France*, returns to Spencer's involvement with caring for grievously wounded soldiers. And John Nash, working in the same large rural studio as his brother, Paul, produced a suspenseful painting called *Oppy Wood, 1917, Evening*. Here, although the shell-pitted scene is desolate, two soldiers are still alive and vigilant in a trench. They gaze out over the ravaged landscape like men yearning for peace and the regeneration of nature, yet two ominous explosions in the distance warn them that nothing is certain.

What were the architectural plans for the Hall of Remembrance, which would have housed all these ambitious, heartfelt and elegiac paintings? According to Muirhead Bone, one of the Committee's principal advisers, it was envisaged as 'a kind of Pavilion' governed by 'a choice modest beauty of conception' and surrounded by a garden on a spectacular, panoramic site at Richmond Hill. He argued that the overall aim ought to centre on a dedication to peace, and music would be performed in one of the Hall's galleries. Charles Holden, the architect invited to prepare a design for the Hall, was an ideal choice. After his inspired and audacious pre-war collaboration with the young Jacob Epstein on the British Medical Association headquarters in The Strand, Holden would again commission Epstein, along with Eric Gill, Henry Moore and other radical sculptors, to make carvings for the post-war headquarters of the Underground Group at 55 Broadway, near St James's Park. Holden may have wanted the sculpture to enhance the facade of the Hall of Remembrance as well, and his preliminary drawing for the building certainly outlines an immensely wide, minimal and cathedral-like structure with its own sculptural presence. Now preserved in the drawings collection of the British Architectural Library, this tantalising sketch confirms that the hall would have been a major work in its own right.

Far from glorifying the conflict and celebrating Britain's role in the eventual victory, Murhead Bone emphasised that the largest space containing Sargent's 'super-picture' ought to culminate in an oratory with a decoration devoted to " 'the coming Brotherhood of Man", for which we all pray'. Holden was very closely in sympathy with such an aim. Deeply affected by the war, he had become a member of the London Ambulance Column and St Paul's Watch in 1916. Two years later he began work as an architect with the Imperial War Graves Commission and ended up designing several of the most eloquent memorials honouring the dead. Among them are the simple stone structures at Corbie, Passchendaele, Tournai and Wimereux, where a memorial seat is incised with lines from John McCrae's poem 'In Flanders Fields'. Perhaps the finest of all is Buttes New British Cemetery in Belgium, where 2,066 British and Imperial troops are buried alongside Holden's memorial, which honours the 382 New Zealanders 'whose graves are known only to God'.

By the autumn of 1918, though, all hopes for realising the visionary Hall of Remembrance scheme had begun to fade. The increasing success of the Allied advance signalled the end of the conflict, and the Committee responsible for the hall acknowledged that it would soon be dissolved. In the end, Beaverbrook reluctantly agreed that the paintings executed for the hall should instead find a home in the collection of the Imperial War Museum. But a fascinating exhibition could now be mounted to celebrate the achievement of everyone involved in the creation of this truly admirable memorial.

Index

Page numbers in *italics* indicate a figure on the corresponding page.

Made in the USA
Las Vegas, NV
29 October 2024

497466fc-33ee-4940-a38d-5eefce9c01d8R01